D1255060

SOCIAL
ENCOUNTERS

SOCIAL ENCOUNTERS:

Readings in Social Interaction

Michael Argyle, editor
Wolfson College
Oxford, England

 ALDINE PUBLISHING COMPANY

ABOUT THE AUTHOR

Michael Argyle is Reader in Social Psychology and Fellow of Wolfson College at Oxford, England. He has taught at Oxford and has held visiting lectureships at universities in the United States, Canada, Africa, Italy, Greece, Germany, and Belgium. His other books include *Social Interaction, The Psychology of Interpersonal Behavior, The Social Psychology of Work,* and *Psychology and Social Problems.* He has been an editor of and published articles in major social psychology journals.

First U.S. edition published 1973 by
Aldine Publishing Company
529 South Wabash
Chicago, Illinois 60605

English edition published 1973 by
Penguin Books Ltd, Harmondsworth,
England

ISBN 0-202-25111-X cloth; 0-202-25112-8 paper
Library of Congress Catalog Number 79-116545

Printed in the United States of America

Contents

Introduction

This collection of Readings is intended as a companion volume to the author's *Social Interaction*. Both books present an approach to social psychology that is rather different from that found in current textbooks on this subject. This new approach is being used by a rapidly growing number of research workers in social psychology and a number of other subjects, including ethology, anthropology and linguistics. The two key ideas are (a) to study the detailed processes of social interaction at the level of the elements of interaction, and (b) to relate social behaviour to its biological basis and cultural setting.

The Readings in this book have been chosen because they are representative studies of different aspects of social interaction, and because they are interesting and important papers in their own right. Within the general approach described above, a range of somewhat different orientations are included. All the selections report empirical findings, and most of them introduce new conceptual notions as well.

One achievement of this recent research has been to establish the basic elements of which social interaction consists; current research is concerned with finding out precisely how these elements function. It is now agreed that the list consists of various signals: verbal and non-verbal, tactile, visible and audible – various kinds of bodily contact, proximity, orientation, bodily posture, physical appearance, facial expression, movements of head and hands, direction of gaze, timing of speech, emotional tone of speech, speech errors, type of utterance and linguistic structure of utterance. Each of these elements can be further analysed and divided into categories or dimensions; each plays a distinctive role in social interaction, though they are closely interconnected.

The new approach to research on social behaviour also takes account of the biological and cultural basis of social interaction. In other words social behaviour is studied in natural settings or replicas of natural settings, for which there are cultural rules familiar to the subjects. Furthermore situations are designed to arouse a definite motivation, for example the participants may be members of a working group or may be attempting to establish sexual or affiliative links.

A new approach to social psychology

The new approach was not developed in a revolutionary spirit, nor was it intended to refute earlier theories or discredit other approaches. Rather its purpose is simply to tackle a baffling and fascinating field of research – the detailed study of social interaction processes. However, from the point of view of this research it is inevitable that other research in the same area should seem unsatisfactory. The dominant approach to social psychology in recent years has been to test rather abstract hypotheses about social behaviour, in 'stripped down' laboratory experiments of an artificial kind; examples are the use of game-playing situations where subjects cannot see each other or where supposed partners do not really exist. It may well be that such experiments omit certain essential ingredients of human social behaviour such as (1) verbal communication, (2) non-verbal communication, (3) a cultural setting with known situational rules, and (4) at least one of the normal motivational bases for interaction. As DeVore says of studies of primates in captivity, 'the conclusions bore as little relation to the behavior of free-ranging groups as would a monograph on middle-class society based solely on the inmates in a maximum-security prison' (p. 30 of this volume).

Similar considerations apply to many laboratory experiments on humans. The results of such experiments may be misleading, or actually wrong, in several ways. In the first place, key elements or processes may be omitted from the situation. The most glaring omissions are those listed above. In addition, there are phenomena that are everyday occurrences in, for example, work groups or families, which have never been seen in laboratory groups. 'Members of laboratory groups do not usually take their clothes off, laugh uproariously, cry, attack or kiss each other, or crawl all over each other, as members of families commonly do' (Argyle, 1969, p. 243). Another source of error is exaggeration in the results of experiments. For example experiments on person perception using static photographs or brief exposure show that physical cues such as spectacles or untidy hair have a marked effect on judgements of personality. However, if observers see target persons interacting for as little as five minutes these effects are greatly reduced or may vanish entirely. Again the results of laboratory experiments may be quite different from the results obtained under more naturalistic conditions. For example experiments on the reinforcement of verbal behaviour under highly controlled laboratory conditions indicate that reinforcement is effective only when the subject becomes aware of what is wanted; under field conditions, however, it seems that learning occurs without awareness.

Research methods

There are several research procedures which avoid the difficulties discussed:

1. Laboratory experiments of a semi-naturalistic kind, in which some

real-life situation is replicated; often a programmed confederate is used in these experiments.

2. Statistical analyses of filmed sequences of behaviour, either in the laboratory or in the outside world.

3. Natural experiments in which members of the public are intercepted by confederates, observed by observers, and become subjects unknown to themselves.

4. Detailed studies of real social groups by participant observation and interview.

5. Questionnaire surveys asking for self-reports on behaviour in different situations or groups.

However, there is a dilemma about how to test some hypotheses. It is sometimes not possible to test a hypothesis without creating a rather unusual and peculiar situation, yet if this is done there is a danger of the experiment becoming invalid. With sufficient skill and ingenuity an experimenter can often test a hypothesis without losing external validity, but it must be confessed that this is sometimes a very difficult dilemma. Other important studies in this field are concerned more with exploration, and discovery of the basic variables, than with testing hypotheses. An example of this kind of research is Birdwhistell on kinesics (p. 93).

Recent research on social interaction has taken a different approach to theory and explanation from that now fashionable in social psychology. Dissonance theory, exchange theory and similar formulations put forward very general and abstract hypotheses about social performance, which are applicable to a wide range of situations. These theories do not however appear to cast much light on the process of social interaction. Furthermore, the experiments stemming from these theories are usually of the 'stripped down' kind, and thus omit many of the essential ingredients of social behaviour (speech, situational rules, etc.); it follows that something must be missing from these theories. It is my opinion that we are not yet ready for general theories of social interaction; what we need to do first is to map out and describe the basic phenomena. We need to know the goals being pursued by people in different situations or groups, the sensory channels of communication and how they are used, the roles of different verbal and non-verbal signals, the effect of situational rules, and so on. Most progress has been made with this task in the field of dyadic interaction; for small social groups and social organizations a lot remains to be found out. There are, however, two kinds of theorizing which are often used in social interaction research.

1. Where similarities with animal social behaviour are found, an evolutionary explanation is given. Hypotheses about human social interaction are

sometimes based on the assumption that processes similar to those found in animals will be discovered.

2. When differences are found between patterns of social behaviour in different cultures, they may be explained in terms of their historical development or of the functions they serve.

However, some features of social behaviour are not very clearly the results either of innate biological processes or of cultural learning; an example is the non-verbal signalling used to control the synchronization of speech (see Kendon, p. 76), perhaps these aspects of interactions are simply the only possible solution to certain universal features of human life given, for example, that we live in groups, possess the power of language, and have certain physiological equipment for sending and receiving signals.

Links with other fields of research

An important feature of these new directions of research in social behaviour has been the strong links established with neighbouring disciplines. Indeed, some of the main advances have been made by research workers outside social psychology, in animal social behaviour, anthropology, psychotherapy, linguistics, and so on. New subdisciplines have been identified, including 'non-verbal communication', 'human ethology', 'kinesics', 'paralinguistics' and 'interpersonal psychiatry'. During the late 1960s these different groups came together and a number of interdisciplinary conferences were held. While 'non-verbal communication' has been the usual title, it is recognized that this is misleading since there is considerable interest in verbal communication too.

The link with animal social behaviour came about through recent ethological studies of the social behaviour of apes and monkeys. During the early 1960s students of animal and human social behaviour were both studying the role of gaze-direction, posture, tone of voice, etc., as social signals, independently of each other. It is now realized that animals and men conduct much of their social behaviour by very similar non-verbal signals, and this has suggested that there may be more of an innate basis to human social behaviour than was previously thought. A second link with animal social behaviour is at the level of group behaviour; both human and non-human primates make friends and find mates, form families, and form cooperative groups with dominance hierarchies for purposes such as work and defence. This may help us understand the interaction patterns found in different kinds of human groups.

The link with sociology and anthropology has come about in two ways. Some anthropologists began to study social behaviour at a more microscopic level than had been customary. For example Watson and Graves (pp. 34-47 of this volume), found variations in the non-verbal signalling used, as well as differences in some of the processes of interaction. Sociologists studying American society, notably Goffman (pp. 202-18), have drawn attention to the elaborate set of rules governing many situations in a culture; such rules have presumably emerged as the result of 'cultural evolution', i.e. the discovery and retention of patterns of behaviour which have been found useful. There is a difference of approach between experimentalists and some sociologists: Goffman and others think that there are not general empirical 'laws' of social behaviour but merely a large number of rules that produce common behaviour in particular situations. On the other hand, most research workers on social interaction assume that there *are* universal empirical laws; they recognize that behaviour is different in different situations, that cultural rules affect behaviour. One way of reconciling the two positions is to say that the *dimensions* of situations have to be taken into account when formulating empirical laws. It would be necessary to explain why there are particular rules in terms of their history and functions.

There are also links between social interaction research and linguistics. Earlier work on linguistics often treated language in isolation from its social setting, and earlier work in social behaviour made very few attempts to analyse the verbal content of utterances. It is now recognized that speech is supported and accompanied by non-verbal signals in a number of ways, and that much can be learned about social behaviour by more detailed study of the structure of utterances. It is known that speech is closely synchronized with bodily movements (see Parts Two and Four), and it has been suggested that gestures may have some 'grammatical' structure of their own.

Fields of research and application

Research on social interaction has been mainly conducted on the simplest social situations – dyadic encounters. However, a certain amount of research on behaviour on small social groups and social organizations has been carried out at this level of analysis (Part Five). There are also important implications for the study of personality (Part Six), and it is necessary to introduce the concept of the self to deal with several aspects of interaction (Part Seven). The main practical application of this research is training people in social skills, in a number of different settings (Part Eight).

Research on social interaction has also shown how the model of man needs to be revised to take account of his social nature. The models of man suggested by learning theory, cognitive theory and psychoanalysis are not adequate in this respect. We know that

for the survival of the group, the satisfaction of biological needs, and the continuation of the species, cooperation in groups is necessary in animals and men;

that there are innate tendencies to respond to others, which in man in particular require experiences in the family for their completion; that there is a system of non-verbal signals for communicating interpersonal intentions and attitudes; that in man there is a second signalling system of language; that interaction is conducted by the two channels of vision and hearing, with the verbal and the non-verbal closely coordinated; and that patterns of communication and interaction are accumulated in each culture as part of the shared solution to the human situation. There is probably one more essential component; it seems likely that there is an innate moral sense which has evolved to keep in-group aggression under control; it has been shown that sympathy appears in young children and that taking account of the point of view of the other is an essential ingredient in interaction. Concern with the views of the other takes a second important form: the self-image is largely constructed from the reactions of others and leads to self-presentation behaviour intended to elicit appropriate reactions in later social situations. Social behaviour is produced as a stream of closely integrated responses subject to continuous correction as a result of feedback, controlled by more or less conscious plans, and subject to partly verbalized rules derived from the culture. It is not supposed that this picture is complete. The full role of cognitive processes in social behaviour has yet to be delineated. For example, there is presumably creativity in social behaviour, as in other kinds of behaviour, but nothing is known about it as yet.

This basic equipment, partly innate, partly acquired from the culture, leads to the formation of interpersonal bonds, small social groups and social structures. Relationships between pairs of people are an essential part of human life; they are built up through a gradual process of trial and error and result in a pattern of interaction which is synchronized and satisfying to both. People interact in small social groups, in the family, at work, and with friends. Here the interaction patterns are more complex, and groups evolve a stable system with norms and differentiation of roles. In larger groups, the roles become formalized and the whole web of interaction follows a regular pattern which is learned by new members; this is called a social structure (Argyle, 1969, pp. 430–31).

Reference

ARGYLE, M. (1969), *Social Interaction*, Methuen; Atherton.

Part One
The Biological and Cultural Roots of Social Interaction

Recent field studies of non-human primates have greatly increased our understanding of human social interaction. The biological purpose of social behaviour can be seen more clearly in these animals; human behaviour is very similar in a number of ways, so insight can be obtained into the probable biological basis of human social behaviour. DeVore (Reading 1) gives an excellent survey of the main varieties of social behaviour and social organization in non-human primates. However, this behaviour is not entirely innate, and in man it is less so, since innate factors are greatly modified by culture. Another very important difference between man and other primates is our ability to use language, which of course greatly affects our social behaviour. There are differences between cultures, both in the languages used and in the systems of non-verbal signalling. Watson and Graves (Reading 2) carried out an excellent study comparing various aspects of non-verbal signalling in pairs of Americans and pairs of Arabs. There are other differences between cultures – rules governing social behaviour, cognitive categories, beliefs and values. One of the main sources of variation *within* cultures is social class. Bernstein has found that there are class differences in the styles of speech used. Bernstein and Henderson (Reading 3) found that middle- and working-class mothers make different use of verbal and non-verbal communication when instructing their children.

1 Irven DeVore

Primate Behavior

I. DeVore, 'Primate behavior', from *International Encyclopedia of the Social Sciences*, vol. 14, 1968, pp. 351-60.

Man is a large, bipedal, diurnal primate closely related to the living great apes. Human behavior is based on a rich social heritage made possible by a tool-dependent culture and the unique properties of language. However, in most of the fundamental features of his social life, such as prolonged care of immature offspring and lifelong association between related adults, man is a typical Old-World primate. Because man is most closely related to the Old-World monkeys and apes, the following discussion is confined primarily to these forms and directed to those issues of most interest to the social sciences.

Living primates

There are about six hundred varieties of living non-human primates, divided into some fifty genera and two hundred species. Because of this extraordinary diversity, ranging from such forms as the small, insectivore-like tree shrews and 'mouse lemurs' to the great apes and man, it is sometimes assumed that the behavior of living primates can be arranged along an evolutionary scale of increasing behavioral similarity to man. However, no living primate is the ancestor of any other, and many varieties have had separate evolutionary histories for tens of millions of years. Every living species has survived by specialized adaptations, and while it is possible to make some broad generalizations about the physical characteristics of prosimians, monkeys and apes (Clark, 1960), behavioral comparisons are more difficult. Washburn and Hamburg (1965) have recently discussed the classification of the primate order from a behavioral point of view.

The many varieties of monkeys alone range in size from creatures weighing less than a pound to others weighing more than one hundred pounds. They have exploited a wide variety of jungle and open woodland habitats, frequently achieving population densities of one hundred or more individuals per square mile. The Old-World monkeys (Cercopithecidae) are divided into two subfamilies, the Cercopithecinae and the Colobinae; the latter group is distinguished by a specialized stomach capable of digesting large quantities of mature leaves. Brief observations have been made of several species of Colobinae, but the only form studied in detail is the common langur of India and Ceylon *Presbytis spp* (Jay, 1965). Among the Cercopithecinae, numerous studies have been made of the two closely related ground-adapted forms, the African baboon (*Papio*) and the Asian macaques (*Macaca*). Of the other two basic groups of Cercopithecinae, the mangabeys (*Cercocebus*) and the guenons, or vervets (*Cercopithecus*), a long-term field study has been made of only one, a ground-adapted species, *Cercopithecus aethiops* (Struhsaker, 1965).

The four apes, the Pongidae, are the gibbon (including the siamang), the orangutan, the gorilla and the chimpanzee. All of the apes differ from the monkeys in that the trunk is 'short, wide and shallow . . . the lumbar region is short . . . and the shoulder and arm muscles are especially adapted to abduction, flexion, and rotation' (Washburn and Hamburg, 1965, p. 9). Because of this adaptation to climbing and the ability to hang or swing from branches, to brachiate, apes have a 'vertical' posture, thus differing from the horizontal, quadrupedal monkeys, and it is no surprise that in their structure and bodily movements the apes closely resemble man. Physically, and to some extent behaviorally, man is most like the African great apes – the gorilla and the chimpanzee. But apes are confined to heavily wooded areas, and some of the behavioral patterns which have enabled man to travel long distances in open country are more closely paralleled in the behavior of terrestrial monkeys, such as baboons and macaques. In fundamental senses such as hearing, eyesight and smell and in the organization of the brain, the viscera and the reproductive organs, man, the apes and the Old-World monkeys share a basic biological pattern which distinguishes them from all other mammals, including New World monkeys and other primates.

Field studies of primates

Although attempts were made to study the African apes soon after their discovery in the nineteenth century, most reports of monkey and ape behavior in the wild remained anecdotal until Carpenter observed the howler monkeys of Panama in 1931. In succeeding years, other field studies were attempted, but these were usually brief; then, in the 1950s, investigators in Japan, the United States and Europe independently initiated a variety of field studies emphasizing long-term, systematic observation of primates living in natural habitats.

Most field studies have been made on monkey species that spend large amounts of time on the ground, where observation conditions are easiest. Because of their similarity to man, all the living apes except the orangutan have been the subject of at least one major field study. Long-term studies of free-ranging groups in monkey colonies have also contributed valuable data. The Japan Monkey Center has kept records of individual monkeys in its colonies since the early 1950s. Beginning with Altmann in 1958 (see Buettner-Janusch *et al.*, 1962), various investigators have restudied the rhesus monkey colony established on Cayo Santiago by Carpenter in 1938; in fact, since 1958 almost all the members of this free-ranging colony have been tattooed for identification. Because the life cycle of primates is so long, field workers cannot ordinarily ascertain sibling or mother–offspring bonds between adults, and yet these relationships are proving to be very important in some species. (For a more complete history of field studies see Southwick, 1963, pp. 1–6; and Washburn, Jay and Lancaster, 1965.)

Laboratory studies of primates, especially of the common Indian rhesus monkeys, have continued without interruption since the 1930s. Contemporary views of such topics as discrimination, operant conditioning, perception, and learning have been summarized by Schrier, Harlow and Stollnitz (1965). Recent studies of hemoglobins, blood serums, chromosomes, the nervous system, and the skin have been reported by Buettner-Janusch (1963–4). There are two journals devoted entirely to primate studies, *Primates* and *Folia primatologica*, and there are many films of primate behavior.

The formerly facile generalizations about monkey and ape behavior are no longer tenable. Although only about a dozen of the several hundred varieties of living primates have been studied to date, it is already clear that primates exploit a wide variety of ecological niches, that they live in different kinds of social groups, and that different species display quite different temperaments. Some species are distributed over large geographical areas, and group structure and behavior have been found to vary significantly between different populations of the same species (Jay, 1965). The unique life history of every individual produces distinctive patterns of temperament and social behavior among the members of a single group. All of these variables make it inevitable that there will be important exceptions to many of the following generalizations.

Primate group structure

Most vertebrate social groups undergo a variety of changes in group composition during the year. Changes are correlated with such phenomena as the abundance of food, the mating season, the birth season and the maturation of offspring. During the mating season adult males may drive off young males and form harems of receptive females; mothers may leave the group altogether when they give birth, living apart until their offspring are able to support themselves, or females with immature offspring may form separate bands of their own. Some or all of these groups may participate in seasonal migrations. The result is a 'population' with changing aggregations of individuals during the year cycle.

The social group of the Old-World monkeys and the apes is very different. Membership in the social group is usually continuous, and group composition may remain stable over many years. Typically, an individual is born, matures, leads its adult life, and dies in the same group. While there are interesting exceptions to these generalizations, they are so characteristic of a wide variety of monkey groups that it is convenient to speak of a distinctive group organization, the 'troop'. A troop so defined is a group of several adults of both sexes, together with juveniles and infants, which maintains a social identity and spatial unity that persists through the annual cycle and transcends the life-span of individual members. Such a troop is easily recognizable to the field observer because its boundaries are typically defended against outsiders. This social organization describes the basic social group of such Old-World monkeys as langurs, baboons, macaques, vervets (*Cercopithecus aethiops*), and colobus; of the New World howler monkey (*Alouatta palliata*), and perhaps spider monkeys (*Ateles geoffroyi*) (see Table 1). Less complete studies suggest that this type of group organization may also be characteristic of at least some species of mangabeys and some other species of *Cercopithecus*. The troop is also characteristic of *Lemur macaco* and probably of some other species of lemur. The description of the troop would apply to the social organization of the mountain gorilla, except that members may move in and out of some mountain gorilla groups rather freely.

Old-World monkey and gorilla troops average about twenty-five individuals, but normal groups may be as small as ten or number more than 200. The fact that primates normally remain in one social group throughout the year means that group members with needs and motivations as different as a small, helpless infant and a large, potentially dangerous adult male must accommodate each other. Among most vertebrates, when antagonisms arise between adults or between adults and mature offspring, usually during mating or birth periods, the result is a change in group structure. In some primate species young adults may change groups or live for a time in an all-male group or as solitary animals. But most remain in their natural group, where mutual tolerance and group cohesion are accomplished by such different behavior patterns as the dominance hierarchy, the persistence of mother–offspring bonds into adult life, an elaborate repertoire of affective communication, and the conservative tradition of the group. In such groups each individual has a status with regard to every other individual, and through the long period of infancy and adolescence, the individual learns to anticipate the responses of other group members and

Table 1 Types of social groups among primates

Type of group	Prosimians	New-World monkeys	Old-World monkeys	Apes	Preagricultural man
Solitary individuals (usually nocturnal or crepuscular)	Tree shrew 'Lesser lemur' Aye-aye Lepilemur Loris[a] Potto[a] Tarsier[a] Galago[b]			Orangutan[a]	
Mated pair with offspring	Hapelemur Indri Avahi Galago[b]	Aotes Callicebus Marmosets[a]		Gibbon	'Family'
One-male group			Patas Theropithecus gelada[c] Papio hamadryas[c]		
Troop, but oriented to one male		Spider monkey[a]	Cercopithecus ascanius[c] Colobus[a] Langurs[d]	Gorilla	
Troop (multiple adults of both sexes)	Lemur macaco Lemur catta Lemur fulvus Propithecus verreauxi	Howler Squirrel monkey[a] Capuchin[a] Spider monkey[a]	Macaques Savannah baboon Vervet Mangabeys[a] Colobus Langurs[d]	Chimpanzee[d]	'Band''
Unstructured aggregation	Galago[b]		Theropithecus gelada[c] Papio hamadryas[d]	Chimpanzee[d]	'Dialect group'

a. Inadequate field data.
b. Changes during annual cycle.
c. Changes during daily cycle.
d. Geographical variation.

behave accordingly. It is in the rich behavioral context of these Old-World primate social groups that many of the behaviors which we have come to consider 'human' were first developed.

In patas monkeys (*Erythrocebus patas*), hamadryas baboons (*Papio hamadryas*), and geladas (*Theropithecus gelada*) the basic social unit comprises several adult females and their offspring but only one adult male. Still another primate grouping pattern is the mated pair with offspring, reported to be found in the Indridae, in some small South American monkeys, and in the gibbon. This form of social organization has been compared to the human family, but it is actually the result of very different behavior patterns. An adult gibbon, for example, is antagonistic toward all other gibbons except its mate and its immature offspring. As a result, each gibbon pair lives apart from all other pairs, and even their own offspring are apparently driven away at maturity. In this respect the gibbon group is more comparable to a mated pair of birds during the breeding season than it is to the human family. (Unlike most birds, the gibbon group is stable and unaffected by seasonal variation.) The human family cannot occur as an isolated pair of adults but is always a subgroup within a larger social unit.

Most of the prosimians are small, arboreal, nocturnal creatures which, like many other such mammals, forage as individuals, coming together only rarely. Yet some, such as *Propithecus verreauxi* and some species of lemurs (such as *Lemur macaco*), live in small troops. The small galago or bushbaby (*Galago senegalensis*) forages singly at night but may sleep in small groups during the day and form mated pairs during part of the year. (The most complete discussion of the classification, social groups, and activity patterns of Madagascar lemurs is in Petter, 1962, and is summarized in Buettner-Janusch et al., 1962, and in DeVore, 1965a.)

Still another form of social group is described for the chimpanzees by Goodall (1965) and by Reynolds and Reynolds (1965). Small subgroups of a population, such as females with young, adult males, and mixed groups of males and females, roam freely in a local area of forest. These clusters are in frequent contact and may gather together, for example, at food trees but do not appear to be organized into large persistent social units. On the other hand, recent observations of chimpanzees by the Japan Monkey Center personnel suggest a group size and organization much like a monkey troop: when crossing open country between forest patches, the chimpanzee group consistently numbered forty-three and contained a nucleus of adult males, females in oestrus, and females with infants. On the basis of brief observations some monkey species, especially in the New World, may also live in loose aggregations. The aggregations of hamadryas baboons are different in that the one-male units remain intact even though more than seven hundred individuals may gather at the same sleeping place (Kummer and Kurt, 1963).

As a result of field studies in progress, it will soon be possible to refine the descriptive categories shown in Table 1 and to add many new species. While the table reveals certain trends, such as the solitary life of many nocturnal prosimians and the frequent occurrence of the 'troop organization' in monkeys, it also illustrates the difficulty of abstracting a model of 'monkey' or 'ape' social organization. Further, gross categories such as those in Table 1 should not obscure major behavioral differences: the frequency, intensity and complexity of social contacts among members of a lemur troop are far fewer than comparable contacts among members of a monkey troop. This list of primate species could be tabulated with respect to characteristics such as habitat, diet and group size (Crook and Gartlan, 1966). For example, with the possible exception of some prosimians, males of all these species are dominant over females, and this is broadly reflected in the degree of sexual dimorphism they display. There is great variation in this characteristic, ranging from the gibbon, in which the sexes are scarcely distinguishable in size, to the baboon and the gorilla, where the male may be two or three times as large as the female. Sexual dimorphism with respect to body size, size of canine teeth, and general robustness of the skeleton and musculature all tend to correlate with the extent to which a species is adapted to the ground. Indeed, the degree to which an Old-World primate species is adapted to life in the trees or to life on the ground is one of the best ways of predicting the size of the group, the degree of sexual dimorphism, the intensity of dominance relations among adults, the use of loud vocalizations in intergroup spacing, and the size of the area over which the social group ranges (DeVore, 1963).

Dominance and aggression

'Dominance' has been defined in many ways by different workers, and further study will undoubtedly show that quite different behaviors have been subsumed under this rubric. Common to all concepts of dominance, however, is the notion that the dominant individual can assert priority over a subordinate in order to gain some desired objective. Although expressions of dominance vary widely from one species to another, between groups within the same species, and even in the same individual at different times, it is clear that dominance interactions are fundamental to primate behavior and that they are specially prominent in the Old-World monkeys, apes and man. It is in the primarily ground-dwelling species such as baboons and macaques that dominance behavior is most apparent, and it is in the social groups of these species that dominance hierarchies exert the most influence in social organization. In these monkeys an adult male is about twice the size of an adult female, and there is typically a pronounced gap between the bottom of the male dominance hierarchy and the top of the female hierarchy. In more arboreal species, females are usually more nearly the size of males, and the dominance hierarchies of the sexes may overlap to some extent. In such species expression of dominance is often less frequent and more subtle, and mere avoidance, for example, may be as important as a challenge or attack in the demonstration of dominance status. In one-male groups the male is larger and more dominant than the females and does not tolerate any other adult males. In the loose aggregation of a species like the chimpanzee, there are frequent dominance interactions between adults, but it has not been reported whether these result in a hierarchy such as gorilla groups show.

The rank of any individual in a dominance hierarchy was formerly considered to be the result of the success of that individual in dominance interactions with each of the other individuals in the group. However, from recent studies of Old-World monkey and ape groups, it appears that dominance status is seldom, if ever, simply the outcome of an interaction between two individuals. Any of a series of circumstances may intervene in the free expression of dominance between two individuals. The mother comes to the aid of her offspring during childhood and, at least among rhesus monkeys, into adult life as well (Sade, 1965). Other individuals frequently join the combatants when a fight starts, and adults who tolerate each other will often support each other when one of them is challenged or attacked (DeVore, 1965b). Thus, an individual's dominance status is the result of a variety of factors, including past success in dominance encounters, the status of its mother, and the number and status of the individuals who will support it when challenged.

Threat behavior

Baboons and macaques, among whom thresholds of aggression are lowest and agonistic encounters most frequent, exhibit the most elaborate repertoire of gestures and vocalizations conveying anger, threat and fear. One form of threat behavior which is common in all the Old-World primates (including man) is the 'redirection of aggression', in which one animal threatens another and the threatened animal redirects the threat to a third individual or even to an inanimate object such as a stone or branch. For example, the loser of a fight between two adult males may chase a more subordinate male or a female or he may shake a tree limb vigorously. If he has chased a female, she will often chase or threaten a more subordinate female or a juvenile. This chain reaction of aggressive acts probably serves to periodically reinforce the various dominance statuses of all the participating group members.

Male dominance

Dominance relationships among adult males in baboon and macaque groups are often stable over many months or even years. A male's status is ultimately based on his strength and fighting ability, and unless the group is very large, the males tend to be arranged in a linear hierarchy, or 'peck order', in which each male is dominant over all individuals beneath him. This stable hierarchy of recognized status serves to reduce the number of agonistic interactions among males. In some savannah baboon, rhesus monkey and Japanese macaque troops, several males in their late prime may be so tolerant of each other that dominance between them is rarely expressed, and in such troops these males may constitute a nucleus in which the members support each other in dominance interactions. As a result, these older males, some of whom would lose a fight to a younger male in individual combat, are able to hold the young males in check by combined action (DeVore, 1965a, pp. 54–71; Imanishi, 1960). It is this nucleus of older supporting males that takes the initiative in protecting the group from outside danger, in repelling individuals who try to join the group, and in breaking up fights among group members. On the contrary, among gorillas and in small monkey groups this initiative is taken by a single dominant, 'alpha' male. Dominance behavior is difficult to understand in captivity, where it seems to be disruptive and anti-social. But in natural surroundings, dominant males protect weaker group members, and females and juveniles seek out the dominant males to sit beside or to groom. So, although the dominance hierarchy depends ultimately on force, it leads to relative peace and stability within the group.

Female dominance

The dominance hierarchy of females tends to be unstable and to depend to some extent on the female reproductive cycle. Females in oestrus are more active and aggressive and are frequently under the protection of a consort male. Among baboons and macaques, adult males are extremely protective of young infants, and this protecting also extends to the mother as long as she is with a young infant. Thus, although it is clear that some adult females are more dominant than others in almost all circumstances, the interference of reproductive cycles in female–female dominance interactions seems to preclude the establishment of stable, linear dominance hierarchies.

Sexual behavior

As in humans, most female monkeys and apes have a menstrual cycle of about thirty days. Because humans do, and monkeys in captivity may, breed at all times of the year, the belief has been widely held that Old-World primates show no seasonal variation in mating activity. Since the publication of Zuckerman's *The Social Life of Monkeys and Apes* (1932), it has often been asserted that the basis of monkey and ape societies is sexual attraction; however, we now know that the non-human primate group performs many functions besides providing its members with sexual outlets.

There are many differences in patterns of sexual behavior between man and the non-human primates. In the first place, in at least some species of macaques, there are sharply defined mating and birth seasons. The data are best for the Japanese macaque and for the rhesus on Cayo Santiago, where records have been kept longest. Lancaster and Lee (1965) show that Old-World monkeys tend to have at least a birth peak, if not a sharply defined birth season. Most monkeys give birth every year, and as in many birds and mammals, their reproductive cycles are presumably affected by such phenomena as day length and temperature. The reproductive cycle of some species, such as the baboons and the apes, is longer than a year, and if marked seasonality of sexual reproductive behavior exists in these species, it has not yet been demonstrated.

Another reason that opportunity for mating is an inadequate explanation of social cohesion in non-human primate groups is the fact that the female is sexually receptive for a relatively small portion of her life. Females will accept a male only on those days of their sexual cycle when they are in oestrus, and sexual cycles are inhibited during pregnancy and lactation. Females and their young constitute the core of monkey groups, and yet the amount of sexual activity in the life of any female, or within any group during the year, is very small. In a species with a mating season, disruptions are most common during this season. At this time extragroup males attempt more actively to join the group, and the existing competition among males already in the group may become more intense. Koford (1966) reports that on Cayo Santiago 66 per cent of all rhesus males who leave a group do so during the mating season. One of the Cayo Santiago groups subdivided into five groups between 1958 and 1964, each subdivision occurring during the mating season. On the other hand, social bonds within groups are probably strongest during the birth season, when mothers are clustered together with their new infants and adult males are actively caring for the infants of the previous year.

Mating patterns

In such species as the gibbon and the patas monkey (and in small groups of any species), only one adult male does the mating, but in most Old-World primate groups the female is potentially accessible to every male in the group during some part of her estrous cycle. In such dominance-oriented species as baboons and macaques, the tendency is for the most dominant male to have priority of access to an estrous female, but his mating activity is usually confined to her period of maximum receptivity. For example, a female baboon is receptive for about twelve days in a thirty-day sexual cycle; the degree of receptivity can be gauged by the amount of tumescence in the sexual skin of the perineal area. During the early period of swelling she is mounted by juvenile and subordinate adult males, and it is only when tumescence is at a maximum that she is sought out by the dominant males. If there are a number of adult males of approximately equal dominance and only one receptive female, the males may threaten and fight for her possession. Although copulations early in her cycle are casual and transitory, dominant adult males usually form a consort pair with a receptive adult female. The pair may remain together for several days, or if there is competition among the males, the pairing may be interrupted after only a few hours. A baboon male's ability to maintain possession of an oestrous female when he is being threatened will depend in part on the support he can expect from other males (DeVore, 1965b). The female must cooperate with the male during copulation, and she is thereby able to exercise some personal preference and to take some initiative in making sexual contacts. Thus, mating patterns in even a sexually dimorphic species like the baboon are more than a simple reflection of the male dominance hierarchy. There are opportunities for subordinate males to copulate before the female becomes attractive to the dominant males; a male's ability to mate may depend on his relationship to other, supporting males; and the female herself is able to exert some initiative.

Prolonged immaturity

By comparison to other mammals of similar size, the period of infant dependency is remarkably long in primates, and the necessity for providing care and protection of immature offspring is a dominant feature of monkey and ape social life. Ordinarily an infant in danger is retrieved by its mother, but adult males of many varieties of monkeys will threaten, distract or attack a potential predator. Aggression toward predators is most prominent in ground-dwelling species such as baboons and macaques; for example, on an average day a baboon group may range as far as two or three miles from the safe refuge of trees.

The birth of an infant not only changes the quantity and quality of its mother's social interaction, but every member of the group is affected in some measure. Adults and juveniles are highly attracted to young infants and repeatedly approach them to inspect, fondle, groom and play with them. The newborn infant primate clings to its mother at all times, imposing substantial behavioral constraints not only on her but on the entire group. This prolongation of preadult life is so biologically expensive for the species that there must be major compensatory advantages. In a recent discussion,

Washburn and Hamburg (1965) have suggested that this prolonged period of immaturity makes it possible for the species to adapt to a wide variety of environmental contexts because of the opportunity it provides for complex learning in the young. A large number of laboratory and field studies support the fact that much of the normal adult behavior of the species must be learned. In nature immature monkeys are in frequent contact with adults of both sexes and with their peers. The major activity of the young primate is 'play', and it is during these long hours of daily play that the juvenile learns both the features of its physical environment and the appropriate responses to the other animals in its social environment. The development of normal sexual behavior, the expression of effective patterns of affection and dominance, and the ability to rear an infant competently are all social skills which must be learned, and monkeys raised in isolation show major deficits in all of these behaviors (Harlow and Harlow, 1965; Mason, 1965). Social deprivation experiments also indicate how even less drastic events in the early life of a young primate reared under normal conditions may lead to the striking individual differences in adult temperament and social skills that are so frequently reported by research workers.

Mother–offspring relations

It has long been obvious to observers that the relationship between a mother and her offspring is the most intense and prolonged in primate life. During the usual field study it is impossible for the observer to know what genealogical relationships may exist between adults or between any group members who are beyond the weanling stage. Rejection by the mother when she weans her infant seems so firm, and the effect on the infant so traumatic, that the tendency has been to assume that their early close bonds have been severed permanently. (Moreover, the mother's attentions are soon redirected to the care of another newborn infant.) But these conclusions are clearly incorrect, at least for some species, as prolonged observation of identified individuals has shown. Studies reported by Imanishi (1960) and Koford (1963) indicate that the rank of a young male in the dominance hierarchy is frequently very closely related to the rank of his mother; high-ranking mothers tend to rear high-ranking male offspring. The evidence is less clear for females, but it seems likely that high-ranking females may also be related as siblings or as mother and daughter.

Sade (1965) has offered the most detailed accounts of the importance of social bonds between uterine kin in rhesus monkeys. The most frequent subgroups are clusters of mature and immature offspring around an old female. These animals not only sit together and groom each other more often than they do other group members, but they frequently support each other in dominance interactions as well. Data indicating the importance of genealogically related subgroups are most convincing for the Japanese macaque and the rhesus on Cayo Santiago, where individual records have been kept for many years, but Jane Goodall (1965) has also described similar clusters of offspring around old female chimpanzees. Troops of Japanese macaques and rhesus monkeys which contain no adult males (except during the mating season) have been reported, but they are rare.

The achievement of high rank by the offspring of dominant females appears to be caused both by childhood experience and by the mother's support of her mature offspring. Infants of dominant females stay with their mothers and other dominant individuals near the center of the group, and in the Japanese macaque they may never go through the period of social peripheralization that is characteristic of most young males. They are born in the middle of the group, grow up there, and remain there as adults, assuming at a young age the roles peculiar to the dominant males at the heart of the group. Also, in day-to-day agonistic interactions, a young male who is supported in aggressive encounters by a dominant mother will simply win more of these encounters than one whose mother is subordinate. Presumably the long period of conditioning during infancy and adolescence strongly reinforces a male's expectation of success or failure in the social dominance interactions of adult life. The question of the effect of genetic inheritance on the achievement of social dominance should be investigated; this could easily be done by cross-fostering experiments, in which the offspring of a subordinate female and a dominant female would be exchanged at birth.

Sade reports that rhesus mothers on Cayo Santiago continue to support their adult sons in dominance interactions with other group members. Furthermore, a mother ordinarily remains dominant over her son all of her life. Apparently correlated with this behavior is the fact that copulation between mother and son is very rare. In one of the few known cases of mother–son incest, the two had engaged in a vicious fight, and the son had subsequently become dominant over his mother before the mating occurred. Although they are not yet well understood, it appears that the complicated patterns of nurturance and dominance behavior between mother and son may inhibit copulation between them and that the aversion to incest may be present among members of a number of Old-World primate species.

Adult male–offspring relations

Paternity in non-human primate groups is rarely known or knowable either to the investigator or to the monkeys. Adult males seek to protect *any* infant from injury either from group members or from predators. However, in some species an adult male may form a special protective relationship with a particular infant. In the Japanese macaque, for example, males frequently establish such a relationship with yearlings when these are rejected by the mother and replaced by a new infant (Itani, 1959). Analogous behavior has been reported in other macaques and baboons (Washburn, Jay and Lancaster, 1965). Among some New-World marmosets a male may carry an infant at all times except when the mother is nursing it. The one-male unit of the hamadryas baboon develops because young adult males forcefully adopt immature females, 'mothering' the females until they reach sexual maturity (Kummer, 1968).

There are no indications from field studies that the adult male in *arboreal* Old-World primates establishes strong social bonds with infants or juveniles beyond protection of infants when the group is threatened by a predator. Even in the ground-adapted patas monkey and in the vervet monkey, the role of the male seems limited to protection or to distracting predators, and the present evidence indicates that more elaborate male–offspring relations arise only in terrestrial primates living in large social groups.

Human and primate social organization

Only a few years ago non-human primate behavior was assumed to be simple, stereotyped and easy to observe; with notable exceptions (Carpenter, 1964), field reports were largely anecdotal accounts by casual observers. Observations of zoo colonies suggested that primate groups were a disorganized rabble, tyrannized by aggressive males and held together only by sexual attraction. From the perspective of modern field studies, the conclusions based only on the behavior of primates in captivity bore as little relation to the social organization of free-ranging groups as would a monograph on middle-class society based solely on a study of inmates in a maximum-security prison.

Social organization is not identical for any two primate species. Human social organization, with its varied cultural manifestations, is unique; but studies of monkeys and apes are helping to distinguish those behavior patterns that are truly unique from those which man shares with his nearest relatives. Before the urban revolution human social organization was centered on small, face-to-face groups of adults involved in the quest for food and the protection of immature offspring, and it is not surprising that patterns of dominance and aggression and of nurturance and affection seem so similar in men, monkeys, and apes. The division of labor by sex, with females specializing in child care and males as protectors, and the performance of different social roles according to status are familiar patterns to the sociologist. [. . .]

Much of the contrast between human and primate social organization is based on human language. Communication in monkeys and apes is a rich complex of vocal, gestural and tactile signals, but the majority of these signals are reflections of changing emotional states among the communicants and are comparable to the communication systems of other animals, not to language (Marler, 1965; Bastian, 1965; Altmann, 1967). Language is so fundamental to human life that it is impossible to dissociate it from other distinctly human behaviors, such as toolmaking and the willingness to share food. Non-human primates do not share food, even with their own infants, but neither do they have tools to gather food or an improved site or camp from which they can disperse during the day in complementary gathering and hunting activities and where they can convene again to share the results of the day's quest.

The most distinctive feature of human social organization, the family, is adaptive only in the context of an economy based on tool use and sharing; presumably it also requires other uniquely human traits such as the ability of the female to mate at all times. On the other hand, many behavior patterns that have been viewed as ramifications of the human family are actually present in the Old-World primates – the maternal affectional system and its extension to uterine kin, the close association of siblings, the protection and nurturance by adult males of the young – and it is no longer so difficult to understand how the human social systems could have evolved. With language, an incest aversion between mother and son became an incest taboo; with language, the already close ties among uterine kin were explicitly recognized and socially extended.

Field and laboratory studies of primates were not begun on a large scale until the 1960s, but they are now attracting the attention of persons in biology, ethology and all branches of the behavioral sciences. Techniques of observation and analysis are constantly being refined, and behavioral studies are being combined with experiments in pharmacology, hormonal studies, and neurophysiology (Washburn and Hamburg, 1968). For example, miniature telemetering devices implanted in the animal have been used to record and direct the behavior of individuals in a free-ranging group. Ethological principles and techniques of observation are being applied to humans and the results compared to studies of non-human primates. There is every indication that in the next few years this renewed interest in the non-human primates will yield results of increasing relevance to the social sciences.

References

ALTMANN, S. A. (ed.) (1967), *Social Communication among Primates*, University of Chicago Press.

BASTIAN, J. R. (1965), 'Primate signalling systems and human languages', in I. DeVore (ed.), *Primate Behavior: Field Studies of Monkeys and Apes*, Holt, Rinehart & Winston.

BUETTNER-JANUSCH, J. (ed.) (1963–4), *Evolutionary and Genetic Biology of Primates*, 2 vols., Academic Press.

BUETTNER-JANUSCH, J., *et al.* (eds.) (1962), 'The relatives of man: modern studies of the relation of the evolution of non-human primates to human evolution', New York Academy of Sciences, *Annals*, col. 102, pp. 181–514.

CARPENTER, C. R. (1964), *Naturalistic Behavior of Non-human Primates*, Pennsylvania State University Press.

CLARK, W. E. LEGROS (1960), *The Antecedents of Man: An Introduction to the Evolution of the Primates*, Quadrangle.

CROOK, J. H., and GARTLAN, J. S. (1966), 'Evolution of primate societies', *Nature*, vol. 210, pp. 1200–1203.

DEVORE, I. (1963), 'A comparison of the ecology and behavior of monkeys and apes', in S. L. Washburn (ed.), *Classification and Human Evolution*, Aldine.

DEVORE, I. (ed.) (1965a), *Primate Behavior: Field Studies of Monkeys and Apes*, Holt, Rinehart & Winston.

DEVORE, I. (1965b), 'Male dominance and mating behavior in baboons', in Conference on Sex and Behavior, Berkeley, Calif., in F. A. Beach (ed.), *Sex and Behavior*, Wiley, pp. 266–89.

GOODALL, J. (1965), 'Chimpanzees of the Gombe Stream Reserve', in I. DeVore (ed.), *Primate Behavior: Field Studies of Monkeys and Apes*, Holt, Rinehart & Winston, pp. 425–73.

HARLOW, H. F., and HARLOW, M. K. (1965), 'The affectional systems', in A. M. Schrier, H. F. Harlow and F. Stollnitz (eds.), *Behavior of Non-human Primates: Modern Research Trends*, Academic Press, vol. 2, pp. 287–334.

IMANISHI, K. (1960), 'Social organization of subhuman primates in their natural habitat', *Current Anthropology*, vol. 1, pp. 393–407.

ITANI, J. (1959), 'Paternal care in the wild Japanese monkey', *Macaca Fuscata Primates*, vol. 2, no. 1, pp. 61–93.

JAY, P. (1965), 'The common langur of North India', in I. DeVore (ed.), *Primate Behavior: Field Studies of Monkeys and Apes*, Holt, Rinehart & Winston, pp. 197–249.

KOFORD, C. B. (1963), 'Rank of mothers and sons in bands of rhesus monkeys', *Science*, New Series, vol. 141, pp. 356–7.

KOFORD, C. B. (1966), 'Population changes in rhesus monkeys: Cayo Santiago 1960–64', *Tulane Studies in Zoology*, vol. 13, no. 1, pp. 1–7.

KUMMER, H. (1968), 'Two basic variations in the social organization of the genus Papio', in P. Jay (ed.), *Primates*, Holt, Rinehart & Winston.

KUMMER, H., and KURT, F. (1963), 'Social units of a free-living population of Hamadryas baboons', *Folia Primatologica*, vol. 1, pp. 4–19.

LANCASTER, J. B., and LEE, R. B. (1965), 'The annual reproduction cycle in monkeys and apes', in I. DeVore (ed.), *Primate Behavior: Field Studies of Monkeys and Apes*, Holt, Rinehart & Winston.

MARLER, P. (1965), 'Communication in monkeys and apes', in I. DeVore (ed.), *Primate Behavior: Field Studies of Monkeys and Apes*, Holt, Rinehart & Winston, pp. 544–84.

MASON, W. A. (1965), 'The social development of monkeys and apes', in I. DeVore (ed.), *Primate Behavior: Field Studies of Monkeys and Apes*, Holt, Rinehart & Winston, pp. 514–43.

PETTER, J. J. (1962), 'Recherches sur l'écologie et l'éthologie des lémurs malgaches', Musée National d'Histoire Naturelle, *Mémoires*, Série A 27, no. 1, pp. 1–146.

REYNOLDS, V., and REYNOLDS, F. (1965), 'Chimpanzees of the Budongo Forest', in I. DeVore (ed.), *Primate Behavior: Field Studies of Monkeys and Apes*, Holt, Rinehart & Winston, pp. 368–424.

SADE, D. S. (1965), 'Some aspects of parent-offspring and sibling relations in a group of rhesus monkeys, with a discussion of grooming', *Amer. J. Physical Anthropol.*, new series vol. 23, pp. 1–17.

SCHRIER, A. M., HARLOW, H. F., and STOLLNITZ, F. (eds.) (1965), *Behavior of Non-human Primates: Modern Research Trends*, 2 vols., Academic Press.

SOUTHWICK, C. H. (ed.) (1963), *Primate Social Behavior; an Enduring Problem: Selected Readings*, Van Nostrand.

STRUHSAKER, T (1965), 'Behavior of the vervet monkey', *Cercopithecus aethiops*, Ph.D. dissertation, University of California.

WASHBURN, S. L., and HAMBURG, D. A. (1965), 'The study of primate behavior', in I. DeVore (ed.), *Primate Behavior: Field Studies of Monkeys and Apes*, Holt, Rinehart & Winston.

WASHBURN, S. L. and HAMBURG, D. A. (1968), 'Aggressive behavior in old world monkeys and apes', in P. Jay (ed.), *Primates*, Holt, Rinehart & Winston.

WASHBURN, S. L., JAY, P. C. and LANCASTER, J. B. (1965), 'Field studies of old world monkeys and apes', *Science*, New Series vol. 150, pp. 1541–7.

ZUCKERMAN, S. (1932), *The Social Life of Monkeys and Apes*, Harcourt, Brace & World.

2 O. Michael Watson and Theodore D. Graves

Quantitative Research in Proxemic Behavior

O. M. Watson and T. D. Graves, 'Quantitative research in proxemic behavior', *American Anthropologist*, vol. 68, 1966, pp. 971–85.

Edward T. Hall, innovator of the term, defines proxemics as 'the study of how man unconsciously structures microspace – the distance between men in the conduct of daily transactions, the organization of space in his houses and buildings, and ultimately the layout of his towns' (1963, p. 1003).

In an article published in 1955, Hall illustrated the difficulties that arise when two systems of proxemic behavior clash. He later presented some of the dynamic aspects of man's structuring of space, linking it with the concept of territoriality (1959, p. 146–64). The paper in which Hall (1963) coined the term 'proxemics' stated further theoretical implications of the study of the structuring of space and provided a system for its notation.

In the works cited above, Hall made the point that members of different cultures, when interacting with each other, cannot be relied upon to attach the same meaning to the same elements of proxemic behavior. The examples he most frequently referred to were the differences between Arabs and Americans. In none of these works, however, did Hall present or mention empirical data used in the measurement of these differences.

Our objectives in pursing this problem were further threefold:

1. To record empirical data quantifying Arab and American proxemic behavior.

2. To test pragmatically Hall's system for the notation of proxemic behavior to try to uncover any weaknesses or ambiguities inherent in the system.

3. To test the validity of Hall's impressionistic observations on Arab and American differences.

Hypotheses

On the basis of Hall's observations, a hypothesis can be made not only that Arabs and Americans differ in proxemic behavior, but about the direction of this difference as well. Hall's descriptive material (1959, 1963) cites many instances of Arab–American differences. The following is a good example (1963, p. 1005):

When approached too closely, Americans removed themselves to a position which turned out to be outside the olfactory zone. . . . Arabs also experienced alienation traceable to a 'suspiciously' low level of the voice, the directing of the breath away from the face, and a much reduced visual contact.

Americans were not only aware of uncomfortable feelings, but the intensity and intimacy of the encounter with Arabs was likely to be anxiety provoking. The Arab look, touch, voice level, the warm moisure of his breath, the penetrating stare of his eyes, all proved to be disturbing.

On the basis of these observations we formulated the following hypotheses:

1. Arabs will exhibit significant differences in proxemic behavior from Americans, with Arabs being closer and more direct in their proxemic behavior than Americans.

2. Within the group of Arabs, persons from any particular Arab country will be more similar to persons from any other Arab country in proxemic behavior than to Americans from any particular region of the United States, the direction of this difference being the same as for overall Arab–American differences.

3. Similarly, Americans from any particular region of the United States will be more similar to Americans from any other region of the United States in proxemic behavior than to persons from any Arab country, the direction of difference again being the same as overall Arab–American differences.

Research strategy

This research was conducted among Arab and American male students studying at the University of Colorado. The Arab students comprised four groups of four students each from Saudi Arabia, the United Arab Republic, Iraq and Kuwait. The American students comprised four regional groups: four students from New York–New Jersey, four from Colorado, four from California and four from the Midwest (Michigan, Illinois and Wisconsin). This made a total of thirty-two persons: sixteen Arabs and sixteen Americans.

A member of each subgroup was enlisted and asked to bring three friends from the same country or US region with him at the scheduled time. Unfortunately, it was impossible to observe all subgroups at a similar time during the day, so there was no control for this factor; all observations were, however, made during the daylight hours. When each group of four students arrived, they were told nothing more than they were going to be observed. They were then directed, two at a time, to an observation room (Figure 1) until observations had been made on the six possible combinations of pairs within the group. The room was bare except for a table and two chairs placed in standardized position in front of the observation window. The students were told to talk about anything that came into their heads, the Arab students being told to speak Arabic. The fact that all four members of each group were friends minimized the possibility of hesitancy in talking to one another. They were observed from behind a one-way glass, and listened to through a microphone inconspicuously placed in the ceiling of the observation room. Each pair was given one or two minutes to 'warm up', and then observations were recorded over a period of five minutes, one line of notation of proxemic behavior per minute. Each group of four students therefore had a total of thirty lines of notation, and each individual had fifteen lines. After all individual scores had been recorded, group means were calculated and various techniques of statistical analysis to be discussed later, were applied.

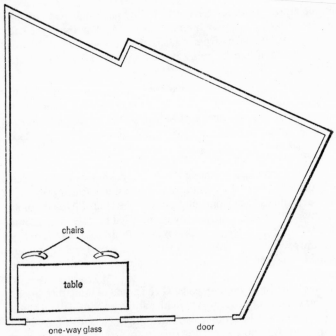

Figure 1 Observation room. Scale: 1″ = 6′

The reliability of the scoring was checked by having a second observer record scores for the first several interactions, and then by cross-checking the two sets of scores. The sets proved to be identical.

After all the data were collected, it was impressionistically obvious that there were large differences between Arab and American proxemic behavior. The Arabs started talking the moment they entered the observation room and didn't stop until we entered and told them that was enough. In a few instances the Arabs told us to wait a minute until they finished their discussion. It could well be that garrulity is a good measure of closeness. The Americans, by contrast, were comparatively restrained in their behavior, but none the less carried on conversation in a fashion that we, as Americans, felt to be typical of Americans.

Operational definitions

Hall (1963, p. 1006) has divided proxemic behavior into eight different categories:

1. Postural-sex identifiers.
2. Sociofugal–sociopetal axis.
3. Kinesthetic factors.
4. Touch code.
5. Visual code.
6. Thermal code.
7. Olfaction code.
8. Voice-loudness scale.

These categories will now be discussed briefly, and operational definitions supplied for each. Hall has treated each category in detail (1963, pp. 1006–18), and the reader is referred there for a deeper understanding of the theoretical and methodological assumptions underlying the categories.

Postural-sex identifiers

This category simply identifies persons as to sex and as to whether they are sitting, standing or prone. Since all subjects in this study were male and since all sat in the chairs provided, this category was not scored as a variable.

Sociofugal–sociopetal axis

This category scores the relation of the axis of one person's shoulders to that of the other. These relationships are scored on a scale of 0 through 8 (Figure 2). The Arabs were expected to be more direct, i.e. to score lower, than Americans.

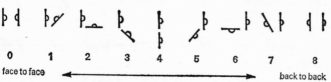

Figure 2 Scoring for variable 1–Axis

Kinesthetic factors

This category relates to the closeness of one person to another, and to the potential of each for holding, grasping or touching the other. There are arrangements in Hall's (1963, p. 1010) scheme for each person to receive a separate kinesthetic score. This would be necessary if the persons observed were of different sizes, i.e. had different potentials for length of reach, etc. The subjects of this research were all of approximately the same size, so only one score was given to each pair of interacting persons, i.e. each of a pair shared the same score. As an aid in scoring, the edge of the table closest to the students was inconspicuously marked with a pencil every six inches. The pairs were scored on the following bases:

1·0. Within body contact distance.
1·5. Just outside this distance.
2·0. Within touching distance with extended forearm.
2·5. Just outside this distance.
3·0. Within touching distance with forearm extended.
3·5. Just outside this distance.
4·0. Within touching distance by reaching.
4·5. Just outside this distance.

Arabs were expected to interact more closely than Americans.

Touch code

This category provides for the amount of contact during each interaction. It is scored as follows:

0. Holding and caressing.
1. Feeling and caressing.
2. Prolonged holding.
3. Holding.
4. Spot touching.
5. Accidental touching.
6. No contact.

Arabs were expected to touch more than Americans.

Visual code

The coding in this category provides an index of the amount of visual contact present. The code is:

1. Sharp (focusing directly on the other person's eyes).
2. Clear (focusing about the other person's head and face).

3. Peripheral (having the other person within the field of vision, but not focusing on his head or face).
4. No visual contact (looking down or gazing into space).

Arabs were expected to have lower scores than Americans, i.e. to display greater and more direct visual contact.

Thermal code

This category provides for the detection of one person's body heat by the other. This would be almost impossible to determine by observation. Heat-sensitive devices or questioning the subjects are about the only ways in which this category can be scored. The latter, more inexpensive technique was chosen. Since none reported detection of the other person's body heat, this category was dispensed with as a variable.

Olfaction code

This category scores for whether the odor of one person is detected by the other. This category, like the preceding one, would be almost impossible to score by observation. Again, subjects were queried as to the detection of odors, and again none reported that they had detected any. This category also was discarded as a variable.

Voice-loudness scale

This category provides a measure for the level of a person's voice during interaction. To make the measurement of this category more reliable, the microphone of a tape recorder equipped with a decimeter was attached to the speaker over which the subjects' voices were heard. The decimeter was divided into ranges, which provided the scoring for this category.

0. Very loud.
1. Loud.
2. Normal plus.
3. Normal.
4. Soft.
5. Very soft.
6. Silent.

Arabs were expected to obtain lower scores, i.e. to talk louder than Americans.

Results

Table 1 presents mean scores on all of the five proxemic variables that could be scored for Arabs as a group, for Americans as a group, and for the various subgroups.

Table 1 Arab and American group means and standard deviations on five measures of proxemic behavior

	Axis		Distance		Touching		Looking		Loudness	
	Mean	SD	Mean	SD	Mean	SD	Mean	SD	Mean	SD
Saudi Arabia n = 4	0·87	0·38	2·99	0·17	5·77	0·07	1·00	0·00	3·07	0·16
UAR n = 4	0·44	0·14	3·07	0·12	5·79	0·11	1·10	0·16	2·67	0·15
Iraq n = 4	0·70	0·14	2·96	0·04	5·82	0·08	1·09	0·08	2·77	0·13
Kuwait n = 4	0·73	0·23	2·97	0·05	5·85	0·08	1·00	0·00	2·78	0·20
Total Arab n = 16 n = 16	0·68	0·27	2·99	0·11	5·80	0·09	1·05	0·09	2·82	0·21
NY-NJ n = 4	2·34	0·12	4·28	0·10	6·00	0·00	2·64	0·14	3·61	0·24
Midwest n = 4	1·50	0·36	4·45	0·04	6·00	0·00	3·07	0·14	3·11	0·08
Colorado n = 4	1·66	0·58	4·34	0·10	6·00	0·00	3·10	0·27	3·58	0·34
California n = 4	2·50	0·03	4·29	0·09	6·00	0·00	2·62	0·11	3·42	0·15
Total American n = 16	2·00	0·54	4·34	0·11	6·00	0·00	2·86	0·28	3·43	0·29

As hypothesized, Arabs confronted each other more directly than Americans when conversing (their mean sociofugal–sociopetal axis scores are lower than for Americans), they sat closer to each other (their mean kinesthetic scores are lower than for Americans), they were more likely to touch each other (no Americans ever touched each other), they looked each other more squarely in the eye (their mean visual scores are lower than for Americans), and they conversed more loudly than Americans. Every one of our hypotheses about the direction of Arab–American differences in proxemic behavior is confirmed, and *no overlapping* is to be found between the distribution of mean scores within the Arab subgroups and within the American subgroups. [. . .]

Axis

Despite the small size of the sample, the magnitude of the difference we found on this variable would have occurred by chance less than five times in ten thousand. Our data therefore provide strong support for our first hypothesis and for Hall's observations. The various Arab subgroups are relatively homogeneous in axis; only three of the six comparisons attained statistical significance, and these at a relatively low level. This is in marked contrast to the sixteen Arab–American subgroup comparisons, all of which were statistically significant and generally at a very high level. This supports our second hypothesis, that persons from the various Arab countries will be more similar to each other than to any regional group of Americans. Four of the six comparisons among American regional groups were statistically significant, and a fifth closely approached significance. This suggests that, with respect to axis, American regional groups are more variable than Arab national groups. But even so, relatively little overlap occurs between the *t* values for intra-American comparisons and those for the Arab–American comparisons. Thus we also have support for our third hypothesis, that persons from various regions of the United States will be more similar to each other than to persons from any Arab country.

Kinesthetics – closeness

Arab–American differences on this variable were even more marked than for axis, and the *t* value falls completely off the tables. Again, greater mean differences are found among American regional groups than among Arab regional groups, though both Americans and Arabs are surprisingly homogeneous. This homogeneity is in marked contrast to the highly significant differences between the Arab–American subgroup comparisons, all sixteen of which achieved the 0·0005 level of significance. Again all three of our hypotheses with regard to distance maintained between persons were strongly supported.

Touching

Only among Arabs did any touching take place during our observations, and this was all of the accidental type. But touches were observed among persons within *each* of the four Arab subgroups and therefore can be interpreted as a general phenomenon among Arabs. The overall Arab–American difference again would have occurred by change less than five times in ten thousand. No significant differences were found between any Arab subgroups, and since no Americans touched during our observations, no differences between American regions were observed either. This is again in marked contrast to the Arab–American comparisons, all sixteen of which yielded significant differences. Again all three of our hypotheses were supported.

Visual directness

This variable yielded the same familiar picture: overall Arab–American differences were highly significant; no significant differences were found between Arab subgroups, and relatively small differences between various American regions; all sixteen Arab–American subgroup comparisons yielded highly significant differences. Again all three hypotheses were supported.

Voice loudness

Although greater heterogeneity was found on this variable among both the Arab and the American subgroups, the overall pattern is very similar to that found on the previous four proxemic variables and strong support was provided for all three of our hypotheses.

In summary, all five of the facets of proxemic behavior defined by Hall for which objective measurement could be achieved yielded highly significant differences between Arabs and Americans in the directions predicted on the basis of Hall's observations. Furthermore, Arab mean scores for the four national groups represented were extremely similar to each other, as were the mean scores of the four American regional groups, though there was more variability among Americans than among Arabs. All three of our guiding hypotheses were given strong empirical support.

Looking at Table 1 more closely, we can see that no one Arab subgroup is consistently more 'American' in proxemic behavior, than any other. The Arabians were most similar to Americans in axis and voice loudness, the UAR students in closeness and visual directness, and those from Kuwait with respect to touching. Similarly, no American regional group was consistently more 'Arab'.

Among the four Arab subgroups, certain consistent patterns of similarity did emerge, however. Group means on all five variables were very similar for the students from Iraq and Kuwait. And the Saudi Arabians and Egyptians, whom we might expect to be quite different in terms of the levels of modernization currently achieved by their countries, were most different of the four subgroups on axis, visual directness and voice loudness. They were similar, however, in distance and touching.

Also, within American regions, except for loudness, the New York–New Jersey group was consistently similar to the California group, in contrast to the Midwest and Colorado groups. This would conform with the similar cosmopolitanism of the two coastal regions. Given the very small sizes of our samples, however, these observations should be considered no more than suggestive clues for future research.

Table 2 Pearson correlations among five measures of proxemic behavior $n = 32$ (16 Americans and 16 Arabs)

	1	2	3	4	5
Variable 1 Axis	×	0·80	0·71	0·77	0·80
Variable 2 Kinesthetics		×	0·87	0·97	0·72
Variable 3 Touching			×	0·83	0·64
Variable 4 Visual directness				×	0·74
Variable 5 Voice loudness					×

A final question – are we really working with multiple dimensions here, or can these various aspects of proxemic behavior be subsumed within a single variable, such as the 'contact' – 'non-contact' dimensions suggested by Hall? For our thirty-two subjects, the uniformly high overall Pearson correlations among the five variables suggest the latter conclusion (Table 2). But these findings are partly an artifact of the gross ethnic group differences observed. *Within* the American and the Arab groups separately, several of these correlations disappeared or even reversed themselves (Table 3). Given our small sample size, we can again draw no firm conclusions, but it appears that patterns of proxemic behavior may prove more complex and variable than casual observation has led us to believe.

Summary and conclusions

Hall's impressions concerning Arab and American differences in proxemic behavior were tested empirically by means of systematic observations of sixteen American and sixteen Arab college students under controlled conditions. Highly significant Arab–American differences emerged in the direction expected, with the Arab students confronting each other more directly than the Americans, moving closer together, more apt to touch

Table 3 Pearson correlations among five measures of proxemic behavior

Variable	Americans only (n = 16)					Arabs only (n = 16)				
	1	2	3	4	5	1	2	3	4	5
1	×	−0·51	0·00	−0·58	0·43	×	−0·33	−0·16	−0·11	0·39
2		×	0·00	0·26	−0·73		×	0·38	−0·04	−0·28
3			×	0·00	0·00			×	−0·10	−0·16
4				×	−0·10				×	−0·54
5					×					×

each other while talking, looking each other more squarely in the eye, and conversing in louder tones. Marked homogeneity among the representatives of four Arab nations was also found; this was also true among the four regions of the United States represented. Nevertheless, interesting patterns of regional differences emerged and appear worthy of further investigation.

Our research, which was exploratory in nature, demonstrates both the feasibility of systematic investigation in this area and its potential power. Improved methods of recording lines of proxemic notation need to be used – such as a digital magnetic tape recorder or even a simple adding machine – that will enable the investigator to keep his eyes on the subjects at all times. A mechanical recording device would also enable the observer to increase the lines of notation to as many as one every five or ten seconds.

It is also obvious that larger samples are needed to increase confidence in the generalizability of our conclusions and to permit the kinds of within-area analysis that proved so provocative. Samples of students from all over the world are contemplated, with the eventual aim of subjecting our observations to a factor analysis. If clusters of subjects belonging to distinct cultural areas emerge, we will obtain interesting definitions of 'Arab' or 'Latin' character in proxemic terms.

When recording techniques have been perfected and when our understanding of the underlying dimensions or dimensions of proxemic behavior have advanced under controlled conditions, observations in the field are also anticipated. The plea advanced for the study of preliterate cultures before they are engulfed by the tide of civilization applies with equal weight to the study of proxemic behavior within these cultures. Observations of proxemics are not common in the ethnographic literature and tend to be limited to non-quantitative descriptions of postural and gestural habits or to remarks by the ethnographer about how the people appear to make spatial distinctions.

Acculturative changes in proxemic behavior are also worthy of systematic study. Do shifts in proxemic behavior occur as people are exposed to patterns different from those in which they were reared? Is there a syndrome of proxemic behavior associated with the urban industrial society toward which developing nations are moving? These remain tantalizing questions for further research.

Finally, almost nothing is yet known about the psychological *meanings* attached to various forms of proxemic behavior. The discomfort aroused by the gross violation of proxemic norms, particularly in cross-cultural situations, has often been noted. But *within* a culture area, are differences in proxemic style – a tendency to confront others more directly, to avoid looking them in the eye more than most, etc. – associated with other person-

ality traits? What kinds of things are communicated by such subtle deviations? We can envision the emergence of a field of 'psychoproxemics' as
challenging to the researcher as psycholinguistics is proving to be.

References

HALL, E. T. (1955), 'The anthropology of manners', *Sci. Amer.*, vol. 162, pp. 85–90.
HALL, E. T. (1959), *The Silent Language*, Fawcett, Greenwich, Conn.
HALL, E. T. (1963), 'A system of notation of proxemic behavior', *Amer. Anthropol.*,
vol. 65, pp. 1003–26.

3 Basil Bernstein and Dorothy Henderson

Social-Class Differences in the Relevance of
Language to Socialization

B. Bernstein and D. Henderson, 'Social-class differences in the relevance of
language to socialization', *Sociology*, vol. 3, 1969, pp. 1–20.

Introduction

One of the most important movements in behavioural science since the war is
the convergence of interest upon the study of basic processes of communication and their regulative functions. The one discipline which appears so far
least affected is sociology. However, from different quarters there are now
signs of growing interest (Grimshaw, 1968; Fishman, 1966; Cicourel, 1964;
Garfinkel, 1967; Hymes, 1967). The study of the educationally disadvantaged has also led to a concentration of research into the process of language
acquisition, into the relationships between language and cognition, and
into the social antecedents and regulative consequences of forms of language
use.

The Sociological Research Unit at the University of London is engaged
upon an exploratory study of forms of familial socialization which affect
orientations towards the use of language. We shall present here the results
of a closed schedule designed to reveal the relative emphasis which members
of social class groups place upon the use of language in different areas of
the socialization of the pre-school child. Although this report is confined
to a study only of the mothers'*orientation* towards the relevance of language,
as this group of mothers have been interviewed twice within a three-year
period and because two speech samples have been collected from their
children when aged five years and seven years, it should prove to be possible
to obtain some measure of both the reliability and validity of the mothers'
reports.

This report is the first step in the analysis of the section of the second
questionnaire given to the mothers which enquired into the orientation of
the mother towards various uses of language. As the other sections were
concerned with the decision-making within the family, its kinship and
community relationships, the procedures of control and role definition,
the relationships between home and school, we can relate the orientation
towards various uses of language to a range of variables.

In the discussion section of the paper we present a model which gives a sociological explanation of social learning in terms of the mediation of the linguistic process in socialization.

Hypotheses

The following hypotheses (derived from Bernstein 1966, and 1968) are to be tested:

1. Both middle class and working class would place greater emphasis upon the use of language in interpersonal aspects of socialization than the emphasis placed upon language in the socialization into basic skills.

2. The shift in emphasis in the use of language from the skill to the person area would be much greater for the middle-class group.

3. Within the skill area the middle class group would place a greater emphasis upon language in the transmission of principles.

Description of the sample

The total sample consists of 311 mothers drawn from two areas: one a working-class area and the other a middle-class area. The r between area and social class of the parents is 0·74. The index of social class was constructed by W. Brandis of the Sociological Research Unit and is based upon the terminal education and occupation of husband and wife. A full description of the Index will be found in Brandis and Henderson (1968). Social class is measured on a ten-point scale 0–9. The sample used in this paper consists of fifty mothers randomly selected from the middle-class area and fifty mothers randomly selected from the working-class area. It was necessary to limit the sample of this study in order that a detailed analysis could be carried out, and to examine possible social-class differences in response to the schedule. In terms of the ten-point scale, the mean social-class position of the middle-class group is 2·8 and the mean social-class position of the working-class group is 6·9.

The closed schedule

The closed schedule consisted of a list of eleven statements which covered the major aspects of socialization. As the schedule was presented, the interviewer put to each mother the question which was printed above the list of statements: 'If parents could not speak, how much *more* difficult do you think it would be for them to do the following things with young children who had not yet started school?' The mother's attention was then directed to the statements and she was asked to assess the difficulty she thought dumb parents would experience in dealing with each situation. A six-point scale was provided: very much more difficult, much more difficult, more difficult, not too difficult, fairly easy, easy. The statements are listed below in the order in which they were presented on the schedule:

1. Teaching them everyday tasks like dressing, and using a knife and fork. (Motor skill)
2. Helping them to make things. (Constructional skill)
3. Drawing their attention to different shapes. (Perceptual skill)
4. Playing games with them. (Dummy)
5. Showing them what is right and wrong. (Moral principles)
6. Letting them know what you are feeling. (Mother-oriented affective)
7. Showing them how things work. (Cognitive)
8. Helping them to work things out for themselves. (Independent-cognitive)
9. Disciplining them. (Control)
10. Showing them how pleased you are with their progress. (Dummy)
11. Dealing with them when they are unhappy. (Child-oriented affective)

Statements 4 and 10 were deliberately inserted as dummy statements designed to move the mother's responses across to 'fairly easy' and 'easy' and thus mitigate the emphasis placed on 'difficulty' in the initial question. In fact, these statements elicited the responses 'fairly easy' or 'easy' from 72 percent of the middle-class mothers and from 76 percent of the working-class mothers. No other statements shifted both groups to the 'easy' points of the scale to this extent. Four of the statements – 1, 2, 3 and 7 – were concerned with the transmission of skills. Five of the statements – 5, 6, 8, 9 and 11 – were concerned with aspects of social control. Statements 1, 2, 3 and 7 will be referred to as the *skill* area of statements, and statements 5, 6, 8, 9 and 11 will be referred to as the *person* area of statements. The points of the scale 'very much more difficult', 'much more difficult' and 'more difficult' will be referred to as the 'difficult' points of the scale, whilst 'fairly easy' and 'easy' will be referred to as the 'easy' points of the scale. 'Not too difficult' will be referred to as the midpoint of the scale.

It will be remembered that the aim of the schedules was to examine the effect of the social-class position of the mothers on their perception of the role of language as a socializing process. In order to obtain such information it was necessary to focus the mother's attention upon the relevance of language across a number of different areas. It was thought that mothers would experience great difficulty if they were simply asked to what extent they relied upon language when dealing with their children. We constructed a general situation such that each mother was faced with a problem of comparison. She also had to assess the difficulty of transmitting skills and dealing with interpersonal processes without language. This focused her attention upon the relevance of the linguistic component of the interaction. At the same time, it was necessary to ensure, as far as possible, that the mother should not feel that the problem was a challenge to her own extra-verbal ingenuity with her child, and so the problem was presented with the general referents *parents* and *young children*. It was equally necessary to preclude the possible use of other linguistic alternatives and therefore we stated the problem in terms of young children who had *not yet started school* and were thus unlikely to be able to read written instructions or explanations.

Method

The analysis was carried out in three stages. In the first stage we examined the population scores, in the second stage we examined the responses of individual mothers within each social class to each statement, and in the third stage analyses of variance were carried out in order to examine the interaction between the social class position of the mothers and their responses within and between the *skill* and *person* areas of statements.

First stage

The population scores enabled us:

1. To examine the distribution of maternal responses across the scale for each statement.

2. To examine the total number of responses across the scale within each area of statements.

3. To compare the total population scores within each area of statements in terms of 'difficult' and 'easy' responses.

We were then in a position to compare differences in patterns of response in relation to the statements.

Second stage

The difference between the number of 'difficult' responses and the number of 'easy' responses to each statement was examined in terms of the social class of the mothers. This procedure also enabled us to compare the 'difficult' to 'easy' responses for each statement with reference to social class.

Third stage

1. A 2×2 analysis of variance on repeated measures was carried out. This

type of analysis enabled us to control for within-person variance as well as for between-people variance and residual variance. Each point on the scale was assigned a score as follows:

Very much more difficult	$+3$
Much more difficult	$+2$
More difficult	$+1$
Not too difficult	0
Fairly easy	-1
Easy	-2

The basic unit of the analysis here was the individual mother's mean response score to the four *skill* statements. This was compared to the mother's mean response score to the five *person* statements. The analysis enabled us to test for significance the differential emphasis upon difficulty in response to each area of statements and its relationship with social class.

2. A 2×5 analysis of variance on repeated measures was carried out on the maternal responses to each of the statements within the *person* area, in order to find out whether there was a significant interaction effect between the social class of the mothers and the individual statements.

3. For the same reason a 2×4 analysis was carried out on the maternal responses to the individual statements within the *skill* area.

Results

First, we will deal briefly with the results which were found when the population scores were examined. It must be emphasized that the main justification for this stage of the analysis was to discover whether differences between the responses to the statements, as well as differences between the social-class groups, were sufficiently large to justify carrying out a more sensitive analysis on the data. We will then deal at greater length with the results of the second and third stages of the analysis.

The population responses

The distribution of the population responses across the scale show that the patterns of distributions differ markedly between the *person* statements and the *skill* statements. The responses cluster at the 'difficult' points of the scale in response to the *person* statements, whereas the distribution is normal, with 'not too difficult' operating as the midpoint, in response to the *skill* statements. Since the two areas of statements were clearly eliciting quite different patterns of response, we decided to compare the summed scores across all the statements within each area for each point of the scale. We then found that although both middle-class and working-class mothers showed a marked move to 'difficult' responses within the *person* area in comparison with their responses within the *skill* area, the relative shift was greater in the case of the middle-class responses. In order to make a more stringent comparison the responses 'very much more difficult' and 'much more difficult' were summed within each social class and compared with the summed responses 'fairly easy' and 'easy'. We found that the social-class differences in response within each area of statements were very great. In particular, the shift of middle-class responses from the *skill* area to the *person* area in terms of the emphasis upon difficulty was just over 5 to 1, whereas the shift of working-class responses from the *skill* area to the *person* area was just under 2 to 1 (Table 1).

Individual responses to statements

In the next stage of the analysis we examined the *individual* responses within each social class to each statement, in terms of the ratios of 'difficult' to 'easy' responses. Again we found that both middle-class and working-class mothers had shifted to the 'difficult' points of the scale in response to the *person* statements. But *within* the *person* area, middle-class mothers placed greater emphasis upon difficulty than did working-class mothers. Within the *skill* area we found a reversal in the pattern of response on the part of middle-class mothers. Middle-class mothers were less likely to give an 'easy' response to the statement 'Showing them how things work' than the working-class mothers. It was also found that more working-class mothers than middle-class mothers gave a 'difficult' response to the statement 'Teaching them everyday tasks like dressing, and using a knife and fork'.

Table 1 **Percentages of summed difficult/easy responses in each area**

		Difficult (0, 1)	Easy (4, 5)	Total no. responses
Middle class	Person statements	48·8	5·2	250
	Skill statements	11·5	30·0	200
Working class	Person statements	33·2	21·2	250
	Skill statements	21·0	20·4	200

The analysis of variance

1. The results of the 2×2 analysis of variance on repeated measures show that the differential emphasis on difficulty between the two areas is highly significant ($F_{1,98} = 294 \cdot 53$, $p > 0 \cdot 001$). Very much greater emphasis was placed upon difficulty within the *person* area of statements than within the *skill* area of statements. However, the analysis also showed that, although greater emphasis was placed on the difficulty of dealing with the situations

described in the *person* area by *all* the mothers, the difference between the responses of the middle-class mothers in relation to the two areas of statements was significantly greater than the difference between the responses of the working-class mothers ($F_{1,98} = 73 \cdot 60$, $p > 0 \cdot 001$). Middle-class mothers placed much *greater* emphasis upon the difficulty or doing the things described in the *person* area than the working-class mothers, but they placed much *less* emphasis upon the difficulty of doing the things described in the *skill* area than the working-class mothers. This highly significant interaction effect illustrates the polarization of the responses of middle-class mothers in relation to the two areas of statements.

We will now turn to the results of the analyses of maternal responses *within* each area.

2. Within the *skill* area the results show that middle-class mothers placed very much less emphasis on language than working-class mothers on the difficulty of doing the things described in these statements, and that this difference in response was highly significant ($F_{1,98} = 228 \cdot 78$, $p > 0 \cdot 001$). This finding replicates the result found by the previous analysis. However, a highly significant interaction effect between the social class of the mothers and responses to individual *skill* statements was revealed by this analysis. Working-class mothers placed significantly greater emphasis on difficulty in response to the statement 'Teaching them everyday tasks like dressing and using a knife and fork', than did middle-class mothers; middle-class

Table 2 **Summary table of mean scores**

| | Statements | | |
	Skill area	Person area	Total $\bar{x}$
$\bar{x}$ Middle class	0·07	1·49	0·78
$\bar{x}$ Working class	0·33	0·80	0·56
Sample $\bar{x}$	0·20	1·04	

mothers, on the other hand, placed significantly greater emphasis on difficulty in response to the statement 'Showing them how things work' than did working-class mothers ($F_{3,294} = 74 \cdot 88$, $p > 0 \cdot 001$).

Table 3 **Summary table of mean scores**

| | Skill statements | | | | |
	1	2	3	7	Total $\bar{x}$
$\bar{x}$ Middle class	−0·48	0·12	0·04	0·62	0·30
$\bar{x}$ Working class	0·48	0·28	0·36	0·36	1·50
Sample $\bar{x}$	0·01	0·20	0·20	0·49	

3. The 2×5 analysis of maternal responses to the five *person* statement shows that middle-class mothers considered that these situations would be more difficult to deal with without language than did working-class mothers. This differential emphasis on difficulty in relation to the *person* statements is highly significant ($F_{1,98} = 14\cdot25$, $p > 0\cdot001$). A highly significant main order effect, *irrespective* of the social class position of the mothers, arose out of differences in response to individual statements ($F_{4,392} = 6\cdot49$, $p > 0\cdot001$).

This result shows that individual statements within the *person* area had elicited very different responses from both middle-class and working-class mothers. We were therefore interested to know how the responses differed *between* the *person* statements. In other words, how were the *person* statements *ranked* in difficulty? The mean scores are presented below as they were ranked in order of difficulty by *all* the mothers in the sample.

Person statements	Mean scores
8. Helping them to work things out for themselves.	1·37
9. Disciplining them.	1·32
5. Showing them what is right and wrong.	1·14
6. Letting them know what you are feeling.	0·98
11. Dealing with them when they are unhappy.	0·91

Summary of results

Differences in response were shown to be due to (*a*) the statements within each area, (*b*) the social class of the mothers, and (*c*) the interaction between social class and individual statements. We find that middle-class mothers

Table 4 Summary table of mean scores

	Person statements					Total $\bar{x}$
	5	6	8	9	11	
$\bar{x}$ Middle class	1·54	1·36	1·56	1·70	1·28	7·44
$\bar{x}$ Working class	0·74	0·60	1·18	0·94	0·54	4·00
Sample $\bar{x}$	1·14	0·98	1·37	1·32	0·91	

consider language less relevant to the situations described by the *skill* statements than do working-class mothers. There is one exception. Middle-class mothers considered that 'Showing them how things work', would be *more* difficult to deal with without language than working-class mothers. Conversely, middle-class mothers place greater emphasis upon language than working-class mothers in response to the *person* statements. However, *all* the mothers considered the *person* situations more difficult to cope with than the *skill* situations. [. . .]

Discussion

The results show that the middle class, relative to the working class, place a greater emphasis upon the use of language in dealing with situations within the person area. The working class, relative to the middle class, place a greater emphasis upon the use of language in the transmission of various skills. However, within the skill area the middle class place a greater emphasis upon the use of language in their response to the statement, 'Showing them how things work', whereas within the same area the working class place a greater emphasis upon the use of language in response to the statement, 'Teaching them everyday tasks like dressing, and using a knife and fork'.

Can these differences in emphasis be accounted for in terms of differences in the relevance of these two *areas* for the social classes? In other words, does the move to language simply reflect the relevance of the area? Or is it the case that both areas respectively have equal relevance to the social classes but their verbal realization is different? It is unlikely that the middle class relative to the working class value basic skills less and yet it is this group which places a reduced emphasis upon language in the skill area. It would be just as difficult to maintain that socialization into relationships between persons is not of *equal* relevance to every subcultural group, although the *form* of that socialization may well vary. On the other hand, the very marked shift by *both* groups towards language in the person area and away from language in the skill area may well reflect the greater importance of control over persons rather than control over the development of skills in the socialization of the very young child. It is therefore unlikely that the shifts in emphasis placed upon the use of language in each of the two areas respectively, by the two social-class groups can be explained in terms of the difference in the relevance of the skill area and the person area. It might be that middle-class mothers can conceive of a variety of ways, other than linguistic, for the acquisition of skills and for this reason these mothers place less emphasis upon language. Whereas the working-class mothers can conceive of fewer alternatives to language for the acquisition of skills. This might seem to be a plausible explanation, but we think that it by no means accounts for the differences between the social classes.

We shall argue that the explanation is to be found in the nature of the social relationship when skills and person relationships are transmitted. If it is the case that in the working class knowledge is transmitted through a social relationship in which the receiver is relatively passive and if, in the middle class, knowledge is transmitted through a social relationship in which the receiver is active, then we might expect the distribution of responses which have been revealed. It may be that motor, perceptual and manipulative skills are acquired by the child in the middle class by his exposure to varied and attractive stimuli which the child explores on his *own* terms. In other words, in the acquisition of motor, perceptual and manipulative skills, the child regulates his own learning in a carefully controlled environment. It is of significance that despite the relatively greater emphasis placed upon language in the skill area by the working-class group, the middle class place greater emphasis upon language in response to the statement, 'Showing them how things work'. It is likely that this statement, for the middle class, raises questions of the transmission of principles, whereas the other three statements within the same area *do not*. If this is the case, then the situation for the middle-class child is particularly fortunate. For, on the one hand, he is socialized into elementary skill learning through role relationships which emphasize autonomy *and* he has access to principles.

In the working-class group, the concept of learning may well be different and, therefore, the form the social relationship takes when skills are acquired would be of a different order. The concept of learning here seems to be less one of self-regulated learning in an arranged environment and more a concept of a didactic theory of learning implying a passive receiver, in which a mother has little alternative but to tell or instruct a child. Although the emphasis in the working-class group, relative to the middle-class, is upon language, presumably upon *telling* or instructing, the child is much less likely to receive explanations of principles. Thus it may be that the working-class child learns skills in terms only of an understanding of the operations they entail, whereas the middle-class child learns both the operations and principles.

Other work of the Sociological Research Unit can be referred to here in support of these hypotheses. Two years prior to the interview in which the present schedule was administered, a sample of 351 middle-class and working-class mothers (of which the sample used in this paper is a subsample) were given a questionnaire in which the mothers were invited to give their views upon a range of experiences relevant to their child's behaviour in the infant school. We found that when middle-class mothers were asked to rank in order of importance six possible uses of toys, they ranked more highly than did the working-class mothers 'To find out about things' (Bernstein and Young, 1967). Further, middle-class mothers saw the role of the infant-school child as an active role, whereas the working-class mothers tended to see this role as a passive one (Jones, 1966). Middle-class mothers, relative to working-class mothers, indicated that 'play' in the infant school had educational significance (Bernstein, 1967).

It would appear than that the difference in the response of middle-class and working-class mothers to the relevance of language in the acquisition of various skills is more likely to arise out of differences in the concept of learning than out of differences between the social classes in terms of the value placed upon the learning of such skills. The socialization of the middle-class child into the acquisition or skills is into both operations and principles which are learned in a social context which emphasizes *autonomy*. In the case of the working-class child, his socialization into skills emphasizes operations rather than principles learned in a social context where the child is accorded *reduced autonomy*.

We will now turn to discuss the differences between the social classes in their emphasis upon the use of language in interpersonal contexts. The results are very clear. Where the context is interpersonal, the middle class, relative to the working class, move markedly towards the use of language. Further, the shift in the emphasis upon language from the skill area to the person area is very much greater in the middle class than in the working class. This, the verbal realization of affects, moral principles and their, application to behaviour, and independence in cognitive functioning is much more likely to be linguistically elaborated in the middle class than in the working class. This is *not* to say that these aspects of socialization do not have the same significance in the working class, only that (according to the mothers' responses) language is of less relevance in the form of the socialization.

Indeed, *both* classes rank the statements (in the person area) in the same order of difficulty.

It is not possible to infer from the mothers' responses what they actually would say to the child, but again we can refer to evidence obtained from the first interview with the mothers two years earlier. This evidence strongly suggests that:

1. The middle-class mothers are more likely than working-class mothers to take up the child's attempts to interact verbally with the mother in a range of contexts.

2. The middle-class mothers are less likely to avoid or evade answering difficult questions put to them by their children.

3. The middle-class mothers are less likely to use coercive methods of control.

4. The middle-class mothers are more likely to explain to the child why they want a change in his behaviour (Bernstein and Brandis, 1968).

Thus, we have good reasons for believing that not only is there a difference between the social classes in their emphasis upon language in contexts of interpersonal control, but there is a difference in the meanings which are verbally realized. It would seem that the internalizing of the principles of the moral order, the relating of this order to the specifics of the child's behaviour, the communication of feeling, is realized far more through language in the middle class than in the working class. The social is made explicit in one group, whereas the social is rendered less explicit in the other. Where the social is made explicit through language then that which is internalized can itself become an object (Mead, 1934). Perhaps here we can begin to see that the form of control over persons in the middle class induces a reflexive relation to the social order, whereas, in the working class, the form of control over persons induces a relatively less reflexive relation to the social order.

The question of the relatively greater emphasis upon the use of language in the interpersonal area raises fundamental questions about the nature of middle-class forms of socialization which would take us beyond the confines of an empirical research report. In Bernstein (1966 and particularly 1968) there is an extensive discussion of the social antecedents of forms of language use and socialization. The view taken in these and other papers is that linguistic codes are realizations of social structure, and both shape the contents of social roles and the process by which they are learned. In short, it has been suggested that the use of elaborated codes renders the implicit explicit, whereas the use of restricted codes reduces the possibility of such explicitness. Thus the codes and their variants regulate the cultural meanings which are rendered both explicit and individuated through the use of language. Whilst there is no evidence in this paper that middle-class mothers use forms of an elaborated code and working-class mothers use forms of a restricted code, Robinson and Rackstraw's analysis (1967) of the answering behaviour of mothers in the main sample indicates grounds for believing that these coding orientations are likely to be found. Further, the works of Bernstein and Brandis (1968) and Cook (1968) show that the forms of control used by the middle class and the working class are consonant with the predictions derived from the sociolinguistic theory. We will have further evidence when Miss Cook's analysis of the speech of the mothers is completed.

We have suggested that in the middle class skills are acquired in such a way that the child has access both to operations and principles. He tends to regulate his own learning in an arranged environment which encourage autonomy in skill acquisition. For this reason the middle-class mothers place less emphasis upon the use of language in the statements within the skill area. In the case of the working-class child, we have argued that he socialized more into the acquisition of operations than into principles through a social relationship which encourages passivity in the learner and so reduces autonomy in skill acquisition. Thus the working-class mothers, relative to middle-class mothers, place greater emphasis upon the use of language when responding to the statements in the skill area. In the case of control over persons, we have suggested that the forms of such control in the middle class arise out of a social structure which is realized through the use of elaborated codes, whereas the forms of control in the subgroup of the working class under examination arise out of a social structure which is realized through forms of a restricted code. As a result, the form of control in the middle class induces a reflexive relation upon the part of the child towards the social order, whereas in the working class the forms of control induce a much less reflexive relation to the social order.

We should point out that a developed reflexive relation to the social order does not necessarily imply role distancing behaviour. In the same way, reduced reflexiveness to a particularistic social order does not necessarily imply that role distancing behaviour will *not* occur in relation to members of a society holding universalistic status.

We can best summarize our interpretation of the results of this analysis and the more general explanation given in this paper, by the use of the following model:

Social structure

↓

Emphasis on language

Orientation	*Role/self-concept*	Middle class	Working class
Persons	Reflexiveness	High	Low
Skills	Autonomy	Low	High
Implicit theory of learning		Self-regulating	Didactic

The model should be read *horizontally* in relation to the areas of orientation and consequent emphasis on language, and *vertically* in relation to implicit theories of learning and emphasis upon language. For example, if there is a *high* emphasis upon the use of language in terms of orientation to *persons* then this will tend to generate *high reflexiveness* of the self-concept; if the emphasis on the use of language is *low* then this will generate *reduced reflexiveness* of the self-concept. In terms of the orientation to *skills*, a *low* emphasis on language will generate *autonomy* in the self-concept, whilst a *high* emphasis on language in this area will *reduce autonomy* in the self-concept. At the same time, the relative emphasis upon the use of language in these two areas perhaps implies different implicit theories of learning. Where the emphasis upon the use of language is *high* in terms of orientation to persons or *low* in terms of orieintation to skills, then the implicit theory of learning is *self-regulating*. Where the emphasis on the use of language is *low* in terms of orientation to persons or *high* in terms of orientation to skills, then the implicit theory of learning is *didactic*. It is important to add that, in this paper, because of the small sample, we have treated the middle class and working class as homogeneous groups. When the total sample is analysed it may be possible to show that there are subgroups within each social-class group who respond differently in relation to these two areas. It is quite impossible that differential emphasis upon the use of language in terms of the acquisition of skills or interpersonal control is related to differences in the form of the social relationships. A subculture may give rise to an implicit theory of learning which is self-regulating in terms of orientation to persons and didactic in terms of orientation to skills, or vice versa. The relationship between culture, linguistic codes, implicit theories of learning and differential emphasis upon the use of language is a matter of investigation. An extensive discussion in Bernstein (1968) deals with the relationship between social structure, forms of social relationship, linguistic codes and different orders of meaning. The hypotheses on which our model is based are derived from this paper.

We can now develop our discussion in regard to possible discontinuities between implicit theories of learning in the home and explicit theories of learning in the school. It is suggested that there may be, for the working-class child in the primary school, two sources of discontinuity; one in the area of skill acquisition and the other in the area of interpersonal relations. If, for example, the school emphasizes autonomy in the acquisition of skills but the implicit concept of learning in the home is didactic in relation to skills, this will be a major source of discontinuity. Similarly, if the school is concerned with the development of reflexive relations in the area of interpersonal relations but the implicit concept of social learning in the home operates to reduce reflexiveness in this areas, then this will be another source of discontinuity. It may be unreasonable to expect children exposed to such discontinuities to respond initially to forms of control which presuppose a culture and socialization very different from their own.

Earlier in this discussion we referred to the fortunate situation of the middle-class child in terms of the results of our analysis. His role relationships emphasize autonomy in the acquisition of skills and reflexiveness in the area of interpersonal relations. He is accorded discretion to *achieve* his social role. On the other hand, the role relationships of the working-class child, in terms of our analysis, reduce his autonomy in the skill area and reduce reflexiveness in the interpersonal area. He has much less discretion – his social role is *assigned*.

In this paper we have shown that maternal definitions of the role of language as a socializing process are dependent upon the area of orientation and that this differential emphasis on the use of language is related to different forms of social relationship within the social structure. Further, we have argued that the differential emphasis on the use of language in relation to certain areas of orientation may reflect different implicit theories of learning which affect the self-concept of the child. We have suggested that these different implicit theories of learning in the home may conflict with the theories of learning in the school, and in this way give rise to major sources of discontinuity between the home and the school.

This analysis has enabled us to contruct a model which gives a sociological explanation of social learning through the mediation of the linguistic process of socialization.

Conclusion

We must emphasize that our data consists of mothers' reports not of their actual behaviour, and that these reports have been obtained through the use of a closed schedule. The analysis of the degree and type of discrimination on the part of the middle-class and working-class mothers gives us reasonable grounds for believing that the scaling procedures and the statements were appropriate. We also believe that the situation construed was such that the 'right' or conventional response was not obvious to the mothers. We have shown that both groups ranked the statements in the person area according to the same gradient of difficult. However, we cannot present at the moment an analysis of possible differences between the social classes in their interpretation of the statements. We may be able to throw some light on social-class differences in the interpretation of the statements when the responses of the mothers to the closed schedule is related to their responses to the other schedules within the language section of the second questionnaire *and* to the results of the analysis of the initial questionnaire.

The findings presented here indicate very clear differences between the social-class groups in their relative emphasis upon language. We hope to be able to utilize the model offered in the conclusion of the discussion to show, when the total sample is analysed, *intraclass* differences in the orientation to the use of language in these two areas of socialization. Perhaps the most important conclusion of this paper is to stress the need for small-scale naturalistic experimental studies of the channels, codes and contexts which control the process of socialization.

In conclusion, it is the case that the three hypotheses given in the introduction have been confirmed. The findings have also revealed that working-class mothers relative to middle-class mothers place a greater emphasis upon language in the acquisition of basic skills. The inferential structure developed into the discussion makes explicit the relationships between macro aspects of social structure and micro aspects of socialization.

References

BERNSTEIN, B. (1966), 'A sociolinguistic approach to social learning', in J. Gould (ed.), *Social Science Survey*, Penguin.

BERNSTEIN, B. (1967), 'Play and the infant school', *Where*, Supplement 11, *Toys*, Christmas.

BERNSTEIN, B. (1968), 'A sociolingustic approach to socialization', in J. Gumperz, and D. Hymes (eds.), *Directions in Sociolinguistics*, Holt, Rinehart & Winston. Also in *Human Contest*, 1 December 1968.

BERNSTEIN, B., and BRANDIS, W. (1968), 'Social-class differences in communication and control', in W. Brandis and D. Henderson (eds.) (University of London Institute of Education, Sociological Research Unit Monograph Series directed by Basil Bernstein), *Primary Socialization, Language and Education, vol. 1, Social Class, Language and Communication*, Routledge & Kegan Paul.

BERNSTEIN, B., and YOUNG, D. (1967), 'Social-class differences in conceptions of of the uses of toys', *Sociology*, vol. 1, no. 2.

BRANDIS, W., and HENDERSON, D. (1968), *Social Class, Language and Communication*, Routledge & Kegan Paul.

CICOUREL, A. V. (1964), *Method and Measurement in Sociology*, Free Press.

COOK, J. (1968), 'Familial processes of communication and control', to be published in the Sociological Research Unit Monograph Series, in preparation.

FISHMAN, J. (1966), *Language Loyalty in the United States*, Mouton.

GARFINKEL, H. (1967), *Studies in Ethnomethodology*, Prentice-Hall.

GRIMSHAW, A. D. (1968), 'Sociolinguistics', in W. Schramm, N. Maccoby, E. Parker, L. Fein (eds.), *Handbook of Communication*, Rand McNally & Co.

HYMES, D. (1967), 'On communicative competence'. This paper is revised from the one presented at the *Research Planning Conference on Language development among Disadvantaged Children*, held under the sponsorship of the Department of Educational Psychology and Guidance, Ferkauf Graduate School, Yeshiva University, 1966. The paper is available from Department of Social Anthropology, University of Pennsylvania, Philadelphia.

JONES, J. (1966), 'Social class and the under-fives', *New Society*, December.

LOEVINGER, J. (1959), 'Patterns of parenthood as theories of learning', *J. Soc. Abnorm. Psychol.*, pp. 148–50.

MEAD, G. H. (1934), *Mind, Self and Society*, University of Chicago Press.

ROBINSON, W. P., and RACKSTRAW, S. J. (1967), 'Variations in mothers' answers to children's questions, as a function of social class, verbal intelligence test scores, and sex', *Sociology*, vol. 1, pp. 259-76.

Part Two
The Elements of Social Behaviour

Research in different aspects of social interaction has shown what the important elements of behaviour are, and how they function. Ervin-Tripp (Reading 4) discusses various aspects of verbal utterances, and the different kinds of utterance, considered as social acts. She does not discuss the non-verbal voice signals which accompany speech-tones of voice, variations in pitch, nor the bodily movements occurring during conversations – these are described in other Readings. One of the most important bodily movements that is coordinated with speech is gaze. Kendon (Reading 5) describes an investigation in which he showed how gaze functions not only as a means of obtaining feedback, but also acts itself as a signal, and in particular is important in governing the synchronizing of speech. This was an intensive exploratory study using a small number of subjects; however the findings have been confirmed and extended in later research. The study of bodily movements was called 'kinesics' by Birdwhistell (Reading 6) gives a summary by him of the present state of this very important field. Much of the work so far has consisted in classifying and labelling the main bodily movements; there has been little experimental research proper into the function of bodily movements, and some investigators think that this may be inappropriate, believing that these signals form a kind of language, and that we need to look for its grammar.

Experimental work has been carried out, however, on the larger movements of posture, orientation and proximity. Mehrabian (Reading 7) has shown experimentally that subjects use these signals if asked to suppose they are interacting with people of high or low status, or with people whom they like or dislike. The results are impressive though the method used was rather artificial.

4 Susan Ervin-Tripp

An Analysis of the Interaction of Language, Topic and Listener

S. Ervin-Tripp, 'An analysis of the interaction of language, topic and listener',
American Anthropologist, vol. 66, 1964, pp. 86–94.

In this paper we shall examine some of the characteristics of sociolinguistic research, and illustrate with a detailed example. The companion field of psycholinguistics (Osgood and Sebeok, 1954; Saporta, 1961) has concentrated heavily on individual psychology: perception, learning, individual differences, pathology. Social psychology has appeared primarily in attitude studies (Osgood, Suci and Tannenbaum, 1957, pp. 189–216), not in psycholinguistic research concerning socialization and acculturation, or small-group and institutional behavior. Thus, in the very fields which overlap most with sociology and sociolinguistics, psycholinguistic research is least developed.

Sociolinguists study verbal behavior in terms of the relations between the setting, the participants, the topic, the functions of the interaction, the form and the values held by the participants about each of these (Hymes, 1962, p. 25). Verbal behavior (talk and its equivalents) is the center of this definition, but of course a complete description of the system must include gestures or pictures when they are functional alternatives to linguistic signs. Verbal behavior is everywhere structured as a highly cohesive system, and therefore it is a convenient starting point. Others might want to deal with a larger set of communicative arts including, for instance, the dance and exchange of tangible objects.

Setting

We shall use the term *setting* here in two senses, that of *locale*, or time and place, and that of *situation*, including the 'standing behavior patterns' (Barker and Wright, 1954, p. 45–6) occurring when people encounter one another. Thus, situations include a family breakfast, a faculty meeting, a party, Thanksgiving dinner, a lecture, a date. Social situations may be restricted by cultural norms which specify the appropriate participants, the physical setting, the topics, the functions of discourse and the style. Obviously, situations vary as to which of these restrictions exist and the degree of permissible variation, so that a sermon may allow less style variation than a party. By altering any of these features, one might either create a reaction of social outrage, change the situation to a new one (date becomes job interview), or enter a situation lacking strong normative attributes and allowing maximal variation.

One of the major problems for sociolinguistics will be the discovery of independent and reliable methods for defining settings. The folk taxonomy of a given society (Conklin, 1962, p. 120) might provide lexical categories for the definition of settings. However, the folk taxonomy may be too gross or too fine to indicate classifications of value to the social scientist. The high degree of regularity of elliptical constructions in waiter-to-cook request forms suggest that there is a setting class for which there is no common name in English; Thanksgiving and Christmas-dinner behavior has common properties though we have no generally accepted superordinate term for both events.

Joos (1962, p. 13) has given a classification of five major setting varieties in his own cultural system; these he defines by style types as intimate, casual, consultative, formal and frozen. The fact that only the first two correspond to common usage suggests that the folk taxonomy may be inadequate for the level of generality Joos sought. It would be desirable to couch the discriminanda of settings in terms permitting cross-cultural comparisons. Joos's hypothesis (1962, p. 10) that all 'national languages' have five styles is testable only if the division of types he described is not arbitrary.

Participants

For most sociolinguistic analyses the important features of participants will be sociological attributes. These include the participants' status in the society, in terms such as sex, age and occupation; their roles relative to one another, such as an employer and his employee, a husband and his wife; and roles specific to the social situation, such as hostess–guest, teacher–pupil, and customer–salesgirl.

In any act of communication, there is a 'sender' and a 'receiver' (Hymes, 1962, p. 25) who together may be called interlocutors. In addition, there may be present an audience which is not the primary addressee of the message. The role of sender, or speaker, is rarely distributed in equal time to all participants. There appear to be four factors which affect the amount of talking of each participant. One factor is the situation. In informal small-group conversation the roles of sender and receiver may alternate; in a sermon the sender role is available to only one participant; in choral responses in a ritual, or in a question period following a lecture, the role of sender is allocated at specific times. A second, related, determinant of the amount of talking is the role the participant has in the group and his social and physical centrality. He may be a therapy patient, chairman, teacher or switchboard operator, so that his formal role requires communication with great frequency; he may informally play such a role, as in the case of a rancounteur, or an expert on the topic at hand. There is a personal constant carried from group to group. The net effect of the second and third factors is that the sending frequency of participants in a group is almost always unequal, and has been shown to have regular mathematical properties in informal discussion groups (Stephen and Mishler, 1952; Bales and Borgatta, 1955). Because relative frequency of speaking is steeply graded, not evenly distributed, in a large group the least frequent speaker may get almost no chances to speak. The 'receiver' role also is unequally distributed even in face-to-face groups, being allocated to the most central, the most powerful, those with highest status, the most frequent speakers, and under conditions where agreement is desired, the most deviant (Hare, 1962, p. 289; Schachter, 1951).

Topic

The manifest content or referent of speech is here called the topic. Topically equivalent sentences may be different in form so that topic is maintained through a paraphrase or translation. Compare these two sentences paraphrased from Watson and Potter (1962, p. 253):
'Every episode of conversation has a focus of attention.'
'There is a single topic in each homogeneous unit of interaction.'

In the terms of Watson and Potter's definitions, these sentences are topically equivalent. Also equivalent are the following: 'Shut up!' 'Please be quiet.' 'Tais-toi.'

Topic includes both gross categories such as subject matter (economics, household affairs, gossip), and the propositional content of utterances. It is the topic which is the concern of cognitive structure studies of kinship systems which differentiate 'grandmother' and 'mother' but not 'mother' and 'mommy'.

Obviously some expressive speech (ouch!) and some routines (hi!) do not have a manifest topic. Such contentless speech could usually be replaced by gestures. In traditional treatments of language, topic is considered essential and typical because of its absence in most non-human and non-linguistic communication. It seems more appropriate to consider referential speech as simply one subcategory of speech. Topically dissimilar utterances or utterances with and without referential content can be functional equivalents. From a functional standpoint, the following could be equivalents in some situations:
'I'm sorry' = 'Excuse me.'
'Hi' = 'How are you?'

Functions of the interaction

Within a given setting, verbal discourse may vary in function. We use 'function' to refer to the effect on the sender of his actions. Skinner (1957, p. 2) has pointed out that in its social uses language may be viewed as operant (rewarded or punished) behavior, which affects the speaker through the mediation of a hearer. The distinction between topic and function is similar to the one between manifest and latent content, as employed in content analysis. A difference is that since in many speech situations the addressee is known, and subsequent behavior of the sender is known, it is more often possible for delineate functions in ordinary speech than in the texts for which content analysis often is employed.

The following system was developed to account for the initiation of dyadic interactions. It is not intended to cover continuous discourse, but merely initiations. The criterion of classification was the hearer response which could terminate the interaction to the satisfaction of the initiator.

1. Requests for goods, services or information

The overt behavior of the hearer is manipulated, e.g. 'What time is it?'
'Please pass the potatoes.' 'Slow down!'

2. Requests for social responses

The desired hearer reactions are often not explicit or even consciously known to the speaker. The subcategories often used are those derived from Murray's need system (1938, p. 315) which includes recognition, dominance, self-abasement, nurturance, affiliation. Behaviorally, overt hearer responses which might be elicited are applause, sympathetic words, laughter, a hug or an angry retort; but often hearer reactions are covert, e.g. 'What a gorgeous dress you're wearing!' 'A weird thing happened to me today.' 'You're a fool.'

3. Offering information or interpretation

Spontaneous instruction evidently based on the belief that the hearer would be gratified to learn. Analogous to spontaneous offer of goods or services, e.g. 'That's Orion. ' 'Did you hear about the fire?'

4. Expressive monologues

Expressions of joy, sorrow, anger; talking to oneself, muttering. The sender reacts to an external stimulus, a feeling, or a problem without attending to the hearer's comments, which may be minimal or absent.

5. Routines

Greetings, thanks, apologies, offers of service by waitresses and salespeople, where the alternatives are extremely restricted, and hence predictable.

6. Avoidance conversations

Conversation is started only because the alternative activity is unpleasant or the sender is satiated; any hearer will do, and topics are highly variable. Water-cooler conversations in an office, coffee breaks during study sessions, bus-stop discourse.

A somewhat similar system was developed by Soskin and John (1963) to classify all the utterances in natural conversations. Their system, for instance, differentiates 'signones', in which the speaker describes his own state or opinions, from 'regnones', in which he tries to influence another's behavior. They point out that 'signones' such as 'I'm still thirsty' or 'that tasted good' may in a benign and nurturant environment be used 'as a consciously manipulative act'. In purely functional terms, such 'signones' are requests for goods, services or information. Thus Soskin and John's classification seems in part to be formal. It is important to treat form separately from function just because there may be systematic discrepancies between manifest and latent function, as indicated in these examples. This point will be discussed further in the next section.

Because functions may not always be explicit, one way to discern latent functions is to examine the sender's reaction to various outcomes. The reason we know that 'Got a match?' is sometimes a social demand rather than a demand for a match is that the speaker may go on chatting even if he fails to get a match. If he primarily wanted a match he would go elsewhere for one. Avoidance conversations are typically masked in the manifest content of other function classes. Small children at bed time may make plausible requests; these could be unmasked if a functionally equivalent alternative response were given – for instance, if one brought a cracker in response to a request for a glass of water. Certain conversational functions perhaps must always be masked in a given society; others must be masked for certain receivers or in certain settings. Masking permits functional ambiguity. A woman's remark to her escort, 'It's cold outside tonight', might be either an expressive monologue or a request for his coat. Presumably such ambiguity may lead to social embarrassment because of differences in interpetation by speaker and hearer.

Formal features of communication

The form of communication may be viewed as having four aspects. The *channel* might be spoken language, writing, telegraphic signals, etc. As we have indicated, gestural signals on occasion may be systematic alternatives to speech and in such cases are part of the significant exchange. The *code* or *variety* consists of a systematic set of linguistic signals which co-occur in defining settings. For spoken languages, alternative codes may be vernaculars or superposed varieties. *Sociolinguistic variants* are those linguistic alternations linguists regard as free variants or optional variants within a code, that is, two different ways of saying the same thing. *Non-linguistic vocal signals* include the range of properties called paralinguistic (Trager, 1958; Pittenger, Hockett and Danehy, 1960) which lack the arbitrary properties of linguistic signals.

Linguists have been concerned primarily with codes rather than with the other three classes of formal variation. A discussion of code distinctions especially pertinent to social variations can be found in Gumperz (1961, 1962). He distinguishes between the *vernacular* (the speech used within the home and with peers) and the *superposed variety* ('the norm in one or more socially definable communication situations'). Superposed varieties include many types, from occupational argots to koines used for trade and regional communication, such as Melanesian Pigdin and Swahili. A special type of vernacular-koine relation exemplified in Greece, German Switzerland, Arab countries and China, had been called *diglossia* by Ferguson (1959). These all are illustrations of code variations.

A speaker in any language community who enters diverse social situations normally has a repertoire of speech alternatives which shift with situation. Yet linguists have generally focused on relatively pure codes. They do this by trying to control the speech situation with the informant and to keep him from using borrowed forms without identifying them. They also may seek out monolinguals who have mastered only one vernacular, and whose speech constitutes therefore a recognizable norm (though not necessarily a highly valued norm in the larger community). Larger communities label some alternative varieties, especially those which either are different enough to interfere with intelligibility, or are identified with specific social groups. 'Folk linguistics' of dialect perception and of classification into language and dialect taxonomies bears on the values attached to speaking in a certain way. As Weinrich has pointed out, 'accent' perception is systematically biased.

It may sometimes be difficult to isolate the features of superposed varieties, because they normally coexist in a single speaker and therefore may interpenetrate. One must seek defining situations demanding rigid adherence to a code (as in prayers) to isolate the features of the code. These may be hard to find in societies like our own with great tolerance for stylistic variability in a given situation. Where the formal difference in varieties is great, as in some diglossias, interpenetration may be more effectively inhibited. Obviously, where code switching and interpenetration or borrowing are permissible, they become available to mark role and topic shifts within a setting (Gumperz, 1964a).

Sociolinguistic variants have received very little attention. Examples are the systematic array of deletions available in answers and requests, as in 'Coffee', *v.* 'Would you give me some coffee, please?'

Request sentences provide some excellent examples of formal variation with functional and topical equivalence. If we use Soskin and John's six categories (1963), we find that requests could take any form, as in the following examples:

'It's cold today.' (structone)
'Lend me your coat.' (regnone) (Also 'would you mind lending . . . ?')
'I'm cold.' (signone)
'That looks like a warm coat you have.' (metrone)
'Br-r-r.' (expressive)
'I wonder if I brought a coat.' (excogitative)

We could also classify these utterances by more conventional grammatical terms, as declarative, imperative and interrogative.

It is clear that the selection of these alternatives is not 'free' but is conditioned by both situational and personal factors. Student observations have shown that the imperative form is used most often to inferiors in occupational settings, and more often for easy than difficult or unusual services. The yes–no question is the most typical request form to superiors. Informants regarding cross-cultural differences have reported great variation in the 'normal' request form to employees in such cases of alternatives as:

'There's dust in the corner,' *v.* 'Sweep the dust from the corner.'
'It's haying time,' *v.* 'Start the haying tomorrow.'

Morphological as well as syntactic options may be available as sociolinguistic variants, as illustrated by Fischer's analysis (1958) of the alternation between the participal suffixes /in/ and /iŋ/. Obviously the choice of referential synonyms (Conklin, 1962) is socially conditioned, as anyone reflecting on English synonyms for body functions will recognize. In fact, the number of referential synonyms may be indicative of the complexity of attitudes towards the referent. Brown and Ford (1961) have observed that the number of terms of address in America is usually directly related to intimacy, nicknames and endearments permitting marking of attitude variations.

The intercorrelation of these variables has been demonstrated in a variety of studies. The following are illustrative.:

1. Participant–function–form. Basil Bernstein (1962) has discovered systematic differences between middle-class and working-class adolescent conversation groups in England. These may be summarized as greater emphasis on offering information and interpretation in middle-class groups and on requests for social responses in working-class groups. The effects on form of these function differences were great. The middle-class boys used fewer personal pronouns, a greater variety of adjectives, a greater variety of subordinate conjunctions, more complex syntax and more pauses.

2. *Participant–form.* Ferguson (1964) has pointed out that in many languages there is a style peculiar to the situation of an adult addressing an infant. The common formal features may include a change in lexicon, simplification of grammar, formation of words by reduplications, simplifying of consonant clusters and general labialization.

Brown and Gilman (1960) examined many aspects, both contemporary and historical, of the selection of 'tu' and 'vous' in French address, and the corresponding terms in Italian and German. They found that the selection was based primarily on the relation of sender and receiver, and that historically the selection had been based on relative power, whereas currently relative intimacy is more important. They found national differences, such as greater emphasis on kin-intimacy in Germany and on camaraderie in France and Italy. They also found that personality and ideology influenced individual differences in the sender's selection.

Joan Rubin (1962) found that the choice of Spanish or Guaraní for address in Paraguay was describable in terms of the same set of dimensions – 'solidarity' and 'power' or status, and sometimes setting. She gives the example of the use of Spanish by men courting woman, and the switch to Guaraní with marriage. Thus in a multilingual society a code shift can mark the same contrasts as a sociolinguistic variation in a single language.

Another kind of participant–form study is illustrated by Putnam and O'Hern's analysis (1955) of the relation between social status, judged by sociological indices, and linguistic features of speech in a Negro community in Washington, D.C. This study has many similarities in method to dialect geography, but adds a procedure of judge's blind ratings of status from tapes, to make a three-way comparison possible between objective status, perceived status, and specific features. Labov (1964) gives a sophisticated analysis of a status–form relation.

3. *Function-setting.* A comparison of interactions of a nine-year-old boy at camp and at home, by Gump, Schoggen and Redl (1963) showed systematic functional changes even in such a subcategory as interactions addressed to adults. The percentage of 'sharing' (which was primarily verbal) was higher at camp, and the percentage of 'submissive' and 'appeal' behavior toward adults was higher at home. Sharing included asking opinion, playing with an adult, competing, telling a story. The child's shifts in behavior may have been effects of the variations in adult-initiated interaction.

Soskin and John (1963, p. 265) used a set of categories which were partially functional in analysing tapes of a couple on vacation, and showed significant variations with setting. Explicitly directive utterances were most frequent by the wife in the cabin, and by the husband out rowing, where he gave her instructions. Informational utterances were most common for both at meal times.

4. Topic–form. In a study of New England children, Fischer (1958) collected evidence of several factors related to the alternation of the participal suffix /iŋ/ *v.* /in/. He found the selection to depend on sender ('typical' *v.* 'good' boy), and on topic of discourse. He heard 'visiting', 'correcting' and 'reading' *v.* 'swimmin', 'chewin' and 'hittin'. The topical distribution suggests that behind the alternation by topic lies an alternation by participants, with /iŋ/ being heard from adults, especially teachers, and /in/ being heard from peers.

Gumperz (1964b) describes the effects of topic on the alternation in Norway between a rural dialect and standard North Norwegian. He found that the type of formal alternation depended on the social properties of the group of addressees.

5. Setting–form. Changes of form with setting have been frequently described. Some excellent examples of a shift between a spoken dialect and a superposed variety are provided by Ferguson (1959), for example the shift from classical to colloquial Arabic which accompanies a shift from formal lecturing to discussion in a classroom. Herman (1961) has given a number of examples of the influence of setting on code selection in Israel, pointing out that immigrants speak Hebrew more often in public than in private situations.

Sociolinguistic variations and paralinguistic features were noted by Andrea Kaciff and Camille Chamberlain who compared children's speech in a preschool playground with their role-playing in a playhouse. The material was reported in an unpublished term paper. They found certain lexical changes, such as the use of role-names in address: 'Go to sleep, baby, say goo-goo.' They found that the children playing the role of the mother adopted a sing-song intonation especially when rebuking the play child. This intonation was not used by the children except in imitative play, and had been observed by another student in a study of adults' speech to other people's children.

In ordinary social life all of these interacting variables tend to vary together. The public setting of the Israeli immigrants included a different audience than the private setting; the address of adults to children is different in participants, topics, and form at once. In using naturalistic situations, we can discern the critical factors in determination of alternations only if we can find in nature comparisons in which other possibly relevant factors are held constant. An example is lecturing *v.* class discussion

diglossia, where the topics, participants and functions may remain the same but only the situation changes, and with it the form. Where it is not possible to find such orderly experimental situations, an appropriate sequel to the ethnographic method is the social experiment.

References

BALES, R. F., and BORGATTA, E. F. (1955), 'A study of group size: size of group as a factor in the interaction profile', in P. Hare, E. F. Borgatta and R. F. Bales (eds.), *Small Groups*, Knopf.

BARKER, R. G. (ed.) (1963), *The Stream of Behavior*, Appleton-Century-Crofts.

BARKER, R. G., and WRIGHT, H. F. (1954), *Midwest and its Children*, Harper & Row.

BERNSTEIN, B. (1962), 'Social class, linguistic codes, and grammatical elements', *Language and Speech*, vol. 5, pp. 221–40.

BROWN, R. W., and FORD, M. (1961), 'Address in American English', *J. abnorm. soc. Psychol.*, vol. 62, pp. 375–85.

BROWN, R. W., and GILMAN, A. (1960), 'The pronouns of power and solidarity', in T. A. Sebeok (ed.), *Style in Language*, Wiley.

CONKLIN, H. C. (1962), 'Lexicographical treatment of folk taxonomies', *International J. Amer. Linguistics*, vol. 28, pp. 119–41.

FERGUSON, C. A. (1959), 'Diglossia', *Word*, vol. 15, pp. 325–40.

FERGUSON, C. A. (1964), 'Baby talk in six languages', *Amer. Anthropol.*, vol. 66, pp. 103–14.

FISCHER, J. L. (1958), 'Social influences on the choice of a linguistic variant', *Word*, vol. 14, pp. 47–56.

GUMP, P. V., SCHOGGEN, P., and REDL, F. (1963), 'The behavior of the same child in different milieus', in R. G. Barker (ed.), *The Stream of Behavior*, Appleton-Century-Crofts.

GUMPERZ, J. J. (1961), 'Speech variation and the study of Indian civilization', *Amer. Anthropol.*, vol. 63, pp. 976–88.

GUMPERZ, J. J. (1962), 'Types of linguistic communities', *Anthropol. Linguistics*, vol. 4, pp. 28–36.

GUMPERZ, J. J. (1964a), 'Hindi-Punjabi code-switching in Delhi', in M. Halle (ed.), *Proceedings of the International Congress of Linguists*, The Hague.

GUMPERZ, J. J. (1964b), 'Linguistic and social interaction in two communities', *Amer. Anthropol.*, vol. 66, pp. 137–53.

HARE, A. P. (1962), *Handbook of Small Group Research*, Free Press.

HERMAN, S. (1961), 'Explorations in the social psychology of language choice', *Human Relations*, vol. 14, pp. 149–64.

HYMES, D. (1962), 'The ethnography of speaking', in T. Gladwin and W. Sturtevant (eds.), *Anthropology and Human Behavior*, Anthropological Society of Washington, pp. 15–53.

JOOS, M. (1962), 'The five clocks', supplement to *Int. J. Amer. Linguistics*, vol. 28, part V.

LABOV, W. (1964), 'Phonological correlates of social stratification', *Amer. Anthrop.*, vol. 66, pp. 164–76.

MURRAY, H. A. (1938), *Explorations in Personality*, Harvard University Press.

OSGOOD, C. E., and SEBEOK, T. A. (1954), 'Psycholinguistics', supplement to *Int. J. Amer. Linguistics*, vol. 20, Memoir 10.

OSGOOD, C. E., SUCI, G. J., and TANNENBAUM, P. H. (1957), *The Measurement of Meaning*, University of Illinois Press.

PITTENGER, R. E., HOCKETT, C. F., and DANEHY, J. J. (1960), *The First Five Minutes*, Ithaca, Paul Martineau.

PUTNAM, G. N., and O'HERN, E. M. (1955), 'The status significance of an isolated urban dialect', *Language Dissertations*, no. 53.

RUBIN, J. (1962), 'Bilingualism in Paraguay', *Anthropol. Linguistics*, vol. 4, pp. 52–8.

SAPORTA, S. (1961), *Psycholinguistics*, Holt, Rinehart & Winston.

SCHACHTER, S. (1951), 'Deviation, rejection, and communication', *J. abnorm. soc. Psychol.*, vol. 46, pp. 190–207.

SKINNER, B. F. (1957), *Verbal Behavior*, Appleton-Century-Crofts.

SOSKIN, W. F., and JOHN, P. V. (1963), 'The study of spontaneous talk', in R. G. Barker (ed.), *The Stream of Behavior*, Appleton-Century-Crofts.

STEPHEN, F. F., and MISHLER, E. G. (1952), 'The distribution of participation in small groups: an exponential approximation', *Amer. Soc. Rev.*, vol. 17, pp. 598–608.

TRAGER, G. (1958), 'Paralanguage: a first approximation', *Studies in Linguistics*, vol. 13, pp. 1–12.

WATSON, J., and POTTER, R. J. (1962), 'An analytic unit for the study of interaction', *Human Relations*, vol. 15, pp. 245–63.

5 Adam Kendon

Some Functions of Gaze-Direction in Social Interaction

A. Kendon, 'Some functions of gaze-direction in social interaction',
Acta Psychologica, vol. 26, 1967, pp. 22–47.

The material gathered and the procedures for analysis

The data to be discussed in this paper have been drawn from sound and
film records of parts of seven two-person conversations, involving thirteen
individuals in all, three of whom were female, and all of whom were undergraduates at the University of Oxford. Each pair, the members of which
were in all cases previously unacquainted, were left together for half an
hour with the instruction to 'get to know one another'. The conversations
were recorded on magnetic tape, and two parts of it were filmed. The subjects
sat across a table, facing one another (about three and a half feet between
them) and to one side of them, on the table, a mirror was placed in such a
way that the camera, which was placed eight feet away behind a screen,
could photograph both subjects in full face, one directly and one in the
mirror. The film was shot at the rate of two frames a second (so that several
minutes of film could be shot at once), and a special piece of apparatus was
attached to send in a signal to the tape recorder each time a frame was
taken. In this way a fairly precise coordination between the film and the
sound record could be made.[1]

The subjects were fully informed of the set-up beforehand. This was
done in the hope that their suspicions and curiosities would be allayed so
that, during the conversation, they would not have to worry too much
about what was going on. In fact few of the subjects had difficulty with the
situation, and in some cases they became very involved with one another
and enjoyed the conversation very much. On being questioned afterwards,
all of them stated that there was some initial awkwardness, but they quickly
came to accept the situation, and were not disturbed by the knowledge
that they were being recorded or by the presence of the apparatus.

The analyses to be reported here are based on a study of five-minute
samples from six of the conversations, all of them taken from the last ten
minutes of it. The sample from the seventh conversation was in two parts.

1. This coordinating device was designed and constructed by Dr E. R. F. W. Cross-
man.

One was seven minutes long, and the other nine minutes, taken from the first and last ten minutes of the conversation respectively.

The films were transcribed, frame by frame, by means of a positional notation using pictographic symbols (Ex and Kendon, 1964). With this notation not only was direction of gaze recorded for each frame but also details of the facial expression, the position of the head, the hands and arms, and the trunk. Analyses of these other aspects of the social performance will be reported elsewhere. A preliminary report has been presented in Kendon (1964). The words uttered, if any, within the half-second interval elapsing between each frame and the one following, were written in against each frame transcription. All of the analyses to be reported here were done from these transcripts. Limitations in the projection apparatus available did not make it possible to do the analyses directly from the films.

No formal reliability studies were made of the work of the transcribers. The transcription of one of the films was done by Dr J. Ex, and the author, who worked in close collaboration, each concentrating on only one of the subjects, but none the less in continual consultation. Four further films were transcribed by the author and a research assistant, again working in close consultation. In all cases, what was aimed at was a transcription on which the transcribers were in complete agreement. Two further films were transcribed by the author for direction of gaze only. Since the author worked on the transcriptions of all of the films studied for this paper, at least they have been done according to a consistent method, though of course other transcribers might have used slightly different criteria in making their descriptions. Also, since this part of the work was purely descriptive, and no interpretation was involved, it is thought likely that discrepancies between different transcribers would be quite small. [. . .]

Direction of gaze in relation to utterance occurrence

It has emerged that an important source of variability in the amount p looks during the course of a conversation is the amount that he speaks, since it was found that the pattern of p's looking behaviour during speaking was quite different from that found during listening. It appeared that whereas during silence p looks in long gazes at q, while speaking he alternated between q- and a-(away) gazes more equal in length. Since it is through the utterance, primarily, that p seeks to pursue his projects in the encounter, whether these concern the material being dealt with in it, or the relationship he has with the other participants, perceptual activity in relation to the occurrence of utterances has considerable interest, for we may expect that it plays a part in the guidance of p's behaviour in the encounter. We shall see too that it may play a part in the guidance of q's behaviour.

Beginning and ending of long utterances

First of all, we shall consider how gaze direction changes as p begins and as he ends a long utterance. A long utterance, for present purposes, is any utterance that last for five seconds or more. Such utterances typically require that q be silent while p is speaking. Shorter utterances are often produced during the other person's utterance, and they tend to fall into the class distinguished by Ogden and Richards (1947) as 'emotive' or, by Soskin and John (1963) as 'relational'. They are, that is, immediate reactions to the other person's ongoing behaviour. They do not involve any planning phase. In their lexical form they suggest that they are always old and well-established speech habits. Long utterances by contrast almost always involve a certain amount of advance planning, even if it is a matter of selecting, from among a number of alternatives, of which a number of well-rehearsed phrases shall be used (cf. discussion in Goldman-Eisler, 1958).

In Figure 1 a diagram is presented, giving an example of a typical long utterance exchange, showing not only changes in gaze direction, but

	NL speech	eyes	brows	mouth	head	gaze	gaze	head	mouth	brows	eyes	JH speech
352	and um	O	⊓⌐	O	□			□ ⊥T	−	W	≍	
3	sometimes	O	⊓⌐	O	⌐□			□ ├	−	W	≍	
4	of course it's	≍	⊓⌐	O	□⊥			□ ├T	=	⊓⌐	O	
355	only one of	≍	m	O	□⊥			□ ├	=	⊓⌐	≍	
6	parents in which	≍	m	O	□⊥			□ ├	=	W	≍	
7	case you can	≍	m	O	□⊥			□ ├	=	W	O	
8	take it	≍	⊓⌐	O	□⊢			□ ├	=	W	O	
9	away and	O	⊓⌐	O	□⊢			□ ├	=	W	≍	
360		O	⊓⌐	O	□⊢			□ ├	=	W	O	
1	let the	O	⊓⌐	O	□⊢			□ ├T	=	W	≍	
2	other one feed them	≍	⊓⌐	O	□⊥			□ ├T	=	W	≍	
3		O	⊓⌐	O	□⊢			□ ├T	=	W	≍	
4	itself	O	⊓⌐	O	□			□ T	◉	W	≍	
5		O	⊓⌐	−	□			□ T├	◉	W	≍	some breed-
6		O	⊓⌐	−	□			□ ├T	◉	W	≍	ers
7		O	⊓⌐	−	□			□ ├T	◉	⊓⌐	≍	um
8		O	⊓⌐	−	□			□ ├T	◉	⊓⌐	≍	pair
9		O	⊓⌐	−	□			□ T	θ	m	≍	with
370		O	⊓⌐	−	□			□ T├	θ	m	≍	infer-
1		O	⊓⌐	−	□			□ ├T	θ	m	O	ior
2		O	⊓⌐	−	□			□ ├	θ	m	O	birds for
3		O	⊓⌐	−	□			□ ├	θ	m	≍	this purp-
4		O	⊓⌐	−	□			□ ⊥T	−	⊓⌐	O	ose
5		O	⊓⌐	−	□			□ ⊥T		⊓⌐	≍	
6		O	⊓⌐	−	□			□ ⊥T	θ	⊓⌐	×	em I mean
7		O	⊓⌐	−	□			□ ├T	θ	W	≍	
8		O	⊓⌐	−	□			□ ├T	θ	W	≍	
9		O	⊓⌐		□			□ ├T	θ	W	≍	those that don't
380												

key

head
□ head erect face pointing forward
⌐□ head turned left
□⌐ head turned right
┤ head tilted left
├ head tilted right
⊥ head tilted back
T head tilted forward

brows
⊓⌐ normal
m raised brows
W puckered or 'frowning' brows

mouth
− closed lips relaxed
O lips relaxed mouth open
◉ lips pouting
= lips drawn tight at corners
⊠ lips pressed forward "pursed"

eyes
O fully open
× narrowed eyes
≍ closed eyes

gaze
□ p looking at q

Figure 1 Partial extract from the film-transcript showing a long utterance exchange

changes in the position of the head and in certain aspects of the facial posture as well. It will be seen first, that as NL ends his utterance the fluctuations in the position of his head come to an end, and he holds his head in a pose little different from the erect position, he looks up at JH before he finishes speaking, and goes on looking at her after he has finished. JH behaves rather differently. Up to 362, and for quite a long period before this, she combines looking at NL with a fairly fixed head posture, one in which she has her head cocked slightly to one side and titled forward. At 361 she utters a faint 'mm', and at 362 she drops her eyelids over her eyes, tilting her head forward in the next frame. She continues to look down, even after she begins to speak at 366. Her head position shows marked changes. This looking away, and other changes, which occur before she begins to speak, coincide with the beginning of the last phrase of NL's utterance, at the point at which, it may be presumed, JH has realized NL is going to finish. Thus it seems that JH is already showing that she is ready to talk before she actually begins to. And NL, in looking steadily at JH before he finishes speaking, is in a position to pick up this advance warning, that she has already, in this case, accepted his offer of the floor.

This example provides all the elements that we have found to occur in many long utterance exchanges. Such exchanges occur quite often in conversations when people are exchanging points of view, comparing experiences or, as in the particular case used for illustration, exploring one another's knowledge of something. When individual cases of this sort are examined, it is found that there is usually some change in the auditor's behaviour before he actually begins to speak, and the person who is bringing a long utterance to an end does so by assuming a characteristic head posture (which is different for different individuals), and by looking steadily at the auditor, before he actually finishes speaking. Such changes in behaviour which precede the utterance itself, clearly make it possible for each participant to anticipate how the other is going to deal with the actual point of change of speaker role, perhaps facilitating the achievement of smoother, or more 'adjusted' changeovers, than might otherwise occur.

The element which has been found to be most typical, and to occur most commonly, is a certain pattern of changes in direction of gaze. Data on this for all of the samples analysed for this study are presented in Figure 2. Here the percentage frequency of q-gaze for each half second is plotted, for three seconds preceding the beginning and the end of the utterance, and for three seconds following its beginning or following its end.

As will be apparent, there is a very clear and quite consistent pattern, namely, that p tends to look away as he begins a long utterance, and in many cases somewhat in advance of it; and that he looks up at his interlocutor as the

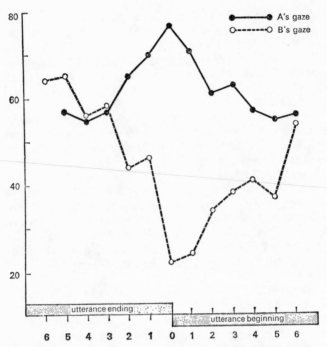

Figure 2 Direction of gaze and the beginning and ending of long utterances. Frequency of q-directed gazes at successive half-second intervals before and after the beginning (broken line) and ending (continuous line) of long utterances. Pooled data from ten individuals, based on a total of sixty eight long utterances

end of the long utterance approaches, usually during the last phrase, and he continues to look thereafter. It was found that of the ninety-five utterances for which beginnings could be observed, over 70 per cent of them were begun with an a-gaze, and that there are only three individuals for whom less than half of their utterances did not begin in this way; and of the ninety-seven utterances for which endings could be observed, there were four individuals for whom less than half of their long utterances ended with a q-gaze.

This relationship may be understood from two points of view. In looking away at the beginning of a long utterance, p is shutting out one important source of input from his interlocutor, and it may be that he is actually withdrawing his attention from him, as he concentrates on planning what he is going to say.[2] When he approaches the end of his utterance, he is

2. We imply here that paying attention to one's interlocutor and planning what to say are incompatible activities. Analyses of the relationship between sensory input

approaching what might be called a choice-point in the interaction sequence. This is a point at which subsequent action he might take will depend largely upon how his interlocutor is behaving. We expect, thus, that p will seek information about his interlocutor at such points, and therefore that he will look at him, as indeed we have found.

From another point of view it should be observed that in so far as looking away at the beginning of an utterance, and looking back as it ends, are regular occurrences, these changes in direction of gaze can come to function as signals to p's interlocutor, marking points of significant change in his stream of behaviour, and, further, may be exploited by p to regulate q's behaviour. Thus, in looking away as he begins an utterance, or before he begins it, in many cases, p may be seen by q to be about to be engaged in an action, and p may indeed look away to forestall any response from q. Similarly, in looking up as he ends an utterance q can perceive that p is now ceasing to talk yet still giving him his attention, and in giving his attention in this way, q can perceive that p now expects some response from him. From p's point of view then, p may be said to be 'offering' q the floor, for in looking steadily at him he indicates that he is now 'open' to his actions, whatever they may be.

In an attempt to corroborate the last part of this interpretation, namely that looking up at the ends of long utterances functions for q as a signal that p is ready for a response from him, we examined the latency with which

Table 1 A comparison between q's responses to p, when q ends his utterances looking, and when he ends them without looking at q. Data from two conversations only, including all utterances

	q *fails to respond or pauses before responding*	q *responds without a pause*	*Total*
p ends utterance			
looking	10	24	34
not looking	29	12	41
	39	36	75

$\chi^2 = 13 \cdot 38$, $df = 1$
$p < 0 \cdot 001$

and motor action in serial tasks such as tracking, and studies of selective listening to speech, support the hypothesis that the human being is to be regarded as capable of dealing with only limited amounts of information at once, and this imposes upon him the necessity of distributing his attention among the several facets of the situation where his activity depends upon processing large amounts of information from several sources simultaneously. This is likely to be the case in social interaction. See the discussion in Broadbent (1958) and Welford (1960).

q's utterances followed those of p's where p did not look up as he ended his utterance. If the interpretation is correct we should expect that in these cases, where p does not look up, q's latencies should be greater than where he does do this. Table 1 presents a comparison of q's responses following utterances ended with a gaze, with those following utterances ended with an a-gaze. These results are taken from two conversations only (these were the only two in which a sufficient number of the two kinds of utterance endings occurred to enable a proper comparison to be made). It will be seen that of those utterances which ended with an extended look 29 per cent were followed by either no response or by an delayed response from q; but of those that ended without p looking up, 71 per cent were followed by either a delayed response or by no response. ($\chi^2 = 13\cdot38$, $df=1$, $p<0\cdot001$.)

Gaze-direction during long utterances

We have seen that p tends to look at q more while he is listening than while he is speaking, and we have seen too that his q-glances during speech tend to be shorter than those observed during listening. It is of some interest to inquire whether there is any association between the structure of p's speech, and where he is looking as he produces it. From the work of Goldman-Eisler (1958), and of Maclay and Osgood (1959) we know something of the significance in changes in rate of speech, and of the occurrence of hesitations and fluent passages. Should a consistent association emerge between direction of gaze and these structural aspects of the utterance, this may add to our understanding of the role of visual information in the regulation of utterance production.

Speech of speech and direction of gaze

Earlier it was suggested that p looked away at the beginning of an extended utterance because such an utterance would require planning, and that p would not be able both to plan what he had to say and monitor q's behaviour simultaneously. As Goldman-Eisler (1954) has shown, although the actual rate of articulation remains remarkably constant, and highly characteristic for a given individual, there are large variations in overall speech rate and these are a function of the amount of hesitation that occurs in the utterance. She has further shown (Goldman-Eisler, 1958) that hesitations tend to precede novel combinations of words, and that they are also more common during speech expressing abstractive and interpretative thought, than during speech in which p is merely describing something (Goldman-Eisler, 1961). This leads her to the suggestion that hesitations occur when there is a lag between the organizational processes by which speech is produced, and actual verbal output. Thus periods of fluent speech correspond to the running off of well organized phrases, or of phrases that are

Table 2 Speech rates and direction of gaze*

Subject	Mean speech rate while looking in syllables per half-second	Mean speech rate while not looking in syllables per half-second	Number of stretches of continuous speech where speech rate was faster while looking than while not looking	Number of stretches of continuous speech where speech rate was slower while looking than while not looking
RB	2·4	2·1	8	2
JS	2·6	2·0	3	1
JH	2·3	1·7	14	4
NL	2·3	1·9	16	10
SJ	3·0	2·3	9	4
W	2·4	2·0	4	0
JS	2·7	2·2	5	2
WJ	2·8	2·4	8	1
Overall mean	2·5	2·03	67 (72·8%)	24 (26·2%)

*Three dyads have been omitted because they did not offer a sufficient number of long stretches of continuous speech for comparison.

prelearned (as, for example, in conventionalized phrases or repeated phrases that form part of an individual's habit of speech), whereas unfluent speech corresponds to the interruption of the processes of speech production by organizing processes (Goldman-Eisler, 1958). If the suggestion made earlier is correct, we should expect that p will be less likely to look at q during those periods when he is engaged in organizing his speech, that is during periods of hesitant speech, than he will when he is speaking fluently, running off a well-organized phrase. We have, therefore, compared the rate of speech production (measured as the number of syllables per half-second) during those portions of the utterance when he is not looking at him. The results are presented in Table 2. The speech rates have been computed for ninety-two different speech stretches taken from eight different individuals. It will be seen first that for all individuals the speech rate is higher during looking than it is during not looking. Second, that for all individuals more than half of the speech stretches examined, and for all of them together three quarters of the speech stretches display faster speaking during looking than during not looking.

It should be noted that this analysis is confined to long utterances, in which only stretches of continuous speech have been considered. Where, as is often the case, a long utterance consists of two or three units of speech separated by a clear phrase boundary pause, these have been treated separately.

Fluent speech, hesitant speech and pausing, and direction of gaze

For the purposes of the present analysis the utterance has been considered to consist of a series of phrases (identifiable as complete grammatical units), each phrase separated from the one that follows it by a short pause, the phrase boundary pause. Within these phrases there are likely to be variations in the fluency with which words are produced. There may be actual breaks in word production (unfilled hesitations), or the break in word production may be filled by a 'hesitation noise' ('um' or 'er', for example), p may break off in mid phrase and repeat what he has just said, or he may retrace his steps, as it were, and correct the phrase he has just produced. These varieties of hesitation have been distinguished by Maclay and Osgood (1959), but for present purposes they have been considered together as 'hesitant speech'. Besides this, 'fluent speech', 'phrase ending', 'phrase pausing' and 'phrase beginning' have been distinguished. For each half second of every long utterance, whether p was looking at q or whether he was not has been noted against the structure of the utterance prevailing at the time. The results are presented in Table 3.

This shows first, that p tends to look at q during fluent speech much more than he does during hesitant speech (50 per cent of the time spent speaking fluently, as compared to only 20·3 per cent of the time spent speaking hesitantly). This finding, of course, coincides with the one reported in the previous section, in so far as fluent speech tends to be fast compared to hesitant speech. Secondly, the table shows that p is more likely to be looking at q at the moment that he ends a phrase, than he is when he resumes speaking after the phrase boundary pause.

What appears to be a typical pattern of gaze-direction change in association with the occurrence of phrase boundary pausing as compared to hesitation, may be seen clearly from the diagram in Figure 3 (p. 86), where a plot is presented of the percentage frequency with which p was found to be looking at q at each successive half second preceding, during and following a phrase boundary pause (upper graph), and a hesitation (lower graph), for two individuals, based upon sixteen minutes of conversation. It will be seen that this figure illustrates graphically what the figures in Table 3 also show, namely that phrase boundary pauses and hesitation pauses differ sharply in how p distributes his gaze when they occur. In the former, p looks at q as he comes to the end of the phrase, he continues to look during the phrase (though the longer the pause lasts the less likely he is to be looking) and then, as the next phrase begins, the tendency is for p to look away again. Hesitations, in contrast, are marked by a decline in the extent to which p looks at q and, unlike the phrase boundary pause, p tends to look back at q as he begins speaking fluently again. The hesitations once over,

Table 3 Direction of gaze and its association with certain aspects of the structure of long utterances

RB	JS	W	SJ	JS	WJ	JH	NL	Total	
227	63	119	203	185	175	547	591	2112	Total amount of fluent speech
117	17	27	40	97	118	345	294	1055	Amount of fluent speech with q-gaze
51·5	26·9	22·7	19·7	52·4	67·4	62·8	49·7	50	Proportion of fluent speech with q-gaze (%)
74	18	31	123	100	35	82	149	612	Total amount of hesitant speech
21	4	8	13	22	8	13	35	124	Amount of hesitant speech with q-gaze
28·4	22·2	25·8	10·6	22	22·9	15·9	23·5	20·3	Proportion of hesitant speech with q-gaze (%)
34	3	19	25	14	25	62	70	252	Number of phrase endings
18	0	5	8	9	23	47	50	150	Number of phrase endings with q-gaze
52·9	0	26·3	32	64·3	92	75·8	71·4	63·5	Proportion of phrase endings with q-gaze (%)
29	3	14	36	15	28	51	50	226	Amount of phrase pausing
9	0	6	11	5	18	29	26	104	Amount of phrase pausing with q-gaze
31·0	0	42·9	30·6	33	64·2	56·9	52	46·0	Proportion of phrase pausings with q-gaze (%)
20	2	11	20	9	21	40	53	176	Number of phrase beginnings
7	0	1	1	5	12	12	15	53	Number of phrase beginnings with q-gaze
35·0	0	9	5	55·6	57·1	30	28·3	30·1	Proportion of phrase beginnings with q-gaze (%)

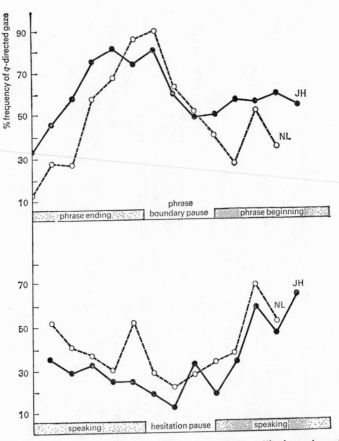

Figure 3 Frequency of q-directed gazes in association with phrase boundary pauses (upper figure) and within phrase hesitations (lower figure) for two individuals. Total sample: forty-eight phrase boundary passes and forty-three hesitation pauses.

p has worked out a phrase to express what he wants to say, and he can run it off, watching q's response to it as he does so.

Phrases, in the sense in which they are referred to here, comprise the minimally meaningful units of an utterance, they are grammatically complete, and it might be said that they constitute the packages in which the speaker ties up what he has to say, and evidence from memory span experiments in which subjects were asked to repeat as much as possible from a passage of speech they had just heard, suggest that this packaging of information assists the listener in his assimilation of the material (Moyra Williams, personal communication). The gaze that is associated with, as it were, the delivery of each phrase, can be seen to have both a checking function for the speaker, in that it is at these points that he is free to check upon how what he is saying is being received by the listener. They may also have a signalling function for the listener, in so far as they mark the boundary of these information packages. They also, we may suppose, mark the points at which p is looking for an accompaniment response from q.

Evidence that the speaker does indeed get some response at these points in his utterance, is provided by an analysis of the distribution of accompaniment signals in relation to certain aspects of the speaker's utterance structure. In Table 4 we have recorded, for each occurrence of an accompaniment signal, what the speaker was doing at the time of the signal. It will be seen that the highest proportion of them (48 per cent) occur during the phrase boundary pause, and that extremely few occur at the point at which speech is resumed after such a pause. Compared with the number that would be expected to occur, if accompaniment signals were produced without any relation to the structure of the speaker's speech, it will be seen that far fewer than would be expected occur during fluent speech, and far more of them occur during phrase boundary pauses.

We may now see something of the part that gaze-direction plays for the interactants, in regulating each other's behaviour. In withdrawing his gaze, p is able to concentrate on the organization of the utterance, and at the same time, by looking away he signals his intention to continue to hold the floor,

Table 4 **Distribution of accompaniment signals in relation to certain aspects of the structure of the speaker's speech**

| | Number of accompaniment signals that occurred during | | | | |
	Fluent speech	Hesitant speech	Phrase ending	Phrases pausing	Speech resumption
	2	1	1	6	0
	2	4	8	2	0
	2	1	1	5	0
	8	9	0	14	1
	1	1	0	1	1
	0	1	0	7	0
	6	2	1	12	0
	2	4	3	15	2
Observed totals	23	23	14	62	4
Expected totals*	90	26	10·8	9·7	7·6

*Calculated on the assumption that they occur at equal time intervals during the speaker's speech without regard to the structure of the speech.

and thereby forestall any attempt at action from his interlocutor. In looking up, which we have seen that he does briefly at phrase endings, and for a longer time at the ends of his utterances, he can at once check on how his interlocutor is responding to what he is saying, and signal to him that he is looking for some response from him. And for his interlocutor, these intermittent glances serve as signals to him, as to when p wants a response from him.

Gaze-direction in relation to the occurrence of short utterances

Long utterances, as we have said, are those utterances which, for their effective production and reception demand that the speaker 'holds the floor' for their duration, and that the listener listens. Such utterances, which last for at least five seconds, and usually for much more than this, involve some degree of planning and organization, and they cannot be responded to properly until they are completed. Short utterances, in contrast, which include accompaniment signals, attempted interruptions, exclamations and short questions, and short answers to questions, have in common that they are simple in their content and that they do not in themselves involve the speaker's claim to the floor, though they may be either a request for the floor, or they may be an advance indication of the speaker's intention to take the floor. For the purposes of the following discussion, we have considered short utterances as falling into the groups mentioned above.

Accompaniment signals. These are the short utterances that the listener produces as an accompaniment to a speaker, when the speaker is speaking at length. There is some evidence to suggest that the speaker does rely upon them for guidance as to how what he is saying is being received by his listener, but very little has been done in the way of classifying the wide variety of forms which accompaniment signals take, or in examining possible differences in their functions. Birdwhistell (1960) reports an investigation of headnods, which are usually coincident with vocalized accompaniment signals, in which he distinguishes between the single, double and triple headnod, and describes how each of these different sorts of headnods have different consequences for the way the speaker organizes his performance. For example, where the single headnod occurs in rapid succession during the course of a phrase within the speaker's utterance, the speaker may slow up and hesitate. Where it occurs in association with the points, of stress in his speech, he will continue. From examples such as these, it is clear that the auditor can exert a fairly detailed control over the speaker's behaviour by the kind of headnods he produces, and how he places them in relation to certain aspects of the structure of his interlocutor's speech. The same is no doubt equally true of verbalized accompaniment signals. Fries (1952) has noted a large number of variants of this form of utterances, though he does not attempt any analysis of the differences in their functions (he even implies that there are no such differences). Here we shall follow a tentative classification, based upon an analysis of where, in relation to the speaker's behaviour the auditor places his attention signals, in which we suggest two main classes of accompaniment signals. These are: the attention signal proper in which *p* appears to do no more than signal to *q* that he is attending, and following what is being said, and what we shall refer to as the 'point granting' or 'assenting' signal. This most often takes the lexical form of 'yes quite' or 'surely' or 'I see' and it occurs when the speaker is developing an argument by presenting a series of points for which he asks the auditor's agreement. Two examples may help to clarify this distinction:

Example 1
SJ: It seems a pity that say someone like that and say someone like Morrison who is performing the same sort of function   *mhm*   um livening the place up a bit it's a pity they're almost lost   *mhm*   to um active politics you know they can air their views and   *yes*   that sort of thing but their power is so limited that   it   seems a great pity somehow   *mhm*.

In this example, taken from a conversation in which the subjects were discussing the functions of the House of Lords, SJ is merely stating his opinions, and his interlocutor's accompaniment signals, which coincide approximately with the ending of each of SJ's points or statements, do no more than indicate that he is still 'with' SJ. These accompaniment signals are examples of the attention signal proper, and they are to be contrasted with 'point granting' or 'agreement' signals, such as occur in the following passage:

Example 2
JS: Well they're put up as absolute dictators aren't they?   *mm yes*   I mean in electing a Prime Minister we say: we make you responsible for what happens to our country   and   *that's true*   therefore indirectly for what happens to us.

Here JS begins his utterance with a rhetorical question, and he then follows this up with a restatement of the argument, which he structures in such a way that his continuing is dependent upon his interlocutor consenting to, or specifically granting him, the points that he is making.

The distinction in terms of their place in relation to the other's discourse seems clear enough. In Table 5 it will be apparent that the distinction in terms of gaze-direction is also quite clear. In almost every case, when *p*

Table 5 Short utterances and gaze-direction

Type of utterance	Number associated with q-gaze	Number associated with a-gaze	Sign test (two-tailed)
Accompaniment signals			
(a) Attention signals	37	16	
(b) Assenting signals	2	25	$p < 0.002$
Short questions	31	10	$p < 0.0005$
Laughter	18	8	$p < 0.04$
Exclamatory utterances			
Positive exclamations (surprise, delight, joy, increased interest)	10	3	
Negative exclamations (horror, disgust, sadness, disagreement, embarrassment)	1	5	

produces an attention signal, he continues to look steadily at q. When he produces an 'agreement' signal, he looks away. This looking away is typically very brief, usually as short as the utterance itself, and it is usually accomplished by merely dropping the eyelids over the eyes, together with a single, or sometimes a double headnod of a rather restricted amplitude.

It should perhaps be noted that within the two main classes of this kind of utterance we have distinguished, there are many further variants which we have not attempted to sort out. For example, in giving the attention signal, p may at the same time hint that he is bored or amused, that he is impatient, that he has not been paying full attention, and so on. These different attitudes may be conveyed by variations in the stress and intonation patterns within the utterances, variations in the relative lengthening or shortening of the syllables, and by variations in the way in which he places his utterances in relation to what the other is saying. What typical kinesic and gaze-direction patterns there are that are associated with such variants is a matter for future investigation. We at present are confident only in the main differences already described.

Exclamations and laughter. By exclamations we mean utterances, whether requested by the speaker or not, that the auditor produces as a direct emotive response to what the speaker is saying or doing. They may be immediately identified by clear deviations from the speaker's speech baseline. Though many exclamations have a lexical character peculiar to them (e.g. 'gosh', 'oh golly', 'heavens' and so forth) they may also take the lexical character of an attention signal, yet are to be identified as exclamations rather than as attention signals through the overlengthening of syllables, overhigh or overlow pitch levels, and various unusual voicings, such as 'squeeze' or whispering. Kinesically, exclamations may readily be distinguished from other accompaniment signals in that they are always associated with relatively marked and prolonged changes in head position, and by a clear change in facial expression.

Associated gaze-direction patterns are given in Table 5. It will be seen that during laughter p is more often looking at q than not. Where he is looking during an exclamation depends upon the kind of feeling being expressed. Where this is one of surprise, delight, increased interest, the exclamation is usually accompanied by a q-gaze. Where the feelings expressed are of horror, disgust, protestation at something the other has said, p is more likely to turn his gaze away. The difference thus, would, appear to be between feelings involving attention and approach, as compared to those involving rejection and withdrawal. There is one class of exclamations, however, which does not appear to fit this scheme. This is where p, the listener, gives expression to a feeling q is also expressing or talking about. For example, NL was describing 'lovely old treasures' dug up in the Sutton Hoo Ship Burial, and as he does do, JH emits a prolonged 'mmm' thereby showing that she is sharing his fascination with the treasures. These sharing exclamations, of which there are only a few examples in our material, are accompanied by a a-gaze (usually due to closing of the eyes, rather than a turning away of the gaze). Perhaps, here in expressing his affective unity with q, p drops his gaze because at this moment he has no further need to monitor q's behaviour: he is sufficiently 'in tune' with him to give expression to the prevailing emotion, without having to check that he has it correctly.

Attempted interruptions. These were rather rare in the material examined, and no clear pattern can be described for them. However, some distinction can be drawn between interruptions which arise when p misinterprets how q is going to behave, and those interruptions which arise when p tries to 'cut in' on q's talking time. In the latter cases, a small battle for the time available may arise and here p and q stare fully at one another as long as the battle lasts.

Short questions. These usually are 'direct' in the sense that p is asking q for some quite specific response to his question. Whether p expects his response to be short or long, however, may depend in part upon the context in which the question is asked, and also upon the way it is asked, in particular as reflected in the particular stress and intonation patterning adopted. In either case, whether p expects a short answer to his question (as when he needs some specific information before he can proceed) or whether he expects a long answer (as where he uses the question as a means of handing the speaker role over to his interlocutor), p will look steadily at q while he asks his question, and where *p* is asking a series of questions, unless he has to pause in thinking of the question, or unless he has to pause in formulating it. In Table 5 where the gaze-direction associated with questions is given, it will be seen that there are a number in which *p* does not look at *q* as he asks his question. In a few cases, such questions are asked hesitantly, and as we have seen, *p* tends to look away during hesitant speech. In certain other cases it seems that the *a*-gaze is associated with questions which are either presumptive, or with questions which broach a subject about which *p* has considerable anxiety. In these instances we may be observing cases of *a*-gaze in which *p* by looking away, is effectively cutting down his level of emotionality, either by cutting down the intensity of the direct relationship he has with *q*, or by reducing information intake from *q*, which would be arousing for him.

References

BIRDWHISTELL, R. L. (1960), 'Critical moments in the psychiatric interview', paper read at the Galesburg State Research Hospital 10th Anniversary Symposium.

BROADBENT, D. E. (1958), *Perception and Communication*, Pergamon Press.

EX, J., and KENDON, A. (1964), 'A notation for facial postures and bodily positions in the social performance', reprinted in M. Argyle (ed.), *Social Interaction*, Methuen.

FRIES, C. C. (1952), *The Structure of English*, Harcourt Brace & World.

GOLDMAN-EISLER, F. (1954), 'On the variability of the speed of talking and on its relation to the length of utterances in conversation', *Brit. J. Psychol.*, vol. 45, pp. 94–107.

GOLDMAN-EISLER, F. (1958), 'Speech analysis and mental processes', *Language and Speech*, vol. 1, pp. 59–75.

GOLDMAN-EISLER, F. (1961), 'The distribution of pause durations in speech', *Language and Speech*, vol. 4, pp. 232–7.

KENDON, A. (1964), 'Progress report of an investigation into aspects of the structure and function of the social performance', Appendix II to First Annual Report to the Dept. of Scientific and Industrial Research of the Social Skills Project, Institute of Experimental Psychology, Oxford University.

MACLAY, H., and OSGOOD, C. E. (1959), 'Hesitation phenomena in English', *Word*, vol. 15, pp. 19–44.

OGDEN, C. A., and RICHARDS, I. A. (1947), *The Meaning of Meaning*, Routledge & Kegan Paul.

SOSKIN, W. F., and JOHN, P. V. (1963), 'The study of spontaneous talk', in R. G. Barker (ed.), *The Stream of Behavior*, Appleton-Century-Crofts.

WELFORD, A. T. (1960), 'The measurement of sensory-motor performance: survey and reappraisal of twelve years' progress', *Ergonomics*, vol. 3, pp. 189–230.

6 Ray L. Birdwhistell

Kinesics

R. L. Birdwhistell, 'Kinesics', from *International Encyclopedia of the Social Sciences*, vol. 8, 1968, pp. 379-85.

Kinesics is the science of body behavioral communication. Any person who has 'learned how to behave in public' and is at all aware of his response to the awkward or inappropriate behavior of others recognizes the importance of body-motion behavior to social interaction. It is more difficult to conceive that body motion and facial expression belong to a learned, coded system and that there is a 'language' of movement comparable to spoken language, both in its structure and in its contribution to a systematically ordered *communicative system*.

Communication is a term used to describe the structured dynamic processes relating to the interconnectedness of living systems. As such, it has much of the indefiniteness and usefulness of terms like 'gravity', 'electromagnetic field', or, perhaps, 'metabolism' in their respective phenomenological contexts. While communication studies must investigate certain biological, social and cultural processes, communication is an essential *aspect* of, not a master category for, such processes. Communication is a multichannel system emergent from, and regulative of, the influenceable multisensory activity of living systems. The spoken and the body-motion languages thus are *infra*communicational systems that are *interdependently merged* with each other and with other comparable codes that utilize other channels; they are operationally communicative. Emphasis upon communication as a multichannel system stresses the difficulty of final objective appraisal of the relative or specific importance of spoken language to communication before we know more about communication. It is unproductively tautological to argue from the fact that language is characteristic of humans to the position that language is the central or the most important communicative code utilized by humans. All infracommunicational channels are equally necessary to the whole of which they are dependent subsystems. To attempt to weigh their relative importance to cultural continuity without more evidence than is now available is somewhat like arguing whether sex or food is more important to speciational continuity.

Communication is a continuous interactive process made of multi-leveled, overlapping, discontinuous segments of behavior. The interaction of communication does not cease when interactants lapse into silence, to begin again with the onset of phonation; other channels continue communicative operations even when the auditory–aural channel is not in use. Humans move in relatively orderly fashion while they vocalize and when they are silent; they can perceive the regularity in the visible movement of others (or at least become aware when it is irregular) and proprioceptively in themselves. They can smell, taste, touch, and otherwise register perception of themselves and their surroundings. When regularities appear, they are not simply mechanical, 'automatic', or happenstantial. Research with visible body motion is convincing us that this behavior is as ordered and coded as is audible phonation. Like language, infracommunicational body motion behavior is a structural system that varies from society to society and must be learned by the membership of a society if it is to interact successfully.

It is as yet unclear how taste, smell, touch, heat and cold, to speak only of the sensory potential of the more obvious communicative channels, are structured and utilized. However, as we gain control of the theory and the methodology (including the technology) prerequisite to their isolation and description, these should prove to have decipherable codes. Body behavioral communication has been the subject of extensive research and major theoretical formulations contributed by descriptive and structural linguists. Yet much of the structural analysis of body-motion behavior had to await the development of the movie camera and the slow-motion projector before elements of kinesic structure could be isolated and demonstrated as significant. Comparably, even the preliminary investigation of the relationships between linguistic and kinesic structure discussed below could not be tested and demonstrated until the linguist and the kinesicist gained control of the sound movie, the tape recorder, the slow-motion projector and the speech stretcher. Engineers are confident that the technology for recording the behavior of other sensory channels is now within the range of possibility. However, such developments are not likely until there is sufficient sophistication about the essential nature of these channels so that the investigator is not drowned in an ocean of insignificant data. Just as linguistic research laid bare data for kinesic investigation, linguistics and kinesics, as they exhaust their respective behavioral fields, should point the way for definitive research in the other communicative channels.

It is within this conceptual framework that some of the results of communicational body motion research are sketched below. The scientific investigation of human body motion communication is a recent development. While a bibliography of thousands of items could be developed which attest to the fact that the graphic artist, the writer, the story teller, the dancer and the ethnographer have long noted the fact that men gesture, posture, move and grimace in interesting, significant and unusual fashions, it does not seem that anyone prior to the twentieth century suspected the structured, languagelike nature of human-body behavior.

Contemporary study

Darwin is often seen as the father of modern communicative studies of body motion. Yet neither in his *Expression of the Emotions in Man and Animals* (1872) nor anywhere else does he seem to have made the qualitative jump between his brilliant observations of animal and human-body motion and expression and these as related to ordered communicative systems. Franz Boas is said by his students to have laid the groundwork for Sapir's brilliant intuition that body motion was coded and that this code had to be learned for successful communication (Sapir, 1931; 1933). Efron (1941), another of Boas's students, conclusively demonstrated the culture-bound nature of south-eastern European, Jewish and Italian gestural complexes. From these insights and from others provided through psychoanalysis and psychiatry, LaBarre (1947) reviewed the literature to discuss 'phatic' communication and the 'pseudo languages' that preceded and surrounded vocal language. However, the beginning of the scientific investigation of the *structured* nature of body motion communication was marked by the publication of the *Introduction to Kinesics* (Birdwhistell, 1952).

More directly relevant to the development of kinesics was the theoretical and methodological progress of the modern descriptive linguists, who in their penetrating and exhaustive analysis of human vocalic behavior presented a model that could be used for the investigation of other kinds of behavior (Bloomfield, 1933; Sapir, 1921; Trager and Smith, 1951). One stimulus to investigate the meaningful variability of human body behavior came from the culture shock induced by the difference between Kutenai and American gestural and expressional patterning. Body-motion research gained maturity and discipline under responsible linguistic tutelage. The recognition that a bilingual Kutenai moved in a consistently and regularly different manner when speaking Kutenai than when speaking English could not be understood until systematic analysis of the structure of American kinesics was undertaken.

Context and meaning

From the outset of kinesic research, investigators have been distracted by the temptation to pursue the phantom of 'meaning'. Each new form or segment of structure isolated during investigations provoked the question, 'What does it mean?' Even linguists, long since chastened by the relative sterility of their own explorations into the semantics of speech forms, seemed to cherish the hope that the kinesicist might present them with an 'expressionary' or a kinecography that would list specific gestural, expressional, or movement complexes, together with their exclusive meanings. It is true that when informants are questioned they may give the investigator an extensive listing of such forms and a range of meaning for each. Cross-cultural comparison quickly reveals that an Arab from Beirut, a Chinese from Taiwan and a Harlem Negro respond quite differently to apparently identical body behaviors. It can be easily established that these differences in response are cultural rather than idiosyncratic; different cultures exploit the potential for body motion in differing ways. Data are accumulating in the literature; particularly worthy of note is the work of Hewes (1955), who has compiled an extensive cross-cultural listing of body posture. However, like other studies of the specialized gestures of particular groups (Saitz and Cervenka, 1962), these belong more properly in the province of ethnographic studies than in the area of kinesics or communication studies. Such lists often have the same relationship to kinesic anthropology that dictionaries do to linguistic anthropology – they are suggestive, but of indirect relevance.

Structural analysis of even the apparently most discrete facial expression (the 'smile' or the 'frown'), the apparently most explicit gesture (the 'nod' or the 'head shake'), or the apparently most indicative posture ('military uprightness' or 'sag') show reports of such behavior to be impressionistic summaries of quite complex and systematically varying particles of activity that are, more importantly, always dependent upon other behaviors. The assemblage of component body behaviors that is reported by informants cannot stand alone any more than the phoneme can stand alone in functional speech behavior. Furthermore, while some informants may have quick responses as to the 'meaning' of such behaviors and others may be goaded into choosing more likely 'meanings 'from a dichotomous battery, when these body behaviors are studied in a natural social setting they prove to depend upon the range of stimuli available in the large context of interactive behavior in which they appear. It appears that these non-lexical forms have the same variability of semantic function as do 'words'. Whatever it is we mean by 'meaning', it is a term which covers the relationship between an isolated event and its appropriate spectrum of surrounds.

Research into the nature of body-motion communication over the past decade has proceeded in two differing but intimately related directions. An attempt has been made to isolate the significant forms of communicative body-motion behavior and, in separate research operations, to gain perspective upon the nature of the levels of context in which these forms function. These latter operations, ultimately concerned with meaning, have

been termed *context analysis*. While research in this area remains exploratory, it is promising. In different ways, the studies of Goffman (1963), that of
Hall (1959), and that of Ruesch (Ruesch and Kees, 1956) have been pioneer-
ing. Their work points toward the rich data that await the investigator who
would systematically describe the structural logic of interpersonal activity
in precise social settings. More cogent to context analysis is the work of
Scheflen (1965). He and others who have followed his lead report the
isolation of interactional units characteristic of the psychotherapeutic
situation. Such studies give promise that minutes-long sequences of communicative behavior may be as structurally marked as are syntactic
sentences ($\frac{1}{2}$ to 4 or 5 seconds in duration) or the kinesic constructions that
are contained within triple-cross kinesic junctures (ranging between 5
seconds and 2 or $2\frac{1}{2}$ minutes). These larger regular shapes of behavioral
sequences increase the possibility of objectively measuring the function of
particular communicative elements in contextual contrasts. Discovering
the structural aspects of the interactive process is necessary to the objective
definition of the 'meaning' of the integral units, the messages carried by
the communicative system. From the point of view of context analysis,
meaning is the behavioral difference occasioned by the presence or the
absence of a particular cue at a particular level of context. The range of
meaning of a particular cue is governed by the range of contexts in which
the cue can be observed to occur.

Units of structure of body motion

Kinesics has been concerned with the exhaustive description and analysis
of the American kinesic structure. Structural linguists have traditionally
approached their data through the word and then, in one set of operations,
engaged in morphological and phonological research, and, in another set,
moved toward the isolation and description of lexemes and syntax. More
recently, linguists have sought to analyse the longer sequences of discourse.
Using an analogous model, kinesic studies have demonstrated that the
'gesture' is a *bound morph* (a stem form) and have gone on to analyse the
position and activity of such forms. The tentative descriptions of kine-
morphology prepared the ground for analysis of behavior into the component *kines* and *kinemes*. As research proceeded, it became increasingly
evident that the American kinesic pattern, at least, was not simply a sequence of these complex kinemorphs (kinemorphic stem plus suffixes).
By conventions of junction, these wordlike forms are combined into
sentencelike sequencies.

Clearly, kinesic forms at each ascending level of analysis resemble
linguistic forms in their duality of patterning (Hockett, 1960). Just as syntactic sentences do not dangle isolated in nature, these extended, linked

sequences of body-motion behavior, the *complex kinemorphic constructions*, do not exhaust the potentials of body activity in communication. These again are building blocks for still longer sequences of behavior, evident in operation but which have thus far resisted analysis. Kinesic forms at each level of analysis (*kinelogical, kinemorphological* and *kinesyntactic*) have distinctive contrastive identity as significant forms and also operate as items of structure.

Over the past century, acoustic phoneticians have developed a sufficient theory and an increasingly complex and reliable technology for the description of the physiological behavior that underlies the production of significant sounds utilized in human speech. It should not be surprising that some students confuse the activity of the apparatus for phonation with the linguistic process. At the present preliminary stage of kinesic research, it is even more difficult to keep the prekinesic activity of the body separate from the structured activity utilized in the kinesic code. Just as we are so impressed with the activity of the lips, the teeth, the tongue, the lungs, the larynx, the pharynx, etc. that we think of them as emitting speech, it is difficult not to be so preoccupied with musculature, bones, fatty tissue, the vascular system and skin that we think of these as emitting body-motion language. Rather these must be regarded as sources of potentials for behavior which are selectively regulated to form the kinesic code. The arm and hand of the telegrapher are of no direct consequence to the telegraphic code.

An example of kinesic communication

As long as the kinesic anthropologist can remain sufficiently disciplined so that he does not confuse the particular activity of a particular part of the body with the code that makes use of certain activities of that body part in certain situations, he can profitably examine the body as an instrument specifically adapted for interactive behavior. Seemingly identical body movements supply the activity for quite different cue classes. To keep the example as simple as possible, movement of the eyebrows is the activity selected for discussion, and only the variables of context and duration are described. The specialized kinesic terminology and annotational conventions may prove confusing to the reader, but the examples chosen should be sufficiently familiar to soften the technicality of the illustration.

One of the more easily detectable *kines* (least perceptible units of body motion) is that of eyebrow lift and return (here transcribed as bbV∧). At times such movement is fleeting; I have been able to detect and record brow movement lasting but thousandths of a second. For instance, the brows may be raised in certain contexts and held for a short duration before returning to the zero or base position. Such positioning may operate as one of the allokines (again using the linguistic analogy, the allokines would be, as allomorphs are, members of a class of events that can be substituted for one another) of the junctural *kineme* (the least cue class) of ($/k/$ /). This bilateral eyebrow raise is quite comparable to, and may during phonation co-occur with, the linguistic single bar of terminally raised pitch, appropriate to the context of 'doubt' or 'question' or as a signal to repeat a message. If we ignore the duration of the action and attend only to the spatial movement of the brows, an identical movement of the brows may be seen in the circumvocal behavior of speakers who select the brows for kinesic stress functions. Intensive experimentation on the relationship between spoken and moved American has demonstrated that there are four degrees of kinesic stress (Birdwhistell, 1965). The brows form one of the positional allokines of the kinemes of stress. Other allokines are provided by the head, hand, foot or body nodding, or the lid closure that accompanies speech.

Thus, the kine eyebrow raise (bb$\wedge$) may be allokinic with the kines of superior headnod (h$\wedge$) or handnod (/$\wedge$), members of the class kineme of kinesic single bar ($/k/$ /) in one context position and an allokine of the form degrees of kinesic stress (/primary, secondary, unstressed or destressed/) in another. These two allokinic roles do not exhaust the cue potential of the brows. Furthermore, with the same muscular involvement, the (bb$\wedge$) may be an allokine of the kineme, the first degree of eyebrow raise (/bb^1/), which combines with other circumfacial kinemes to form a kinemorph.

I fully appreciate the reader's difficulty in picturing these abstractions. The point made here may be comprehended if the reader will conceive of a conversation in which an animated speaker is being attended to by an interested auditor. The eyebrows of the speaker rise and fall as he speaks (kinesic stress kinemes). From time to time, the speaker's eyes 'focus' upon the face of the auditor and he pauses in his speech and raises his brow ($/k/$ /). He may continue vocalization following the single head nod (/hn/) of the auditor. During one sequence of the conversation, the auditor may 'de-expressionalize' into the complex kinemorph of dead pan (// O //) the speaker, without signaling response, may continue vocalization until the auditor raises his brows (/bb^1/), while sustaining the dead pan (// O //), to form the kinemorph $\left(// \dfrac{bb^1}{O} // \right)$. At this point, the speaker hesitates in his speech flow, drops his head and lids $\left(// \dfrac{h\vee\wedge}{\overline{\Theta\Theta}\vee\wedge} // \right)$, and after several vocal false starts repeats part of his lexication. In the situations that we have observed, several conversationalists returned in discourse correction to the topic under discussion at the onset of the auditor's dead pan (//N$\rightarrow$O//).

These three kinesic activities do not exhaust the cue potential of the eyebrows. Like the scalp, the eyebrows, while mobile in position in the young, gradually become relatively stationary in *base* placement (the point from which movement is initiated and the point of return following movement). As measured at the most superior aspect of the hirsute brow, there is a possible range of almost one half inch for brow placement. While the diakinesic (comparable to language dialect) range is less marked in Americans, any observant traveler in England can mark the contrast between the high placement of the brows among people of certain regional and economic groups (many Englishmen look to the American as though they were perpetually surprised) and the low-brow placement in other areas and at different socio-economic levels (so-called beetle-browed). Such brow and scalp placement is learned behavior and is, on the one hand, an aspect of unique identity, and thus part of signature behavior, and, on the other, contributes to the common appearance of family, group, and regional members. The latter represents signature behavior at another level. From this example of certain eyebrow behaviors and from this view of communication it becomes clear that communicative units may vary in duration from milliseconds to years. It may be argued that individual appearances, such as diakinesic variation, are not to be classified as communicative behavior. Such a position, focusing on short sequences, would also deny the communicative role of dialect and individual speaking style. However, any regular and systematically variable learned behavior that redundantly contributes to the definition of an aspect of the code is in itself part of a larger code and must be understood if we are to comprehend the structure of the interactive process. As we have long realized intuitively, there is more that goes on in any conversation than is present in the immediate interaction. It is the researcher's duty to adapt his observations to the shapes of nature.

Future research

Kinesics has been preoccupied with the description and analysis of body positions and movements. It has been possible to isolate and test thirty-four kinemes in the American kinesic system. While such a prediction is risky, there may be no more than fifty base units in the system. However, as kinesic research proceeds to gain security from cross-cultural studies it is going to have to pay systematic attention to other body associated phenomena. Such matters as the oiliness, wetness and dryness of the skin, tension and laxity of the skin and musculature, variable and shifting vascularity in the skin's surface, and shifts in the underlying fatty tissue are all going to have to be studied intensively and systematically. All of our present observations, and these have been extensive but crude and non-conclusive, lead us to believe that these are coded in both long and short durational cue complexes. While at the moment these behaviors are assigned to paralanguage, a catchball category for insufficiently analysed behavior, there seems every reason to believe that they will be subject to isolation, analysis and communicative assignment. In this perspective particular attention must be paid to the work of Hall and Westcott. Using what may be an unnecessarily limiting dyadic model, Hall, in his conception of *proxemics* (Hall, 1963), places emphasis on the human use of space arrangements as a coded system of transactional process. His work forces attention on all primary telecommunicative processes. Westcott (1964), in his discussion of *streptistics*, is attempting to order the various channels and their operative codes in structural relation to each other. These approaches, when taken together, with the accumulating data from kinesic and linguistic anthropology lay the groundwork for communication analysis.

References

BIRDWHISTELL, R. L. (1952), *Introduction to Kinesics*, University of Louisville Press.

BIRDWHISTELL, R. L. (1965), 'Communication without words', unpublished manuscript.

BLOOMFIELD, L. (1933; 1951), *Language*, rev. edn, Holt, Rinehart & Winston.

DARWIN, C. (1872; 1965), F. Darwin (ed.), *The Expression of the Emotions in Man and Animals*, Philisophical Library.

EFRON, D. (1941), *Gesture and Environment*, Kings Crown Press.

GOFFMAN, E. (1963), *Behavior in Public Places*, Free Press.

HALL, E. T. (1959), *The Silent Language*, Doubleday. (A paperback edition was published in 1961 by Fawcett.)

HALL, E. T. (1963), 'A system for the notation of proxemic behavior', *Amer. Anthropol.*, new series vol. 65, pp. 1003–26.

HEWES, G. (1955), 'World distribution of certain postural habits', *Amer. Anthropol.*, new series vol. 57, pp. 231–44.

HOCKETT, C. F. (1960), 'Logical considerations in the study of animal communication', in Symposium on Animal Sounds and Communication, Indiana University, 1958, *Animals Sounds and Communication*, American Institute of Biological Sciences.

LABARRE, W. (1947), 'The cultural basis of emotions and gestures', *J. Personal.*, vol. 16, pp. 49–68.

LABARRE, W. (1954), *The Human Animal*, University of Chicago Press. (See especially pages 165–8 on 'Paralinguistics,' and page 349 on 'Kinesics'.)

RUESCH, J., and KEES, W. (1956), *Nonverbal Communication*, University of California Press.

SAITZ, R. L., and CERVENKA, E. J. (1962), *Colombian and North American Gesture: A Constrastive Inventory*, Centro Colombo Americano.

SAPIR, E. A. (1921), *Language: An Introduction to the Study of Speech*, Harcourt, Brace & World.

SAPIR, E. A. (1931), 'Communication', in *Encyclopaedia of the Social Sciences*, vol. 4, Macmillan, pp. 78–80.

SAPIR, E. A. (1933), 'Language', in *Encyclopaedia of the Social Sciences*, vol. 9, pp. 155–68.

SCHEFLEN, A. E. (1965), *Stream and Structure of Communicational Behavior: Context Analysis of a Psychotherapy Session*, Behavioral Studies Monograph no. 1, Philadelphia: Eastern Pennsylvania Psychiatric Institute.

TRAGER, G. L., and SMITH, H. L. Jr (1951; 1962), *An Outline of English Structure*, American Council of Learned Societies.

WESTCOTT, R. W. (1964), 'Strepital communication: A study of nonvocal sound production among man and animals', unpublished manuscript.

7 Albert Mehrabian

Inference of Attitudes from the Posture, Orientation and
Distance of a Communicator

A. Mehrabian, 'Inference of attitudes from the posture, orientation and distance of
a communicator', *Journal of Consulting and Clinical Psychology*, vol. 32, 1968,
pp. 296–308.

The studies to be presented deal with the attitude-communicating significance of a number of postural, orientation and distance cues emitted by a
communicator while seated or standing. There have been a few introductory
attempts to conceptualize the relationships of the posture, orientation and
distance between communicators to their attitudes towards each other. In
his informal discussion of the significance of distance between communicators, Hall (1959) noted the presence of implicit norms within any culture
regarding permissible ranges of distance between two speakers. If the distance between two speakers exceeds or is less than these limits, then negative
attitudes are either elicited or inferred. Subsequently, Hall (1963) subsumed
distance, touching and orientation (i.e. angle through which the median
plane of a speaker is turned away from his addressee) cues under the rubric
of 'proxemics'. Mehrabian (1967) suggested that the concept of proxemics
can be used to refer to the degree of closeness, directness or immediacy of
the non-verbal interaction between two communicators. In this context, a
number of non-verbal cues occurring in a communication situation can be
conceptually ordered and interrelated. The distance, eye contact, openness
of arms or legs, touching and holding, forward–back lean of trunk, and
directness of orientation of a speaker towards his addressee can be considered examples of proxemic variables. Mehrabian (1967) also hypothesized that within Hall's (1964) permissible ranges (e.g. the permissible
ranges for distance between communicators in the different social situations
which Hall investigated) greater proximity of a speaker toward his addressee
communicates a more positive speaker attitude to the addressee.

There is some experimental evidence relating the non-verbal proxemic
variables to attitudes. James (1932) used photographs of a masked male
model as stimuli. He asked his Ss about the attitude being expressed by each
posture and the portions of the posture which were most significant. He
used 347 photographs in which the positions of head, trunk, feet, knees,
and arms were systematically varied – certain combinations being eliminated due to their awkward quality. He selected thirty of these photographs

on the basis of the highest agreement among his three Ss' judgements of the attitude being communicated. Two additional experiments in which Ss interpreted the set of thirty selected postures yielded the following four postural categories:

(a) approach, an attentive posture communicated by a forward lean of the body; (b) withdrawal, a negative, refusing or repulsed posture communicated by drawing back or turning away; (c) expansion, a proud, conceited, arrogant or disdainful posture communicated by an expanded chest, erect or backward-leaning trunk, erect head and raised shoulders; and (d) contraction, a depressed, downcast or dejected posture communicated by a forward-leaning trunk, a bowed head, drooping shoulders and a sunken chest. For each of these four generic categories, the head and trunk positions were found to be the most important indicators. However, specific discriminations within each category were determined by the position of hands and arms. In his third experiment, James (1932) found that postures were generally interpreted in the same way whether S viewed the posture and interpreted it or whether S viewed and imitated the posture and then interpreted it. Finally, James found that a decoder-S's response could be affected by the situation in which the posture occurred.

James's categories of approach and withdrawal are related to the present concern in that they include the proxemic variables of forward–back lean of trunk and directness of orientation. His findings support the hypothesis that a forward lean communicates a relatively positive attitude, whereas a backward lean or turning away communicates a more negative attitude. Finally, James's expansion (i.e. proud, conceited, arrogant or disdainful) category seems relevant to the communication of status differences as well as attitudes. Thus, an expansive arms-akimbo position can be hypothesized to communicate a negative attitude and a higher status relative to an addressee.

Exline (1963) and Exline, Gray and Schuette (1965) found that there is more eye contact of a communicator with an addressee when there is greater preference for, or more positive attitude toward, the addressee. These results were found in both non-competitive discussion and interview situations. Machotka (1965) informally noted relationships between several postural variables and attitudes. In his study, drawings of groups of people who had assumed various postures relative to one another were judged by Ss who were asked to infer social relationships. For example, he found that openness of arms indicate warmth and that eye contact indicates concern with the addressee. Little (1965) found that a smaller distance between communicator and addressee is associated with more positive attitudes. Furthermore, Argyle and Dean (1965) found that, for a given degree of communicator attitude toward his addressee, directness of orientation decreases as closeness increases. The latter finding suggests that directness of orientation and closeness additively reflect degree of communicator attitude toward, or intimacy with the addressee, and, therefore, increases (or decreases) in the former are associated with compensatory decreases (or increases) in the latter when attitude is constant. In connection with the latter interpretation, it is interesting to note that Lott and Sommer (1967) found that when there is a status differential between communicators (which may correspond to less intimacy) the selected seating distance is greater than when the communicators are of equal status. Another implication of the Lott and Sommer study for the hypotheses of the present study is that when a communicator is addressing a different-status addressee he is not expected to assume significantly different distances *vis-à-vis* high-compared to low-status addressees.

Argyle and Kendon (1967) summarized the experimental literature relating posture, orientation, and distance to attitudes and status relationships between communicators. Their review indicates that in addition to the proxemic variables there is another postural cue, degree of tension, which can relate to status differences between communicators. Schlosberg (1954) posited the relaxation–tension dimension as a basic factor in emotional expression. A direct relationship between the degree of relaxation of a communicator's posture and the relative status of the communicator and his addressee is suggested by Goffman (1961), who noted that higher status participants (e.g. psychiatrists) are more relaxed in psychiatric staff meetings than are lower status participants (e.g. interns).

The following four experiments are designed to further explore the relationships of postural, orientation, and distance cues to attitude and status relationships among communicators. The first three experiments employ a different methodology from the fourth in that Ss serve as decoders, whereas in the fourth experiment Ss serve as encoders of communication. In the decoding experiments, Ss are asked to judge the communicative significance of photographic stimuli presented by E; these stimuli being varied along the postural, distance and orientation dimensions. In the fourth, encoding, experiment, Ss are asked to communicate attitude and status differences using posture, orientation and distance, and E records their behavior. They are requested to imagine themselves in situations involving different kinds of addressees and to assume postures which they actually would if they were interacting with these addressees.

One of the objects of the present study is to assess the relative merits and relationship of encoding and decoding methodologies in investigations of 'implicit' (e.g. postural, facial, vocal or sarcastic) communications of attitude.

The list of hypotheses below is an attempt to summarize the implications of available data which relate postural, orientation and distance variables to attitudes and status differences between communicators. Each of the hypotheses is relevant to at least one of the following experiments.

The following factors communicate and are associated with a more positive communicator attitude toward his addressee: (a) a smaller distance to the addressee, (b) more eye contact with the addressee, (c) a more direct orientation to the addressee, that is, a turn toward rather than away from the addressee, (d) an open and accessible rather than a closed and inaccessible posture, (e) a relaxed rather than a tense posture, (f) a more forward lean of the torso toward the addressee while seated, and (g) a relative absence of the arms akimbo position while standing.

Two additional hypotheses relate to status differences: (h) a communicator is more tense in communicating to a high- compared to a low-status addressee, and (i) for standing postures, an arms-akimbo position is more probable when the addressee is of low status than when he is of high status.

[Three experiments on the perception of interpersonal attitudes from photographs are omitted in this reprinting.]

Encoding experiment

In the following experiment, which employed an encoding methodology, Ss were asked to imagine themselves in situations involving different kinds of addressee and to stand in the ways in which they would if they were actually interacting with these addressees. The four independent factors in the experiment were encoder-communicator attitude towards the addressee (positive versus negative), addressee status (high versus low), addressee sex and encoder sex. The dependent measures were eye contact, distance, head orientation, shoulder orientation, arm openness, leg openness, arm position (hanging versus akimbo), head raised or lowered, hand relaxation, and leg relaxation. The instructions and scoring criteria presented in the method section below serve to further define these independent and dependent variables.

Method

Subjects. Fifty-two University of California undergraduates served as Ss. The Ss were equally divided as to sex.

Procedure and instructions. The experimental room was 17×18 feet in size and was selected to allow equal movement in either the lateral or straight-ahead directions. There were three tables, two armchairs, and one hat rack in the room. The door to the room was situated along one of the longer walls. Directly across from the door, and 2·5 feet from the wall opposite the door, there was an empty hat rack. All the furniture was against the walls, giving S considerable freedom of movement in the positions he assumed within the experimental room. Perpendicular to the wall retaining the door, and to the left of the door, there was a one-way mirror which allowed judges to rate Ss behavior from an adjacent room.

The experimental materials, which consisted of a blank cardboard mask, instructions, eight cards, and a small box, were placed on a table in the room. The mask was large enough to cover S's face completely and had narrow slits for vision.

The experiment was individually administered to each S. The S was led into the experimental room by a male *E* and was asked to place his books and coat on top of a table and to take a seat in the adjacent armchair. The *E* gave the first page of the two pages of instructions to S and told him that they were self-explanatory. The *E* then left the room, and S remained alone for the rest of the experiment. The instructions were as follows:

Instructions Page 1
We are trying to study ways in which people communicate feelings toward each other. We have written these instructions so that you can follow them on your own without us being present.

In this room there is a coat rack. You are to imagine that there is a person facing the door standing about where the coat-rack is. You will be told different things about the sex, status, and your attitude toward this imaginary person in each part of the experiment.

After the imaginary person is described, your task is to stand the way that you would if you were really talking with the person. It is necessary that you do your best to stand in a way that you would if you were really with the described person. You will have as much time as you need to think and to get into the position you feel is the natural one. Feel free to move to anywhere in the room and to assume any posture – as long as you feel that it is the natural one. Remember it is your standing and not your facial expression which is important. In order to help you keep your mind off your facial expression you will wear the cardboard mask which is on the table. After you have read about each imaginary situation, thought about it, moved to where you want to stand, put on the mask, and assumed the posture which feels right; say 'Ready.' Hold the posture until you hear two taps on the glass of the one-way mirror.

You are now ready to begin. On the table there is a stack of eight cards. Each one describes a different situation. In each situation, you will know the sex of the imaginary person, whether you like or dislike this person, and whether the person is of higher or lower status than you. [. . .]

The eight cards used by S contained all possible combinations of the three within-S conditions. For example, one card was as follows: 'Imagine that you are talking to a *male of higher status* than yourself whom you *like*.' The order of the eight cards (and therefore the eight within-S conditions) was random for each S.

Observational procedures. Three judges independently rated the behavior of S from an adjacent room through the one-way mirror. Partitions separated the judges while they were rating. All three judges were not told anything about the intent or the hypotheses of the experiment. Furthermore, it was not possible for any judge to know which condition was being administered to an S at a given point in the sequence of eight conditions; that is, the order of the cards for each S was unknown to the judges.

In each experimental condition, eleven ratings of S's behavior were made by each judge. The judges typically took about one minute to obtain the eleven ratings with the use of the scoring criteria summarized in Table 1. In addition to the verbal instructions contained in Table 1, judges also had diagrams illustrating the scoring of the eye contact, distance, and orientation measures.

Table 1 **Scoring criteria for a standing posture**

1. Openness of arms

0 Arms crossed
1 Hands or arms touching in front and at or above waistline
2 Hands or arms touching in front and below waistline
3 Front portion of body covered by one or both hands, but not in ways specified under scores of 0, 1 or 2
4 Arms hanging or one or both arms akimbo
5 Hands touching in back, hands in back pockets, or hands in side pockets

2. Openness of legs

0 One leg crossed in front of the other
1 Only foot portion of one leg crossed in front of the other
2 Legs or feet uncrossed

3. Relaxation of hands

0 Very tense: hands are tightly clasped or fists are tightly clenched or hands are in motion, for example, fingers drumming, or hands are clasping anything tightly
1 Moderately tense: hands are loosely clasped or are in loose fists, or are clasping any object or part of the body loosely
2 Relaxed: fingers are extended but not stiff; hands in pockets

4. Relaxation of legs

0 Symmetrical stance of legs with insteps touching
1 Symmetrical stance of legs with insteps not touching
2 Asymmetrical stance of legs with one or both feet partially lifted off the floor
3 Assymmetrical stance of legs with both feet resting flat on the floor

5. Eye contact

0 The subject is looking toward an area such that his gaze would probably not meet that of the imaginary addressee
1 The subject is looking toward an area where the imaginary addressee's eyes would probably be

6. Head orientation: the number of degrees that the median plane of the head of the subject-communicator needs to be turned so as to be parallel to the median plane of the head of the addressee and facing toward the addressee's direction. Take the smaller angle of the two possible angles. Use only 10-degree units.

7. Shoulder orientation: the number of degrees that the median plane of the upper torso of the subject-communicator needs to be turned so as to be parallel to the median plane of the head of the addressee and facing toward the addressee's direction. Take the smaller angle of the two possible angles. Use only 10-degree units.

8. Straight-ahead distance: measured from front line of imaginary addressee (i.e. coat rack) in terms of number of tiles to nearest half, up to a line which is perpendicular to the straight ahead and which passes near the center portion of the foot on which the communicator is resting. If he is resting on both feet, then a point in between the two feet is used.

9. Lateral distance: measured similarly to 8.

10. Up-down head tilt: score 0 for head tilted down such that the line of vision forms 10 degrees or more with the horizontal, 1 for line of vision horizontal, and 2 for line of vision pointing 10 degrees or more above horizontal.

11. Arm position: scores of 0, 1 or 2 corresponding to number of arms in akimbo position.

Results

Reliability. Average product-moment correlations obtained from the three judges' ratings of each dimension are as follows: 0·55, eye contact; 0·99, total distance; 0·91, head orientation; 0·89, shoulder orientation; 0·70, up-down head tilt; 0·97, arm openness; 0·95, leg openness; 0·99, arm position; 0·66, hand relaxation; and 0·62, leg relaxation. These correlations were deemed satisfactory, and therefore none of the dependent measures was eliminated due to unreliability. The mean rating of the three judges for each of the dependent variables in a condition was employed in the analyses reported in the following sections.

Eye contact. A score of zero was assigned for no eye contact, and a score of unity was assigned for the presence of eye contact. A $2 \times 2 \times 2 \times 2 \times 26$

analysis of variance was performed on the mean judgements of eye contact obtained from the three judges. In this design, there were two levels each of attitude, Addressee Status, Addressee Sex and Encoder Sex; there were twenty-six Ss nested under each level of the encoder sex factor, and there were repeated measures on the first three factors. The results of the analysis of variance of the eye-contact scores indicate significant effects due to addressee sex ($F = 7.5$, $df = 1/50$, $MS_e = 0.19$, $P > 0.01$), addressee status ($F = 19.0$, $df = 1/50$, $MS_e = 0.21$, $p > 0.01$), Encoder Sex $\times$ Addressee Status ($F = 4.1$, $df = 1/50$, $MS_e = 0.21$, $p > 0.05$), and Encoder Sex $\times$ Attitude ($F = 5.1$, $df = 1/50$, $MS_e = 0.34$, $p > 0.05$). The means corresponding to these effects indicate that there is more eye contact with male addressees (0.66) than with female addressees (0.54). There is also more eye contact with high-status addressees (0.70) than with low-status addressees (0.50). Comparisons of the four means corresponding to the Encoder Sex $\times$ Addressee Status interaction indicate that male encoders have significantly more eye contact with a high-status addressee (0.75) than with a low-status addressee (0.47), and, similarly, female encoders have significantly more eye contact with a high-status addressee (0.64) than with a low-status addressee (0.53). This difference, however, is greater for male than for female encoders, as indicated by the significant Encoder Sex $\times$ Addressees Status interaction. Comparisons of the four means corresponding to the Encoder Sex $\times$ Attitude interaction indicate that male encoders have significantly more eye contact with liked addressees (0.73) than with disliked addressees (0.50). However, female encoders do not have significantly more eye contact with liked addressees (0.57) than with disliked addressees (0.60).

Distance. The straight-ahead and lateral distances were used to obtain the total distance of S from the addressees. The unit of measurement of distance was the length of a side of the 9 $\times$ 9 inch tiles covering the floor. The design employed for the present analysis, as well as all subsequent analyses of variance, was identical to that already reported for the analysis of the eye-contact measure. The analysis of variance of the distance scores yields significant effects due to addressee sex ($F = 10.8$, $df = 1/50$, $MS_e = 1.4$, $p < 0.01$), attitude ($F = 22.8$, $df = 1/50$, $MS_e = 2.3$, $p < 0.01$), and Encoder Sex $\times$ Addressee Sex $\times$ Attitude ($F = 5.7$, $df = 1/50$, $MS_e = 1.5$, $p < 0.05$). The means corresponding to these effects indicate that encoders stand closer to female addressees (4.04) than to male addressees (4.43). Also, encoders stand closer to liked addressees (3.88) than to disliked addressees (4.59). To examine the Encoder Sex $\times$ Addressee Sex $\times$ Attitude interaction, separate analyses were performed on the male and female encoder data. No significant Addressee Sex $\times$ Attitude interaction is obtained for the male encoders. There is, however, a significant Addressee Sex $\times$ Attitude interaction for the female encoders ($F = 5\cdot9$, $df = 1/25$, $MS_e = 2\cdot0$, $p < 0\cdot05$). The latter effect for female encoders is due to the following: Female encoders do not stand significantly closer to liked male addressees (4·39) than to disliked male addressees (4·58). However, they do stand significantly closer to liked female addressees (3·60) than to disliked female addressees (4·76).

Orientation measures. Head- and shoulder-orientation measures correlate 0·93 with each other and correlate −0·43 and −0·41 with eye contact, respectively. Analysis of variance for head-orientation scores yields results which are similar to the following reported for shoulder-orientation scores: there is one significant effect due to addressee status ($F = 9\cdot4$, $df = 1/50$, $MS_e = 350$, $p < 0\cdot01$). There is a more direct shoulder orientation to a high-status addressee (21·6 degrees) than to a low-status addressee (27·2 degrees).

Head tilt. This measure was obtained in such a way that greater numbers correspond to a more head-raised position, while lower numbers correspond to a more head-lowered position. A score of unity corresponds to a head in a level position. Analysis of variance of the head-tilt scores shows significance due to addressee status ($F = 20\cdot6$, $df = 1/50$, $MS_e = 0\cdot25$, $p < 0\cdot01$) and Encoder Sex × Addressee Sex ($F = 4\cdot3$, $df = 1/50$, $MS_e = 0\cdot17$, $p < 0\cdot05$). The head of an encoder tends to be raised higher in communicating to a high-status addressee (0·97) than in communicating to a low-status addressee (0·75). Comparisons of the cell means corresponding to the Encoder Sex × Addressee Sex interaction indicate that male encoders raise their heads significantly more when communicating to male addressees (0·88) than when communicating to female addressees (0·71). However, female encoders do not show a significantly different degree of head tilt when communicating to male addressees (0·93) than when communicating to female addressees (0·93).

Openness measures. Both openness measures were obtained in such a way that larger numbers correspond to greater openness. The product-moment correlation of the arm-openness scores with the leg-openness scores is −0·09, which is not significant. Analysis of variance of the arm-openness scores for male and female encoders does not yield any significant effects, although there are some effects approaching significance. A separate analysis of the male encoder data shows no significant effects, whereas the analysis of the female encoder data shows significance due to addressee status ($F = 5\cdot1$, $df = 1/25$, $MS_e = 2\cdot4$, $p < 0\cdot05$) and Addressee Sex × Attitude ($F = 5\cdot4$, $df = 1/25$, $MS_e = 1\cdot5$, $p < 0\cdot05$). Female encoders show more arm openness with high-status addressees (3·46) than with the low-status addressees (2·97). Comparisons of the means corresponding to the Addressee Sex × Attitude interaction indicate that female encoders show more arm openness with liked (3·40) than with disliked (2·88) male addressees. However, there is no significant difference in the arm openness of female encoders when they communicate with liked (3·15) versus disliked (3·41) female addressees.

Analysis of variance of the leg-openness scores shows a significant effect due to Encoder Sex × Addressee Status ($F = 4·1$, $df = 1/50$, $MS_e = 0·15$, $p < 0·05$). Comparisons of the cell means corresponding to this interaction indicate that male encoders show significantly less leg openness with low-status (1·86) than with high-status (1·99) addressees. However, female encoders do not show a significantly different degree of leg openness with low-status (1·99) compared to high-status addressees (1·97). It will be recalled that for leg openness a score of zero corresponds to 'one leg crosses other', a score of 1 corresponds to 'one foot crosses other', and a score of 2 corresponds to 'legs and feet uncrossed'. Thus, the obtained means indicate that female encoders rarely place one foot or leg in front of the other while standing, whereas male encoders occasionally do so when they communicate to a low-status addressee.

Arm position. For this measure, a score of zero was assigned when neither arm was akimbo, a score of 1 was assigned when one arm was akimbo, and a score of 2 was assigned when both arms were akimbo. Analysis of variance of the arm-position scores shows significance due to encoder sex ($F = 5·0$, $df = 1/50$, $MS_e = 0·42$, $p < 0·05$), addressee status ($F = 8·7$, $df = 1/50$, $MS_e = 0·22$, $p < 0·01$), and attitude ($F = 4·8$, $df = 1/50$, $MS_e = 0·33$, $p < 0·05$). Male encoders have a greater tendency to use an arms-akimbo position (0·24) than female encoders (0·10). There is a greater tendency to use an arms-akimbo position with low-status addressees (0·24) than with high-status addressees (0·10), and there is a greater tendency to use an arms-akimbo position with disliked addressees (0·23) than with liked addressees (0·11).

Relaxation measures. Both the hand- and leg-relaxation measures were obtained in a way such that greater numbers correspond to a greater degree of relaxation. The correlation of the hand-relaxation and leg-relaxation scores is −0·02. Analysis of variance of the hand-relaxation scores shows significance due to addressee status ($F = 3·8$, $df = 1/50$, $MS_e = 0·27$, $p < 0·07$). Hand relaxation is greater in communication to low-status (1·24) than high-status (1·14) addressees.

Analysis of variance of the leg-relaxation scores shows significance due to encoder sex ($F = 5·4$, $df = 1/50$, $MS_e = 1·9$, $p < 0·05$) and addressee status ($F = 16 \cdot 1$, $df = 1/50$, $MS_e = 0 \cdot 9$, $p < 0 \cdot 01$). Female encoders show more leg relaxation ($2 \cdot 19$) than male encoders ($1 \cdot 88$). Also, there is more leg relaxation in communication with low-status ($2 \cdot 22$) than with high-status ($1 \cdot 85$) addressees.

Summary of results. As in the case of the decoding experiments, the results of the present experiment can also be summarized in equation form, however, with the use of a different statistical procedure. The application of discriminant analysis (see Anderson and Bancroft, 1955) yields the following pair of equations for the differentiation of positive versus negative attitude of male and female encoders who are in a standing position. For males, the equation is:

Positive Attitude
$= 2 \cdot 90$ (eye contact)$-1 \cdot 35$ (arm position)
$\qquad -1 \cdot 34$ (distance).   **1**

The corresponding equation for females is:

Positive Attitude
$= -5 \cdot 89$ (arm position)$-1 \cdot 07$ (distance)
$\qquad +0 \cdot 40$ (arm openness).   **2**

Discriminant analysis also yields the following pair of equations for the differentiation of the relative status of the addressee from the posture of an encoder who is standing. For males, the equation is:

Addressee Status $= 6 \cdot 00$ (head tilt)
$+3 \cdot 25$ (leg openness)$+2 \cdot 50$ (eye contact)
$-2 \cdot 45$ (arm position)$-1 \cdot 16$ (leg relaxation)
$\qquad -0 \cdot 89$ (hand relaxation)
$\qquad -0 \cdot 04$ (shoulder orientation).   **3**

The corresponding equation for females is:

Addressee Status $= -4 \cdot 64$ (hand relaxation)
$-3 \cdot 69$ (arm position)$-2 \cdot 74$ (leg relaxation)
$+2 \cdot 13$ (head tilt)$+2 \cdot 02$ (eye contact)
$\qquad +1 \cdot 43$ (arm openness)
$\qquad -0 \cdot 01$ (shoulder orientation).   **4**

As in the computation of the equations in the decoding studies, once again in the present analyses only those factors were included which the analyses of variance indicated as being significantly related to attitude (in the case of equations **1** and **3**) and status (in the case of equations **3** and **4**). For example, equation **1** indicates that more eye contact, a relative absence of an arms-akimbo position, and a smaller distance are part of an attempt to communicate a more positive attitude when the communicator is male and is standing. Furthermore, the coefficients in equation 1 indicate that the effects of eye contact are more important than those of arm position or distance which have approximately equal effects. (Incidentally, the absolute, but not the relative, values of the coefficients in equations 1–4 are arbitrary.) Again, equation 4 indicates that less hand relaxation, a relative absence of an arms-akimbo position, less leg relaxation, head in a level position, more eye contact, more arm openness, and more direct shoulder orientation occur in communications of a standing female with a higher status addressee. Finally, equations 3 and 4 indicate that shoulder orientation has a negligible coefficient.

Discussion

The methodologies employed in the above studies require some comment. The first three experiments [not reprinted here] employ a decoding methodology; that is, various combinations of postural cues are presented to Ss who infer (or decode) the communicators' attitude. There are a number of disadvantages associated with a decoding methodology. The use of static photographs can only yield information about attitudes inferred from stationary postures. A second disadvantage is that the interactive effects of posture with movements such as gestures cannot be studied. Finally, the isolated presentation of postural cues to Ss is likely to highlight the effects of these cues in everyday communications which would typically include verbal cues, facial cues and movements. The advantage of a decoding methodology, however, is that it provides a basis for the comparison of the effects on inferred attitude of a number of postural, orientation, and distance cues, singly or in combination. Furthermore, it allows the investigation of the relative effects of these cues for various communicator and addressee groups (e.g. different sex or age groups). Finally, possible confounding effects of communications in other channels (e.g. facial expressions, verbalization or gestures) can be eliminated. In sum, a decoding methodology yields a considerable amount of information due to the possibility of systematic control of a large number of variables. However, this information can only be cautiously extended to inference of attitude in everyday communication situations.

The fourth experiment employs a role-playing methodology in which Ss are asked to assume that they are in specific situations instead of E trying to create such situations in the experiment. Regarding the use of such role-playing methodologies in experimentation on attitude change, Brown noted,

The role-playing design does seem to permit the testing of detailed implications in a model of attitude change without relying on elaborate techniques of deception. We believe that a role-playing subject will behave in a way that corresponds more closely to the life situation than a hoodwinked subject will (1962, p. 74).

Brown's comments seem appropriate for the selection of methodologies in the study of implicit attitude communications as well.

A decoding method allows the investigation of the interactive effects of several postural cues and communicator characteristics, whereas an encoding method cannot include the systematic study of interactions among postural cues. However, the requirement of factorial designs for the study of the interactions of a decoding study limits the number of cues which can be investigated. This is because the number of experimental conditions corresponding to a factorial design involving more than six or seven factors is unmanageably large, and higher order interactions are difficult to interpret. The encoding method only provides the possibility of studying the interactive effects of one postural cue with communicator and addressee characteristics at a time. However, there is no limit to the number of postural cues which can be readily included and interpreted in such a design. The use of discriminant analysis, in conjunction with an encoding method, can provide information about the relative strengths of the various postural cues for discriminating attitudes or status relationships.

Before proceeding to an interview of the findings from the four experiments, it is necessary to note that the present study constitutes an exploratory searching for relationships among attitude, status, communicator age and sex, and postural variables. The relationships which have been obtained are not cross-validated for the most part. More specifically, although some of the main effects from the various experiments are congruent, a large number of the higher order interactions obtained in the decoding studies require cross-validation and need to be cautiously interpreted. Finally, the methodologies, despite their suitability for such exploratory study of a large number of relationships, are essentially artificial in nature. Therefore, the obtained relationships need to be considered with these limitations until further research with different kinds of methodologies becomes available.

The findings from all three of the decoding experiments suggest that greater relaxation, a forward lean of trunk towards one's addressee, and a smaller distance to the addressee communicate a more positive attitude to the addressee than a backward lean of posture and a larger distance. The findings do not provide much support for the hypotheses which relate more open posture and more direct orientation to more positive attitude inferred by an addressee. The latter two variables, that is, openness and orientation, however, do interact with several of the other variables included in the experiments in determining inferred attitudes. While tentative generalizations regarding these interactions effects have already been made in the results sections above, detailed interpretations of these interactions should await further replications of these exploratory findings.

The findings from the encoding experiment suggest that for male communicators (in the order of their importance) more eye contact, smaller distance, and a relative absence of an arms-akimbo position are part of an attempt to communicate a positive attitude. For females, the corresponding cues (also in order of importance) are a relative absence of an arms-akimbo position, smaller distance and arms openness. Also, a male communicator can convey his lower, in contrast to higher, status relative to his addressee using the following cues (in order of their importance): head tilt close to horizontal rather than head hanging, a relative absence of the crossing of one leg or foot in front of the other, more eye contact, a relative absence of an arms-akimbo position, less leg relaxation, less hand relaxation, and more direct shoulder orientation. For female communicators the corresponding list (also in order of importance) is less hand relaxation, a relative absence of an arms akimbo position, less leg relaxation, head tilt close to horizontal rather than head hanging, more eye contact, greater arm openness, and more direct shoulder orientation.

The findings of the fourth experiment also suggest that arm and leg openness while standing are more appropriately considered relaxation rather than proxemic indices. In other words, the folding of arms or the crossing of one foot or leg in front of the other are less formal and possibly more relaxed postures than postures approximating the 'standing at attention' posture which corresponds to the more open end of the arm-or-leg-openness continuum. Thus, subsequent measures of arm and leg relaxation while standing can include folding of arms or crossing of legs as criteria of relaxation. Since these openness measures are reliable, they can improve the reliability of the arm and leg relaxation measures.

A comparison of the moderately relaxed versus tense conditions of the first experiment and the variations in degree of relaxation exhibited by Ss in the fourth experiment suggests that the tense condition employed in the first experiment was quite extreme compared to the degrees of relaxation–tension exhibited spontaneously in the fourth experiment. The variations in degree of relaxation in the first experiment range from moderately relaxed to very tense, whereas such variations in the fourth experiment range from very relaxed to moderately relaxed. The findings, which relate relaxation to attitudes, can therefore be summarized as follows: a tense posture relative to a moderately relaxed posture communicates a more negative attitude. However, in a standing position, a moderately relaxed posture is not associated with a different attitude from a very relaxed posture.

In sum, among the hypotheses, those relating directness of orientation to attitude and openness of posture to attitude are not supported. In addition, the hypothesis relating relaxation to attitude needs to be modified in accordance with the previous paragraph. The remaining hypotheses relating attitudes to posture are supported. Also, both hypotheses relating status relationships to posture are supported; however, as already noted, Experiment IV provides additional relationships between status and postures.

Some further comments regarding choice of methodology in experiments of implicit attitude communication are required. A thorough study of communication in any medium would require both encoding and decoding strategies, that is, how is a given feeling or internal state of a communicator represented in different classes of behavior, and how are these different classes of behavior interpreted by other members of the same communication group? One approach to the study of implicit communications could employ an encoding method first to chart the most important variables involved. Next, more detailed investigations of the interrelationships among communication cues and communicator and addressee characteristics could be studied with the use of decoding methods. The stimuli used in the decoding studies could thus be based on communication cues obtained in the encoding studies.

Within the limits that have been noted, there are some possible applications of the findings of the present study. The normative data can be used to investigate the degree of nonconsensual quality of postural communication of an individual in the same experimental situations. Hypotheses relating degree of psychopathology to deviant implicit communication patterns can be studied. Also, the possibly greater degree of inconsistency of postural versus verbal communications of maladjusted compared to normal individuals can be investigated.

Another application of the above findings is in the study of deceitful communication. Given the above categories for the description of posture, variations in posture during deceitful versus truthful communications can be explored. It is possible that postural indices of negative attitude occur more frequently in deceitful than in truthful communications. The occurrence of negative postural indices associated with deceitful communication would be assumed to be due to negative attitudes toward the communication situation.

References

ANDERSON, R. L., and BANCROFT, T. A. (1955), *Statistical Theory in Research*, McGraw-Hill.

ARGYLE, M., and DEAN, J. (1965), 'Eye contact, distance and affiliation', *Sociometry*, vol. 28, pp. 289–304.

ARGYLE, M., and KENDON, A., (1967), 'The experimental analysis of social performance', in L. Berkowitz (ed.), *Advances in Experimental Social Psychology*, vol. 3, Academic Press.

BROWN, R. (1962), 'Models of attitude change', in R. Brown, E. Galanter, E. H. Hess and G. Mandler (eds.), *New Directions in Psychology*, Holt, Rinehart & Winston.

EXLINE, R. V. (1963), 'Explorations in process of person perception: Visual interaction in relationship to competition, sex, and need for affiliation', *J. Pers.*, vol. 31, pp. 1–20.

EXLINE, R. V., GRAY, D., and SCHUETTE, D. (1965), 'Visual behavior in a dyad as affected by interview content and sex of respondent', *J. pers. soc. Psychol.*, vol. 1, pp. 201–9.

GOFFMAN, E. (1961), *Encounters*, Bobbs-Merrill.

HALL, E. T. (1959), *The Silent Language*, Doubleday.

HALL, E. T. (1963), 'A system for the notation of proxemic behavior', *Amer. Anthropol.*, vol. 65, pp. 1003–26.

HALL, E. T. (1964), 'Silent assumptions in social communication', *Disorders of Communication*, vol. 42, pp. 41–55.

JAMES, W. T. (1932), 'A study of the expression of bodily posture', *J. General Psychol.*, vol. 7, pp. 405–37.

LITTLE, K. B. (1965), 'Personal space', *J. exper. soc. Psychol.*, vol. 1, pp. 237–47.

LOTT, D. F., and SOMMER, R. (1967), 'Seating arrangements and status', *J. pers. soc. Psychol.*, vol. 7, pp. 90–94.

MACHOTKA, P. (1965), 'Body movement as communication', *Behavioral Science Research*, vol. 2, pp. 33–66.

MEHRABIAN, A. (1967), 'Orientation behaviors and nonverbal attitude communication', *J. Communication*, vol. 17, pp. 324–32.

SCHLOSBERG, H. (1954), 'Three dimensions of emotion', *Psychol. Rev.*, vol. 61, pp. 81–8.

Part Three
Perception of the Other during Interaction

During social interaction those involved receive a great deal of information about the reactions, emotions, attitudes and personalities of the others present. Beldoch (Reading 8) reports a study of the ability to identify emotions from tone of voice and other non-verbal media. This is found to be a general ability, in which there are large individual differences. It should be noted however that the subjects were not actually engaged in interaction during the experiment, and other complicating factors may appear during interaction. It is well-known that facial expression may be a misleading guide to emotions, since people control their expressions. Ekman and Friesen (Reading 9) report a study of the expression of emotions by the hands and other parts of the body. They find that when a person keeps the expression of an emotion out of his face there is 'leakage' to other parts of his body and that the emotion can be identified by observers who cannot see the head. When one person (A) perceives another (B), he may be trying to assess B's properties, or he may be more interested in B's perceptions of A, as for example when A is being interviewed by B. Laing and his colleagues (Reading 10) describe a technique for assessing the accuracy of such perceptions and of various elaborations arising out of A's and B's perceptions of one another.

8 Michael Beldoch

Sensitivity to Expression of Emotional Meaning in Three
Modes of Communication

M. Beldoch, 'Sensitivity to expression of emotional meaning in three modes of
communication', in J. R. Davitz *et al.*, *The Communication of Emotional
Meaning*, McGraw-Hill, 1964, pp. 31–42.

Although previous studies have identified individual differences in ability
to recognize emotional expressions, each of these researches has been
concerned with only a single mode of communication. Thus, for example,
Davitz and Davitz (1959a) reported a wide range of accuracy in identifying
vocal expressions, but there is no evidence about the relationship of sensitivity to vocal messages and sensitivity in other modes of communication.
The present study, therefore, was designed to investigate the interrelationships among abilities to identify non-verbal emotional expressions in three
modes of communication: vocal, musical and graphic.

At the outset of this research, there was no substantial basis for making
any specific prediction about the interrelationships of sensitivity in the
three modes studied. Perhaps, like intelligence, emotional sensitivity might
be characterized by a general factor which operated in a variety of media,
as Spearman's *g* seems to account for some part of the variance in most
intellectual tasks. On the other hand, it was just as reasonable to predict
that emotional sensitivity was a specific function of the particular mode of
expression, so that measures of sensitivity to vocal cues would be independent of sensitivity to either musical or graphic communications. This
research was thus designed as a cross-validation study in an effort to define,
with reasonable confidence, the particular pattern of emotional sensitivities
which exist in relation to the various modes of non-verbal expression.

Procedure

In measuring abilities to identify expressions of emotional meaning via
different media, there was initially the dual problem of determining whether
or not ability in each of the modes is a stable characteristic and of developing
a reliable measure for each mode.

Speech instrument

Previous work (Davitz and Davitz, 1959b; Fairbanks and Pronevost, 1939)
using vocal communication provided important guides in developing the

measure to assess sensitivity to vocal expression. Three male and two female speakers tape-recorded recitations of the same three-sentence paragraph in an attempt to communicate twelve different emotions: admiration; affection; amusement; anger; boredom; despair; disgust; fear; impatience; joy; love; worship. The paragraph, 'I am going out now. I won't be back all afternoon. If anyone calls, just tell them I'm not here,' was selected for its apparent neutrality so far as specific emotional content was concerned.

The twelve emotions as communicated by the five speakers constituted a pool of sixty items from which the final items for the vocal test were selected. Two criteria were established for determining whether or not a given expression communicated the intended emotional meaning:

1. The number of listeners who identified the item correctly, in terms of speaker's intention, had to exceed that which would be expected by chance at the 0·01 level.

2. A plurality of listeners had to respond in the category of meaning intended by the speaker.

The total pool of sixty items were played to fifty-eight subjects (Ss) on two separate occasions one week apart. They were provided with the list of emotions and were told that each emotional meaning could appear once, more than once, or not at all. On the basis of these data, an item analysis of responses to the sixty items was carried out, utilizing the two criteria for selecting items. The final instrument consisted of thirty-seven of the original sixty items, involving ten of the twelve categories of emotional meaning. Affection and worship were dropped from the final instrument because not enough identifications of these emotions were obtained to warrant inclusion in the final instrument. Of the thirty-seven items finally selected, the fifty-eight Ss correctly identified a mean of 22·2 on the first test and 24·2 on the retest, with a test-retest correlation for total accuracy of 0·74.

Graphic art instrument

The steps followed in developing a reliable measure of communication via the vocal mode served as a model for the construction of the instruments for other modalities. Artists were asked to create abstract representations of the ten emotions used in the speech tape, and to avoid using obvious kinds of symbolization such as heart shapes to convey love, etc. The art work was shown on two separate occasions one week apart to samples similar in composition to those used in developing the speech instrument. After item analysis to eliminate paintings and drawings which did not communicate the artist's intention the final graphic art instrument consisted of twenty-six samples of colored art work and twenty-four pencil-line drawings, all free from any content cues or obvious symbolization. Test-retest correlation for this instrument was 0·48.

Music instrument

The music instrument was developed in a manner similar to the speech instrument. Musicians were asked to create and tape record on the instrument of their choice short compositions, ten to twenty seconds in length, each tape attempting to communicate one of the ten emotions. The fifty-item tape was then played to twenty-six Ss and replayed to twenty of the Ss one week later. Following the procedure and criteria described in the development of the speech instrument, an item analysis of the forty-eight papers yielded twenty-six items, and a rescoring of the papers according to these items yielded a test-retest correlation of 0·52 ($N = 20$; $p < 0·05$).

Procedure for principal study

The final presentation included a tape recording of thirty-seven items of content-standard speech, a twenty-six-item tape of recorded original musical selections, and an opaque projection of fifty graphic items, twenty-six in color and twenty-four in pencil. The test-retest correlations derived from the preliminary study were relatively low according to usual psychometric criteria. However, estimates of internal consistency based on split-half reliability coefficients for the experimental sample of eighty-nine Ss were somewhat higher. These coefficients were: 0·75 for speech, 0·67 for music, and 0·62 for art.

In addition to these instruments, a forty-item vocabulary test (Thorn-dike, 1942) was administered to obtain an estimate of verbal intelligence. A three-hundred-item Adjective Check List, developed by Harrison Gough, was completed by all Ss in the final sample in an attempt to identify some of the self-reported personality correlates of the traits measured by the art, music and speech instruments. Finally, the subjects answered a questionnaire relevant to their background, training and interest in drama, music and painting.

Subjects

The subjects of the principal study were eighty-nine men and women students attending Teachers College, Columbia University. For the purpose of the cross-validation design they were divided randomly into two groups. Group A contained forty-five subjects; group B forty-four subjects. Group A consisted of twenty-three males ($\overline{X}$ age $= 29·35$) and twenty-two females ($\overline{X}$ age $= 32·95$); group B consisted of twenty males ($\overline{X}$ age $= 31·07$) and twenty-four females ($\overline{X}$ age $= 34·63$). Vocabulary scores for groups A and

B were not significantly different (group A, $\bar{X} = 24 \cdot 21$, SD $= 5 \cdot 68$; group B, $\bar{X} = 24 \cdot 83$, SD $= 5 \cdot 70$; $t = 0 \cdot 49$, $p < 0 \cdot 05$).

Results

This study concerned itself with interrelationships among abilities to identify emotional meanings expressed in different media, and the relationship of self-reported personality characteristics as well as various background factors to the several measures of emotional sensitivity.

Correlations among media

Table 1 presents the product moment correlations obtained between scores on the speech and music, speech and art, and music and art instruments for groups A and B. From this table it can be seen that there is a clearly positive interrelationship among scores representing responses to the three media. The design of this study required the testing of hypotheses generated by group A by cross-validation on group B. The results for group B were analysed by product moment correlation using one-tailed tests of significance since direction could now be predicted. As indicated in Table 1, the results of this analysis support the initial finding that scores in all three media are positively interrelated.

Table 1 Intercorrelations among scores on speech, music, and art instruments

Group and variable	Music	Art
Group A[a]		
Speech	0·64**	0·56**
Music		0·53**
Group B[b]		
Speech	0·43**	0·27*
Music		0·55**

[a] Two-tailed tests.   * Significant at 0·05
[b] One-tailed tests.   ** Significant at 0·01

Instruments

The relationship of verbal intelligence and ability to identify expressions of feelings was investigated by product moment correlations between scores on the vocabulary test and scores on each test of emotional sensitivity. As indicated in Table 2, verbal intelligence is positively related to scores in all three media for both groups A and B.

Table 2 **Correlations of vocabulary scores with separate media and total score**

	Correlation with vocabulary	
Variable	Group A[a]	Group B[b]
Speech	0·46**	0·31*
Music	0·32*	0·47**
Art	0·41**	0·69**
Total	0·50**	0·62**

[a] Two-tailed tests.   * Significant at 0·05
[b] One-tailed tests.   ** Significant at 0·01

Since there were significant correlations between each of the separate media and the vocabulary scores, it was decided to compute partial correlations between the three media, holding the effects of the vocabulary scores constant.

As indicated in Table 3, controlling for verbal intelligence, the correla-

Table 3 **Partial correlations between media, controlling for the effects of verbal intelligence**

Group and variable	Music	Art
Group A[a]		
Speech	0·59**	0·46**
Music		0·46**
Group B[b]		
Speech	0·34*	0·08
Music		0·38**

[a] Two-tailed tests.   * Significant at 0·05
[b] One-tailed tests.   ** Significant at 0·01

tions between speech and music and between music and art are significant for both group A and group B. However, the positive relationship between speech and art, though significant for group A, was not supported by the cross-validation.

Relationship to self-reported sensitivity

Forty of the forty-five subjects in group A completed a six-step rating scale included in the general questionnaire Ss filled out as part of the research procedure. This item read, 'I am (very, quite, fairly, moderately, a bit, not at all) sensitive to other peoples' emotional expressions.' Ss were instructed to check the word or words in the brackets that best described their own sensitivity. The distribution of responses to the rating scale was such that by combining the number of subjects who responded to this item by checking either 'very' or 'quite', and by combining the number of respondents who checked any of the other alternatives, a median test analysis of the results for the separate media and for the total score was possible. The results indicated that total scores as well as scores on the speech and graphic art instruments are positively related to self-reported emotional sensitivity, but scores on the music instrument are independent of self-reported sensitivity.

Another attempt to measure self-reported personality correlates of ability to identify emotional expression was investigated by means of a three-hundred-item Adjective Check List. This list was administered to all subjects in an attempt to find out if Ss who scored above the median on the combined speech, music and art instruments checked different adjectives than those who scored below the median. An item analysis of the three-hundred adjectives based on group A yielded two adjectives which were significantly more often checked by high scorers: leisurely and outgoing. Five adjectives were significantly more often checked by low scorers: aggressive, interests narrow, painstaking, simple and thrifty. However, when these seven adjectives were cross-validated on group B, none of the seven were significant at the 0·05 level.

Effect of training and background

An attempt was made to evaluate the effects of training, current interest in, and degree of reported enjoyment received from the various media on scores on the art, music and speech instruments. Answers to items on the questionnaires eliciting information about these areas were subjected to chi-square analysis. Of the nine analyses done, only one was significant at the 0·05 level. Such a findings could easily be due to chance in that the probability of finding one hypothesis out of nine confirmed at the 0·05 level when all of the hypotheses are drawn from a single common source is between 0·30 and 0·40 (Sakoda, Cohen and Beall, 1954). Therefore, it would seem warranted to conclude that training, current interest in, and degree of enjoyment received from the various media do not significantly affect scores on the art, music, or speech instruments.

Two additional analyses of the data were carried out. Table 4 lists the mean scores for men and women on the speech, music and art instruments and for total scores. No significant differences between the sexes were obtained from any set of scores.

Table 4 Means and standard deviations for men and women, and significance of sex differences

Instrument	Men Mean	SD	Women Mean	SD	t	p
Speech	20·7	4·0	19·6	5·7	0·97	>0·05
Music	12·3	2·8	11·3	3·5	1·38	>0·05
Art	13·7	4·7	13·9	5·0	0·16	>0·05
Total	46·8	8·1	44·8	12·5	0·85	>0·05

Discussion

At the outset of this study there was no information available upon which to base a prediction about the relationships among abilities to identify the communication of emotional meaning in various media. It is now evident that there exists a general ability to identify emotional communications which transcends a given medium of expression. Thus, those individuals who better identify emotional expressions in content-standard speech also tend to identify expressions more accurately in graphic and musical modes. Ability to identify non-verbal emotional expressions, therefore, is a relatively stable human characteristic which can be measured with some reliability and which generalizes over specific modes of communication.

However, a finding of equal, or perhaps greater, importance emerges from the study in relation to the operation carried out to control for intelligence. Verbal intelligence was related to all three measures of the ability to identify emotional expressions, although partialling out verbal intelligence did not eliminate all of the significant intercorrelations among the measures. Thus, although verbal intelligence is positively related to the ability to identify emotions expressed in the three media, verbal intelligence alone does not account for the common variance among the three measures of sensitivity.

Intelligence in this study was measured by a vocabulary test. The ability to identify the intended emotion, on the other hand, was measured by three content-standard or content-free tests. But both kinds of measures involved responding to symbolic stimuli. On the vocabulary test, of course, the Ss responded to linguistic symbols; in the tests of emotional sensitivity, the Ss responded to vocal, graphic and musical symbols. Regardless of the test, however, Ss were required to understand the symbolic meaning of each item, i.e. to identify the meaning of each vocabulary item in terms of a multiple choice among several words, and to identify the meaning of each vocal, musical and graphic item in terms of a multiple choice of ten different feelings. Thus, all of the measures involved symbolic processes, and the results might best be conceptualized in terms of a general theory of symbolization.

Michael Beldoch 127

Discursive and non-discursive symbols

The theory of symbolic processes developed by Susanne Langer (1942; 1953) seems particularly appropriate to this study in view of her distinction between discursive and non-discursive symbols, for this distinction may clarify the relationship between verbal intelligence and the ability to identify emotional expressions.

A knowledge of word meanings, according to Langer's theory, is a knowledge of discursive symbols, which correlate names or concepts and things, are verifiable, duplicable, and have a defined syntax and order. Non-discursive symbols, on the other hand, depend upon personal perceptions, on intuition, and on direct insight for understanding. They cannot be verified or duplicated, do not have 'dictionary meanings', and do not have a socially defined syntax and order.

Miss Langer interprets art as communication in the non-discursive mode. The artist is concerned with the expression of feelings even though he may not at the moment of expression actually be experiencing the emotion in question; specifically, he creates forms symbolic of human feeling. Although it would be unreasonable to assume that the persons in this study who produced the vocal, graphic and musical items were creating symbols which would generally be recognized as art objects, in the sense that they did indeed produce forms that communicated emotional meanings, one might assume a parallel between the non-discursive symbols of Langer's theory of art and items contained in our three tests of emotional sensitivity. Thus, the three tests of ability to identify intended emotions seems to fall within the realm of non-discursive symbols, for they involved expressions of feeling on the basis of formal, or content-free properties of each mode of communication. In contrast, the measure of verbal intelligence would seem to involve, according to Langer's view, discursive symbolization. Therefore, the correlations between verbal intelligence and the three measures of ability to identify expression of emotion may reflect a relationship between abilities to deal with symbols both in the discursive and non-discursive modes of communication. If this interpretation is valid, the results suggest that these two kinds of symbolic ability are positively related, but have considerable independent variance, and both kinds of ability may very well be involved in the communication of emotional meanings in everyday, human interaction.

Conceptualizing the ability to identify communication of emotions in terms of a symbolic ability, related to but different from, the usual measures of intelligence, may help rescue the concept of 'emotional sensitivity' from the mysterious, and perhaps unknowable realm of empathy, 'third ears', and other notions which have been proposed to account for observed differences in ability to identify communications of feeling. For in terms of this point of view, emotional sensitivity involves symbolic processes which can be investigated empirically, with the aim of discovering the general principles of 'emotional intelligence' in perhaps much the same way as psychologists have discovered the principles underlying discursive intellectual functioning. Langer cogently emphasized throughout her work that non-discursive symbolization is governed by a logic, a set of principles, which is different from that of discursive symbolization, but is not theoretically any more mysterious, unknowable, or less open to empirical investigation. If emotional sensitivity, therefore, can legitimately be accounted for in terms of non-discursive symbolization, the task of research is to discover the psychological principles of this kind of ability, just as Spearman, Thurstone, and others have discovered the principles of discursive intelligence.

Correlates of sensitivity

Psychologists are already familiar with many of the correlates of discursive symbolic ability; most of what is measured when a subject is given a standard test of intelligence concerns this area of symbolic behavior. But what are the correlates of non-discursive symbolic activity?

The fact that high-scoring Ss describe themselves as more sensitive than low-scoring Ss probably reflects the more or less accurate feedback as a consequence of correctly responding to emotional communication in everyday life. Awareness of one's own emotional sensitivity or insensitivity probably is an important aspect of interpersonal adjustment. The results of this study do not support the familiar and popular notion about the superiority of women's intuition; men and women did not differ significantly on any of the music, art or speech measures or on the total sensitivity score. Nor did training or background courses in the three media contribute to success in identifying the communication of feelings in the media. In addition, the attempt to isolate relatively gross personality variables as they relate to this ability met with largely null results. [. . .]

Summary

It was the central purpose of this study to examine by means of a cross-validation design the interrelationships that exist among abilities to identify the communication of feelings in different media.

Although there has been considerable interest through the years in the ability to identify emotional communication in a variety of media, there has been no research on the interrelationships that exist among abilities to identify such communications in different media. It was the central purpose of this study to examine such relationships by means of a cross-validation design.

Tape recordings of male and female speakers reciting the same neutral paragraph in an attempt to communicate various emotional states were presented to evening-college students on two separate occasions. Item analyses of responses to the tapes which were conducted and a final tape developed which included only items which were more often identified as the speaker's intended emotion than any other choice. A similar technique was used with recordings of musical phrases created and played by musicians in an attempt to communicate the same emotions. Abstract art created by artists to convey these emotions was shown by opaque projection to still another group of evening students and the same criteria used to select items that successfully communicated the artists' intention. Reliability coefficients for each instrument were in the 0·60s and 0·70s, indicating that the measures in the three media were internally consistent.

The final study presented to eighty-nine men and women graduate students in Teachers College tape recorded speech selections and musical phrases, opaque projections of abstract art, a three-hundred-item Adjective Check List, and a questionnaire which elicited background information with regard to the Ss training, participation in and enjoyment derived from the separate media. A six-step self-report scale of sensitivity to other people's emotional expressions and a forty-word vocabulary test as a measure of intelligence completed the materials used in this study.

Significant intercorrelations were obtained among the abilities to identify the expression of feelings in all three media. Vocabulary scores also correlated significantly with ability in all three modes and with total score, although when controlling for vocabulary scores, two of the three significant relationships among abilities in the three media remained significant. Background training or current interest in the arts did not contribute to success with any of the instruments. None of the adjectives on the check list discriminated between high and low scorers on the sensitivity measures, but self-reported sensitivity did distinguish between groups, the high scorers describing themselves as more sensitive than the low scorers.

The results of the study were discussed in terms of Langer's distinction between discursive and non-discursive symbolic activity. Intelligence is most often measured by tasks in the discursive mode, such as knowing the meaning of words. Non-discursive symbols, on the other hand, are communicated by their formal properties, and are the kind used by artists and in the process of intuition. This research suggests that abilities in the discursive and non-discursive modes have some common variance, but that they are in many ways independent of each other. The implications for further research focus on understanding the correlates of ability in the non-discursive mode, especially as they may relate to cognitive and conceptual function and malfunction.

References

DAVITZ, J., and DAVITZ, L. (1959a), 'The communication of feelings by content-free speech', *J. Communication*, vol. 9, pp. 6–13.

DAVITZ, J., and DAVITZ, L. (1959b), 'Correlates of accuracy in the communication of feelings', *J. Communication*, vol. 9, pp. 110–17.

FAIRBANKS, G., and PRONEVOST, W. (1939), 'An experimental study of the pitch characteristics of the voice during the expression of emotion', *Speech Monographs*, vol. 6, pp. 87–104.

HOLT, R. R., and LUBORSKY, L. (1958), *Personality Patterns of Psychiatrists*, Basic Books.

LANGER, S. K. (1942), *Philosophy in a New Key*, Harvard University Press.

LANGER, S. K. (1953), *Feeling and Form*, Scribners.

SAKODA, J. N., COHEN, B. H., and BEALL, G. (1954), 'Test of significance of a series of statistical tests', *Psychol. Bull.*, vol. 51, pp. 172–5.

THORNDIKE, R. L. (1942), 'Two screening tests of verbal intelligence', *J. app. Psychol.*, vol. 26, pp. 128–35.

9 Paul Ekman and Wallace V. Friesen

Non-Verbal Leakage and Clues to Deception

P. Ekman and W. V. Friesen, 'Non-verbal leakage and clues to deception', *Psychiatry*, vol. 32, 1969, pp. 88–105.

In the last few years there has been a resurgence of interest in facial expression and body movement, both in research relevant to psychotherapy (see Argyle, 1967; Birdwhistell, 1959; Dittman, Parloff and Boomer, 1965; Freedman and Hoffman, 1967; Mahl, 1968; Ruesch and Kees, 1956), and in the development of psychotherapeutic techniques which emphasize this mode of behavior (see Gruenberg, Liston and Wayne, 1967; Paredes and Cornelison, 1967; Wilmer, 1967). Most of the research has shown that the kind of information which can be gleaned from the patient's words – information about affects, attitudes, interpersonal styles, psychodynamics – can also be derived from his concomitant non-verbal behavior. Yet, if body movements and facial expressions were only redundant with verbal behavior, there would be little need for the therapist to carefully attend to it, or the psychotherapy researcher to bear the burden of recording and analysing visual records. In 1968 we argued that the central problem for those investigators interested in the application of their work to psychotherapy research or practice was to provide evidence of how non-verbal behavior can provide information which differs from that provided by words. We suggested that demographic variables, changes in ego states, situational variables and message content would all be relevant in determining when actions speak louder than words. In this article we will explore only one of these variables, the interaction situation, and will consider how within deception interactions differences in neuroanatomy and cultural influences combine to produce specific types of body movements and facial expressions which escape efforts to deceive and emerge as *leakage* or *deception clues*.

The proposal that non-verbal behavior may escape efforts to deceive, may evade self-censoring, or may betray dissimulation is by no means new. Darwin wrote:

Some actions ordinarily associated through habit with certain states of mind may be partially repressed through the will, and in such cases the muscles which are least under the separate control of the will are the most liable still to act, causing movements which we recognize as expressive. In certain other cases the checking of one habitual movement requires other slight movements; and these are likewise expressive (1872, pp. 48–9).

Darwin did not, however, clearly specify which movements are susceptible to control of the 'will', and which escape such control or are themselves a product of the control.

Freud was persuaded of the importance of non-verbal behavior when he wrote:

He that has eyes to see and ears to hear may convince himself that no mortal can keep a secret. If his lips are silent, he chatters with his finger-tips; betrayal oozes out of him at every pore (1905, p. 94).

But Freud was less concerned with non-verbal behavior than with the intricacies of verbal behavior, and such forms of verbal leakage as slips of the tongue and dreams.

Goffman is the contemporary writer whose general framework is most relevant to deception and non-verbal behavior. Social interactions are all in a sense deceptive; the participants are engaged in a dramatic performance to manage impressions that are given off.

The legitimate performances of everyday life are not 'acted' or 'put on' in the sense that the performer knows in advance just what he is going to do, and does this solely because of the effect it is likely to have. The expressions it is felt that he is giving off will be especially 'inaccessible' to him. But as in the case of less legitimate performers, the incapacity of the ordinary individual to formulate in advance the movements of his eyes and body does not mean that he will not express himself through these devices in a way that is dramatized and pre-formed in his repertoire of acts. In short, we all act better than we know how (1959, pp. 73–4).

Our view of deception situations differs from Goffman's in emphasis; we will isolate specific types of interactions which differ from other performances in terms of the focus upon withholding information and dissimulating. Goffman has also described how non-verbal actions may inadvertently distract from the performance. He considers unmeant gestures as problems in that the audience may treat them seriously, questioning the honesty of a performance because of accidental expressive cues. We will emphasize the other side of the coin, how certain non-verbal acts should be treated as important evidence that the performance is deceptive and the information being provided is false.

We will distinguish two types of deception, and then consider three dimensions which distinguish deceptive situations from other forms of social interaction. We will then postulate differences in the sending capacity of the face, hands and feet based largely upon neuroanatomical considerations, and discuss how these sending differences combine with sociocultural variables to bring about differences among face, hands and feet in internal and external feedback. These differences in feedback form the basis for our predictions about the types of non-verbal activities which provide leakage and deception clues. Finally, we will present evidence from our study of psychiatric interviews which illustrates our general hypotheses.

Definitions

We will consider two forms of deception: alter-deception, where ego, the deceiver, conceals information from the other interactant, alter; and self-deception, where ego is the object of his own deception, concealing information from himself. Alter is not deceived if he perceives either deception clues or leakage. Deception clues tip him off that deception is in progress but do not reveal the concealed information; the betrayal of that withheld information we call leakage. Alter may become aware of deception clues or leakage regardless of whether ego is aware of their occurrence or of alter's cognizance of them. During alter-deception, if ego realizes alter is on to him, he may give up his deception; or he may continue it, since explicit acknowledgement of engaging in deception may be more embarrassing than maintaining a deception tacitly discovered. During self-deception, it is likely that alter may be aware of deception clues and leakage of which ego is oblivious; if ego becomes aware of his own deception clues he may have an uncanny feeling that something is amiss, or that he has some conflicting feelings; presumably ego does not become aware of his own leakage during self-deception because to learn the information he has concealed from himself would produce severe anxiety.

Ego plans his behavior during alter-deception and is usually quite aware of what he wishes to conceal from alter. The information withheld might refer to ego's feelings and attitudes toward alter, or toward some other person or object; or it might be about some past activity or future plan of his own, or of alter's, or of some third party of interest to alter. Ego has two choices, if he is to succeed in his deception: inhibit or simulate. Most often he will do both. Simply inhibiting, cutting off communication entirely, is the safest way to prevent leakage, but it usually is a giveaway to alter that something is amiss. Instead ego will attempt to maintain the communicative flow, pretending that nothing is being concealed while he carefully and selectively omits certain messages.

Simulation comes about for three reasons. The first reason, just described, is that the gaps left by omitting specific messages must be filled if the gaps are not to be become conspicuous deception clues. A second motive for simulation is to maintain a barrier against the breakthrough of inhibited behavior. When there is considerable pressure behind the matters being concealed the only way to prevent their leakage is by simulating antithetical feelings. A neutral face probably will not succeed in masking uproarious laughter, particularly if there is continuing mirthful provocation; the trace of the smile, the quiver in the corners of the lips, can best be withheld over time by setting the jaw, biting the lip or compressing the lips.

A third reason for simulation is more intrinsic to the structure of the social setting and the goal of the deception. Most deceptive situations not only dictate the need to conceal one item of information but also require the substitution of a false message. It is not sufficient, for example, for the job applicant to inhibit signs of nervousness or inexperience, or for the hospital-ized depressive patient to inhibit signs of melancholia; the goal of the deception requires that to gain employment the applicant simulate cool confidence, that to gain release from the hospital the patient simulate feelings of optimism, well-being and insight. The extent of simulating is thus related to how extensive the lie may be, how many gaps are created by omission, how much motivational force is associated with the informa-tion concealed, and how extensive the requirements are for substituted false messages in order to achieve the goal of the deception. Later we will describe how simulations may be improperly performed because of defects in internal feedback about certain types of non-verbal behavior, and how such imperfect non-verbal simulations are major forms of deception clues.

While alter-deception involves a dyad in which one member deceives the other, self-deception is a more individual phenomenon, where the presence of the other person is not necessarily relevant to the deception. Alter is not the primary target; instead the purpose of the deception is to conceal information from the self-aware part of the self. There is a division within the individual such that one part of the self can inhibit and conceal in-formation from the more conscious or self-aware part of the individual. Such a formulation of individual behavior is, of course, completely con-sistent with the psychoanalytic theory of defense mechanisms. The term 'blocking' would be applied to those self-deceptive situations in which ego realizes that he has concealed something from himself, or that he can't remember something, or that he can't describe or be sure of how he feels. The terms 'repression' or 'dissociation' would refer to a more complete manifestation of self-deception, where ego is totally unaware that part of his self has engaged in concealing information from the self-aware part. And the situation of ambivalence has similarities, which we will discuss later, in both alter- and self-deception.

Simulation typically accompanies the inhibition of information in self-deception. In order for ego to maintain the required image of himself and the desired social face to others, it is usually not sufficient that he conceal certain information; he must adopt as his own, feelings and attitudes which help disconfirm the matters being withheld. The person who dissociates anger not only may need to omit all such feelings, but also may need to appear to himself and others as altruistic and generous. The simulated behavior during self-deception differs from the simulation during alter-deception; it is less explicitly managed and the false message is actually felt, but it is not all that is felt. The simulation and its degree of genuineness is much like the feelings involved in the psychoanalytic defence mechanism of reaction-formation, and this is far more actually experienced than the simulations of alter-deception. [. . .]

Sending capacity, external feedback and internal feedback

The *sending capacity* of a part of the body can be measured by three indexes: average transmission time, number of discriminable stimulus patterns which can be emitted, and visibility. In these terms the face is the best sender, the feet/legs the worst. The face has the shortest potential transmission time; most 'macro' facial expressions, those that can be easily seen and readily labeled in terms of emotion, last less than a second, often about half a second. 'Micro' facial expressions are even shorter; by definition their duration is so short that they are at the threshold of recognition unless slow-motion projection is utilized. The facial musculature allows for a great number of discriminable stimuli patterns, far more than are provided by legs/feet. The face has the greatest visibility; it is covered only by sunglasses, make-up or hair, except in cultures that frequently use masks or veils. It is difficult to hide the face without being obvious about concealment; there are no inhibition maneuvers for the face equivalent to putting the hands in the pocket or sitting upon them. A frozen, immobile poker face is more noticeable than are interlocked fingers or tensely held feet.

The feet and legs are in almost all respects the worst non-verbal senders. Their transmission time is slow, far slower than that for the face or hands. The number of discriminable stimulus patterns which can be emitted is also limited. When a person is standing, his foot movements are restricted by the requirements of staying erect; even when seated, he is limited to what foot and leg movements can occur without his falling or sliding out of the chair. Feet/legs are not very visible; the toes are usually covered by socks and shoes, much of the leg by pants or a skirt (the popularity of mini-skirts makes for some change in visibility, although inhibitions about looking may still apply). In Western society at least, furniture is usually arranged so that the feet or legs cannot be easily viewed, and people become uncomfortable during conversations if they are totally exposed without the screen of a desk, table or speaker's podium. Even when furniture does not directly interfere with the gaze, seating distance usually does. While talking, people usually sit or stand too close for inspection of the feet/legs area to take place without a noticeable look downwards.

Anatomically, hands are intermediate between face and feet/legs, and this is also true of their sending capacity. Although small hand movements may be as brief as most macro facial expressions, most hand activity, whether it be in space or touching the body, requires a longer duration for performance. The independent movements of the ten fingers, the differential spatial patterns which may be described, the accelerations, the choice of areas of the body to contact, and the actions which may occur at the apex of the movement provide the hands with many more discriminable stimulus patterns than the legs/feet, perhaps as many as the face. Hands are much more visible than the legs/feet, rarely covered by clothing or obscured by furniture, but, unlike the face, they can easily be hidden.

External feedback from alter closely parallels these differences in sending capacity. External feedback can be defined as behavior by alter which ego is likely to perceive as reactive to his own non-verbal behavior. The most obvious external feedback would be alter's verbal comment on ego's non-verbal behavior; alter's gaze direction may also provide external feedback to ego, at least in terms of alter's interest in a non-verbal act. There can be other forms of external feedback, such as imitative behavior or other changes in verbal or non-verbal behavior which are responsive to ego's non-verbal behavior, but ego usually will not associate them with his own non-verbal behavior. The term 'external feedback' does not refer to what alter perceives, but more narrowly to those aspects of alter's behavior which explicitly inform ego what alter has perceived and evaluated.

The most external feedback is provided for the face; people are most willing to comment verbally on and hold the person responsible for what is shown facially. There is less external feedback directed at the hands, and very little to the feet/legs, which not only are rarely the subject of verbal comment but also are rarely the conspicuous target of eye gaze. The differences in sending capacity among body areas may partially explain these differences in external feedback: people look most at the best sender, the face. But there are other reasons for looking at and commenting on facial behavior. As the input site for seeing, hearing, smelling, tasting, breathing and ingesting, and the output site for words, most other sounds, and lip-reading cues, it commands attention. In Western culture there is almost a fetish about facial attractiveness; at least part of the self is identified with the face; there is belief in the ability to read character and intelligence from facial cues; and the most idiosyncratic personal sector of the individual is thought to reside in or be reflected in the face. The face is the primary site for the display of affects, and in particular for eye-contacts, which are important in regulating the relationship between ego and alter.

There are, however, limits to the attention that can be directed toward the face. The face cannot be watched as continually as the voice can supposedly be listened to. If alter looks too long he suggests intimacy or a power struggle; if he looks too little he suggests disinterest, dishonesty or suspicion. In Western society a dyadic conversation usually occurs in a seating position where the rest positions of the faces are not directly *vis-à-vis*. People sit at slight angles to each other rather than directly face to face, particularly if no table is interposed. Looking at the other person requires an act, moving the eyes or the head from center, and the act ends by returning to the resting position where it is easy not to look or not to be looked at. Seating a dyad in direct face-to-face confrontation can produce the same discomfort as removing all screens blocking the view of the body below the waist. Such seating positions connote interrogation and severe role inequality.

Alter may give external feedback regarding ego's hands if those hands are moving in space, particularly if they are enacting what we have called 'illustrator' movements, motions which in some fashion illustrate what is being verbalized. But there is a taboo about being caught looking at hand acts when they involve contact with the body, particularly if hands contact a body orifice or genital area. It is not that people are polite and constrained and don't do these things their parents would scold about; but people are polite observers. When the rules of Emily Post are broken and people rub, pick or massage their noses, ears, anus, or crotch, they believe that others won't look, and this is generally true. Rudeness seems to reside as much in watching such behavior as in emitting it. An interesting sidelight on this phenomenon is found in interactions between drivers of automobiles. Many people act in their cars as if they had the privacy of their bathrooms, and a convention has developed of not looking through the open window or clear glass at such bathroom behavior, so that the 'embarrassed' party is not the groomer but the one caught watching the grooming.

Even less external feedback is given to the feet/legs than to the hands. Alter might directly comment on a facial expression, describing or mimicking it and asking ego what it means, and might similarly comment on a hand movement in space. But just as it would be extraordinary for alter to ask about ego's nose picking, ear scratching, or genital rubbing, so it would be unusual for him to comment on leg squeezing or foot arching. These differences in what alter will comment upon are paralleled in any looking behavior which occurs in a fashion easily noted by ego.

Let us repeat that in this discussion of external feedback we have not meant to claim that alter will not see hand movements or leg/foot movements; he may, just as he may actually see facial behaviors on which he does not provide feedback. Instead, our use of the term 'external feedback' rather than 'visual focus' was to limit our concern to those behaviors of alter which conspicuously provide information to ego that ego's non-verbal behavior is the subject of alter's scrutiny and evaluation. In such terms, the face receives more commentary than the hands or the legs/feet.

Internal feedback, our conscious awareness of what we are doing and our ability to recall, repeat or specifically enact a planned sequence of motor behavior, parallels both sending capacity and external feedback in terms of the differences among face, hands and feet. People have the greatest internal feedback about their face, next most about their hands and least about their legs and feet. Why might this be so? As we have explained, the face, as the best sender, receives the most external feedback; such feedback may teach ego to pay more attention to his face, amplifying and focusing upon whatever internal feedback cues are available. Conversely, ego may learn that people pay little attention to his legs/feet, and therefore conclude that he can afford to be less vigilant about what he does in this body area.

Further, our verbal vocabulary is most extensive for facial behaviors, next most for hands, and least for legs/feet. While it is reasonable to presume that the verbal labels develop because of the greater sending capacity of the face and the need for a simple means of communicating about facial messages, the existence of labels amplifies any already existing differences, in that cognitive processes of retrieval, sorting and recognition of logical or temporal relationships are aided by the availability of a simple means of referring to or tagging non-verbal events.

Another consideration is that just as people are held responsible for what they show facially, so they take more responsibility for what is shown in their face. Most people identify at least some part of their self with their face, but do so to a much lesser degree with other areas of the body.

A last consideration relates to the neuroanatomical properties of the face, hands and legs/feet. Internal feedback may be more developed and accentuated for the face than for hands and legs/feet because of the relative rapidity of facial muscular movements, and because of the possible neural linkage of the facial muscles as affect programs, as suggested by Silvan Tomkins. Ego may have to monitor facial behaviors very closely because they are such a fast system, capable of being ennervated by involuntary as well as voluntary events.

Our hypotheses about the non-verbal sources for leakage and deception clues can be derived from what has been outlined about sending capacity, internal feedback and external feedback. Ego will not expend much effort inhibiting or dissimulating with areas of the body largely ignored by alter.

Paul Ekman and Wallace V. Friesen 139

Equally important, ego cannot inhibit or dissimulate actions in areas of the body about which he has learned to disregard internal feedback or in which he receives little internal feedback. If an action is to be withheld, that area of the body must be closely monitored; if a false message is to be sent, then ego must be able to retrieve easily information about actions he has customarily employed to express the particular feeling he wishes to convey misleadingly at this moment. [. . .]

Leakage and deception clues

Earlier we traced how sending capacity and external and internal feedback are greater for the face than for the hands and feet. From this we hypothesized that ego will attempt much less inhibition or dissimulation in the areas of the hands and feet. Thus, the face is likely to be the major nonverbal liar, maximally redundant with the verbal behavior during deception, subject to lies of both omission and commission. The chief exceptions are micro facial displays, which can serve as leakage or deception clues. Because the face is such a fast sending system, even during alter-deception, there may be affect displays which begin to emerge before ego is fully aware of them and can squelch them. Other forms of deception clues in the face are imperfectly performed simulations of affect. These might include performances of too long duration, with too extensive a scope to the expression, or without the usual blend of affects. Examples are the smile that lasts too long, the frown that is too severe, the look of fear that is not sufficiently blended with surprise.

The full affect reduced time micro displays may well be those which ego is not aware of, while the squelched micro displays may be those which ego senses and interrupts in mid performance. If that is so, we would expect the time reduced full affect displays to be more prevalent in self-deception than in alter-deception, and the reverse to be true of the micro, squelched affect displays.

In a sense the face is equipped to lie the most and leak the most, and thus can be a very confusing source of information during deception. Generally, ego can get away with and best perpetuate deception through his face. Although he must monitor quickly and work continually to inhibit this fast responsive system, he has most awareness of his facial displays and is usually well practised in the display rules for modulating facial affects. In contrast to either the hands or legs/feet, the face is the major site for lies of commission, for simulated messages; ego has the internal feedback to retrieve information about what facial muscles to move to create the appearance of an affect which he does not feel at present. The success of facial deception depends upon alter's ignoring or disregarding the leakage through micro displays and the rough edges on the simulated displays. The evidence cited earlier suggests that most persons do disregard such important forms of leakage and deception clues, and one would expect the usual observer of the face typically to be misled. One would expect the keen observer, on the other hand, to receive contradictory information from facial cues: simulated messages, micro leakage of information which contradicts the simulations, and deception clues of squelched displays and improperly performed simulations.

The hands are easier to inhibit than the face; as mentioned earlier, they can be hidden from view without the hiding itself becoming salient as a deception clue. But the hands, unlike the face, are not fakers; most people will not use their hands to dissimulate. The hands commit lies of omission but not of commission. Major forms of leakage in the hands are the adaptors, particularly the self-adaptors. While facially smiling and pleasant, ego may be tearing at a fingernail, digging into his cheek, protectively holding his knees, and so forth. Self-adaptors can also serve as deception clues, betraying discomfort about the deception. Alter-adaptors in the hands and legs/feet can provide leakage or deception clues – for example, a fist can leak interest in attack, a beseeching hand movement can leak fear which is otherwise disavowed. Object-adaptors can provide deception clues, such as the restless tapping of a cigarette; or leakage, such as the displacement of a withheld anger into the snapping of a pencil.

The legs/feet, which have a limited repertoire of information, are a primary source of both leakage and deception clues. Like the hands, they are relatively easy to inhibit, although not as totally as the hands, and the legs/feet are employed even less than the hands in dissimulations. Leakage in the legs/feet could include aggressive foot kicks, flirtatious leg displays, autoerotic or soothing leg squeezing, abortive restless flight movements. Deception clues can be seen in tense leg positions, frequent shift of leg posture, and in restless or repetitive leg and foot acts.

Another form of deception clues in both the hands and legs/feet results from ego's neglecting to perform simulations which should accompany the verbal and facial simulations. The lack of the usually associated self- and alter-adaptors, the lack of the usual illustrative hand movements, can create the impression in alter that ego does not really mean what he says; ego just doesn't look natural. But, generally, these areas of the body are not watched too closely by alter, and deficiencies can pass.

To summarize, the availability of leakage and description clues reverses the pattern described for differences in sending capacity, internal feedback and external feedback. .The worst sender, the legs/feet, is also the least responded to and the least within ego's awareness, and thus a good source for leakage and deception clues. The best sender, the face, is most closely watched by alter, most carefully monitored by ego, most subject to inhibition and dissimilation, and thus the most confusing source of information during deception; apart from micro expressions, it is not a major source of leakage and deception clues. The hands are intermediate on both counts, as a source of leakage and deception clues, and in regard to sending capacity and internal and external feedback.

Illustrative experiments

We have conducted some preliminary experiments employing records of natural occurrences of deception. Sound motion-picture films had already been collected of 120 brief interviews with forty female psychiatric inpatients at different points in their hospitalization. The films of each patient, the interviewer's notes about her, the ward records, and information obtained after her discharge were examined in order to isolate interviews in which the patient had probably been engaging in either self- or alter-deception. We could be certain that deception occurred and could specify the concealed information on only three interviews.

The basic design of the experiments was to show a film of one of the interviews silently to one of two different groups of naïve observers, one group viewing only the face and head, the other viewing the body from the neck down. The observers were not told they were seeing a psychiatric patient; the film was identified as a record of a conversation. After viewing the film, both groups of observers described their impressions by checking words from Gough's Adjective Check List, three hundred words descriptive of attitudes, traits, affects, manners. To test hypotheses about the source of leakage of withheld information, the information conveyed by head/face cues was contrasted with information conveyed by body cues.

An example of alter-deception

Patient A was admitted to the hospital with depressed affect, angry outbursts, screaming, threats of suicide; there was disagreement about whether the diagnosis was agitated depression or schizophrenia. She was given amitriptyline hydrochloride and psychotherapy. Within two and a half weeks she had begun an attempt to manage her affect expression, and to inhibit the display of her anxiety, anger and dysphoria. Films were taken on the first day of hospitalization, in the middle of hospitalization and shortly before discharge. At the middle of hospitalization it appeared that Miss A was engaged in alter-deception, attempting to conceal information about how upset she still actually was, and simulating optimism, control of affect, and feelings of well-being. Our evidence that such deception occurred during this interview included the interviewer's impression and the ward psychiatrist's impression; the patient's behavior at the conclusion of the interview when she broke down, cried and admitted she did not feel as well as she had earlier claimed; and posthospitalization discussions of this film with the patient.

Hypothesis. The observers who view the face/head cues, more than those who view the body cues, will miss concealed information about depression and agitation, and instead will pick up the simulated message about well-being. While we anticipated that there would be both micro leakage and deception clues in the face, we expected that naïve observers viewing the head/face at normal projection speed would fail to pick up these occurrences and would instead be more misled by the patient's deception than those who viewed the body.

The head/face version of the film was viewed by eighteen observers; twenty-eight observers viewed the body version of the film. In data analysis a word from the Adjective Check List was considered a 'head' message if it was checked by $\geqslant 50$ per cent of the observers who saw the head, $\leqslant 49$ per cent of the observers who saw the body, and if there was $\geqslant 20$ per cent difference in the head and body percentages. The same criterion was used for determining a 'body' message. A word was considered to be a message for both head and body if it was checked by $\geqslant 50$ per cent of both head and body observers and if there was $\leqslant 19$ per cent difference in the head and body percentages.

Table 1 shows the head messages, body messages, and messages common to both cue areas. Our hypothesis is supported only in part. While the head messages contained the expected dissimulated information and the body messages conveyed the expected concealed information, the messages conveyed by *both* head and body contained some of what we expected to be concealed (anxious, confused, worrying, etc.). We believe that this was due to the fact that near the end of the film the patient ceased her efforts to deceive and cried openly, thus providing previously concealed information in her face.

Self-deception: example

The same patient, Miss A, was in a hypomanic state shortly before discharge. At this time she engaged in a great deal of girlish, seductive, flirtatious behavior, showing coquettish interest in the males she encountered. On the basis of her verbal behavior in the interview, the impressions of the interviewer, and posthospitalization discussions with the patient, who within a few months had a recurrence of her depression, the flirtatious, immature seductiveness seemed quite outside of her awareness.

Hypothesis. The observers who view only the head/face will tend to see only the appearance of a healthy, cooperative patient, while those who view the body will perceive the coquettish, excited, seductive picture.

Paul Ekman and Wallace V. Friesen 143

Table 1 Alter-deception: patient A, withholding information about depression and agitation, simulating health and well-being. (percentage ratings)

Head messages	Head	Body	Body messages	Head	Body	Head and body messages	Head	Body
Sensitive	83	36	Tense	44	82	Anxious	89	100
Friendly	50	14	Excitable	22	79	Emotional	89	82
Cooperative	50	14	High strung	39	75	Confused	72	82
Self-punishing	50	02	Fearful	33	68	Defensive	72	71
			Hurried	0	61	Worrying	50	68
			Changeable	39	61	Dissatisfied	56	57
			Awkward	33	61	Despondent	56	56
			Complaining	11	54			
			Touchy	28	54			
			Affected	33	54			
			Restless	06	50			
			Impulsive	17	50			
			Impatient	0	50			
			Rigid	17	50			

Table 2 Self-deception: patient A, withholding information about seductive, immature, impulsive behavior, and simulating cooperativeness. (percentage ratings)

Head messages	Head	Body	Body messages	Head	Body	Head and body messages	Head	Body
Talkative	68	30	Confused	48	83	Emotional	65	83
Alert	65	39	Awkward	47	78	Active	74	74
Cheerful	61	30	Excitable	42	78	Changeable	68	74
Cooperative	59	35	Restless	32	74	Nervous	65	74
Serious	52	22	Impulsive	39	65	Defensive	52	61
			High strung	29	65			
			Feminine	32	65			

The head/face version was seen by thirty-one observers; twenty-three observers saw the body version of the film. Table 2 shows the results of the comparative analysis of head and body messages. These results provide some support for the hypothesis; the expected differences in head and body messages appear to have been conveyed, and the messages conveyed by both head and body do not contain the information which we expected to be concealed.

In other research on this film we found many legs/feet movements which we considered to be flirtatious, autoerotic, and appropriate to a woman much younger than the patient. We showed just the legs/feet movements of this film to another group of observers, and when we compared their impressions with those of persons who had seen just the head/face, the legs/feet messages generally supported our impression. We also found that the observers of the legs/feet guessed that the patient was in her teens, while those who saw the face/head guessed her to be in her thirties. This difference in age perception was not found when comparing observers of head and observers of feet for the same patient's admission-to-the-hospital film. [. . .]

These studies show a difference in the information conveyed by the head as compared to the hands/legs/feet, which is in the direction predicted by our formulation of leakage and deception clues. They do not, however, directly test our theory; there is no comparison of the information conveyed by non-verbal and verbal behavior, no comparison of the micro and macro facial displays, and no determination of whether the specific hand and legs/feet acts which we described as sources of leakage and deception clues were actually responsible for conveying the messages listed in the tables. Further, they suffer from an uncertainty, which probably can never be fully resolved in studying naturalistic occurrences of deception, about whether we were correct in our assessment of what information was withheld and what was dissimulated. To remedy some of these deficiencies, our work in progress is employing an experimental, laboratory, dyadic interaction in which ego is immersed in a positive or negative affect-inducing experience and instructed to engage in alter-deception by simulating positive affect when experiencing negative affect, and vice versa.

Before closing, some mention should be made of the major exceptions to what we have presented. There are some people who do not leak very much, if at all; they are professional, convincing non-verbal liars – for example, the professional dancer or actor, the skilled courtroom lawyer, the shrewd diplomat or negotiator, and the successful (sometimes psychopathically so) used-car salesman. An explanation of why there is less non-verbal leakage with the dancer and actor can be inferred from the earlier discussion of internal and external feedback. The dancer and actor have focused their attention on the use of their body as a communicative instrument; they have heightened their internal awareness of their non-verbal behavior and engaged in continual training which involves focused external feedback from coach, director, audience, about the effectiveness of their simulations. Thus, they are exceptions to our formulation because they have what most people lack, the feedback necessary to monitor, tune, and thus disguise through the non-verbal channel. [. . .]

There are a number of applications of this description of leakage and deception clues. People could be trained to become better non-verbal liars, utilizing videotape feedback to enhance their internal feedback, and focusing external feedback to help them plug up leaks and better eliminate deception clues; the most benevolent use of such procedures would be in the dramatic arts. Our description of deceptive situations should help begin to specify those types of interactions or points during an interaction when ego and alter might best attend to non-verbal behavior or as a source of information which will be least repetitive with the verbal behavior. Moreoover, we have suggested specific types of behaviors or which the diagnostician or clinician should look; these may be useful either in evaluation or as a focus in bringing problems to the attention of the patient. Training could be developed which would improve recognition of micro expressions as well as alert the observer to particular non-verbal acts. Knowledge of non-verberal leakage and deception clues could also perhaps be utilized in an attempt to develop lie detection procedures which rely upon non-verbal behavior.

It is interesting to note that our formulation of the origin of leakage and deception clues contains a suggestion that the phenomenon may considerably change – and may even partially disappear – as attention is brought to bear upon it. If the reader believes what has been said, then when he is engaged as ego in deceptive situations he may monitor his own behavior more closely, and be more alert about what to inhibit and which body areas to scrutinize; paradoxically, the leakage through hands and legs/feet should be relatively easy to eliminate once a person is aware of it. In the role of alter he should also be more attentive to the areas of leakage in others. If we are correct, such an increase in both internal and external feedback may start to diminish the information revealed through non-verbal leakage and clues to deception.

References

ARGYLE, M. (1967), *The Psychology of Interpersonal Behaviour*, Penguin.
BIRDWHISTELL, R. L. (1959), 'Contribution of linguistic-kinesic studies to the understanding of schizophrenia', in A. Auerback (ed.), *Schizophrenia: An Integrated Approach*, Ronald Press.
DARWIN, C. (1872), *The Expression of the Emotions in Man and Animals*, Philosophical Library, 1955.

DITTMAN, A. T., PARLOFF, M. B., and BOOMER, D. S. (1965), 'Facial and bodily expression: a study of receptivity of emotional cues', *Psychiatry*, vol. 28, pp. 239–44.

EKMAN, P., and FRIESEN, W. V. (1968), 'Non-verbal behavior in psychotherapy research', in J. Shlien (ed.), *Research in Psychotherapy*, vol. 3, American Psychological Association.

FREEDMAN, N., and HOFFMAN, S. P. (1967), 'Kinetic behavior in altered clinical states: approach to objective analysis of motor behavior during clinical interviews', *Perceptual and Motor Skills*, vol. 24, pp. 527–39.

FREUD, S. (1905), 'Fragment of an analysis of a case of hysteria,' *Collected Papers*, vol. 3, Basic Books, 1959.

GOFFMAN, E. (1959), *The Presentation of Self in Everyday Life*, Doubleday.

GRUENBERG, P. B., LISTON, E. H., and WAYNE, G. J. (1967), 'Intensive supervision of psychotherapy with videotape recording', paper presented at the meetings of the American Psychiatric Association.

MAHL, G. F. (1969), 'Gestures and body movements in interviews', in J. Shlien (ed.), *Research in Psychotherapy*, vol. 3, American Psychological Association.

PAREDES, A. F., and CORNELISON, F. S. (1967), 'An audiovisual method for eliciting attitude changes in alcoholics', panel on videotape feedback, presented at the meetings of the American Psychiatric Association.

RUESCH, J., and KEES, W. (1956), *Non-Verbal Communication*, University of California Press.

WILMER, H. A. (1967), 'Television as participant observer', paper presented at the meetings of the American Psychiatric Association.

10 R. D. Laing, H. Phillipson and A. R. Lee

The Interpersonal Perception Method

Excerpt from R. D. Laing, H. Phillipson and A. R. Lee, *Interpersonal Perception*, Tavistock, 1966, pp. 49–66.

The Interpersonal Perception Method makes use of sixty dyadic issues around each of which twelve questions require to be answered. The average time required to complete the seven hundred and twenty questions is seventy minutes. Each member of the dyad answers the questions separately. Where it is convenient and appropriate both members may answer the questions at the same time and in the same room.

The issues

The sixty issues are presented as phrases that express interaction and interexperience. All can be used with self and self–other reference. They were culled from a larger group of some two thousand words and phrases that were derived from a small standard dictionary. The list was reduced by eliminating redundancies, synonyms and antonyms, and later, after experience with three hundred and then one hundred and sixty remaining issues, eighty-four were chosen, excluding those that were most difficult for subjects to understand. Finally these eighty-four issues were reduced to sixty following test-retest studies and item analyses.

The sixty issues used range from those which tend to foster interdependence with autonomy to those which tend to be destructive of such 'healthy' processes. Within this range the issues may be grouped into six categories, according to the extent to which they express:

A Interdependence and autonomy.
B Warm concern and support.
C Disparagement and disappointment.
D Contentions: fight/flight.
E Contradiction and confusion.
F Extreme denial of autonomy.

No one, of course, will be so naïve as to assume that a couple who give unqualifiedly positive answers to issues, say, in categories A and B, and unqualifiedly negative answers to issues in C to F (as some couples do) are by that token an ideally happily married pair. 'Straight flushes' of positive replies to all the issues that ideally seem to demand them are just as likely to indicate reciprocal idealization and denial, or simply stereotyped robot-like responsiveness that indicates how little real interplay is occurring.

What we do suppose, however, is that were two people really to be and do with each other what they suppose that they are and are doing when they fill in the issues in category A positively, then one could legitimately characterize their relationship as one that balances separation and autonomy on the one hand, and interrelatedness on the other, in a way that in our society we tend to regard as 'good' or 'desirable'. These items express the fact or illusion of genuine 'mutuality' of relationship, based on a responsive acceptance of the other as a human being whom one respects, loves, cherishes, understands. Autonomy is expressed by the fact that the issues of 'depend on' and 'take responsibility for' are focused on the self-self direction. Self feels that, both for self and for the self of the other, each has a source of strength from within, and is capable of taking responsibility for one's own person, while, at the same time and indeed by the same token, being responsive towards the other.

The issues in category B express warm concern and support, not qualified or tempered, however, by autonomy as in category A. Thus, while the issues of dependence and taking responsibility figure in category A in their pp and oo directions only, in category B they appear in directions po and op. This epitomizes the distinction between category A and category B. The absence of an explicit feeling or separateness is expressed again by the issue 'is at one with'. We are not, however, trying to draw any hard and fast distinctions, and the 'function' of each issue can be understood in each individual dyad only by studying its place in the overall picture given by their combined protocols.

While the issues in categories A and B if answered affirmatively would indicate that the persons themselves are conveying a predominantly satisfied view of themselves and their relationship, the issues in category C express disparagement and disappointment. These fourteen items give each person ample scope to explicitly express negative viewpoints about themselves or the other in specific respects. The issues in category D focus more on straight contentions, conflict, competition. In unmitigated form they would indicate a couple fighting or breaking off the fight, dominated by the fight–flight phantasy described by Bion (1961). Category E issues enable the subjects to express perceptions of masking and confusion rather than avowedly open warfare (Laing, 1965).

The category F issues focus on the issue of autonomy, but this time in its negative aspects. Here the issue is the perception, or the phantasy, of being unwillingly engulfed by the other (or by a part of oneself), or of being an agent in engulfing the other.

Classification of the sixty issues

Directions: *po op pp oo*

A *Interdependence and autonomy*

1. understands	21. lets be self
4. depends on	28. is honest with
6. takes seriously	36. can face conflicts
12. respects	40. thinks a lot of
15. loves	45. readily forgives
19. takes responsibility for	53. believes in

A−

11. is afraid of	44. has a warped view of
35. worries about	

B *Warm concern and support*

4. depends on (po, op only)	34. is good to
9. takes good care of	37. is at one with
19. takes responsibility for (po, op only)	43. likes
	60. is kind to

B−

14. is mean with	30. analyses
22. couldn't care less about	50. is detached from

C₁ *Disparagement* & C₂ *Disappointment*

C₁ *Disparagement*	C₂ *Disappointment*
18. torments	7. is disappointed in
20. finds fault with	23. pities
27. mocks	24. doubts
39. blames	32. lets down
49. belittles	33. expects too much of
51. makes a clown out of	42. has lost hope for future
54. humiliates	55. is sorry for

C−

46. puts on a pedestal

D *Contentions: fight/flight*

5. can't come to terms with	17. fights with
8. can't stand	26. gets on nerves
10. would like to get away from	29. hates
16. tries to outdo	47. is bitter towards

E Contradicting and confusing	
25. makes contradictory demands on	52. bewilders
41. deceives	59. gets into a false position
48. creates difficulties for	

F Extreme denial of autonomy	
2. makes up mind for	38. won't let be
3. is wrapped up in	56. makes into a puppet
13. makes centre of world	57. spoils
31. treats like a machine	58. owes everything to

As we have said these are not hard and fast groupings but ones we have found useful in giving order to our assessment of dyads.

The questionnaire containing the sixty issues is presented in Part Three as it would be used by the 'he' in a 'he–she' dyad. The instructions to the subject are also reproduced.

The two perspectives and their two directions

Following the rationale developed in the early chapters it will be clear that any question around our sixty issues has to be stated from a specific perspective if it is to be meaningful within a dyad. In addition it has to be pointed in a specific direction.

A dyad contains two epicentres of experience, two points of view, two perspectives, e.g. Peter's perspective and Paul's, husband's and wife's, p's and o's. Sometimes when referring to these two perspectives different nuances are employed such as Peter's view of Paul, what Peter 'feels' about Paul, what husband 'thinks' of wife, how husband (H) 'sees' wife (W) and so on.

From each of these two points of view or perspectives, questions may be pointed in two directions, those directed at Peter, from his own perspective and from Paul's and those directed at Paul, from his own perspective and from Peter's.

Thus we have:

Peter's view of himself
Peter's view of Paul

and

Paul's view of himself
Paul's view of Peter

In shorthand   and

1. Peter →Peter   3. Paul →Paul
or   p → p   or   o → o
or   H → H   or   W → W
and   and
2. Peter →Paul   4. Paul →Peter
or   p → o   or   o → p
or   H → W   or   W → H

In terms of one of the issues we use in our method, 'loves', the questions that concern the dyad are:

Peter loves himself
Peter loves Paul
Paul loves himself
Paul loves Peter

But in any dyadic interaction these questions are the concern of both Peter and Paul. They are, in fact, questions about four relationships that comprise Peter's and Paul's interperceptions and interexperience around this issue.

The four relationships as seen from each perspective

We have seen already that each point of view is directed to *relationships*. They are concerned with four relationships. We sometimes speak of *phases* of relationships for each of the following four relationships within the dyadic system:

1. Husband's relationship with himself   (HH)
2. Husband's relationship with wife   (HW)
3. Wife's relationship with herself   (WW)
4. Wife's relationship with husband   (WH)

Note, in expressing these relationships in 'shorthand', no arrows are used, the order is left to right corresponding to subject–object, and parentheses are used.

We can now express the direct perspective of H and W on each of these four directions of relationships as follows.

H →(HH)   husband's point of view on
H →(HW)   or what husband thinks of
H →(WW)   or husband's perspective on
H →(WH)   or how husband sees . . .

and

$$W \to (WW)$$
$$W \to (WH)$$
$$W \to (HH)$$
$$W \to (HW)$$

We can put H's point of view and W's point of view on these relationships together in the following way:

$$H \to (HH) \gets W$$
$$H \to (HW) \gets W$$
$$H \to (WW) \gets W$$
$$H \to (WH) \gets W$$

Now, so far we have represented only the *direct* perspectives of H and W. But, in addition, we are concerned with *meta* and *meta-meta*perspectives.

Metaperspectives and meta-metaperspectives

The husband's conduct is not guided only by husband's view of wife, but also by what husband thinks of wife's view of husband. Actually, in colloquial speech, 'what I think of you' probably includes 'what I think you think of me'. Here, however, we shall distinguish between husband's simple or direct or first-level perspective or view of wife, and a more complicated indirect second-level perspective, namely, husband's view of wife's view of him.

In our discursive account of some of the issues involved in the intermeshing of perspectives within a dyadic system in the previous chapters, we saw that perspectives or points of view recede logically to infinity. In the construction of the method we have made provision for three levels of perspective.

That is to say, if (X) stands for any issue:

husband's view of (X)	direct perspective
husband's view of wife's view of (X)	metaperspective
husband's view of wife's view of his view of (X)	meta-metaperspective

and similarly for wife.

That is:

wife's view of (X)	direct perspective
wife's view of husband's view of (X)	metaperspective
wife's view of husband's view of her view of (X)	meta-metaperspective

If the issue is (X), the different orders or levels of husband's perspective on (X) are represented as follows:

H (X)	direct perspective	H's view of (X)
H W (X)	metaperspective	H's view of W's view of (X)
H W H (X)	meta-metaperspective	H's view of W's view of H's view of (X)

and for wife's perspective:

W (X)	direct perspective	W's view of (X)
W H X	metaperspective	W's view of H's view of (X)
W H W (X)	meta-metaperspective	W's view of H's view of W's view of (X)

Both husband's and wife's perspectives can be represented together in shorthand as:

H (X) W	direct perspective
H W (X) H W	metaperspective
H W H (X) W H W	meta-metaperspective

An interesting practical problem arises here with regard to the best way to formulate the questions so that they would be most readily understood.

Let us suppose that husband and wife are answering the test, and that each of them (Jack and Jill), is asked three types of question, on direct, meta and meta-metalevels of perspective:

1. What do you think about (X)?
2. What do you think he or she thinks about (X)?
3. What do you think he or she thinks you think about (X)?

These questions can be put in a variety of ways. For instance:

Do *you* love *him*?

or

Would you say '*I* love *him*'?

On the metalevel:

Do you think he thinks *you* love *him*?

or

How would he answer the question '*she* loves *me*'?

On the meta-metalevel:

Do you think he thinks you think *you* love *him*?

or

How will he think you have answered the question '*I* love *him*'?

That is, depending on from whose point of view Jack and Jill are regarded, each may be called I, me, you, him or her.

After trying out a number of different versions, we found that most people grasped the questions best when all the relationships were put in terms of first person and third person, using the second person as our form of address to the test subject. So our questions were finally all cast in the form of the following:

A. How true do you think the following are?
1. She loves me.
2. I love her.
3. She loves herself.
4. I love myself.

B. How would she answer the following?
1. 'I love him.'
2. 'He loves me.'
3. 'I love myself.'
4. 'He loves himself.'

C. How would she think you have answered the following?
1. She loves me.
2. I love her.
3. She loves herself.
4. I love myself.

[. . .]

Patterns of conjunction and disjunction

One of the facets of reality we can explore by the IPM is the extent to which the dyad as a system may possess properties (e.g. patterns of conjunction and disjunction) unbeknown to either of its members, which may, however, influence the way they interact and interexperience themselves in this situation. There are a number of formal *reciprocally matched comparisons* that can be made in this dyadic system.

Two kinds of analyses are now possible:

1. Non-reciprocally matched comparisons.
2. Reciprocally matched comparisons.

In a non-reciprocally matched comparison one simply gathers information about how each person sees the other and constructs a profile of his viewpoint. For example, a husband might see his wife as cold and mean but very bright, or a wife might see her husband as weak and wishy-washy but quite charming. By this method we gather a set of characteristics that each person attributes to self and to other, to the meta-metalevel of perspective. This is truly descriptive material. We are not, however, greatly interested in this type of information alone.

We are primarily interested in the pattern that emerges when we match H's views (direct, meta, meta-meta) and with W's views (direct, meta, meta-meta) of the same questions and issues. The moment we match one person's view against another person's view we are in a completely different arena. It no longer matters *per se* if a husband sees his wife as kind or mean to him. What matters instead is whether or not the husband's view of how his wife treats him is concordant or disconcordant with how she sees herself to be treating him, and how she sees him as viewing her treatment of him. It is the pattern of concordant or disconcordant attributions made at each level of analysis which now becomes significant, not one person's set of attributions considered in isolation.

By the method of *reciprocally matched comparison* we have direct access to the relationship itself, as well as to each person in relationship. By reciprocally matched comparison, the profile that our technique discloses is the *profile of the relationship between two points of view*.

The following are the reciprocally matched comparisons that seems likely to be the most important.

Comparison between one person's view and another's on the same issue tells us whether they are in *agreement* or *disagreement*.

If one person is aware of the other's point of view, we say he *understands* him. And if he fails to recognize the other's point of view, we say he *misunderstands*.

In agreement and disagreement we are comparing *direct perspectives on the same issues*.

In understanding and misunderstanding we are comparing the one person's *metaperspective* with the other person's *direct perspective* on the same issue.

Represented in shorthand, agreement or disagreement is found by the comparison

H→(X): W→(X)

in

H (HH): W (HH)
H (HW): W (HW)
H (WW): W (WW)
H (WH): W (WH)

and understanding or misunderstanding is found by the comparison

$H \rightarrow (X)$: $W \rightarrow H \rightarrow (X)$

that is, does W understand H?

or

$W \rightarrow (X)$: $H \rightarrow W \rightarrow (X)$

that is, does H understand W?

Now, we have no constant term for the comparison between third and second order perspectives, but, as we have seen they are just as relevant to the way the dyad is kept in a steady state as the first two levels.

Let us remind ourselves that comparison of H's metaperspective with W's direct perspective tells us whether H understands W.

If H's metaperspective is now compared with W's meta-metaperspective, we learn whether W *realizes that she is understood or not*. This is represented by the comparison

$H \rightarrow W \rightarrow (X)$: $W \rightarrow H \rightarrow W \rightarrow (X)$

that is, does W realize or fail to realize that H understands or misunderstands W?

or

$W \rightarrow H \rightarrow (X)$: $H \rightarrow W \rightarrow H \rightarrow (X)$

that is, does H realize or fail to realize that W understands or misunderstands H?

That is to say, if what I feel about something is compared to what I think you think I feel, I see whether I feel that you understand me or not. Clearly, my feelings of being understood (conjunction between my direct perspective and my meta-metaperspective) or my feeling of being misunderstood (disjunction between my direct and meta-metaperspectives) may in either case be correct or incorrect.

I may

feel understood correctly.
feel understood incorrectly.
feel misunderstood correctly.
feel misunderstood incorrectly.

Whether or not I am correct or incorrect to feel understood or misunderstood is given by comparing my meta-metaperspective with the *other* person's metaperspective. We shall discuss these very important conjunctions and disjunctions more fully below.

Henceforth we shall use the terms realize, realization or failure to realize, failure of realization as technical terms for conjunction or disjunction between the one person's meta-meta and the *other* person's metalevels of perspective.

To summarize:

1. Comparison between the one person's direct perspective and the other person's direct perspective on the same issue, gives *agreement* or *disagreement*.

2. Comparison between the one person's metaperspective and the other person's direct perspective on the same issue gives *understanding* or *misunderstanding*.

3. Comparison between the one person's meta-metaperspective and his *own* direct perspective gives the feeling of *being understood* or of *being misunderstood*.

4. Comparison between the one person's meta-metaperspective and the other person's metaperspective on the same issue gives *realization* or *failure of realization*. Whether or not this is a realization or failure of realization of understanding or misunderstanding entails a comparison *of all three levels*. [. . .]

Some IPM profiles

	H	W	H	(X)	W	H	W
Agreement			+		+		
Agreement and understanding		+	+		+	+	
Agreement, bilateral understanding and realization of being understood	+	+	+		+	+	+
Unilateral failure to realize that one is understood	−	+	+		+	+	+
	+	−	−		+	+	+
Bilateral failure to realize that one is understood	−	+	+		−	−	+
	−	+	+		+	+	−
Unilateral impression that one is understood when one isn't	+	−	+		+	+	+
	+	+	+		−	+	−
Agreement that is unilaterally not recognized			−		+	+	+
and this failure is in turn not realized	+	−	+		+	+	+

We can see already that *only the total spiral derived from the matching of both individuals gives us a profile of the dyad as a system at any point in time.*

References

BION, W. R. (1961), *Experiences in Group and Other Papers*, Tavistock.
LAING, R. D. (1965), 'Family and individual structure', in P. Lomas (ed.), *Psychoanalytic Approaches to the Family*, Hogarth Press.

Part Four
Two-Person Interaction

A number of different processes occur in interaction between two
persons. Indeed the same processes take place in larger groups too,
but they can be studied most easily in groups of two. One of the
simplest of these processes is 'response-matching'. Rosenfeld
(Reading 11) describes an experiment in which subjects smiled and
nodded more in response to a smiling and nodding partner.
Rosenfeld describes this as 'reciprocation', which is more commonly
used to refer to the slower and more deliberate exchanges of rewards.
Pairs of people develop an 'equilibrium' level of relationship, which is
somewhat resistant to change. Argyle and Dean (Reading 12) predicted
that if two people are placed further apart they will look at each other
more, to compensate for a loss of intimacy. This result was obtained,
and has been confirmed in a number of later experiments (Argyle and
Ingham, 1972). Several theorists have suggested that interactors 'take
the role of the other', or should do so in order to interact successfully.
One of the few experiments to test this expectation is that by Feffer
and Suchotliff (Reading 13). They approached the problem from a
Piagetian standpoint, and developed a test of ability to see several
perspectives. They found that high scorers did better at a laboratory
communication problem. However, performances at this problem cannot
be regarded as a general measure of social competence – which does
not exist.

  Goffman (Reading 14) approaches two-person interaction from a
quite different point of view. He carries out rather informal fieldwork
in order to discover the structure of certain sequences of behaviour –
as one might try to discover the rules and ideas underlying a game or a
religious ceremony. Two examples are given here – greeting and
farewell, and the 'remedial sequence'. Since the results are not
established in the usual way, perhaps they should be regarded as
hypotheses awaiting further confirmation.

Several other aspects of two-person interaction, such as reinforcement, feedback, and self-presentation, are described in *Social Interaction*, chapter 5.

Reference

ARGYLE, M., and INGHAM, R. (1972), 'Gaze, mutual gaze and proximity', *Semiotica*, vol. 6, pp. 32–49.

11 Howard M. Rosenfeld

Non-Verbal Reciprocation of Approval: An Experimental Analysis

H. M. Rosenfeld, 'Non-verbal reciprocation of approval: an experimental analysis', *Journal of Experimental Psychology*, vol. 3, 1967, pp. 102–11.

Several classes of verbal and non-verbal response have been employed effectively as social reinforcers in experiments on verbal conditioning (Krasner, 1958). Recent research on three such categories – smiles, positive head nods and brief verbal recognitions such as 'mm-hmm' – has indicated that they play similar roles in free social interaction (Rosenfeld, 1966a, 1966b). These responses were more often emitted by subjects motivated to seek approval from peers than by control groups; and the responses tended to bring about approving reactions from the peers to whom they were directed. A less expected finding was that when pairs of unacquainted peers were observed in free interaction, the rates of performance of the non-verbal approval-related responses by the two members of dyads were significantly intercorrelated. Smiles occurred at highly similar levels within the dyad during initial acquaintance periods and maintained this high simplicity over repeated encounters. Positive head nods gradually increased in their intradyadic similarity with repeated encounters. Gesticulations of the hand, interpreted as an indicator of intensity of motivation, also showed evidence of intrapair similarity.

Given such findings, it is tempting to speculate that approving responses are normatively reciprocated in our society, and that this process provides interpersonal feedback which may play a significant role in the maintenance of free interaction. However, several alternative explanations of the evidence obtained so far are plausible. For example, rather than directly reciprocating smiles or nods, two persons may express them simultaneously in response to the content of a verbal statement. Or similarity between persons on a given response dimension could be confounded with similarity in total output of responses. Thus, the current study was designed to rule out these alternatives and to determine if reciprocation of the approval-related responses could be demonstrated.[1]

1. The term 'reciprocation' is used here merely to label the temporal causal contingency between members of a dyad in the performance of a given response class. No further explanatory mechanisms are implied at this time.

To vary rates of presentation of the approval-related responses by a stimulus person, while controlling the rate and content of his other responses, an interview procedure was constructed. For efficiency, the three approval-related responses and gesticulations were varied simultaneously. It was predicted that these responses would be expressed more often by subjects whose interviewers regularly emitted such responses than by subjects whose interviewers either withheld such responses or who displayed disapproving responses instead.

Two other classes of behavior of the subjects were of particular interest in the present study – self-manipulatory responses and verbal disfluencies. These two response classes, which have been interpreted as indicators of anxiety (Boomer and Goodrich, 1963; Kasl and Mahl, 1965), were expected to be less common in subjects interviewed by an approving interviewer than in any other condition.

Method
Subjects

Subjects were forty-eight students, ranging in age from fourteen to sixteen years, selected to fall within one standard deviation of the mean IQ score of their ninth-grade class. The sample consisted of an equal number of males and females.

Experimental procedures

The interviewer presented questions from a standard list to the subject over a five-minute period. The interview consisted in brief inquiries, and follow-up probes, into events relevant to the daily lives of the subjects. The standard items included requests for descriptions and evaluations of classes the subjects were taking in school and their after-school activities, and opinions about teaching practices, discipline problems, and institutions in the community. An interviewer of each sex was randomly assigned half of the subjects of each sex. Two interviewers were employed primarily to reduce the potential effect of idiosyncratic personal characteristics.

Four different modes of interviewer response to the answers of the subject comprised the experimental treatments of the study. In the *approving condition* the interviewer immediately followed each utterance[2] of the subject with as many of the following four responses as he (or she) could perform in a natural fashion, smile, positive head nod, gesticulation, and brief verbal indication of attention. In the *disapproving condition*, the inter-

2. In our formal analyses of data, 'utterance' was defined linguistically in terms of pause, change in inflection, and grammatical completion (Davis, 1937, p. 44). However the interviewers, who were not trained in linguistic analysis, were asked only to attend immediately to each completed response of the subject.

viewer followed each utterance of the subject with as many of the following responses as he could appropriately perform: frown, negative head nod, and short disparaging comment. In the *mixed condition*, the interviewer used the approving responses in the first half of the interview, and switched to the disapproving responses in the second half. In the *non-responsive condition* the interviewer failed to respond to the subject's answers in either the approving or disapproving modes, remaining as non-responsive as possible both verbally and gesturally. In each condition, a new question or probe was introduced by the interviewer at the end of a brief but noticeable silence on the part of the subject. During a short training period, the various approving and disapproving response classes were described to the interviewers in common-sense terms. The interviewers were permitted to perform the responses in the manner that was most natural to them. They were not informed of the hypotheses.

Subjects were transported in small groups from their school to a laboratory conveniently located in a research department of a local institution for retarded children. While a given subject was in the interview room, the remaining subjects waited in a separate room. Sessions were run in one day to prevent information about the task from reaching untested subjects. Questions about the institution were included in the interview schedule to make the subjects' presence there appear plausible to them. Subjects were randomly assigned to conditions, which were run repeatedly in the sequence described above.

Recording of responses

Smiles, positive head nods and gesticulations emitted by subjects were recorded by an observer who had established high reliability in marking their occurrence in the earlier studies. He also marked two additional responses for which he was trained – negative head nods and self-manipulations, the latter referring to any motion of the hands or fingers in contact with the body. Working definitions of the non-verbal responses and the simple observational procedures for recording them are presented elsewhere (Rosenfeld, 1966a). The observer also operated a tape recorder from which transcriptions could be made of verbal responses in the interviews. To reduce bias in observation, the observer was assigned the ostensible task of gathering normative data on the frequency of occurrence of the non-verbal responses (which he previously had observed only among college students) in the younger population samples in the current study.

The tape-recorded verbal responses were transcribed by a typist who was asked to note every verbalization of interviewer and subject, including mispronunciations and lengthy pauses. The transcriptions were then compared with the tapes, corrected, and content-analysed by an assistant who was previously trained in the reliable scoring of speech disturbances (Kasl and Mahl, 1956) and various grammatical and lexical categories (Rosenfeld, 1966b). The verbal responses of subjects of greatest interest was 'recognition', which may be summarized here as a broad class of usually brief responses to an utterance which indicate attentiveness to the other person, but apparently add no other information to the conversation. Recognitions include commonly-used 'verbal reinforcers' such as 'mm-hmm', and less commonly researched attentional responses such as 'I see', 'no kidding?' and 'really?' when no other communicative functions are apparent.

Results

All of the verbal and non-verbal response categories of interviewers and subjects that provided adequate frequency distributions were submitted to a $4 \times 2 \times 2 \times 2$ analysis of variance – treatments, by sex of subject, by sex of interviewer, by time period.[3] More specific analyses were made by applying Duncan's multiple comparison test (Edwards, 1960) to differences between cell means. While there were occasional effects of sex of subject and sex of interviewer on particular responses, these sex variables seldom interacted with each other or with the experimental treatment. Also, the design did not permit unconfounded interpretations of causal direction of sex effects, since both interviewers and subjects could vary in their responses to each other. For the sake of clarity, the presentation of results will be limited to the effects of treatments and time periods within treatments. Time periods are included primarily because each half of the mixed condition comprised a different treatment.

Responses of interviewers

Except for withholding responses to subject utterances in the non-responsive condition, the interviewers were expected to keep their amount of verbal participation relatively constant across treatments. Analyses of variance of frequencies of interviewer utterances and words indicated no significant effect of treatments on either measure of verbal output. A comparison of treatment, means, however, did show one significant difference: in the non-responsive condition the interviewers made fewer utterances than in any of the other three conditions. When interviewer utterances were subclassified into questions, recognitions, and a residual category, the only significant findings by analysis of variance was that recognitions

3. Non-parametric statistics were also used to analyse treatment effects on positive head nods and gesticulations because of their infrequent occurrence in some conditions. The results were identical in p-levels to those obtained by analysis of variance. A 'significant' statistical finding in this report refers to the 0·05 or less probability level, two tails, unless otherwise qualified.

were affected by treatments and by the interaction of treatments and time periods. Multiple comparison tests revealed that interviewer recognitions were significantly higher in the two time periods of the approving condition and in the approving half of the mixed condition than in any of the other treatment periods.

Responses of subjects

Subjects were expected to smile, nod positively, gesticulate and verbally 'recognize' the interviewer more in both halves of the approving condition and the approving half of the mixed condition than in any other treatment period. Recognitions by subjects occurred too infrequently to permit analysis. Gesticulations were relatively uncommon, although they were significantly more frequent in the approving and in the mixed conditions than in either the disapproving or the nonresponsive conditions. Smiles and positive head nods both showed significant treatment effects and significant interactions of treatments and time periods. Multiple comparison tests revealed that each of these two responses operated as predicted. As Figure 1 indicates, they were significantly more frequent in the three approving periods than in any other period.

Significant effects of treatments were also found on *total* non-verbal responses, which was significantly correlated with the specific category frequencies. To eliminate this possible confounding, the non-verbal response categories were also analysed as percentages of total non-verbal responses of the subject. Table 1 shows that the treatment effect, and the

Table 1 Analyses of variance of interviewee non-verbal responses as a function of interviewer treatment and time period

Source[b]	df	All non-verbal responses	% Smiles	% Positive head nods	% Self-manipulations
		F scores for non-verbal responses[a]			
Treatment	3	4·58***	6·49***	5·79***	3·98**
Time period	1	0·56	18·65***	3·66	2·04
Treatment × period	3	2·72*	3·98**	2·57*	2·59*

[a] Percentages of negative head nods and gesticulations are not shown because of their low frequency distributions.
[b] Sex of interviewer, sex of subject, and their interactions are omitted here (see text).
    * $p < 0.10$.
  ** $p < 0.05$.
*** $p < 0.01$.

treatment by time interactions, remained significant for percentage of smiles and, to a weaker degree, for percentage of positive head nods. Again,

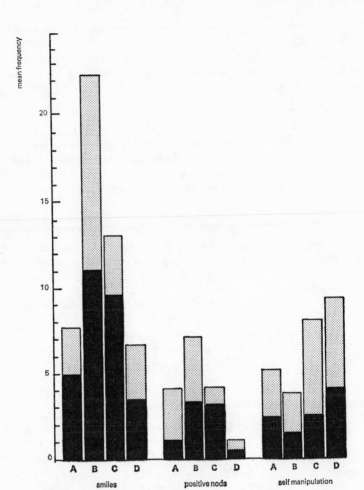

treatments

A non-responsive
B approving
C mixed.
D disapproving
■ 1st period
▨ 2nd period

Figure 1 Effects of experimental treatments on frequencies of non-verbal responses

these two responses were distributed precisely as predicted – significantly higher in each of the three approving periods than in any other period. The percentage of gesticulations was significantly higher in the approving condition than in the non-responsive condition.

The treatments did not have significant effects on the raw frequencies of self manipulation ($p < 0.20$), although Figure 1 shows that the predicted order of treatment effects occurred. Analysis of variance of percentages of self manipulations (Table 1) showed a significant main effect of treatments. Comparisons of the four treatment means revealed that subjects in the approving condition engaged in a significantly lower percentage of self manipulations than did subjects in any other condition.

A more extensive analysis of verbal responses of subjects showed no significant effect of treatments on total utterances or words, although subjects tended to talk most in the approving periods. Of particular interest was the effect of treatments on aspects of speech disturbance (Kasl and Mahl, 1965). Analyses of variance showed no significant effect of treatments on the total ratio of speech disturbances to words spoken. However, when the speech disturbance ratio was divided into 'ah' and 'non-ah' subcategories the latter was found to be affected by treatments at the 0.1 level of confidence. The non-ah ratio was significantly higher in the disapproving condition than in any other condition.

Discussion

Although the non-verbal responses of the interviewers were not observed formally during the experimental sessions, some indirect objective evidence of the validity of the roles played by the interviewers was available from transcriptions of the tape recordings. Recognitions – conceived as a broad class of social reinforcers expressed in conversation – should have been emitted more often by interviewers when they were attempting to express approval than at any other time. This proved to be the case. No other subcategory of interviewer utterance significantly differentiated the four roles of the interviewers. Total interviewer utterances were comparable across treatments except, as expected, for their somewhat reduced level in the non-responsive condition. Thus, the attempt to prevent the amount and content of interviewer responses from confounding their various treatment-roles appears to have been successful.

Several response classes of subjects occurred too infrequently to permit meaningful statistical analyses. One of these – negative head nods – also had occurred at a similarly low level in previous observations of college student dyads in free interaction (Rosenfeld, 1966a). Gesticulations and recognitions were less frequent in the current study than in the earlier studies. The rare occurrence of recognitions by subjects may have been due to the structure of the interviews, a large portion of which consisted in asking the subject questions calling for particular informational content in response. The gesticulation rate, which tends to indicate general motivational level (Ekman, 1965; Rosenfeld, 1966a; 1966b), may have been unexpectedly low because of the relatively passivity of the role of interviewee. However, the distribution of gesticulations across treatment was consistent with the reciprocation hypothesis.

The two approval-related responses of subjects that did occur regularly – smiles and positive head nods – were emitted precisely as predicted. They were significantly more common in the approving periods of the interviews than in the disapproving or non-responsive periods; and this effect was upheld both between and within subject groups. Given that smiles and positive head nods were relatively uncommon among subjects in the disapproving condition, in which the interviewer was gesturally active, it is unlikely that the subject's rate of smiling or nodding can be attributed to the sheer non-verbal activity of his interviewer. Also, there were no differences in frequencies of utterances between the approving and disapproving periods. Thus, assuming that the interviewers smiled and nodded primarily in the approving periods, and that the amount and content of conversation was approximately equivalent across conditions, it is concluded that the subjects were indeed reciprocating forms of approval expressed by the interviewers. The fact that smiles apparently were more highly reciprocated than were positive head nods coincides with the finding of an earlier study that in free interaction smiles were more similar in frequency of occurrence between members of dyads than were nods, especially during early acquaintance (Rosenfeld, 1966a).

Previous research also indicated that a subject's self manipulations were disapproved of by the person with whom he was conversing (Rosenfeld, 1966a). In the present study self manipulations were most common among subjects in the disapproving periods and least common in the approving periods. Thus it would appear that not only do self manipulations by a subject lead to disapproval from others, but also that disapproval from others leads to self manipulations by the subject.

Another potential indicator of anxiety was available at the spoken level – the non-ah speech disturbance ratio (Kasl and Mahl, 1965). The non-ah ratio was significantly higher in the disapproving condition than in any other condition. Thus disapproving responses by the interviewer produced an increase in anxiety-related responses at both the vocal and gestural levels.

Thus, a person motivated to gain or maintain another individual's approval can receive immediate feedback about his effectiveness in several ways. If the person's responses are followed by a high or increasing level of smiling, nodding, and perhaps gesticulating by the other, then the person's response style should be reinforced. If the other withholds such feedback after having provided it earlier, the person's response style should be extinguished. If the other fails to provide smiles and positive head nods throughout the interaction, the person may not know whether the other disapproves of his behavior or whether he just is habitually non-reinforcing. Thus, the person may emit smiles and nods to determine if reciprocation will occur. If it does, the person may continue his style of interaction, assuming covert approval from the other.[4] If not reciprocated, the person may change his tactics to determine if a new approach will increase approving gestures by the other, or increase the likelihood of reciprocation of approving responses. Besides the failure to obtain reciprocation of normatively reciprocated responses, the person may interpret changes in other classes of response by the other individual as negative feedback. One of these is self manipulation; another is the non-ah speech disturbance ratio.

Many questions about the responses that were reciprocated in this study remain to be answered. What topological and contextual constraints are necessary for smiles and positive head nods to be perceived as approving? How common is the use of such responses across social groups, and how consistent are their approval-related functions? How is the reciprocation process related to different mechanisms of behavioral contagion (c.f Wheeler, 1966)? The role of awareness, which has been raised in the area of verbal conditioning in particular (Spielberger and DeNike, 1966), also may be raised with regard to non-verbal reciprocation processes. From their rate of occurrence and their positive evaluation in American advertising, one would surmise that we are very conscious and concerned about the expression of smiles. On the other hand, previous research and informal observations by the author have quite consistently indicated that persons other than professional operant conditioners are seldom aware of either their own rates of positive head nodding or those of the persons they converse with. Most of these problems can be approached by objective behavioral procedures. The direct study of the approval-seeking process in free social interaction has some obvious advantages over research that is focused primarily on personality assessment in situations removed from social interaction, or experimental studies that limit response possibilities to the degree that they bear little resemblance to common varieties of human social behavior.

4. It is recognized that certain forms of smiles and positive head nods, and their expression in certain contexts, may function as aversive stimuli.

References

BOOMER, D. S., and GOODRICH, D. W. (1963), 'Speech disturbance and body movement in interviews', *J. nerv. ment. Dis.*, vol. 136, pp. 263–6.

DAVIS, E. A. (1937), *The Development of Linguistic Skill in Twins, Singletons with Siblings, and Only Children from Age Five to Ten Years*, University of Minnesota Press.

EDWARDS, A. (1960), *Experimental Design in Psychological Research*, Holt, Rinehart & Winston.

EKMAN, P. (1965), 'Differential communication of affect by head and body cues', *J. pers. soc. Psychol.*, vol. 2, pp. 727-35.

KASL, S. V., and MAHL, G. F. (1965), 'The relationship of disturbances and hesitations in spontaneous speech to anxiety', *J. pers. soc. Psychol.*, vol. 1, pp. 425–33.

KRASNER, L. (1958), 'Studies of the conditioning of verbal behavior', *Psychol. Bull.*, vol. 55, pp. 148–70.

ROSENFELD, H. M. (1966a), 'Instrumental affiliative functions of facial and gestural expressions', *J. pers. soc. Psychol.*, vol. 4, pp. 65–72.

ROSENFELD, H. M. (1966b), 'Approval-seeking and approval-inducing functions of verbal and non-verbal responses in the dyad', *J. pers. soc. Psychol.*, vol. 4, pp. 597–605.

SPIELBERGER, C. D., and DeNIKE, L. D. (1966), 'Descriptive behaviorism versus cognitive theory in verbal operant conditioning', *Psychol. Rev.*, vol. 73, pp. 302-26.

WHEELER, L. (1966), 'Toward a theory of behavioral contagion', *Psychol. Rev.*, vol. 73, pp. 179–92.

12 Michael Argyle and Janet Dean

Eye Contact, Distance and Affiliation

M. Argyle and J. Dean, 'Eye contact, distance and affiliation', *Sociometry*,
vol. 28, 1965, pp. 289-304.

During social interaction, people look each other in the eye, repeatedly but
for short periods. If we may anticipate, people look most while they are
listening, and use glances of about 3 to 10 seconds in length. When glances
are longer than this, anxiety is aroused. Without eye-contact (EC),[1] people
do not feel that they are fully in communication. Simmel has described it
as 'a wholly new and unique union between two people', and remarked
that it 'represents the most perfect reciprocity in the entire field of human
relationship' (Simmel, 1921). A certain amount is already known about the
empirical determinants of EC, and this will be reviewed below. Rather less
is known about the psychological processes which produce EC, or the
functions which it serves; the most important alternatives are discussed in
the third section. We shall develop a set of hypotheses relating EC to the
need for affiliation, and then report some experiments which test these
hypotheses.

The determinants of gaze

The amount of gaze which takes place in an encounter varies from zero to
100 per cent of the time available, and some of the sources of variation are
known. In some of the experiments cited it is more appropriate to speak of
'gaze direction', since what was measured was whether the subject looked
up, regardless of whether the other person was looking back. In other
experiments, a confederate was used who gazed all the time at the subject,
so that gaze direction is the same as eye contact.

Point in the conversation 1. In all investigations where this has been studied
it is found that there is more gaze when the subject is listening than when
he is speaking, typically with a ratio of $2\frac{1}{2}$ or 3:1. Furthermore people look
up, at the end of their speeches and of phrases within them, and look away
at the start of long utterances (Kendon, 1964; Exline, Gray and Schuette,
1965; Nielsen, 1962).

Nature of topic 2. There is more gaze when less personal topics are discussed

1. We shall use 'gaze' to refer to a person looking another in the eyes, and 'eye contact'
to refer to a mutual gaze.

(Exline, Gray and Schuette, 1965) and when the material is cognitively straightforward. There is less during unfluent and hesitating passages (Exline, 1963).

3. *Individual differences* in looking are very great. Women are found to engage in more gaze, in a variety of situations (Exline, 1963). Some patients suffer from 'aversion of gaze' (Reimer, 1955) and it has been found that autistic children avoid masks of human faces too (Hutt and Ounsted, 1966). There are cross-cultural differences, varying from taboos on gaze, to much greater amounts of intimacy than are common in Western countries.

4. *Relations between a pair of people.* There is more gaze if A likes B (Exline and Winters, 1965), and if they are cooperating rather than competing (Exline, 1963). There is less gaze if there is tension in the relationship, as when a soldier is being disciplined by an officer (Goffman, 1963, p. 96), or if A has recently deceived B (Exline *et al.*, 1961).

5. *The developmental history of gaze.* Observations of infants show that the smiling response to certain aspects of the human face develops in the first weeks of life. Spitz carried out experiments with masks, and found that in the second month a representation of the top of the head, including the eyes, would produce smiling (Spitz, 1946). Wolff observed that gaze first appeared between the twenty-fifth and twenty-eighth day; when this occurred it stopped the baby's random activity, and was found rewarding by the mothers, who now regarded the baby as 'fun to play with' (Wolff, 1963, pp. 122–3). Just as the young of other species imprint the mother and follow her around, it has been suggested that the immobile human infant follows the mother's face with its eyes (Gray, 1958).

Functions of E C

There is no one theory that can explain all of the above findings. It has been pointed out that gaze can have a variety of subjective meanings – such as friendship, sexual attraction, hate and a struggle for dominance (Feldman, 1959, p. 233). We shall consider here the main functions which E C may serve.

Information seeking. If social behavior is looked at as a kind of motor skill, we must inquire how the performer obtains the necessary feedback on the reactions of the other. Speech and paralinguistic material convey a great deal, but it is possible to get a lot more by careful inspection of the other's face, especially in the region of the eyes. Such feedback is needed most at the end of speeches, to see how these have been received. The speaker looks away at the beginning of his speeches and when he has to think about what he is saying, because the extra input from gaze is distracting.

Signalling that the channel is open. During EC each person knows that the other is attending primarily to him, and that further interaction can proceed. A flicker of the eye towards a third party may indicate that the channel is closed. This can be regarded as a rather special case of the first process, in that information is obtained about the other's direction of attention. EC also places a person under some obligation to interact; thus, when a chairman or waiter allows his eye to be caught he places himself under the power of the eye-catcher (Goffman, 1963, p. 94).

Concealment and exhibitionism. Some patients, according to Laing, lack adequate feelings of self-regard and ego-identity, and have a great desire to be seen, in order to be 'loved and confirmed as a person' (Laing, 1960a, chapter 8). Some people want to be seen, and EC is the proof that they are being seen. Others do not want to be seen, and feel 'impaled before the glance of another' (Scheutz, 1948), feel they are depersonalized or turned to stone by becoming an object for another's perception (Laing, 1960b, pp. 48, 78). This fear of being seen may be due to a fear of being rejected, based on past experience, or a desire to conceal inner states – which in turn would lead to rejection. The latter is supported by the finding that subjects who had been induced to cheat gazed less (Exline *et al.*, 1961).

Establishment and recognition of social relationship. If A gazes at B, this will have a different impact, depending on his facial expression. If there is EC, both may know that A's attitude to B is one of sexual attraction, friendship, hate, dominance or submission. There may be a rapid sequence of communications, in which EC plays a central part, and which serves to establish the relationship between A and B. For example, suppose A wants to dominate B: A stares at B with the appropriate expression; B may accept A's dominance by a submissive expression and looking away; or B may outstare A, or simply withdraw by looking coldly away. Hess has found that emotional arousal leads to enlargement of the pupils, and that men are more attracted by girls with enlarged pupils (hence the use of bella-donna), though they are quite unaware that this is the cue to which they are responding (Hess, 1965).

The affiliative conflict theory. In this section we shall introduce some ideas which will explain some of the gaze phenomena which are so far unexplained.

1. There are both approach and avoidance forces behind gaze. The approach forces include the need for feedback, discussed above, and sheer affiliative needs: for example, gaze can be used as a reinforcer in the operative conditioning of verbal behavior (Krasner, 1958). It may be innately satisfying as suggested above. The avoidance components include the fear of being

seen, the fear of revealing inner states, and the fear of seeing the rejecting responses of others, which were discussed above.

2. If there are both approach and avoidance drives behind EC, Miller's conflict analysis is applicable (Miller, 1944, pp. 431–65), and it would be expected that there should be an equilibrium level of EC for a person coming into social contact with some second person, and that if EC rises above that amount it will be anxiety-rousing. (Of course the equilibrium amount of EC, and the equilibrium distance may not be the same for the two people; they will then work out some compromise solution, more or less satisfactory to both. In the experiments to be reported here, however, we shall hold the behavior of one person constant.)

3. It is supposed that similar considerations apply to other types of behavior which are linked with affiliative motivation. Thus there will be an equilibrium point of physical closeness, of intimacy of conversation, and of amount of smiling. The more these behaviors occur, the more affiliative motivation is satisfied, but if they go too far, anxiety is created.

4. It is suggested that an equilibrium develops for 'Intimacy', where this is a joint function of eye contact, physical proximity, intimacy of topic, smiling, etc. This equilibrium would be at a certain degree of intimacy for any pair of people. We deduce that if one of the components of intimacy is changed, one or more of the others will shift in the reverse direction in order to maintain the equilibrium. Thus,

$$\text{Intimacy} = f \begin{cases} \text{eye contact} \\ \text{physical proximity} \\ \text{intimacy of topic} \\ \text{amount of smiling} \\ \text{etc.} \end{cases}$$

5. Twelve empirical deductions follow from this formulation. For example if amount of smiling is reduced, and intimacy of topic and physical proximity are held constant, EC should be increased to restore the equilibrium level.

6. If equilibrium for intimacy is disturbed along one of its dimensions, attempts will first be made to restore it by adjusting the others. If this is not possible because all are held constant, or because the deviation is too extreme, the subject will feel uncomfortable in one of two ways. If the disturbance is in the direction of too much intimacy, the avoidance forces will predominate, and the subject will feel anxiety about rejection or revealing inner states; if in the direction of less intimacy, he will simply feel deprived of affiliative satisfactions.

An experiment has already been reported that confirms one of these twelve deductions. Exline (Exline *et al.*, 1961) found that there was more E C when the topic of conversation was less intimate. We shall report two experiments testing two more of these deductions. Another experiment by Exline confirms the postulated connection between E C and 'intimacy': those who were caused to like a confederate engaged in more E C with him (Exline and Winters, 1965).

An experiment on E C and equilibrium for distance

There is some evidence for an equilibrium level of physical proximity. For the purposes of any particular form of interaction, people take up a position a certain distance from one another. Hall reports that Americans will not stand nearer than eighteen to twenty inches when talking to a stranger of the same sex. If they have to stand closer than this preferred distance, they will turn and face each other at right-angles, or stand side-to-side (Hall, 1955). Steinzor found that subjects in groups of ten were least likely to speak to those nearest to them, and most likely to address those two or three places away (Steinzor, 1950). As well as minimum distances for E C and social interaction, there are also maximum ones. Sommer found that people did not like sitting more than five and a half feet apart when conversing in a rather large hall, and would move to another position if further apart. The preferred position for conversation at a table was at two corner seats, so that the participants were physically close, but not directly facing one another (Sommer, 1962).

Americans may stand at eighteen to twenty inches, but people from Latin America and the Middle East will stand much closer. Hall reports how conversations at international gatherings result in Americans retreating backwards or gyrating round in circles (Hall, 1955). Members of some primitive societies in Africa and Indonesia come closer still and maintain bodily contact during conversation (Ardener, personal communication). Every animal species has its characteristic individual distance, closer than which they will not go, as well as a maximum social distance between members of the group. For some the minimum distance is zero, as for some kinds of monkeys; for the flamingo it is two feet, and so on (Hediger, 1955, pp. 66, 83).

In order to carry out the later experiment it was necessary to know where the equilibrium point was for local subjects and conditions. And it was predicted from the affiliative conflict theory that the equilibrium point for approach would be closer if the other person's eyes were shut.

Method

Subjects were invited to take part in a perceptual experiment, and asked to stand 'as close as is comfortable to see well' two physical objects, both the same size as a human head (a book and a plaster head of William Mc-Dougall). Then followed three other displays in different orders for different subjects: (1) a cut-out life-sized photograph of the face of the first author, (2) the first author with eyes shut and (3) with eyes open. In (1) and (3) the object was looking straight at the subject with a pleasant-to-neutral expression; in (2) and (3) the object was seated in a chair. Displays 1–3 were given in all six orders. The subjects were six adult acquaintances (three male, three female), and six child acquaintances (three male, three female, aged five to twelve). Distances eye-to-eye were measured by a long ruler. It was hoped that the disguise of the experiment as a study of vision would prevent such measurements being disturbing.

Results and discussion

As is shown in Table 1, subjects stand eleven inches closer to the photograph than to the person, and six inches closer to a person whose eyes are shut than to a person whose eyes are open. The second effect is more marked for adults than for children, and children stand closer in all three conditions.

Table 1 Position in inches of nearest approach under different conditions

Subjects	n	Photo	Eyes shut	Eyes open
Adults	6	35·7	34·0	42·7
Children	6	16·9	27·6	31·4
Total	12	26·3	30·8	37·1

There were no reversals for the six adults, and only one for the six children. Applying a binomial test, both the photo/eyes-open differences and the eyes-open/eyes-shut differences are significant at $p < 0.003$. Other tests of significance give a rather lower value in view of the large individual differences, but for adults only a on Mann–Whitney test the eyes-open/eyes-shut difference is significant at $p < 0.05$.

The main effect of order is that it makes a difference whether the 'eyes-shut' condition follows or precedes the 'eyes-open' condition. The finding is that when 'eyes-shut' comes first, both distances are less ($p < 0.05$). This suggests a persistence of the social system which is first established.

An experiment to determine the effects of distance on eye contact

There is some evidence that EC is reduced when proximity is greater. When proximity is very great, as in lifts and buses, interaction and EC often cease entirely. Goffman reports that EC is common when approaching a stranger on a pavement, while it is decided on which side to pass, but that 'civil inattention' is given when the stranger gets to a distance of eight feet (Goffman, 1963).

The present experiment was designed to test one of the twelve deductions from our affiliative theory of EC, viz. that if spatial proximity is increased, EC will be reduced. If it is assumed that intimacy is a function of length of glance as well as of total EC, it follows that with greater proximity glances will become shorter.

Method

The method first employed by Exline was used, in which two people take part in a conversation, one of whom is a confederate who gazes continually at the other, a genuine subject.

Subjects were asked to come and take part in an 'experiment on conversations'. They were introduced to a person who appeared to be another subject but who was actually a confederate of the experimenter. The two were asked to discuss a TAT card and make up a story about it in three minutes. Three conversations were held, and the chairs were placed so that the distance between them was two feet, six feet and ten feet, eye-to-eye, in different orders for different pairs. In two preliminary experiments, the pairs were placed facing one another. In the final version of the experiment to be reported here, they were placed at ninety degrees, behind tables; this has the advantage that EC is more 'voluntary', and the gazing of the confederate is less apparent.

The independent variable was the distance between subjects. Each pair held three conversations, at distances of two feet, six feet and ten feet. The chairs and tables were placed so that subjects could not deviate very far from these distances by leaning backwards or forwards. Subject and confederate were asked to move their chairs between conditions to positions marked by chalk. The experimenter said 'And for the next conversation I'd like you to move your chairs and sit . . . here . . . and . . . here'.

The dependent variables were the amount of EC in three minutes, and the average length of glances. Since the confederate gazed continuously, the amount of EC taking place depended entirely on him, and it was only necessary to record the duration of his looking at the confederate. The observers were placed behind a one-way screen as shown in Figure 1.

The observers were looking directly into the eyes of the subject, and could tell with some accuracy when he looked at the confederate. The amount of EC in the three-minute conversations was recorded on cumulative stop watches. During the early trials two observers were used, but the agreement was so close that later we relied on one. A second observer counted the number of glances made by the subject during the three minutes. It has been suggested that at greater distance it is less clear whether the subject is really

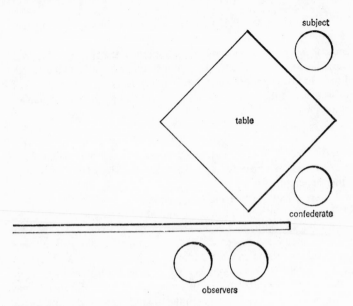

Figure 1 Arrangements of subjects and observers

looking at the eyes of the confederate, or at other parts of his head, so that the amount of EC at greater distances may be over-estimated. However Gibson and Pick (1963) have found that subjects can tell with considerable accuracy whether a second person is looking them in the eye: when the other was two metres distance, shifts of fixation of ten centimetres were clearly discriminable. Exline found that an observer agreed highly with a confederate as to whether EC was taking place (Exline *et al.*, 1961), and that there was very high agreement between observers ($r = 0.98$). It was our experience that for the majority of subjects there was no difficulty in telling whether EC was occurring or not; they did not spend much time fixating other parts of the head. In later studies with schizophrenics we have had greater difficulty. We also found that a subject's eyes were very stable when he was gazing, rather than scanning the rest of the confederate's face. During gaze there is a steady fixation, and this can generally be identified.

Instructions given to each pair were as follows: 'This is an experiment to find out how two people come to an agreement during a conversation. We would like you both to look at this picture, and then you will have three minutes to make up a joint story about what you think is happening. We shall be listening to your discussion from the next room'.

Eighty subjects were used, twenty-four of them in the main experiment,

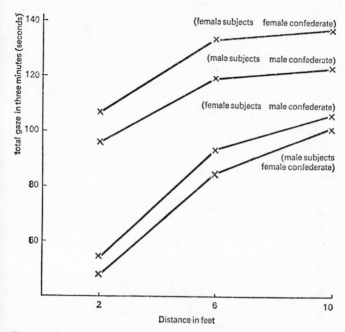

Figure 2 Relation between EC and Distance for different combinations of confederate and subject

half of each sex. The subjects in the main experiment were all graduate students in subjects other than psychology. There were four confederates, two of each sex, and these young people of similar age and background to the subjects. Some deception was used to make it appear that they were genuine subjects: they were instructed to talk about half the time and to adopt a pleasant-to-neutral expression.

At the end of the experiment, subjects were interviewed, mainly to discover if they had noticed that the confederate was gazing all the time, or whether they had guessed the point of the experiment, and to explain the experiment to them.

Results

The experimental procedure was thought to be satisfactory, in that perfectly normal conversations took place, and only one or two persons realized that they were being gazed at, or that they were talking to a confederate; and their results were no different from those of other subjects. The main findings on total EC and length of glance are given in the analyses of variance shown in Table 2 and Figure 2.

Table 2 Analyses of variance for main experiment on total EC and length of glance

Source	Total eye contact					Average length of glances				
	s.s.	df	m.s.	F	p	s.s.	df	m.s.	F	p
Distance	20,824	2	10,412	16·12	0·001	211·4	2	105·7	8·13	0·01
Sex of Subject (SS)	1271	1	1271	1·97	n.s.	10·0	1	10·0	0·77	n.s.
Sex of Confed. (SC)	263	1	263	0·41	n.s.	13·1	1	13·1	1·01	n.s.
Sequence (Seq.)	16,230	5	3246	5·03	0·025	145·3	5	29·1	2·24	0·06
Distance x SS	64	2	32	0·05	n.s.	8·3	2	4·2	0·32	n.s.
Distance x SC	40	2	20	0·03	n.s.	6·1	2	3·0	0·23	n.s.
Distance x Seq.	905	10	91	0·14	n.s.	40·5	10	4·1	0·31	n.s.
SS x SC	22,349	1	22,349	34·59	0·001	219·6	1	219·6	16·90	0·01
SS x Seq.	14,758	5	2952	4·57	0·025	479·4	5	95·9	7·38	0·01
SC x Seq.	22,779	5	4556	7·05	0·01	676·6	5	135·3	10·41	0·01
Dist. x SS x SC	1423	2	711	1·10	n.s.	16·7	2	8·4	0·64	n.s.
Dist. x SS x Seq.	2795	10	280	0·43	n.s.	85·8	10	8·6	0·66	n.s.
Dist. x SC x Seq.	3673	10	367	0·57	n.s.	64·5	10	6·5	0·50	n.s.
SS x SC x Seq.	19,450	5	3890	6·02	0·01	316·7	5	63·3	4·87	0·025
Residual	6460	10	646			130·0	10	13·0		
Total	133,284	71				2424·1	71			

The experiment has been replicated four times, with variations in task and conditions, and using different subjects, confederates, observers and experimenters. The first two experiments used a head-on position of the subjects: the effects of this are discussed later. The third experiment is the one reported here, and incorporated a number of improvements in technique, such as using tables and chairs that prevented the subjects from changing the distance between them. The fourth is an experiment by E. R. Porter using pairs of males throughout, and varying certain other conditions. The effect of distance was similar in all these rather different versions of the experiment.

Distance and total EC. The prediction that EC will decrease with spatial proximity is confirmed for all four combinations of sexes ($p < 0.001$). It is somewhat more marked for opposite-sex pairs. These results are shown in Figure 2 (p. 181). It can be seen that EC varies from about 30 per cent to 75 per cent of the time in the different conditions, i.e. we are dealing with major sources of variance. These results were replicated in the preliminary experiments, using a different angle between subjects. The effects of distance were more marked at 90 degrees than 180 degrees between the subjects ($p < 0.05$, females only).

It was found that the effect of distance is greatest for subjects with short EC (averaged for all three distances): $p = 0.38$ ($p < 0.05$). Is this due to the greater shift and lower EC for opposite-sex pairs? If separate correlations are calculated, it is found that the shift/EC correlation is -0.30 (n.s.) for opposite-sex pairs, and 0.00 for same-sex pairs. It appears that the more fundamental relation is between sensitivity to distance and low EC, which in turn could explain the greater effect for opposite-sex pairs.

Distance and length of glances. Length of glance increased with distance from 5·5 seconds at two feet to 8·8 at six feet and 9·6 at ten feet ($p < 0.01$). Thus the main difference occurred between two feet and six feet. These averages are rather unsatisfactory indices for certain subjects who had one or two very long glances, perhaps trying to outstare the confederate.

Sex differences. It was expected that female subjects would show more EC than males. This was found (see Figure 2), but the differences although consistent were small and non-significant. The same is true of length of glances. Sex of confederate as a variable was a negligible source of variance. However, sex of subject and sex of confederate interact strongly ($p < 0.001$): there is much less EC with mixed-sex pairs. This is most marked at two feet. Length of glances is less for opposite-sex pairs: 3·7 seconds as opposed to 7·2 seconds for same-sex pairs at two feet.

Sequence of conditions. It was found in the experiment on distance equilibrium, and in the first two versions of the present experiment, that the social relationship established in the first condition persisted in the later ones. Thus if two feet was the first condition there would be less EC throughout all three conditions. This was *not* found in the experiment we are reporting here. Although sequence (2–6–10, 2–10–6, etc.), and order (1st, 2nd or 3rd condition), are both significant sources of variance, we conclude that this must be due to nonrandom sampling of subjects, as no meaningful pattern could be discovered. There were only four subjects for each of the six sequences compared.

Observational results concerning equilibrium tendencies. It was expected that at very close distances efforts would first be made to reduce intimacy by reducing EC, etc., but that anxiety would be shown if such steps were not enough. In the two feet condition, EC never quite fell to zero, but signs of tension were observed in all subjects, especially when facing each other directly. They tried to increase the distance – by leaning backwards – which was prevented by chairs in the main experiment. They engaged in various gestures apparently to reduce EC or to distract attention: looking down, shading the eyes with the hand, narrowing the eyes, scratching the head, smoking (prevented in final version), blowing the nose, etc. At the ten feet position, on the other hand, subjects were inclined to lean forwards, as would be expected from the equilibrium theory. This was prevented by tables in the main experiment.

We should consider how far the conditions of the experiment may have distorted the results. The situation was odd in at least one respect; namely the confederate stared continuously. This would probably be interpreted by the subject as seeking greater intimacy; had the confederate adopted a more hostile expression, it might have been seen as an attempt to dominate. Thus the amount of intimacy in the situation was entirely under the control of the subject. However, many subjects were not aware that the confederate *was* gazing continuously; and this was particularly true of subjects with short EC, for whom the effect of distance was most marked.

Discussion

How far do our results support the existence of equilibrium positions for distance or EC? The first experiment found that subjects would only approach to a certain degree of physical proximity; the second experiment found that those at two feet tried to increase the distance, and those at ten feet to reduce it, by leaning backwards and forwards respectively. Subjects at two feet were in a state of discomfort and tension. There are no comparable data to demonstrate an equilibrium for EC, but in our second experiment, where EC was entirely under the subject's control, we found a consistent level of EC for each subject, and that this was a function of our experimental conditions, varying from 30 to 75 per cent of the time. There were very great individual differences, from 0 to 100 per cent of the time.

How far have our tests of hypotheses, derived from the theory, confirmed that theory? In the first experiment it was found (for adults) that A would stand 8·7 inches nearer B when B's eyes were shut – a difference of about 23 per cent of the mean distance. In the second experiment, it was found that EC was reduced at closer distances. The effect was greatest between two feet and six feet, for subjects who were low in EC, and for opposite-sex pairs, this being possibly a special case of the former. EC changed from 30 per cent to 58 per cent of the time for opposite-sex pairs, from 55 per cent to 72 per cent for same-sex pairs. Clearly this hypothesis is also confirmed, though there are further complications not envisaged by the theory.

There is an apparent difficulty over the finding that EC did not fall to zero in the two feet condition. Placing two people two feet apart is a major disturbance of equilibrium, and considerable reduction of gaze, smiling, etc., would be needed in compensation. The fact that subjects were very uncomfortable at two feet shows that equilibrium was not satisfactorily restored. There seem to be two possibilities:

1. There is a separate equilibrium for gaze, distance etc., they cannot *fully* compensate for one another, as our theory supposed; or

2. There are such strong positive forces behind gaze that it is difficult to reduce it to zero.

These forces are the need for *some* feedback, to ensure that the channel is still open, and to avoid sheer rudeness in view of the conventional social pressures to engage in some EC. In the preliminary experiments, in which subjects sat directly facing each other, there was nearly as much EC at two feet as at six feet. We thought that this might be due to the difficulty of avoiding EC without rudeness at two feet, and we used a ninety-degree position in the main experiment to make EC more voluntary. In fact there was a much greater drop in EC between six feet and two feet with this arrangement, which supports the interpretation above. In subsequent studies with schizophrenics, to be reported elsewhere, some subjects *did* reduce their gaze to zero at two feet.

The finding that opposite-sex pairs show *less* EC and use shorter glances is contradictory to the general expectations of the theory, since it may be presumed that the approach drives are stronger with opposite-sex pairs. In fact, there was rather more arousal in the opposite sex pairs, and conversation was more lively. Of course, opposite-sex pairs in other contexts *do* engage in a lot of EC, but this may be only when intimacy really has developed. In our situation the subjects were initially strangers. Another aspect of EC may need to be postulated to account for our result. EC between opposite-sex pairs of this age, in this culture, probably carries the additional implication of sexual attraction, and this may be especially true of long glances. In order to keep this attraction within bounds in the laboratory setting, EC may have been reduced.

Since the information and feedback-seeking aspects of gaze are reasonably well established, it is worth inquiring whether our results could be explained in these terms. The greater EC at greater distances could perhaps be due to the increased difficulty of perception. It may also be more necessary to keep signalling to the other that one is still attending, i.e. that the channel is still open. We found that EC invariably fell off in the second half of each three-minute conversation. This could be because the necessary feedback had by then been obtained; in addition, subjects were at this stage thinking hard for more ideas, and EC would have constituted a distraction. On the other hand, this theory offers no explanation for the existence of an equilibrium position, or for the emotional aspects of EC, and it is believed that the affiliative-conflict theory is required in addition to the information-seeking analysis.

Summary

Previous evidence on the determinants of eye-contact was reviewed, and it was concluded that gaze serves a number of functions. One of the most important of these is the quest for feedback during social interaction, together with that of signalling that the channel is open.

A second theory was proposed, that EC is a component of intimacy and is equivalent to physical proximity. These, and other aspects of intimacy are governed by both approach and avoidance forces, and are kept in a condition of equilibrium for any two people. Experiments were reported which provide evidence of such an equilibrium for physical proximity and for eye contact.

It is postulated that if this equilibrium is disturbed along one of its constituent dimensions, e.g. by increasing physical proximity, there will be compensatory changes along the other dimensions. It has already been shown that greater intimacy of topic leads to less eye contact. We have now shown that reducing eye contact makes greater proximity possible, and that greater proximity reduces eye contact.

References

Exline, R. V. (1963), 'Explorations in the process of person perception: visual interaction in relation to competition, sex and the need for affiliation', *J. Pers.*, vol. 31, pp. 1–20.

EXLINE, R. V., GRAY, D., and SCHUETTE, D. (1965), 'Visual behavior in a dyad as affected by interview content and sex of respondent', *J. pers. soc. Psychol.*, vol. 1, pp. 201–9.

EXLINE, R. V., THIBAUT, J., BRANNON, C., and GUMPERT, P. (1961), 'Visual interaction in relation to Machiavellianism and an unethical act', *Amer. Psychol.*, vol. 16, p. 396.

EXLINE, R. V., and WINTERS, L. C. (1965), 'Affective relations and mutual glances in dyads', in S. Tomkins and C. Izzard (eds.), *Affect, Cognition and Personality*, Springer.

FELDMAN, S. S. (1959), *Mannerisms of Speech and Gesture in Everyday Life*, International University Press.

GIBSON, J. J., and PICK, A. D. (1963), 'Perception of another person's looking behavior', *Amer. J. Psychol.*, vol. 76, pp. 386–94.

GOFFMAN, E. (1963), *Behavior in Public Places*, Free Press.

GRAY, P. H. (1958), 'Theory and evidence of imprinting in human infants', *J. Psychol.*, vol. 46, pp. 155–66.

HALL, E. T. (1955), 'The anthropology of manners', *Scient. Amer.*, vol. 192, pp. 84–90.

HEDIGER, H. (1955), *Studies of the Psychology and Behavior of Captive Animals in Zoos and Circuses*, Butterworth.

HESS, E. H. (1965), 'Attitude and pupil size', *Scient. Amer.*, vol. 212, pp. 46–54.

HUTT, C., and OUNSTED, C. (1966), 'The biological significance of gaze-aversion with particular reference to the sydrome of infantile autims, *Behav. Sci.*, vol. 2, pp. 346–56.

KENDON, A. (1964), 'The distribution of visual attention in two-person encounters', Report to Department of Scientific and Industrial Research, London.

KRASNER, L. (1958), 'Studies on the conditioning of verbal behavior', *Psychol. Bull.*, vol. 55, pp. 148–70.

LAING, R. D. (1960a), *The Self and Others*, Tavistock.

LAING, R. D. (1960b), *The Divided Self*, Tavistock.

MILLER, N. E. (1944), 'Experimental studies in conflict', in J. McV. Hunt (ed.), *Personality and the Behavior Disorders*, vol. 1, Ronald.

NIELSEN, G. (1962), *Studies in Self Confrontation*, Monksgaard.

REIMER, M. D. (1955), 'Abnormalities of the gaze: a classification', *Psychiat. Q.*, vol. 29, pp. 659–72.

SCHEUTZ, A. (1948), 'Sartre's theory of the alter ego', *Philosophy phenom. Res.*, vol. 9, pp. 181–99.

SIMMEL, G. (1921), 'Sociology of the senses: visual interaction', in R. E. Park and E. W. Burgess (eds.), *Introduction to the Science of Sociology*, University of Chicago Press.

SOMMER, R. (1962), 'The distance for comfortable conversations: a further study', *Sociometry*, vol 25, pp. 111–16.

SPITZ, R. A. (1946), 'The smiling response: a contribution to the ontogenesis of social relations', *Genet. Psychol. Monogr.*, vol. 34, pp. 57–125.

STEINZOR, B. (1950), 'The spatial factor in face to face discussion groups', *J. abnorm. soc. Psychol.*, vol. 45, pp. 552–5.

WOLFF, P. H. (1963), 'Observations on the early development of smiling', in B. M. Foss (ed.), *Determinants of Infant Behaviour*, vol. 2, Methuen.

13 Melvin Feffer and Leonard Suchotliff

Decentering Implications of Social Interactions

M. Feffer and L. Suchotliff, 'Decentering implications of social interactions', *Journal of Personality and Social Psychology*, vol. 4, 1966, pp. 415–22.

Although Piaget (1948, 1962) has considered interpersonal behavior within a cognitive-developmental framework, his thinking has been primarily directed toward the analysis of such impersonal cognitive categories of experience as space, time, and number. The present study represents an attempt to bring these 'cold-blooded aspects of cognition' (Flavell, 1963) into contact with the interpersonal domain. As such it represents a continuation of past empirical studies (Feffer, 1959; Feffer and Gourevitch, 1960) which have been similarly directed toward the goal of extending the implications of Piaget's concepts to the interpersonal area. To this end, the present study focuses upon some characteristics of social interaction as interpreted in terms of Piaget's decentering concept.

Within Piaget's (1950) framework, cognitive processes are viewed as reflecting greater maturity and adaptiveness to the degree that immediate sense impressions are subordinated to thought in organizing experience. In particular, Piaget sharply contrasts perception and thought in terms of decentering activity. He advances the notion that distortion is inherent in the act of focusing or centering upon a given aspect of the perceptual field. Although the successive distortions involved in decentering (shifting focus from one part of the perceptual field to another) serve to correct or balance each other, the correction of distortion is only partial due to the sequential nature of the centrations. Mature ideation or thought, however, allows for a much more thorough correction of the distortion inherent in any given focus by enabling the individual to consider a number of aspects of a situation in relation to each other at the same time, that is, simultaneous decentering.

Although the decentering concept has been relatively restricted within Piaget's framework to an interpretation of such impersonal cognitive functioning as the child's developing concept of quantity (Piaget, 1950), it can be extended to interpersonal behavior in terms of the following formulation. The dovetailing of responses involved in effective social interaction requires that each participating individual modify his intended behavior in the light of his anticipation of the other's reaction to this behavior. In order to accurately anticipate this reaction, one must be able to view his intended behavior from the perspective of the other. Modifying one's behavior in the light of this anticipation further requires that one must also view the intended action from his own perspective at the same time. The cognitive organization of the individual capable of effective social interaction can, accordingly, be interpreted as one in which different viewpoints are considered simultaneously in relation to each other such that the distortions engendered by a given perspective or centering is equilibrated or corrected by another perspective. In contrast, individuals who are only able to focus sequentially upon their behavior from a single viewpoint at a time should have difficulty in appropriately modifying their responses in such a situation. This formulation is basic to the hypothesis governing the present study, namely, that effective social interaction is a function of each participating individual's ability to consider his behavior simultaneously from different viewpoints.

An initial extension of the decentering concept to the cognitive structuring of interpersonal content received support in a study by Feffer and Gourevitch (1960). Children of various chronological ages were given a projective role-taking task (RTT), which elicits interpersonal content, and a series of impersonal cognitive tasks developed by Piaget and his co-workers. It was found in this study, as well as in a follow-up study by Candell (1965), that a developmental ordering of role-taking behavior in terms of the decentering concept showed a predicted progression with age as well as predicted relationships with the independent assessments of decentering activity on the impersonal cognitive tasks. Wolfe (1963) and Buchsbaum (1965) have also reported an increasing predominance of mature decentering in the structuring of interpersonal content as a function of increasing chronological age. It should be noted, however, that in all these studies the assessment of interpersonal decentering activity was limited to RTT performance, that is to say, to the projective material of the individual subject. The present study represents a more direct extension of the decentering concept to interpersonal behavior in that it focuses upon the decentering implications of interaction between two individuals.

Method

The sample consisted of thirty-six male and female students enrolled in an undergraduate course in psychology. Subjects were first given a group version of the RTT in order to determine their decentering ability in the structuring of interpersonal content. They were then paired into eighteen dyads on the basis of similar decentering ability. These dyads were subsequently evaluated in regard to effectiveness on a task requiring cooperative social interaction (password). Following the password situation, each subject was given the WAIS vocabulary, a word-association test, and a word-fluency test.

RTT

The RTT has served in past studies as a basis for evaluating, in decentering terms, the individual's structuring of interpersonal content. The RTT requires that the subject make up initial stories for a number of ambiguous scenes. After the stories are completed, each scene is again presented, and the subject is asked to retell the initial story from the viewpoint of each of his characters.

In the group procedure, three TAT-like pictures were projected upon a screen. The instructions for the initial story telling were as follows:

This is a test of imagination, one form of intelligence. I am going to show you some pictures, one at a time; your task will be to make up as dramatic a story as you can for each. Tell what led up to the event shown in the picture, describe what is happening at the moment, what the characters are thinking and feeling, and then give the outcome. Write your thoughts as they come to your mind. You will have about four minutes for each story. Please number your stories as you go along. Make sure your handwriting is legible. If you have any questions, raise your hand.

After presentation of the three pictures, the following instructions were given:

Now you are going to see the same pictures again, but this time make believe that you are each one of the people in the story you made up. Here is the first picture. [The first picture was again projected upon the screen.] I want you to make believe that you are this person [examiner pointed to a predetermined figure] and you are right in the situation. Retell the story from the point of view of this person. That is, tell the story again, but this time as though you were really this person. You have up to three minutes. Use a new sheet of paper for each character. [After three minutes, examiner pointed to a second predetermined figure.] Now make believe that you are this person. Tell the story as though you were really this person. [After another three minutes, examiner pointed to the third figure.] This time tell the story as though you were this person.

The RTT is evaluated in terms of the degree to which the subject is able to refocus upon his initial story from the perspectives of his characters while at the same time maintaining continuity between his various versions of the initial story. It is assumed that the change and continuity which define successful role-taking performances are indicative of the subject's ability to consider his behavior simultaneously from different viewpoints. Thus, a subtle degree of coordination between versions of the initial story is interpreted as a type of decentering which is simultaneously modulated by previous and anticipated centerings; in contrast, inconsistency or discontinuity between the characters' viewpoints is interpreted as a form of sequential decentering, that is, a shift in focus that is not concomitantly guided by other centerings.

These general considerations serve as the basis for the specific categories whereby R T T decentering activity is evaluated. These categories are ordered in terms of the number and subtlety of attributed which are coordinated from the various viewpoints. The basic categories are as follows:

Simple refocusing. The requirement for this category is a change in the subject's description of an actor (a given story character) from that actor's viewpoint as compared to the subject's description of that actor in the initial story. For example, if the father is described as having 'had a bad day at the office' in the initial story, and as 'hungry' in the father's role, this is taken as evidence that an inconsistent refocusing has taken place. A more consistent or coordinate focusing is indicated by the subject's description of father from father's viewpoint as 'unhappy'.

Character elaboration. In order to be classified under this category, there must be some evidence of a refocusing upon a given actor from more than one viewpoint. As in the previous category, this change may be made with various degrees of thematic consistency. For example, if the subject describes father as 'unhappy' from father's viewpoint, and 'petted the dog' from mother's viewpoint, then an inconsistent character elaboration is indicated. That is, there is a refocusing upon father from each vantage point, but the two viewpoints are not coordinated. On the other hand, coordination is indicated in the subject's description of father as 'unhappy' from father's viewpoint, and 'felt lousy' from mother's viewpoint, that is, a consistent character elaboration.

Perspective elaboration. The requirement for consistent character elaboration has to be met, that is, change yet consistency between the descriptions of a given actor from the various perspectives. In addition, these descriptions should differ appropriately from role to role in the sense that the description of an actor in his own role should have an 'inner' orientation as contrasted to an external description of that actor from a viewpoint other than his own. For example, the subject in father's role describes father as 'unhappy because he thought he was going to get a raise that day and it didn't work out'. That is, as father he offers reasons for his feelings which, as the father, he is more likely to know. The subject as mother, on the other hand, describes father in external superficial terms: 'He looked sad'. In contrast, the character elaboration described in the previous category, although consistent, does not fulfill the requirement for perspective elaboration because of the mother's inappropriate inner orientation with regard to father, that is, 'felt lousy'. Different levels within the perspective elaboration category are based upon the subtlety find fineness of coordination between inner and outer descriptions.

Change of perspective. This category requires an overall synthesis between two perspective elaborations. That is, the two roles must have a particular relationship to each other such that the internal orientation of one is appropriately reflected in the external orientation of the other and vice versa. For example, the subject in the role of father describes father from an internal orientation: 'He's unhappy because he thought he was going to get a raise that day and it didn't work out.' This description finds its external counterpart in the subject's description of father in mother's role: 'He looked sad'. At the same time, the subject in the role of mother describes mother from an internal orientation, that is 'tired because she had washed the floor that day', which is consistently reflected in the external description of mother by father, that is, 'didn't seem too pleased to see him'. Different levels of change of perspective are based upon the subtlety of coordination between inner and outer descriptions.

Since it was necessary to complete the testing of subjects before the semester ended, the senior investigator evaluated the subject's RTT performance on one of the three cards of the series. This card depicts a bar-room scene in which a seated female figure is observing a male and female who are standing and who seem to be arguing. This picture was chosen since, of the three cards, it had elicited the widest range and most differentiated set of scores in a pilot study. Each subject was assigned a score based upon the highest RTT category evidenced in his performance. Subjects of the same sex who attained similar scores were paired into dyads and were subsequently tested (from one month to two months after the RTT) in the password situation by the junior investigator who was unaware of the dyad's RTT level.

Social interaction situation (*password*)

In the password situation, a stack of eighteen 3 × 5 index cards was placed before each member of the dyad. A single word was printed on each card. One member of the dyad, as donor, was required to communicate his test word to his partner, the recipient, via one-word association clues. The recipient, in turn, was required to guess at the test word in the form of one-word responses to each association clue of the donor. This form of interaction continued until the test word was communicated, or until a ninety-second time limit was reached, at which point the word on the next card was attempted. Effectiveness of social interaction was defined for the purpose of the present study by the length of time and the number of clues necessary for the dyad to solve their common problem, that is, the communication of the list of thirty-six test words.

A number of considerations governed the choice of the password situation as the basis for evaluating effectiveness of social interaction. On a descriptive level, the password game represented a form of interaction which could be standardized and experimentally manipulated, and which afforded quantitative estimates of effectiveness. More important, however, was the consideration that the password situation represented an analogue of the type of social interaction previously formulated in decentering terms, particularly with regard to the donor's role. The donor's relative adequacy in communicating the test word was viewed as being based upon his ability to select, from the myriad of association possibilities available to him, the association clue with the most information value to the recipient. This selection, in turn, was considered to be a function of the donor's ability to modify his intended behavior not only in the light of a general instructional set (that of communicating the test word), but also in the light of his anticipation of the recipient's possible response as well as the recipient's previous responses. It appeared necessary for the recipient, on the other hand, to modify possible responses in the light of previous clues, his past responses, and the general instructional set of guessing the test word. The progressive modification and dovetailing of responses thus required to communicate and receive the test word appeared to rest importantly upon the relative ability of each participant to attend simultaneously to aspects of his experience from more than one viewpoint.

Since the aim of the study was to extend the decentering notion directly to social interaction, a major consideration was whether, in the password situation, it was the characteristic of interaction, as such, that constituted the source of experimental variation. Two forms of password, representing differing degrees of interaction, were designed to meet this question. The first, termed the 'loud' condition, was a face-to-face situation in which the recipient responded verbally to the verbal clue of the donor. The donor was then free to give an additional verbal clue if the response of the recipient was not correct. Instructions for the loud condition were as follows:

The object of this task is to attempt to communicate to your partner the words on the cards in front of you. The words are to be communicated by the use of one-word clues. For example, I have to communicate 'hat' to you. I say CAP, you say 'bottle'; then I might say CHAPEAU, and, hopefully, you would get the word 'hat'. After the donor (the one who knows the word) gives a clue, he must wait until his partner responds before giving the next clue. All clues and answers must be of one word, and to each clue given only one guess is permitted. In order to guess again, the person must await a new clue. If the recipient cannot think of a word, he can say PASS, and this allows the donor to give another clue. No part or form of the word may be used as a clue; for example, CHEMIST cannot be used for 'chemistry', STEAL cannot be used for 'stolen', and MONK cannot be used for 'monkey'. A previously given word may be repeated by either player. The exact form of the word must be gotten, for example, 'muddy' for MUD is not correct, and play must continue until MUD is gotten. You are allowed one-and a half minutes to try to get each word. You will be timed, and I will stop you at the end of one and a half minutes.

The second form of password interaction, the 'silent' condition, restricted the amount of feedback for both donor and recipient. Although the donor continued to give verbal association clues under this condition, his back was to the recipient who *wrote* his response. The following instructions were given for the silent condition:

At times I will ask the donor to turn around when giving the clues and the recipient to write his responses down instead of saying them [instructions repeated as necessary]. I will say 'continue' if the recipient does not write down the correct word. Thus, you must wait for me to say 'continue' before giving the next clue. I will stop you when the recipient gets the word or when time runs out. If the recipient cannot think of a word, he can write down the word 'pass'. This will allow the donor to continue.

As may be seen in Table 1, each subject served as both recipient and donor under loud and silent conditions. Each dyad communicated thirty-six words, twenty-four under the loud condition and twelve under the silent condition. In addition, in order to avoid possible contamination between word content and the form of password interaction (whether loud or silent), two groups of dyads were formed from the eighteen dyads. Both Group I ($N = 8$) and Group II ($N = 10$) had the same word list. One series of twelve words, however, which was passed under the loud condition by Group I, was passed under the silent condition by Group II, while a second series of twelve words passed under the silent condition by Group I was passed under the loud condition by Group II. The two series of words, in addition, were equated for familiarity in terms of the Thorndike-Lorge (1944) word count and for difficulty in terms of the results of a pilot study. The loud and silent conditions under which these particular series of words were passed will henceforth be termed 'equated-loud' and 'equated-silent' conditions. The equated-loud and equated-silent conditions were thus similar in all respects other than degree of interaction or informational feedback.

Controls

Somewhat independent of the question as to whether it is the interactive quality of the password situation which is contributing systematic variation in dyad performance is the possibility that a given variable having little or

Table 1 Characteristics of password situation

Test word[a]	Donor–recipient direction[b]	Form of interaction[c]
earth	A B	L-L
infection	B A	L-L
relax	B A	S-L
ivory	A B	L-S
stingy	A B	L-L
guilty	B A	L-S
gloom	B A	L-L
selfish	A B	S-L
Bible	A B	L-S
breast	B A	L-L
carve	B A	L-S
suck	A B	L-L
butcher	A B	L-L
kite	B A	S-L
spaghetti	B A	S-L
smash	A B	L-S
skate	A B	S-L
burden	B A	L-S
moss	B A	L-L
take	A B	S-L
sob	A B	L-S
pure	B A	S-L
argue	B A	L-S
slang	A B	L-L
confess	A B	S-L
label	B A	L-S
reliable	B A	S-L
sloppy	A B	L-S
suicide	A B	S-L
street	B A	S-L
juicy	B A	L-L
fail	A B	L-L
butterfly	A B	L-S
compass	B A	L-L
chalk	B A	L-S
bush	A B	S-L

[a] Test words were presented in the order listed.

[b] First letter refers to donor, second letter to recipient, for example, BA = B passes to A.

[c] S-L = passed by silent method in Group I and loud method in Group II. L-S = passed by loud method in Group I and silent method in Group II. L-L = passed by loud method in Group I *and* Group II.

indirect conceptual relevance to decentering might be the basis of the predicted relationship between RTT and password performance. Three variables were examined as being germane in this regard. The first, verbal intelligence, was evaluated by means of the WAIS Vocabulary under standard conditions of administration. The second, verbal fluency, was assessed in terms of the number of words beginning with the letter P that the subject could produce in one minute. The third variable, degree of similarity, has frequently been evaluated in terms of the extent to which subjects respond to personality inventory items in similar ways; it seemed more appropriate, however, given the one-word association clues of the password situation, to evaluate degree of similarity as reflected in similar associations. Accordingly, each subject was given a word-association test under standard conditions. Each dyad was scored in terms of degree of shared associations or 'overlap', that is, the number of times the members of the dyad gave the same response to a given word-association item. A fourth variable, that of sex differences was initially considered as a possible contaminating factor. This was eliminated, however, when it was found that males and females did not differ significantly in regard to RTT performance.

Predictions

It will be recalled that the hypothesis governing the present study is that effective social interaction is a function of each participating individual's ability to consider his behavior simultaneously from different viewpoints. Given the particular procedure of the study, it was predicted that those dyads which were comprised of higher RTT scorers would evidence more effective password performance under the loud password condition than those dyads which were comprised of lower RTT scorers. It was further predicted that the association between password and RTT would be evidenced under the equated-loud rather than under the equated-silent condition.

Results

As may be seen in Table 2, the predicted relationship between RTT decentering scores and measures of password effectiveness was confirmed in that the higher scoring RTT dyads passed words more quickly and with fewer clues under the loud condition than did the lower scoring RTT dyads. This association, moreover, was evidenced under the equated-loud but not under the equated-silent condition. Thus dyad differences stemming from the interactive nature of the password situation appeared to be systematically related to RTT differences. The results are thus consistent with the hypothesis of the study.

The data were further analysed with regard to the possibility that variables

Table 2 Relationship between RTT decentering scores and password performance

Password condition	Group I $N = 8$		Group II $N = 10$		Combined probability	
	Time	Trials	Time	Trials	Time	Trials
Overall loud	0·65[a]	0·50	0·28	0·50	<0·05>0·02	<0·02>0·01
Equated loud	0·55	0·38	0·40	0·35	<0·05>0·02	<0·10>0·05
Equated silent	−0·12	−0·04	0·12	−0·02	>0·50	>0·50

[a] The Kendall tau was used because it afforded precise probability estimates that could be combined by the Fisher method of combining probabilities. Probability estimates are one-tailed.

other than decentering might have accounted for the relationship between RTT and password scoring. Password effectiveness in terms of time was examined since this variable showed the clearest differences in the comparison of the equated-loud and equated-silent conditions. As may be seen in Table 3, of the three control variables so considered, neither verbal fluency scores nor WAIS Vocabulary scores were significantly related to either RTT or password measures. It was thus inferred that these variables did not contribute essentially to the association between password and RTT performance. However, the third variable, degree of associative overlap, was significantly related to the password score and showed a trend in regard to the RTT measure. In further analysing the nature of the associative overlap, it was found that of the fifty-three words on which shared associations occurred, 94 per cent of the overlap occurred on the most popular response to each word. The remaining 6 per cent occurred on the second most popular response to each word. There was, accordingly, no overlap with respect to any responses other than the two most popular response associations to a given test word. It is possible, therefore, that the more basic variable underlying the relationship between overlap and password performance is the extent to which the subject responds with popular associations on the word-association test. This possibility is consistent with the findings reported in Table 4. A popularity score was determined for each response to the word-association test based upon the frequency with which that association was given by the total group. Each dyad was assigned the mean popularity score of its members' word-association responses. As may be seen in Table 4, popularity of response was significantly associated with RTT functioning and password effectiveness under the equated-loud but not the equated-silent condition, a pattern similar to and actually somewhat more accentuated than that between overlap, RTT functioning, and password effectiveness.

Discussion

The relationship between popularity of associative response and password effectiveness is subject to different interpretations. One possibility is that effective password performance as defined in the present study is based upon, or at least facilitated by, the possession by both individuals of the same (popular) associations to the password items. This interpretation would place more emphasis upon some type of automatic correspondence of associations than upon the active modification and dovetailing of associative responses as implied by the decentering concept. The position encounters certain difficulties, however, one of which is that the popularity score is related to password performance under the loud and not the silent condition. If effectiveness of password interaction were simply a function

Table 3 Relationship between control measures, RTT decentering, and password effectiveness

| | RTT decentering | | | Password effectiveness (time) | | | | | |
| | | | | Equated loud | | | Equated silent | | |
Control measures	Group I $N=8$	Group II $N=10$	Combined probability	Group I $N=8$	Group II $N=10$	Combined probability	Group I $N=8$	Group II $N=10$	Combined probability
Verbal fluency	−0·12[a]	0·30	>0·50	0·44	0·04	<0·20>0·10	0·48	0·40	>0·50
WAIS Vocabulary	0·21	−0·08	>0·50	−0·38	−0·02	<0·30>0·20	0·07	0·21	<0·50>0·30
Word-association overlap	0·35	0·34	<0·20>0·10	0·66	0·44	<0·02>0·01	0·15	0·24	<0·30>0·20

[a] The Kendall tau was used because it afforded precise probability estimates that could be combined by the Fisher method of combining probabilities. Probability estimates are one-tailed. In the case of correlations of opposite sign, a rough estimate of combined probability was afforded by averaging r to z transformations.

Table 4 Relationship between popularity of response measure, RTT decentering, and password effectiveness

| | RTT decentering | | | Password effectiveness (time) | | | | | |
| | | | | Equated loud | | | Equated silent | | |
Control measures	Group I $N=8$	Group II $N=10$	Combined probability	Group I $N=8$	Group II $N=10$	Combined probability	Group I $N=8$	Group II $N=10$	Combined probability
Popularity of response measure	0·31[a]	0·51	<0·05>0·02	0·66	0·54	<0·01>0·001	−0·37	0·23	>0·50

of both individuals' possession of the same associations to the test words, then some degree of facilitation would be expected under the silent condition as well as the loud condition. An additional difficulty encountered by this interpretation is that it leaves in question the findings concerning popularity of associative response and RTT performance. That is, it is not clear from this position how being able to produce popular associations is related to the ability to coordinate different viewpoints.

An alternative interpretation of the relationship between the popularity measure and password performance may be derived from Rapaport's (1946) approach to the processes involved in the word-association test. He has suggested that the instructions of the word-association test engender an anticipation or task set which both selects from and is influenced by the multitude of association possibilities triggered by the stimulus word. This reciprocal modification between task set and associative network is considered to be the basis of a popular response conceptually coordinate with the stimulus word. Rapaport suggests further that if the strength of the task set is attenuated, as in certain forms of maladaptive behavior, then part reactions which are normally modulated in their expression by the presence of the task set find abortive expression as idiosyncratic responses. In its emphasis upon a reciprocal modification between task set and associative network, Rapaport's formulation bears a strong resemblance to the decentering concept, particularly as applied to the password situation. Accordingly, it suggests an alternative interpretation congruent with the formulation of the present study, namely, that the empirical relationships between popularity of associative response, effectiveness of password performance under the loud condition, and level of RTT performance are based upon a common decentering dimension.

The results of the present study are thus interpreted as providing support for the extension of the decentering concept to social interaction. As such, the findings underscore an assumption which is tacit in much social psychological research, namely, that the psychological organization of the individual is the basic unit of analysis in social interaction. It is relevant to point out in this regard that the RTT, which has been used as the measure of individual processes in this study of social interaction, is a unique combination of projective content and formal assessment of decentering activity. If one makes the projective assumption that the characters which the subject creates on the RTT represent aspects of the self-organization, then such decentering defects as evidenced in discontinuity between specific perspectives may at the same time be taken as indicative of a disjunctive relationship between particular aspects of the self. The RTT, therefore, may be particularly well suited for analysing those attributes of self-organization which underlie forms of symptomatic social interaction. The symptom of assaultiveness may be taken as a case in point. This maladaptive form of social interaction can be viewed in decentering terms as a distortion of an interpersonal relationship in which a role of dominance takes on an unmodulated brutal form of expression by virtue of the individual's being unable to take simultaneously the reciprocal role of submission. One would expect that individuals who evidence this type of primitive sequential decentering in their social behavior would have particular difficulty in coordinating the perspectives of dominant and submissive characters in their RTT performance. This conception of symptomatic behavior is elaborated upon elsewhere and is currently being subjected to empirical evaluation with appropriate clinical groups. It is hoped that the results of these studies will provide further information concerning the relationship between individual processes and social interaction as interpreted in terms of the decentering concept.

References

BUCHSBAUM, B. (1965), 'The effects of frustration of interrupted play on cognitive level as a function of age', unpublished doctoral dissertation, Yeshiva University.

CANDELL, P. (1965), 'Social egocentrism as a function of cognitive development and social withdrawal', unpublished honors thesis, Clark University.

FEFFER, M. (1959), 'The cognitive implications of role-taking behavior', *J. Pers.*, vol. 27, pp. 152–68.

FEFFER, M., and GOUREVITCH, V. (1960), 'Cognitive aspects of role-taking in children', *J. Pers.*, vol., 28, pp. 384–96.

FLAVELL, J. (1963), *The Development Psychology of Jean Piaget*, Van Nostrand.

PIAGET, J. (1948), *The Moral Judgement of the Child*, Free Press.

PIAGET, J. (1950), *The Psychology of Intelligence*, Harcourt, Brace & World.

PIAGET, J. (1962), *Plays, Dreams, and Imitation in the Child*, Norton.

RAPAPORT, D. (1946), *Diagnostic Psychological Testing*, vol. 2, Year Book Publishers.

THORNDIKE, R. L., and LORGE, I. (1944), *The Teacher's Word Book of 30,000 Words*, Teachers College, Columbia University, Bureau of Publications.

WOLFE, R. (1963), 'The role of conceptual systems in cognitive functioning at varying levels of age and intelligence', *J. Pers.*, vol. 31, pp. 108–23.

14 Erving Goffman

Relations in Public

Excerpts from E. Goffman, *Relations in Public*, 1971, pp. 80–91, 138–48; Allen Lane The Penguin Press.

Having progressed from the lay term 'greeting' to the concept 'access ritual', let us examine some of the things that can be said about this behavior.

As is true of other arrangements within the domain of public order, the expectation that an access ritual will be performed by a certain person at a certain moment establishes a time–person slot such that anything issuing from him at that moment can be very closely and imaginatively read for a functional equivalent of an access ritual. Certainly physical gestures can be used instead of words and a wide range of constraining contingencies will be seen as sufficient reason to allow use of quite atypical equivalents. Indeed, a jokester can suppress all response to a salutation while looking into the faces of those who provide it and know that if he breaks into a smile just at the point when his return salutation should have ended, that the others will display a little laugh to show that they get the point that a friendly joke was being played. The jokester, in brief, can count on those who make the first move retrospectively reading the *absence* of any reply as a joking statement that was going on all the time. Social nature abhors an empty slot. Anything can be dumped in it and read as the anticipated reply. It is in this light that we are to understand the oft-remarked fact that when A asks B how he is feeling, the questioning is not to be taken literally; a question is not being asked, a greeting is being extended.[1] The answer provided is not an answer but an independent greeting, one available to second speakers. If identificatory sympathy alone were involved, then we might expect some reciprocity as in the following sequence:

A: 'How are you?'

1. One qualification ought perhaps to be allowed. When the recipient of a greeting is a hopeless invalid with a painful disease or someone who has just sustained an overwhelming personal loss, the greeter may feel a trifle uneasy about using the standard form, 'How are you?' Halfway through the offering the greeter might find himself giving feeling to his words, and that, of course, would be disastrous. Emily Post recognizes that the recipient, too, might be uneasy about using the standard return in these circumstances and recommends, 'All right, thank you.'

B: 'Fine, thanks.'
B: 'And how are you?'
A: 'Fine, thanks.'

But in passing greetings, in fact, we often find *in toto* the following:

A: 'How are you?'
B: 'Fine.'

which denies reciprocity. Or solely the following:

A: 'How are you?'
B: 'How are you?'

which omits all answering. Indeed, if the context is right, then one individual's statement can be taken as a functional equivalent for the full interchange. Thus, when one individual races past another in order, say, to catch up with some friends, the racer may be thrown a hello whose tone and gesture will suggest that it is understood that no answer will be possible, or he himself may initiate the ritual with a wave of his hand and a half-twist of his upper trunk, a greeting the reply to which his forward movement will obviously prevent him from witnessing. Thus the following:

A: 'Helloooo'
B: (gone)

A: 'Can't stop'
B: —

We find these apparently incomplete variants because they are functionally equivalent to the complete form.

Although I have classed various greetings together, it is obvious that a significant difference exists among them. The 'hi' one laconically employs when passing a neighbor each day would not be appropriate, indeed would be a sign of trouble in a relationship, if extended to someone known to have been away a long time or known to have been a great distance away and cut off from contact.[2] Instead of 'hi's', 'hello's' would probably be exchanged, followed by a spate of grooming talk. The restoration of one self to another self would have to be celebrated.

What is said here about greetings can also be said about farewells. If the

2. Before the advent of jet airplanes, the time during which an individual was away from his neighborhood and the distance over which he had travelled were nicely correlated; both variables could be managed in the same simple ritual equation. One of the novel aspects of the recent space voyages (it is said there are others) is that men who warranted the biggest goodbye and hello in the world had been gone for only a few days.

leave-takers are merely going back into the same felt probability of contact from which they came, and if this probability is high, then a phrase such as 'see you' or 'so long' may well be employed; on the phone, currently, it is 'b'bye'. But if the departure is to a place which for a time will render contact costly, then something more serious is likely to be said, namely, 'Goodbye'.[3] And similarly, when one 'moves on' from a conversational circle during a party or business occasion, there being an expectation that coparticipation in conversation will soon recur, an 'excuse me' or a hand gesture may be all that is given.

In considering the appropriate expansiveness of access rituals, I have tacitly kept constant the closeness of the relationship binding the two individuals who perform the display to each other. But obviously, of course, a long-absent neighbor will ordinarily be owed less of a show than a long-absent brother. However, relationships themselves carry an implication of probability of contact, and so the two factors, degree of access and closeness of relationship, are not independent. This is nicely seen in traditional etiquette, which seemed to recognize that the farewell given a stranger should be distinctive, in part, perhaps, because he might never be met with again:

A lady terminates an interview with a stranger who has come to see her on business, by bidding him 'Good afternoon'. On like occasions she would say 'Good morning' or 'Good evening', but not 'Good-bye' or 'Good night' – both of which are said to friends (Post, 1937, p. 21).

In any case, it must be admitted that rituals of greeting and farewell are responsiveness not merely to the issue of access but also to the kind of ritual licence binding the performers; thus, presumably 'Hi' would not be appropriate coming from a subordinate to a very sacred official, even though the two parties enjoyed an environment in which contact between them was, and was known to be, frequent.

As suggested earlier, the implication is that in many cases an appreciation of the probability and costs of contact is built into a relationship, and, in consequence, any return to a wonted ease of contact upon the termination of distancing circumstances warrants special celebration.[4]

3. Our term 'farewell' connotes a potentially permanent leave-taking, but now has a literary cast; the same can be said of the French 'adieu'.
4. This argument partly clears up an interesting ritual problem. When persons who are barely acquainted or not quite acquainted happen upon each other as tourists in a foreign land, they are likely to exchange expansive greetings and shows of pleasure and surprise at the prospect of being in each other's company. Why? One reason, I think, is that the two are suddenly forced into the status of persons close enough to know when there has been a marked increase in cost of contact between them – since it is now apparent to each that were he at home he would never be able to make contact

Given the above, we are to see that the following structural problem arises. On reattaining easy contact after an unusual separation, individuals owe each other an expansive greeting. However, the performance of this display will necessarily coincide with an increased likelihood of more frequent subsequent contact. If on each of these following contacts a full display were performed, the participants would soon find activity becoming clogged with ritual. An understanding must be available, then, whereby individuals can progressively leave off their initial obligation; there must be an 'attenuation rule'. Nowhere can this be seen more prettily than in the conduct of long-separated, closely related friends who newly come together during a social occasion. On first contact, an expansive greeting will occur. A moment later when the next proximity occurs, a reduced version of the initial display will be provided. Each succeeding contact will be managed with an increasingly attenuated greeting until after a time the two will exhibit the standard minimal middle-class social recognition only – a rapid grimace involving little change in eye expression, the two ends of the mouth stretching a little in a cheek flick. (After this point has been reached, the two may cooperate, of course, in seeing to it that one of them can act as though his eyes have not fallen on the other, thereby obviating all display, even the most attenuated.)

It should be noted that although an attenuation rule must be available in order to manage greetings, such a rule is not needed in regard to closing salutations simply because once a farewell occurs, departure is likely, which means that if matters go as expected, contact will be broken and additional ritual for the time becomes impossible.[5]

Another issue. When accessibility is about to shift markedly in either direction – typically involving geography – parties to a relationship may make special arrangements to come together for a sociable period just to mark the transition. Thus whenever close friends newly find themselves in the same country, region, city or neighborhood, they will often make a point of getting in touch, directly or by phone or mail, in order to mark the fact. Similarly, when a friend departs for a job in another state, enters the army, is to leave for an extended trip, or changes neighborhood or place of work, then the departure is likely to receive some ritualization: farewell parties are held and gifts may be given. Note that these ritual occasions are slotted into activity

---

with the other. But since at this very moment of discovery it costs nothing at all to groom each other, the opportunity to do so can hardly be forborne.

5. Attenuation has also been considered by ethologists in an evolutionary time frame in regard to changes in species performance and use of particular displays. Here see Moynihan, (1970).

at an opportune time. In case of greetings, there will be an economy of effort in waiting for easy contact before a supportive display is performed (and correspondingly, a heightened affront in not so using the opportunity); similarly, the point of leave-taking is the last moment when getting in touch is possible at reduced rates.

These expansive access ceremonies draw attention to an interesting issue, which linguists call embedding. The ritual recognition that is accorded a significant change in access (especially geographical access) can itself be a period of high access, as in the case of social parties, dinners-out, or telephone calls. But these little periods of open contact, being something in their own right and not merely the functional equivalent, say, of a gift, must themselves be marked and bounded by opening and closing salutations following the rule for handling periods of heightened access, whatsoever their cause. That the reason for being together is to celebrate a felt shift in access does not alter matters. Obviously, on first making contact with a friend on the occasion of a farewell dinner for him, one still says hello or its equivalent. One does not initiate the encounter or social occasion with a goodbye. And the final closing salutation will contain within it at least two notes, one attesting to a small period of open access that is about to terminate and a second, no doubt the more significant, attesting to the beginning of a shift downward in the economy and likelihood of such a contact occurring.

Access ceremonies of the extended kind exhibit in a marked way what is often found in brief salutations also, namely, a division in ceremonial labor: the division between guest and host. Leave-takers typically leave someone who remains to represent the prior social world, and those newly arriving are typically in a guest or visitor relation to those amongst whom they newly come. The same in fact can often be said about social occasions and the period of open access which they provide: the premises are likely to be under the jurisdiction of someone who is therefore in the host role, and the others who participate are likely to be in a guest role. The complication here is that what is owed an individual in terms of one's relationship to him can be different from what is owed him in his situationally generated role as guest. Indeed these obligations can be in opposition. Thus when a stranger from another city is brought along to a dinner by someone who himself is merely a guest, the host will be under special obligation to make the stranger welcome, and this to the degree that the stranger might doubt the appropriateness of his presence. In any case, we are to see that an opening greeting may take the asymmetrical form of a welcome, just as a closing salutation can take the asymmetrical form of a 'well-go', involving a nice-to-have-had-you on one side and a thanks-for-everything on the other.

Access ceremonies held in private homes have a relevantly troublesome feature. To greet someone in one's house who has recently come from far away is not to have availed oneself of prior opportunities that necessarily occurred when he came within practical reach. For one's house cannot be gotten to without first coming into one's country and city and neighborhood. Similarly, to say goodbye to a loved-one from one's doorstep when the leave-taker is to become quite inaccessible for a period is to disavail oneself of the opportunity to follow along with him to a somewhat later point in his departure, which is almost inevitably a practical possibility. These greetings and farewells understandably, then, want of something. And it is understandable that courtesy will often require that the arrival be met at the airport or station or dock – this being the first practical contact point – and be said goodbye to in the same setting. Long-distance travel by car solves this problem, particularly when the vehicle can be parked close outside the door.

Saying that greetings come at the beginning of increased access and farewells at the end, does not cover all the structural differences between these two rituals. Another is suggested here.

Since a greeting marks the initiation of a period of easier contact, the participants may be concerned to constrain their enthusiasm so that a misleading indication of what is to be expected will not occur. Closing salutations figure differently. Since the participants can assume that they soon will be less available to each other, at least for a time, the way is opened for supportive accesses which otherwise might create burdensome anticipations – a concern which often inhibits individuals from treating their associates too well. High praise and substantial offerings can be accorded since there will be no chance for this level of giving to be established as the norm. Desires for increased closeness and involvement can be expressed safely because there will be no chance to realize them. Reservations the senders-off have about the merit of the leave-taker are erased, because soon close evaluation will not be an issue. At the same time, the participants can demonstrate and affirm with only one down-payment that they are persons who give weight to the feelings and fate of others. The one qualification here, of course, is that favors extended at the beginning of increased access are likely to be easier to reciprocate than those extended at the beginning of decreased access, and this may influence the giver's decision as to when to give.

In the context of this difference between greetings and farewells, we can properly see another. In the main, greetings are oriented to the lapsed time of no contact that is now terminated, and once these rituals are performed, their significance cannot be undercut. A second and third recontacting following close on the first can carry a little reflected warmth as a means of preventing embarrassment to the initial greeting. And should anticipated contact fail to occur for extraneous reasons, disappointment can be felt, and there the matter can rest. Farewells, on the other hand, are situated in a fundamentally different way in regard to the management of relationships. A farewell is oriented not to the termination of the social occasion or sociable moment wherein it takes place but to the sharp decrease that is about to occur in the possibility of such comings-together again occurring – at least for a time. And the more lengthy and absolute the predicted separation, the more expansive the ritual. Yet no matter how long and complete the anticipated separation, the fact that the participants are at the moment in easy access situates them favorably for the separation not to occur as planned. Farewells, in short, inevitably expose the participants to unanticipated recontacting. And should this occur, the performers will find that the ritual already performed is improperly profuse for what has turned out to be a short absence; yet there is no way to take it back. And if the actual departure then comes, the need will arise for a performance that has already been completed. Something has been 'worked through' which now must be, but cannot be, worked through again. A twinge of anomie results, the kind that comes about when ritual statements are made that undermine the idiom itself. All of this is exacerbated by the fact that when a person is accessible to others to a given degree, the social life that results takes this into consideration. Once he alters this accessibility downward, his social place begins to close up over him. Returning unexpectedly, he finds that there has begun to be no room for him.

Examples of the disordering effect of failed departures are numerous. An individual leaving a social party, having been given a handsome well-go by the host, discovers a block away that he must return to retrieve something left behind; the greeting that is due him on re-establishing easy access must be attempted in the face of a recently performed farewell which now proves to have been performed in vain. Another example often noted occurs in connection with ocean voyages. Shipboard friendships can be enthusiastically established, bringing together persons who would otherwise stay clear of each other, because it is evident that bondedness need not continue after the voyage. Promises to meet soon can be warmly exchanged when the ship docks, it being half-understood that these promises cannot or need not be honored. The activity associated with disembarkation, however, provides an arena where ensured farewelling cannot be accomplished because there is no way to identify in advance the point of last easy contact. Almost inevitably the full farewell is performed and then recontact occurs shortly. Something similar occurs when a friend is taken to a train and followed to the platform. The final farewell is readied and the stage cleared for its performance, but if the train does not pull out on cue, the developmental rhythm held natural for emotions is broken; the stayer and goer must face each other in the wings, the deadness of the wait an embarrassment to the animation which is to occur as the train pulls out.

Another standard example of spoiled ritual is the office departure ceremony. An employee leaving for another job in a different city or about to retire may be treated to some sort of party and a farewell gift collectively paid for. On unexpectedly having to stay, or to return after a very brief absence, the recipient will find that he has caused himself and the givers to participate in an inappropriate statement, yet one that cannot be unsaid. (The final example here, of course, is the Enoch Arden case in which a person returning unexpectedly finds not only that his place is no longer available to him, but that another person has filled it, thereby creating what may be worse than a sociological demise, namely, a sociological double.)[6]

There is yet another difference between greetings and farewells that is worth considering. The display owed a close friend at his departure upon a long and perilous voyage is nicely balanced in its way by what is owed him upon his safe return; the same balance is found between the muted greeting of two neighbors when stopping for a back-fence chat and the muted farewells they exchange upon termination of the small talk. Indeed, it might be thought that for every type of greeting there is a corresponding type of farewell. But this is not the case, and the reason is supplied by a very obvious feature of relationships. For relationships must begin and end. They can begin with a social introduction, and when they do, this greeting-like ritual must necessarily be light because there is yet hardly any relationship to warrant something deeper – at least ordinarily. Relationships *can* end through a process of very gradual attenuation, but they can also end violently, either because of bad feelings or because circumstances such as death or geography are about to make the participants totally inaccessible to each other. In these latter cases, a farewell can occur that marks the simultaneous termination of a moment or two of being in touch and the relationship that made being in

6. Failed departures, greeting obligations and attenuation rules can together give rise to some jumbled occasions. For example, in the United States in higher academic circles, fast travel, soft money and expanding occupational choice have led to considerable job mobility over distances, especially between the coasts, under circumstances where once a man has departed with suitable ceremony, he is likely to bob up again very soon on business, and then again and again and again. His first revisit is often marked with considerable social ritual; his ties are still warm, there is a chance he will change his mind and return, and there is an urge to ceremonially reinstate him as a member of the community. On the second revisit considerably less is made of him. By the third and the fourth, the attenuation rule will begin to govern, and his closest local friend may become his only one. Those involved will begin to seek for ritual rules that are in keeping with jet air travel.

touch in that way possible. The poignancy of such a ritual hardly has a parallel or opposite expression in what can occur in greetings.[7]

A last difference. Preparation for a greeting can be done at one's ease, since the person to be greeted is not then present to examine the preparatory effort and the feelings generated by having to engage in it. Preparation for a farewell can be a much more delicate operation, since one party may be less inclined than the other to get on with the inevitable, thereby obliging the other party to instigate the process in advance by cues that are effective but not blatant.[8] [. . .]

The structure of the remedial interchange

This analysis began on the most magisterial note I can attempt: moral rules and their function as the link between self and society. This led, with little loss of abstractness, to a consideration of deviations from the rules and the ritual dialogue that provides a remedy. But now it has been argued that moral claims are made with respect to a multitude of minor territories of the self, and that correctives for infraction are to be found in body gloss – the indignities of overacted gesticulation. This brings the study of remedial activity into the street, into the little interactions that are forgotten about as soon as they occur, into what serious students of society never collect, into the slop of social life. That is right where I want to continue to consider it, but now the focus will be on activity that occurs within encounters, activity involving statement-like moves directed to particular others who respond in a replying-like fashion so that something clearly like a dialogue results. In what follows, an attempt is made to build up a picture of immediate remedial interaction systematically, one step at a time. Some explication of the obvious is required and some repetition. My excuse for introducing detail really should be an apology for providing so little of it; for phenomenally speaking, remedial interchanges are of enormous importance. Middle-class children in our society are taught to preface every statement to an adult with a request or by-your-leave and to terminate every encounter, if not every interchange, with some version of thank you. They are taught a formal approach to social life; it is impressed upon them that all dealings, important or unimportant, extended or momentary, between the acquainted or unacquainted, mediated or face-to-face, in work or play, are to be treated as similar and isolable in that all are to be transacted from within ritual brackets. Transactions and dealings that share nothing else at all are made to

7. The exception occurs when an offspring introduces his new spouse to his parents, or when a parent introduces his new mate to his child by a previous spouse. Here full relationships may be ready to be taken up, awaiting only introductions.
8. Suggested by William Labov (in correspondence).

share this; all are to be tied up with the same ribbon. These teachings are reinforced throughout life. Among adults in our society almost every kind of transaction, including every coming together into a moment of talk, is opened and closed by ritual, if not remedial then supportive. This infuses into every area of life – harsh, easy, personal and impersonal – a constant checking back to, and reminder of, a small number of central beliefs about the rights and character of persons.

Start the analysis, then, with a little street incident:

One pedestrian trips over another, says 'Sorry', as he passes, is answered with 'Okay', and each goes on his way.

It appears that three different elements are involved in the incident. First, as already suggested, are the virtual considerations: offence, offender and victim. Here, at worst, the offender can be seen as someone with no control over his body, no reign on his intent, and the victim as someone over whose territoriality no one need concern himself; or, in slightly different circumstances, the offender can give the impression that he might be trying to create a showdown purposely. Second is the ritual work that is performed in the situation. Here the apology and its acceptance. Third is the 'deed', the act – real, not virtual – which otherwise might be an offence but for the ritual that is performed in association with it, this work functioning to modify the worst possible implications of what in fact has occurred. A deed, then, is an act whose meaning is addressed by ritual work that is designed to establish what this meaning will be, the work itself being oriented to a worst possible reading of the deed; it is an act claimed as something not to be seen in any light other than the one provided by the remedial activity. In the incident under question, the deed is the striking of one foot by another, and the reading that is pressed is that it was an unintentional act expressing minor clumsiness, for which the actor is sorry.

By according one turn at talking to a line, by letting letters stand for persons, and by allowing the end of the transcription to mark the end of the ritual work that seemed directly oriented to the incident in question, the entire interaction can be recorded as follows:

Deed: A trips over B

A   'Sorry'

B   'S'okay'[9]

9. The interchanges in this paper are drawn from notes taken on actual interaction, except where quite stereotyped or apocryphal interplay is cited. I have done this because it is easier to record interactions or cull them than to make them up. In all cases, however, their intended values is not as records of what actually happened, but as illustrations of what would be easily understandable if they had happened and had happened with the interpretive significance I give them.

The ritual work described allows the participants to go on their way, if not with satisfaction that matters are closed, then at least with the right to act as if they feel that matters are closed and that ritual equilibrium has been restored. If any discontent remains within either party, presumably it will have to be expressed or exhibited at some other time. In other words, after the ritual work, the incident can be treated as though it were closed. So the 'round' that has occurred is also a complete interchange.

It would seem that instead of providing an apology, the virtual offender could play through the sequence by providing an account ('Have to catch that train.'), or a request ('May I get through?'), or a combination of two or three ('Sorry, may I get through, I have to catch a train.'), and that at some level of analysis, these function in exactly the same way as does an apology. Instead, then, of speaking of an apology (or an account or a request), we might speak of a 'remedy', designating by this term what is common to the way in which the three ritual moves function in the remedial dialogue.

Similarly, whereas it might be said that the virtual victim accepted an apology, or granted a request, or saw an account as sufficient, it is plain that here, too, a functional equivalence is found. In fact, if we treat as the same, things that have the same ritual consequences, then still other possibilities must be added. In the case of requests, the person asked can give an 'acceptable' reason why his granting of it must be postponed or even denied. Such an 'accounted denial' need but express that the asker was right in making his request and that the person asked is sympathetic to the plea; thereby the ritual implications of a denial can be held in check even though the asker is literally denied. Here, too, we need a term for referring to the responses to a remedy by what is common functionally to them. For want of a better word, I shall speak here of 'relief'.

remedy A   'Would you pass the milk?'
  relief B   'Gee, I'm sorry. There doesn't
      seem to be any left in the pitcher.'

It is apparent that when the victim provides a sign that the remedy offered by the offender is sufficient, then this places the offender under some obligation to show gratitude or thankfulness, this counting as a third basic move in the remedial sequence. In brief, appreciation or thanks can be given:

    remedy A   'Would you pass the milk?'
      relief B   'Here.'
  appreciation A   'Thanks.'[10]

10. It has been argued that in the West historically, there were two basic appreciations. One, involving our current terms, expressed that the receiver also could be a giver. The other, using phrases such as 'God bless you', expressed gross inequality, namely, that the recipient never would be in a position to reciprocate the relief, at least not to he who had given it to him. Here see the comment by Bourguignon (1962).

Note, this appreciation is owed the victim not merely as evidence that the offender is fully alive to the virtual offence and desirous of dissociating himself from the sort of person who would commit it, but also as proof that he is alive to the norms and practices associated with the management of negative sanctions. Appreciation, then, informs the victim that his act as someone who generously handles his role in sanctioning is respected and, incidentally, provides evidence that the offender possesses at least one of the traits of character of a worthy person, namely aliveness to favors done him.[11] Again we have a general term covering acts that are phenomenally different but functionally equivalent, that is, they fall into the same slot in the remedial sequence and perform the same work in ritual interchanges. It is understandable, then, that an accounted denial, being ritually equivalent to the granting of a request, should lead the person thus denied to terminate the interchange with an appreciation move, in this case phrases such as 'Thanks anyway', 'That's all right', or 'I understand'

Following this third move is sometimes found a fourth, namely, an act on

11. Signs of thanks or gratitude often function also as a means of closing out an encounter. This leads to some otherwise strange behavior. Employers who draw an employee aside to tell him privately that he is being let go may find that the termination interview is terminated by the employee thanking the employer. Similarly, Walter Clark, a student of the Berkeley police, reports that when an officer gives a traffic ticket to a motorist, the latter often will terminate his dealings with the officer by saying 'Thank you', which can puzzle the recipient and make him feel that to respond with 'You're welcome' would be awkward. No doubt a factor here is that the motorist may feel he has not been treated as badly as he might, which, indeed, is often the case, since officers routinely understate actual speed on a ticket in order to have a basis of control over those they ticket. In part, however, employees being fired and motorists being fined say thank you because that is a way encounters are closed out. The same seems to be the case in regard to the airline hijacker who pays for the drink he orders and thanks the pilot when the latter, on request, offers a light (*Philadelphia Bulletin*, 14 April 1969). I might add (as previously implied) that since requests provide proper ways of initiating certain encounters and interchanges, we can find politeness at both ends of a transaction in circumstances where this might not be expected. Thus, during the Great Train Robbery when the handcuffed fireman was allowed to smoke, the following apparently took place: 'Then seeing the tempting smoke rising from the fireman's lowly position, the robber [guarding him] said, longingly, "I want one, if you have one to spare." The fireman politely passed up his lighter; and the man who had just robbed a train of millions, having cadged a light and a fag, thanked him courteously for both' (Fordham, 1965, p. 88). The close analysis of what robbers *actually* say when they confront their victims hardly has begun. Newspapers print purported records of savageries and marked gallantries, but ordinary details go unreported. How, for example, does a robber ask a victim where the bathroom is? How does he initiate the interchange? How does he terminate it? If a robber chooses to answer a ringing phone, what does he say? And how does he sign off? Where, if anywhere, is ritual bracketing not employed? The point, of course, is that we are not dealing here with 'politeness', but rather with rules for opening and closing encounters and interchanges.

the part of the victim that repeats in diminished form the relief he provided as the second move, shows appreciation of the appreciation shown him, and rather fully terminates the interchange. In current American speech, examples of this are: 'You're welcome', 'That's all right', 'Think nothing of it', or 'It's okay'. The effect is that the victim graciously makes light both of what he has foregone or suffered and of the quality of character he must have to make light of this sort of thing. This move I shall call a 'minimization'. It completes the full expansion of the basic remedial cycle, describable as follows:

Deed: A virtually offends B
      remedy A 'Can I use your phone to make a local call?'
        relief B 'Sure, go ahead.'
  appreciation A 'That's very good of you.'
  minimization B 'It's okay.'

Between the first round in the remedial cycle (remedy and relief), and the second (appreciation and minimization) is a shift in concern from the issue of the norm that was violated to the way the participants handle their management of infractions. Note, too, that between the first and second round there is in effect a rule of attenuation, a rapid diminution of ritual activity associated with the ritually relevant event. Relief creates the need for appreciation; the latter creates the need for a minimization. But by the time this fourth move is made, the participants can let go and go on with the other business at hand. And there is good reason for this. As will be considered later, any ritual move can be seen as putting the mover in some kind of jeopardy and thereby generating a need for a saving response from the other parties. Every second move thus becomes itself a first move requiring its own second move. If each succeeding move were not attenuated quickly, ritual would come to take all of everyone's time. Each occasion on which a remedy was provided would lock the provider and recipient into an interminable 'After you, Alphonse' routine. Understandably then, remedial interchanges often terminate after the second move, that is, after relief is given, and when appreciation *is* provided, the final move in the full sequence, namely, minimization, may not occur (resulting in a three-move interchange) or do so in an almost imperceptible form.

Until now, the discussion has tacitly assumed that a turn at talking (what in linguistics is sometimes called, with unclear warrant, an 'utterance') and a ritual move are much the same, all of what an individual does and says during his turn at bat constituting one ritual move. But when we examine actual turns at talking, this often proves not to be the case:

A 'I'm taking the rake. Okay? Thanks.'
B 'Sure. Nothing at all.'

What we appear to have here are turns at talk, each of which involves more than one ritual move of an interchange in progress. (The first turn involves a request and an appreciation, the second, relief and minimization.) In short:

A request/appreciation
B relief/minimization

If, instead, B omitted the 'Nothing at all', then the interchange would have the following structure:

A request/appreciation
B relief/—

and if B omitted the 'Sure', then, as follows:

A request/appreciation
B —/minimization

The remedial interchanges thus far described could be ones that 'exhaust' the encounters in which they occur; a state of talk is opened with the first move of the interchange and closed with the last. (The same could be said for many 'supportive interchanges', involving the exchange of greetings and the like; they, too, can exhaust the encounter in which they occur.) Such 'encounter interchanges' are extremely common, comprising, it seems, the bulk of the focused interaction that occurs in public places, but, of course, there are encounters that are merely opened by such an interchange, or merely closed, the encounter itself containing many interchanges. If, for purposes of analysis, we can assume that the encounter proceeds by these ritually closed spurts and is compounded entirely from them,[12] then the question arises as to how these interchanges are linked or chained.[13] If we restrict ourselves to two-person talk and to two-move interchanges, that is, ones made up entirely from one exchange or round, and if we use superscripts to designate second and further interchanges, some rough answers can be suggested.

Two linkages seem obvious and basic. First, he who makes the initial move in one interchange can make the initial move in the next interchange:

A^1 'Where have you been?'
B^1 'The bookstore.'
A^2 'Get anything?'
B^2 'No.'

12. This argument is made in Goffman (1955).
13. I take the term 'chain' and the question it implies from Harvey Sacks. In his unpublished papers he considers, for example, the organization of rounds involving more than two speakers.

Second, he who makes the terminal move in one interchange can make the initial move in the next:

A[1]   'Where have you been?'
B[1]/B[2]   'The bookstore./Did you fix the tap?'
  A[2]   'No.'

The latter form involves a turn at talking that contains two moves. It suggests a third possibility, one already considered in connection with moves within an interchange, namely, an opening turn at talking that itself contains two first moves, leading to a second turn at talking that contains two second moves. This is commonly found in service encounters. Once a customer enters the area or 'post'[14] where his presence functions as a summons, the server is likely to provide a greeting and an offer of service, thus combining the beginning of a supportive interchange with the beginning of a remedial one. The same sort of linking is found in encounters between friends:

A[1]/A[2]   'Hi./Say, I owe you five bucks. Here.'
B[1]/B[2]   'Hi./I'd forgotten.'

Finally, there is a linkage that corresponds closely with what linguists call 'embedding', here meaning the inclusion of one interchange within brackets established by another:[15]

A[1]   'What'll ya have?'
B[2]   'Ya got those almond things?'
A[2]   'Not today, honey.'
B[1]   'Black coffee and a toasted muffin.'

  Once some basic linkages are described, we can expand the analysis by including interchanges containing more than two moves and linkages between the linkages, but although it is easy to record and transcribe these lattices, it is less easy to find additional reasons for doing so.

  Earlier it was suggested that in the fully expanded remedial cycle – remedy, relief, appreciation, minimization – the second pair of moves involves a shift in concern from the instigating virtual offence to the manner employed in dealing with it, and that these two moves (appreciation and minimization) are likely to be attenuated. Given these differences between the first and second round of the full remedial cycle, we can anticipate a degree of organizational looseness between them. At least at certain levels of determination,

  14. This term is taken from an unpublished paper (1968) by Marilyn Merritt, 'On the service encounter'.
  15. Here I draw on the very nice treatment by Emanual Schegloff of Columbia University in a forthcoming paper. His term for it is 'insertion sequence'.

it appears that the participants in a remedial interchange have a choice as to whether they will terminate matters with one round or go on to introduce a second.

This looseness suggests a parallel in the linkage of interchanges in an encounter. For it seems to be the case that when one or both of the participants in a conversation are not particularly primed for its maintenance, the talk will proceed by two-move couplets, each fairly closed ritually, with considerable choice as to whether any current round will be followed by a next. Consider, for example, one student (A) borrowing a pen from another student (B), the pen turning out to be one with a nib, and consider the apparent arbitrariness of the length of the chain:

A^1 'Pen?'
B^1 'Here.'
A^2 'I like that nib.'
B^2 'I always use that kind.'
A^3 'Me, I always lose them.'
B^3 'That's the trouble.'
A^4 'Still.'
B^4 'Ya.'
A^5 'It's very light.'
B^5 'It's light.'

The same could be said about standard interrogation-type encounters not directly remedial in character in which a chain of three-move interchanges can be expanded or contracted almost at the interrogator's will, he being the one to take two-move turns at talking:

A^1	'Did you read *Red Harvest*?'
B^1	'No, I missed that one.'
A^1/A^2	'Terrific./Did you read *The Glass Key*?'
B^2	'No, but I saw the picture. I liked it.'
A^2/A^3	'Was better than the book./You see "The Maltese Falcon"?'
B^3	'Ya, it was swell.'
A^3/A^4	'It was better than the book, too./You like Ambler?'
B^4	'I've read him all, but I don't know, I don't think I like him much.'
$A^4/$etc.	'I like him. /etc.'

Here again we can see the thrust of naturalistic analysis. Although the sentence is the traditional unit of linguistic study, it is apparent that a turn at talking may contain more than one of them; and yet a turn at talking is a natural unit in some respects. This unit itself may operate as one functionally differentiated move (such as a remedy or an appreciation) within the sequence of moves that comprise an interchange so that move and turn can be the same; but a single turn can also contain two such moves. Moreover, a single turn at talking can, as illustrated, contain the terminating move of one interchange and the opening move of another. Any technique, then, of quantitative analysis that takes the sentence as its codable unit, or even the turn at talking, is likely to average out some of the significant realities of the interaction.

References

BOURGUIGNON, E. (1962), 'On the dyadic contract', *Amer. Anthropol.*, vol. 64, no. 6, p. 1301.

FORDHAM, P. (1965), *The Robbers' Tale*, Hodder & Stoughton.

GOFFMAN, E. (1955), 'On face-work', *Psychiat.*, vol. 18, pp. 213–31.

MOYNIHAN, M. (1970), 'Control, suppression, decay, disappearance and replacement of displays', *J. Theoretical Biology*, vol. 29, pp. 85–112.

POST, E. (1937), *Etiquette*, Funk & Wagnalls; new edn, Cassells, 1969.

Part Five
Interaction in Groups and Organizations

Small social groups show all the phenomena found in groups of two. Bales (Reading 15) reports some of the results and ideas emerging from his studies of laboratory groups of five, using his twelve categories. This provides very interesting evidence about interaction sequences, and the development of equilibrium. It does not take account of specific non-verbal signals, which were not known about when this research was done. Sherif and Sherif (Reading 16) report a quite different kind of small group research – a field study of real groups of friends by interview and observation in the field. They obtained very useful information about conformity to different kinds of norm. The results should be treated as suggestive until confirmed by more rigorous inquiry.

In social organizations a number of new phenomena appear. The members have formal positions, and are related to each other as leaders and followers, or through the work-flow system. Blau and Scott (Reading 17) discuss the problems of hierarchical structures, and report a study of patterns of consultation and helping in a working hierarchy. A lot of thought is being put into how to change hierarchical structures to designs that are more efficient and more acceptable. One of the most important social skills inside organizations is leadership, at different levels. Fleishman and Harris (Reading 18) report a study showing the relations between two dimensions of supervisory style, and various measures of the job satisfaction of subordinates. This study is of particular interest in view of the great effect on the satisfaction measures, and because of the curvilinear relationships obtained – the worst supervisors had a particularly marked effect. Other studies have confirmed these results, and have also shown similar though smaller effects on productivity. The technology affects the organizational design, and hence the pattern of interaction and the organizational effectiveness. Emery and Trist (Reading 19) report two of the Tavistock's studies which showed that the same technology can be handled by different social systems. The most effective social systems had cooperative work-teams with a complete range of complementary skills.

15 Robert F. Bales

The Equilibrium Problems in Small Groups

Excerpt from T. Parsons, R. F. Bales and E. A. Shils (eds.), *Working Papers in the Theory of Action*, Free Press, 1953, pp. 115–34.

The profile of activity and the equilibrium problem

One of the interesting characteristics of interaction is the distribution of total number of acts among the twelve categories, according to quality. A distribution of this kind in percentage rates based on the total is called a profile. An illustrative comparison of group profiles of two five-man groups working on the standard diagnostic task is shown in Table 1.

Table 1 Profile of a 'satisfied' and a 'dissatisfied' group on case discussion task

Type of act	Meeting profiles in percentage rates			
	Satis-fied[a]	Dissatis-fied[b]	Average of the two	Average rates by sections
1 Shows solidarity	0·7	0·8	0·7	
2 Shows tension Release	7·9	6·8	7·3	25·0
3 Agrees	24·9	9·6	17·0	
4 Gives Suggestion	8·2	3·6	5·9	
5 Gives Opinion	26·7	30·5	28·7	56·7
6 Gives Orientation	22·4	21·9	22·1	
7 Asks for Orientation	1·7	5·7	3·8	
8 Asks for Opinion	1·7	2·2	2·0	6·9
9 Asks for Suggestion	0·5	1·6	1·1	
10 Disagrees	4·0	12·4	8·3	
11 Shows Tension	1·0	2·6	1·8	11·4
12 Shows Antagonism	0·3	2·2	1·3	
Percentage Total	100·0	100·0	100·0	100·0
Raw Score Total	719	767	1486	

[a] The highest of sixteen groups. The members rated their own satisfaction with their solution after the meeting at an average of 10·4 on a scale running from 0 to a highest possible rating of 12.

[b] The lowest of sixteen groups. Comparable satisfaction rating in this group was 2·6.

In the present illustration the 'satisfied' group attained a higher rate of suggestions, more often followed by positive reactions and less often by negative reactions and questions than did the 'dissatisfied' group.

The profiles produced by groups, however, are not completely and radically different from each other. The profile produced by the average of these two illustrative groups is more or less typical of averages of larger aggregates under laboratory standard conditions. Attempted answers, that is, giving orientation, opinion and suggestion, are always more numerous than their cognate questions, that is, asking for orientation, opinion or suggestion. Similarly, positive reactions, that is agreement, showing tension release, and solidarity, are usually more numerous than negative reactions, i.e. showing disagreement, tension and antagonism. Intuitively one would feel that the process would surely be self-defeating and self-limiting if there were more questions than answers and more negative reactions than positive.

On the average, for groups we have examined, the relations of amounts by sections are about as they are in the illustration. The relations between the amounts can be viewed as the final result of a repetitive series of cycles, each of which consists of: (1) an initial disturbance of the system (precipitated by the introduction of a new idea, or opinion, or suggestion into the group) followed by (2) a 'dwindling series of feedbacks' and corrections as the disturbance is terminated, equilibrated or assimilated by other parts or members of the system. Attempted answers, or as one might call them for the moment, 'initial acts', account for a little over half (or 57 per cent) of the total activity, with positive and negative reactions and questions accounting for the other half, roughly.

Looking at the *Reaction* side alone, and assuming it to be 50 per cent of the total, about half the reactions (or 25 per cent of the total) are positive and presumably terminate the disturbance introduced by the initial action. The other half of the time the reaction fails to terminate the disturbance. Of this non-terminating portion again, about half (or 12 per cent of the total) are negative reactions, which typically precipitate another attempted answer, thus beginning a repetition of the cycle. Of the remaining hypothetical 13 per cent or so, about half (or 7 per cent) are questions, which also typically precipitate another attempted answer. If about 7 per cent of attempted answers are in direct response to questions, these might well be called 'reactions', thus leaving the relation of 'initial acts' to 'reactions', thus leaving the relation of 'initial acts' to 'reactions' about 50–50, as assumed above. One might say that quantitatively (as well as qualitatively, by definition) interaction is a process consisting of action followed by reaction. The balance of action with reaction is one of the equilibrium problems of the system.

Act-to-act tendencies and the equilibrium problem

A more detailed understanding of the equilibrating tendencies by which the characteristic profile arises may be obtained by examining the frequencies with which each type of activity tends to be followed by each other type. Two input–output matrices showing these act-to-act tendencies are presented in Tables 2 and 3. These particular matrices were obtained by tabulation from the interaction tapes of the total sixteen sessions of the four five-man groups of the present observation series. The total number of output acts occurring after each input type of act is considered as 100 per cent, and the probabilities for each type of output act are derived by a percentage breakdown.

It will be noted that two matrices are presented, one called a matrix of proactive tendencies, and the other a matrix of reactive tendencies. A single matrix could be produced, of course, by omitting this distinction, but such a matrix would ignore the fact that the action 'changes hands' at certain points, from one member to another. And this fact is crucial, since the equilibrium problem of social systems is not simply one of a certain 'balance' in the relation of qualitatively different types of acts to each other, as shown by the profile. It is at the same time, and just as intrinsically, a problem of a certain balance in the way in which these activities are distributed between separate members. The distinction beteen 'proaction' and 'reaction', for the matrices presented, hinges on the member-to-member oscillation of activity. Very simply, an act which is a direct continuation by the *same* member who has produced the last act is called 'proactive'. An act which follows immediately the last act of *another* member is called 'reactive'.

The distinction is based on a suggestion by Murray:

I ... suggest ... that the term *proaction*, in contrast to *reaction*, be used to designate an action that is not initiated by the confronting external situation but spontaneously from within. An action of this sort is likely to be part of a serial program, one that is guided by some directional force (aim) which is subsidiary to a more distally oriented aim. As a rule, a proaction is not merely homeostatic, in the sense that it serves to restore the organism to a previously enjoyed equilibrium or state of well-being. If successful, it results in the addition or production of something – another bit of physical construction, let us say, or more money in the bank, or greater social cohesion, or another chapter of a novel, or the statement of a new theory. The integrates of serials, of plans, strategies, and intended proactions directed toward distal goals constitute a large portion of the ego system, the *establishment* of personality which inhibits impulses and renounces courses of action that interfere with progresss along the elected paths of life (Murray, 1951, pp. 439–40).

The operational definition of the distinction for purposes of tabulating from interaction records does not correspond perfectly to Murray's theoretical

Table 2 Matrix of proactive tendencies output probabilities for a given input, sixteen meetings of five-man groups

Category of prior act (input type)	Category of following act (output)												Total per cent
	1	2	3	4	5	6	7	8	9	10	11	12	
1 Shows solidarity, raises other's status, gives help, reward		6·8	9·1	22·7	29·5	18·2		4·5	2·2			6·8	99·8
2 Shows tension release, jokes laughs, shows satisfaction	1·6	37·5	1·6	6·3	21·9	9·4	0·8	1·6	2·3	3·1	3·9	10·2	100·2
3 Agrees, shows passive acceptance, understands, concurs, complies	3·0	4·6	6·6	9·7	41·6	22·1	2·8	2·1	0·7	5·1	0·8	0·8	99·9
4 Gives suggestion, direction, implying autonomy for other	2·6	4·8	1·6	55·6	19·3	9·6	1·0	2·6	0·6	1·0	1·0	0·3	100
5 Gives opinion, evaluation, analysis, expresses feeling, wish	2·3	4·4	1·6	5·0	60·1	17·0	1·8	4·4	0·7	0·9	1·4	0·3	99·9
6 Gives orientation, information, repeats, clarifies, confirms	0·2	2·1	0·2	3·4	22·6	61·4	4·7	2·8	1·3	0·4	0·8	0·2	100·1
7 Asks for orientation, information, repetition, confirmation	1·1	1·1	1·1	6·5	19·4	38·7	21·5	7·5	1·1	1·1	1·1		100·2
8 Asks for opinion, evaluation, analysis, expression of feeling		3·2		9·7	31·2	26·9	4·3	19·4	2·2	2·2	1·1		100·2
9 Asks for suggestion, direction, possible ways of action	3·2	6·5		16·1	22·6	19·4	3·2		19·4	6·5		3·2	100·1
10 Disagrees, shows passive rejection, formality, withholds help	1·2	2·5	1·6	6·6	51·4	21·8	4·1	2·5	0·8	1·6	5·3	0·4	99·8
11 Shows tension, asks for help, withdraws 'out of field'		4·2	2·1	8·3	45·8	35·4		2·1			2·1		100·0
12 Shows antagonism, deflates other's status, defends or asserts self	5·9	27·5		5·9	19·6	7·8	5·9	2·0			3·9	21·6	100·1

Table 3 Matrix of reactive tendencies output probabilities for a given input, sixteen meetings of five-man groups

Category of prior act (input type)	Category of following act (output)												Total per cent
	1	2	3	4	5	6	7	8	9	10	11	12	
1 Shows solidarity, raises other's status, gives help, reward	28.4	11.9	3.0	13.4	14.9	11.9	4.5	4.5	1.5	3.0	1.5	3.0	100.0
2 Shows tension release, jokes, laughs, shows satisfaction	0.7	68.2	3.2	3.1	10.2	6.7	2.2	1.5	0.3	1.7	0.6	1.5	99.9
3 Agrees, shows passive acceptance, understands, concurs, complies	0.6	2.7	15.9	8.5	40.8	21.4	2.3	3.0	0.9	2.7	1.0	0.2	100.0
4 Gives suggestion, direction, implying autonomy for other	1.3	6.7	46.0	8.6	9.2	8.8	2.3	1.5	1.5	12.4	1.3	0.4	100.0
5 Gives opinion, evaluation, analysis, expresses feeling, wish	0.6	4.3	48.9	2.2	19.2	6.3	2.3	2.8	0.3	11.8	0.6	0.6	99.9
6 Gives orientation, information, repeats, clarifies, confirms	0.6	5.8	35.0	3.6	15.2	24.0	5.6	1.3	0.4	5.7	1.1	1.7	100.0
7 Asks for orientation, information, repetition, confirmation		1.0	3.6	0.7	10.0	73.7	5.6	1.0	0.3	1.6		0.7	100.2
8 Asks for opinion, evaluation, analysis, expression of feeling	1.5	5.4	9.2	2.4	45.9	13.2	10.7	3.0	0.5	4.4	2.0	2.0	100.2
9 Asks for suggestion, direction, possible ways of action		13.2		35.8	28.3	9.4	1.9	1.9		3.8	3.8	1.9	100.0
10 Disagrees, shows passive rejection, formality, withholds help	0.3	6.6	12.4	5.2	25.0	13.5	3.6	2.0	0.3	24.2	3.9	3.0	100.0
11 Shows tension, asks for help, withdraws 'out of field'	4.1	7.2	5.2	2.1	39.2	22.7	2.1	4.1		4.1	9.3		100.1
12 Shows antagonism, deflates other's status, defends or asserts self	1.0	18.1	4.8	3.8	12.4	11.4	1.0	3.8		5.7	1.9	36.2	100.1

distinction, but the basic idea is the same. In face-to-face interaction it is true by and large that the first act of a person following the last act of some other is 'provoked' by the last act of the other as the 'stimulus' and thus has a 'reactive' quality. Conversely, it is sufficiently true that as a person continues talking his activity tends to change to a 'proactive' quality, directed adaptively and instrumentally to the achievement of more distant aims. The activity is now *directed toward* the external confronting situation, including the situation external to the group as a whole, rather than immediately *initiated by* it, as in the 'reactive case'. It might be noted in passing that the term 'initiation of action' is ambiguous, in that it is often defined empirically as the total of *all* types of activity 'given out' by a specific individual, but usually carries the theoretical *connotation* of 'proaction'.

The matrix of proactive tendencies shows very clearly that when the same person continues talking, after having given an act of orientation, opinion or suggestion, the probability is very high that he will continue with the same type of activity (probabilities of about 0·61, 0·60 and 0·55) presumably in a connected 'serial program', to use Murray's term. When he does not continue with the same precise category of activity, the probability is still relatively high that he will carry on in one of the three types called attempted answers. If his preceding act was a question of some type, and he continues himself instead of yielding the floor to some other, the highest probabilities are that he will either repeat or go directly ahead with an attempted answer. Indeed, the tendencies to continue proactively in the attempted answer area are very strong, even when the member has begun his participation with a reaction to the other. As we all know, an act of agreement is often a way of 'getting one's foot in the door' in order to go ahead and present one's own ideas. And similarly, when one has given a disagreement, he is very likely to go ahead and 'tell why'. In both of these cases, the tendency to present the argument in terms of 'opinion' rather than 'facts' is notable.

If the preceding reaction was far over on the affective side, however, there are appreciable tendencies for the member to continue in the affective area. If one's former act was a display of antagonism, the present act is likely to be another, unless it passes over into tension release, either of which is more probable than a direct return to the task area. Similarly, when the last act was one of tension release, the next act is likely to be *another* act of tension release, and the tendency to continue with an act of antagonism (possibly a joking one) is still appreciable. Once such a cycle of antagonism and tension release is set in motion, it appears to have a tendency to continue until presumably the major potential of implicit tension is 'bled off' to a substantially lower level. Similar cycles also appear between showing solidarity and showing tension release, although they do not appear on this matrix because of our scoring convention (now changed) of scoring 'jokes' in category two, as well as laughs. We now score the jokes themselves in either category one, or category twelve, according to whether the butt of the joke is outside the immediate group, or a member of it. This convention appears to us now to more satisfactorily represent affective dynamics of the process, but as a result of the change we obtain considerably more scores in category one than previously, and a few more in category twelve. The implication of the scoring change is simply that we now assume, on the basis of experience and intuition, that one of the reasons the number of acts in these two categories was formerly so low (of the order of 1 or 2 per cent) is that in our particular type of groups, the management of positive and negative affect is typically accomplished in a 'joking' rather than in a 'serious' manner. Whether joking or serious, however, these cycles of affective activity, once started, have a tendency to 'carry on', just as do the 'serials' of instrumental-adaptive activity.

As we think of the matter, the instrumental-adaptive activity of the preceding participant tends to build up tensions in the present participant to some point where he enters the process and changes to activity of an expressive-integrative relevance, which tends to 'bleed off' the tension to some point at which he changes the focus himself and continues again with instrumental-adaptive activity. The problem of equilibrium is essentially the problem of establishing arrangements (or an 'orbit of activity') whereby the system goes through a repetitive cycle, within which all of the disturbances created in one phase are reduced in some other. The dilemma of all action systems is that no one disturbance can be reduced without creating another.

The individual personality is such an action system, and some of its cyclical tendencies can be seen in the proactive matrix. The combination of two or more personalities in interaction, however, is also an action system. Indeed, this is the level on which the systematic properties can be seen most fully articulated in overt observable behavior. The 'switch-over' from reactive to proactive behavior can be seen in the individual person as he continues his participation, but the switch-over from proactive to reactive is most notable at those junctures in the process when the action changes hands. What happens to the quality of action when the action changes hands may be seen in the matrix of reactive tendencies.

When the prior act of another member has been an attempted answer, the highest probabilities are that the present act will be a positive reaction, specifically an agreement, rather than a continuation in the task area, although there are appreciable tendencies for the reacting person to continue directly with further opinion or information. Probabilities of positive reactions (for these groups) far outweigh probabilities of negative reactions, and this is generally true, though occasionally we observe groups where it is not the case.

Theoretically, we tend to assume that a preponderance of positive reactions over negative is a *condition* of equilibrium or maintenance of the steady state of the system. The reasoning goes something like this: We assume that the instrumental-adaptive goals of the system involve the maintenance of a certain level of accomplishment output, and that this level *tends to fall* without the constant application of effort, energy and activity applied successfully to the realities of the external situation. But the level of *accomplishment* cannot be maintained for long without also maintaining the level of diffuse *satisfaction*, which depends upon the achievement of expressive-integrative goals. The full stable 'orbit' will have to include tension release, gratification and a feedback of positive sanctions to the person(s) performing the instrumental activities, in such a way as to 'reinforce' them (in the learning theory sense), either in keeping them doing what they are doing, or in keeping them generalizing appropriately from their former accomplishments. Negative reactions tend to inhibit the behavior which preceded, but do not provide the basis for establishing a stable, positively defined orbit. Nor does generalization from negative reactions help appreciably in finding a positively defined orbit. It simply tends to cancel out or inhibit possible untried orbits, while the unstable 'seeking' or 'trial and error' fluctuation of the system continues.

Furthermore, each failure, and each negative reaction, tends to result *in its own right* in disturbance, and thus reduces the satisfaction levels directly. Assuming a quantitative equivalence of units of action observed (a shaky, but not inconceivable assumption), one might conclude that at least one positive reaction would be required for each negative reaction, simply to counteract the disturbances introduced by the negative reactions. On these assumptions, if positive reactions are only equal to negative reactions, the system barely manages to counteract the disturbances introduced by the 'friction' of its own controlling apparatus, and the accomplishment and satisfaction levels will tend to sink because of lack of effort and instrumental activity applied constructively and successfully to the situation of the system. One concludes that the accomplishment and satisfaction levels can only be maintained in a steady state if an orbit is found in which positive reactions preponderate over negative. The degree to which they must do so in order to maintain steady levels will then depend upon such factors as levels of expectation or aspiration, the stringency of situational demands, and the abilities or resources of the actors in relation to aspirations and situational demands.

One obvious inference from this theoretical formulation is that the levels of satisfaction of members at the end of a problem-solving attempt will be a function of the degree to which positive reactions have outweighed negative reactions during the process. The two illustrative profiles given earlier demonstrate this relation. There are a considerable number of ways of constructing single indices from the balance of rates in the profiles which give reasonably good predictions of satisfaction. We do not yet know which of these is best in general. Several we have tried tend to yield correlations with average satisfaction at the end of meetings ranging from about 0·6 to 0·8.

Another possible inference is that the satisfaction ratings of individual members will tend to be a function of the preponderance of positive reactions received over negative reactions received by that member. We have not thoroughly explored this hypothesis as yet but there are some indications that higher-status members tend to receive higher relative proportions of positive reactions, and in general have higher-satisfaction ratings. The degree of satisfaction, we believe, as a working hypothesis, tends to be highest with the members of highest status, and to grade down as status grades down. On the basis of the theory, however, one should definitely not expect perfect correlations, either between total group profiles and average post-meeting satisfactions, or between positive reactions received by individual members and their individual post-meeting satisfactions. The reason is that starting levels are typically not known, and that other factors such as stringency of situational demands, abilities or resources of the members, and the content and stringency of levels of expectation or aspiration are believed to be involved also. Much work remains to be done in this direction.

On the matrix of reactive tendencies it will be noted that the tendency to reply to an attempted answer of the other with a positive or negative reaction increases from a prior act of giving orientation to one of giving opinion, to one of giving a suggestion. One might say that the 'urgency' of giving a positive or negative reaction increases as the proaction becomes more 'directive' or 'constricting'. An act of giving orientation has only a probability of about 0·06 of provoking a disagreement. An act of opinion, however, has a probability of about 0·12 and an act of suggestion has a little higher probability. But an act of suggestion is a little less likely than an act of opinion to provoke an agreement. If one makes an index by representing the probability of disagreement as a percentage of the probability of agreement the index rises from 0·16 in response to an act of orientation, to 0·24 in response to an act of opinion, to 0·26 in response to an act of suggestion. The difference between the last two is very small, but in the expected direction. It should be pointed out that on the proactive matrix the probability that a member will follow a disagreement with an act of opinion is very high, 0·51. Consequently, the replies to opinion on the reactive matrix are often replies to an opinion which was in support of a still prior disagreement. If one took the trouble to segregate those cases where the acts of orientation, opinion and suggestion are given without prior disagreement, it is likely that the differences between them would be greater.

The notions that proaction is likely to provoke reaction, that the probability of reaction increases as the process passes from problems of orientation, to evaluation, to control, and that the reaction will tend to swing to the negative side as the implications of the acts become more 'directive' and 'constrictive' are fundamental to the theory of equilibrium problems in small groups. The problem appears in many guises, and solutions are worked out in many directions, as will appear later in the discussion of the way in which participation tends to get distributed between members, the way in which quality of activity tends to move through a series of phases constituting a closed cycle in time, the way in which number of members affects the process, the way in which differentiated roles tend to appear, and the way in which the structure of roles tends to shift though a series of meetings.

On the matrix of reactive tendencies the probabilities that a question from the other will provoke a complementary or cognate attempted answer are seen to be very high. There is perhaps nothing very remarkable about this, but it does provide evidence of a kind of 'reasonable continuity' in the process – the persistence of the system in an instrumental-adaptive direction of movement, once started, in spite of the fact that the action changes hands from one member to another. Questions provide a means of turning the process into the instrumental-adaptive direction of movement, with a low probability of provoking an affective reaction, and are an extremely effective way of turning the initiative over to the other.

Our impression is, however, that in our groups the number of questions which arise out of a self-conscious anticipatory attempt to guide the process in this way is comparatively small. They probably appear more often after strains arise out of earlier failures, as a result of disagreement, argument and 'backtracking' from premature attempts to proceed more 'directively'. Questions provide a 'neutral way out' – a 'patch-up' procedure of last recourse when negative reactions are anticipated if one goes ahead himself. At least this way of looking at the process gives a reasonable explanation as to why the rates of questions are in general so low (about half that of negative reactions). Questions constitute the last of the 'dwindling series of feedbacks' mentioned earlier, and tend to be called into play only after more direct and obvious feedback controls have failed to equilibrate the system. Since they tend to prevent the asker from going ahead to give his own ideas, they provide little opportunity to raise one's status, but rather hand this opportunity over to the other. Thus, one might suppose, where competition is high (as it is generally in our initially leaderless groups) there will be a tendency to avoid them except as a last resort. Those who have a fixed high status, and those who have essentially accepted a low status, can 'afford' to ask questions, but not those who are in the thick of competition.

The tendency for antagonism to provoke antagonism is even more marked when the action changes hands (in the reactive matrix) than when the same person continues (in the proactive matrix). Similarly, in the reactive matrix, showing solidarity tends to provoke a like reaction. Either type of marked affect tends to lead to tension release, and this type of activity, when once tripped off, is more likely to continue than any other type. 'Laughter is contagious' as the saying goes. In the present context it is another instance of the tendency of the system, once started, to continue in a given direction of movement until checked by other factors. It is interpreted as a mechanism by which massive changes in the tension level take place in a short length of time, and typically appears only periodically, with intervening periods of tension build-up, as will be pointed out later in the discussion of phase movement.

The interpretation of the rate of tension release for given groups is a vexed problem. According to our present thinking, a 'moderate rate' (around 7 or 8 per cent) is associated with successful equilibration after normal hazards. Very low rates lead us to expect high residual tension, and very high rates lead us to look for extraordinary sources of tension. Levels of satisfaction as measured by post-meeting questions would appear to give us some *entrée* to this problem, but the complex determinants of satisfaction have already been pointed out.

These problems of interpretation are general, however, not specific to certain types of acts or results of acts. The whole implication of an equilibrium theory as an interpretive device is that the determinants of any part of the process, or any result of it, are complex, and should be sought in some kind of complicated balance of the system as a whole, rather than in a maximization or minimization of supposedly isolated factors. The understanding of a *repeated* phenomenon in this type of approach lies in showing how it fits into a system, or constellation of interlocking systems, as one link in a closed, repetitive cycle of activities or orbit which constitutes the moving steady state of the system as its equilibrium is persistently disturbed and reestablished.

The who-to-whom matrix and the equilibrium problem

A further unfolding of the equilibrium problem may be seen by a closer examination of the way in which participation tends to be distributed among members. The total number of different possible combinations of who is speaking and to whom for a given time period is called a 'who-to-whom matrix'. The scoring system recognizes acts addressed to the 'group as a whole' as well as to specific individuals.

An aggregate matrix of a collection of eighteen sessions of six-man groups (all types of activity) is presented in Table 4 as an illustration. The aggregate matrix is produced by rank ordering the members of each separate session according to the total amounts of participation given out, and then summing together all rank one men, all rank two men, all rank one men speaking to all rank two men, etc.

Table 4 Aggregate who-to-whom matrix for eighteen sessions of six-man groups,[a] all types of activity

Rank order of person originating act	Speaking to individuals of each rank:						Total to individuals	To group as a whole	Total initiated
	1	2	3	4	5	6			
1		1238	961	545	445	317	3506	5661	9167
2	1748		443	310	175	102	2778	1211	3989
3	1371	415		305	125	69	2285	742	3027
4	952	310	282		83	49	1676	676	2352
5	662	224	144	83		28	1141	443	1584
6	470	126	114	65	44		819	373	1192
Total received	5203	2313	1944	1308	872	565	12,205	9106	21,311

[a] These groups were observed before the standard laboratory task was evolved. The general features of the standard groups are similar.

The pattern of distribution is different in detail under different conditions. For example, groups with no designated leader generally tend to have more equal participation than groups with designated leaders of higher status. However, in spite of these differences, the distribution of total amounts of participation of each member, as well as the pattern of who talks how much to whom (and how, qualitatively), seems to be subject to system-influences, which tend to produce similarities from group to group, and some regular gradations by group size.

These generalizations may be illustrated in part by reference to Table 4. If the personnel are arrayed in rank order according to the total amount they speak ('basic initiating rank') we then find that they are spoken to in amounts proportionate to their rank order. Roughly speaking, each man receives back about half as much as he puts out in total. It will be remembered that something like half of all interaction is 'reactive' and each man spends a certain portion of his time reacting to the initial acts of others. The amount of time spent reacting to specific other individuals rather than proacting to the group as a whole, however, differs according to the rank of the member. The profiles of participants tend to change systematically as we proceed downward in rank. High-ranking men tend to have more proactive attempted answers in their profiles and to address more acts to the group as a whole than lower-ranking men, while low-ranking men have more 'reactions', both positive and negative, and address more of their acts to specific individuals. Quantitative differentiation in participation is accompanied by, or is symptomatic of, qualitative differentiation of roles of members. For example, the top man tends to give out more information and opinion to specific individuals than he receives, while, on the contrary, low men give out more agreement, disagreement, and requests for information than they receive.

If this is true one might expect quantity of participation to be related to the status hierarchy of the members. We typically find that the order produced by ranking individuals according to their 'basic initiating rank' on total amounts of participation is fairly highly correlated with the order produced by their own ratings of each other as to 'productivity', i.e. who has the best ideas, and who does the most to guide the discussion effectively. Similar findings are reported by Norfleet (1948) and Bass (1949) with correlations of about 0·95 in each case. Strodtbeck (1951) finds in addition a fairly dependable connection between amount of activity given out and probability of winning in contested decisions, which is a kind of measure of power of influence. The empirical correlation between status in some generalized sense and amounts of participation given out and received seems to be pretty well established, but perfect correlation is definitely not to be expected in general.

Such approximate generalizations, once established, can typically be used to produce further valuable diagnostic information, as will be shown later. Any specific group, or some particular types of groups, may present exceptions, in one or more particulars, depending on the conditions operating. Exceptions to the empirical rule give the investigator the cue to look for exceptional conditions. For example, we have often found particular exceptions to the expected correlation between amount given out and amount received in cases where one of the members disagrees with the others persistently, and so tends to attract or receive a disproportionate amount of communication. Festinger and Thibaut (1950) have produced this effect experimentally. We have found similar exceptions to the generalization when two highly interactive and agreeing members form a sub-group or coalition *vis-à-vis* a third neglected or rejected member.

Size of group is obviously an important condition affecting the distribution of activities. From present indications it appears that the top man in groups larger than five or so tends to speak considerably more to the group as a whole than to specific individuals in the group, as in Table 4. All other members tend to speak more to specific individuals (and particularly to the top man) than to the group as a whole. Each man tends to speak to each other man in an amount which is a probability function of both his own rank on outwardly directed remarks, and the rank of the other on the receiving of communication (Keller, 1951). As groups increase in size, a larger and larger proportion of the activity tends to be addressed to the top man, and a smaller and smaller proportion to other members. In turn, as size increases, the top man tends to address more and more of his remarks to the group as a whole, and to exceed by larger amounts his proportionate share. The communication pattern tends to 'centralize', in other words, around a leader through whom most of the communication flows.

But if the situation is one in which *inter*action is expected by the participators, there would seem to be a top ceiling for the top man somewhere around 50 per cent, apparently connected with the general tendency for interaction under such expectations to come to a system-closure, such that each 'action' of one member, as it were, tends to be countered with a 'reaction' from some other. Even if the top man is initiating most of the action, he still has to expect that he will receive a 'feedback of reactions', both of a positive and negative sort, that will tend to equal the amount of action he initiates. It may very well be that the expectation of 'equality' which is so often present in groups of our culture, refers rather to this overall balance of action and reaction than to an equality of amounts of output of all members, which in practice, is never found.

Thus it can be seen that the differentiation between members as to specialized roles and status, is intimately related to the equilibrium problem. The tendency for the system, once started, to continue moving in the same direction until checked by opposing forces, is reflected in the tendency of given members to continue proacting until checked by other members. Negative reactions appear to act as such a check, presumably through learning mechanisms. Their regular appearance should be viewed as a check on the widening of status differences, as well as a result of 'objective mistakes' and task attempts which fail to appeal on other grounds. But if, as we have hypothesized, the system cannot maintain a steady state without a preponderance of positive reactions over negative, then in the equilibrated system more task attempts will be rewarded than punished, and they will be attempts by specific persons.

Here enters the crucial importance of 'generalization' in the learning theory sense. In so far as a given person 'gets on the right track' and receives positive reactions from other members, he will be reinforced in his direction of movement, and will tend to keep on talking. He will 'generalize' from the premises, logical and emotional, which underlay his original successful attempt. This is the 'growing point' of the system of common symbols or group culture, as well as of role differentiation. And reciprocally, the other members will 'generalize' from his earlier attempts, gratifying in some sense to them, to an expectation of further effective behavior on his part. The member begins to build a 'specialized role'. In so far as the activity he performs is felt to be important in terms of the functional problems of the group, its goals and value norms, the 'status' of the member will begin to rise. There will be a 'generalization' from the specific *performance* of the person to a *qualitative ascribed* 'position' in the group which bears a rank relation to other positions similarly developed. It is apparently in some such terms that one may understand the tendencies toward gross differentiation of amounts of participation given and received, the qualitative differences by rank, and above all, the emergence of a 'top man' in larger groups, with an amount and quality of activity radically discontinuous with the more or less equal rank intervals between the other men. A system cannot achieve a steady state without generalization, but the operation of generalization produces a differentiation of roles which introduces new strains. The price of accomplishment is differentiated status.

It should not be assumed, however, that once generalization in its various aspects has resulted in an ascribed status and role for a man, that his position is now stable. There are apparently a number of ways in which it may be undermined and subject to later shifts, two of which may be mentioned as likely. The first is that the effects of his role-specialized behavior, even if it does not change, put other members under ambivalent strains of some sort which gradually lead them to shift their perception of, attitudes toward, or behavior addressed to him. The second is that the psychological effects of holding a given position may result in gradual *changes* in his behavior (either by 'overconfidence', 'dissatisfaction' or in some other way) which finally 'break through' stereotyped perceptions of his previously established role and become obvious to the other members, with a resulting shift in their attitudes toward him. In other words, the problem of equilibrium is relevant on the more macroscopic levels of role structure and in longer changes over time, as well as on the more microscopic levels we have so far discussed.

References

BASS, B. H. (1949), 'An analysis of leaderless group discussion', *J. appl. Psychol.*, vol. 33, pp 527-33.
FESTINGER, L., and THIBAUT, J. (1950), 'Interpersonal communication in small groups', in L. Festinger *et al.* (eds.), *Theory and Experiment in Social Communication*, University of Michigan Press.

KELLER, J. B. (1951), 'Comment on "Channels of communication in small groups"', *Amer. Soc. Rev.*, vol. 16, no. 6, pp. 842–3.

MURRAY, H. A. (1951), 'Towards a classification of interactions', in T. Parsons and E. A. Shils (eds.), *Toward a General Theory of Action*, Harvard University Press.

NORFLEET, B. (1948), 'Interpersonal relations and group productivity', *J. Soc. Issues*, vol. 4, no. 2, pp. 66–9.

STRODTBECK, F. L. (1951), 'Husband–wife interaction over revealed differences', *Amer. Soc. Rev.* vol. 16, no. 4, pp. 468–73.

16 Muzafer Sherif and Carolyn W. Sherif

Acceptable and Unacceptable Behavior Defined by Group Norms

Excerpt from M. Sherif and C. W. Sherif, *Reference Groups*, Harper & Row, 1964, pp. 167–80.

Procedures

Observers were instructed at this *third phase of their observations* to concentrate on recording any and all regularities in the words or actions of group members, as well as external signs of membership, such as dress, insignia, decoration. They were told to note the relative *frequencies* of similar behaviors and expressed evaluations of individual actions, group performance, and of persons and objects outside of the group. In particular, they were to note exceptions to the common practices – who followed them and who did not, who agreed and who did not. Instances of praise, blame, punishment were to be noted, the members who initiated, supported, concurred, or objected being specified.

Further material related to member attitudes, self-conceptions, present and future goals was obtained after observations were completed. In interviews with members, the observer could find out more about their membership, stated attitudes and expressed goals. These were in many cases supplemented by interviews with parents and teachers, and records of schools, social agencies and police. With these and observational data, let us examine the group practices and products for which the latitude of acceptance was most restricted and reaction to deviation most severe.

Insignia of group membership

All but four of the twelve groups had names by which members referred to themselves. Three of the four which lacked names functioned in areas of middle or high rank; and none of them regularly engaged in interteam sports competitions, although they did play games among themselves. However, most members of a group (1) in a high-rank area had belonged to a secret fraternity, officially abolished by school authorities but continuing to function 'underground'. All but one of the members had been forbidden by parents to continue fraternity membership. They all regretted this and often expressed the wish that they could rejoin. In a sense, even these boys had an identity as former 'Alpha Beta Deltas'.

The groups which had a name in use for a considerable time were either

1. Groups whose explicit purpose was athletic competition and/or
2. Groups in areas of the city where conflicts among adolescent groups were relatively frequent. They were *not* all identified by police as 'delinquent'.

The role of intergroup conflict in sharpening the identity of a group and in its adoption of a name is strikingly apparent in group 2: the name 'Los Apaches' was adopted by this group in the middle 1950s before the present membership was adolescent. Before that time, there were several groups within the area. These groups were friendly toward one another, and would get together when attacked from the outside. The oldest brothers of the present leader were members when it adopted the name 'Los Apaches'. In fact, one of the leader's older brothers is referred to as 'El Apache'.

Interestingly enough, this colorful and bellicose designation, in which members took great pride, was not even entirely an in-group product. Here, in the observer's words, is how it was acquired:

During a fight with the Lakeside [gang], in which a member of the Lakeside was fatally wounded, a member shouted the words 'Los Apaches' as they were chased by policeman. The next day, the local newspapers gave an account of how a gang by the name of 'Los Apaches' had defeated the Lakeside. The name Los Apaches stuck with the group thenceforth – present-day members take interest in reading the newspaper in search of articles regarding Los Apaches.

Insignia of membership, like names, were associated with intergroup rivalry. The fraternity boys of group 2 had put away their pins, but they still felt it was the best fraternity – even far superior to college fraternities. When the boys in group 3 acquired basketball shirts, there was great excitement and serious consideration to the matter of selecting insignia. The observer wrote that there was no discussion about which member should have what numeral. When the box of shirts arrived, the three top status members stepped forward, the leader sorting through the shirts first to pick his numeral, then the others following in order of status to select theirs from those remaining.

Tattoos were common insignia of group membership in low rank neighborhoods with Spanish-speaking population. The location of the tattoo (e.g. between the thumb and forefinger) and the Pattern (e.g. a cross between quotation marks) were distinctive to the group. A former member of Los Apaches who is now a settled and employed member of the neighborhood told the observer that he now regretted having a tattoo, but that at the time it seemed the thing to do and he would have been considered 'chicken' if he hadn't had one.

Such insignia of membership (tattoos, articles of clothing) made the question of whether one was or was not a group member a clearcut matter. In at least one group (2), the practice of fighting as a test of entry into the group was also employed on occasion.

However, the most general criterion of membership in all groups was simply whether other members accepted a boy when he hung around with them, and how frequently he was included in their plans. As we shall see, if he violated norms in matters of consequence to the group, such a general criterion made it relatively simple to exclude him.

The lack of tangible insignia of membership at times made particular individuals uncertain of their standing. A fraternity member had a badge, but the hanger-on in a high-rank group who lacked a car and money had occasion to wonder if mere tolerance of his presence meant he was 'in' or not. Similarly, in a low rank area, members of group 4 discussed whether or not a member had belonged to a group formerly existing in their neighborhood. The boy said that he had; the others disagreed, two of them on the basis of their own association with the group.

In summary, the data on insignia of membership support the generalization that the sharpness of the delineation between those who are 'in' and those who are not is to a significant degree a function of intergroup rivalry. Tangible signs of membership serve to make the distinction formal. Members of groups which had tangible insignia of membership were also much more exclusive in their contacts, habitually avoiding, ignoring or expelling outsiders who ventured with unaggressive intent into their circle.

Clothing and possessions

Among the narrowest ranges of individual variation permitted in the groups was the latitude of acceptable clothing. The norms for dress and hair style in these groups were not, on the whole, distinctive to the groups, but were highly differentiated between groups in different areas. Because of this and because apparel may appear to be a relatively inconsequential matter to males, it might appear that clothing and hair style were not related to group membership.

Apparel and hair style are closely related to important motives which brought the boys together, and the norms governing them did become group affairs. The fact that they vary with rank of the area in the city is simply one example of the norms of a setting becoming the norms for a group within it. There is ample evidence that appearance was a matter of definite concern to these boys, as a symbol of being a maturing male and of being counted as a group member. Members of a group in a high-rank area (1) wore the 'Ivy League' styles of college students uniformly. Those in a neighboring area characterized by lower income and greater urbanization, but attending or graduated from the same school (5), wore blue jeans pushed down to the hips, no belt, and 'flat-top' haircuts with rather long sideburns. The greatest difference from these styles was found in the low-rank areas in cities with large Spanish-speaking population and in the areas with the poorest and least acculturated population.

The norm for dress in the low rank, less acculturated areas (e.g. groups 6 and 2) on occasions when the members went out socially was a dark suit, with pegged trousers, vest and expensive shoes ($25 to $30). The shoes were a matter of particular interest and desire. In fact, on three occasions, the observer of group 2 reported that members had beaten up men to rob them of their *shoes*. The observer of group 6 found frequent discussions of expensive brands of clothing, especially shoes. For a time, it was fashionable to remove the heels from the shoes, whether purchased or otherwise acquired.

Concerns over conformity to acceptable modes of personal appearance are revealed in several reported instances of deviation. In group 5, one member wore his hair in a very long, full style with much hair dressing. His father and the recreational director of the youth center where the group congregated repeatedly told, urged and ordered him to have it cut. His fellow members told him that no girl would have anything to do with him if he did not change the style, then began to insult him about it deliberately. Following a particularly humiliating instance of hazing, the boy went to have his haircut. Upon his return, he was greeted like a hero and praised warmly for the style he had chosen (a flat-top like the others).

A member of group 2 badly needed a new suit for a social event and, having no money for one, was overjoyed when the observer offered to lend him one. However, when he saw that the suit was gray, not black, he thanked the observer and went away without it. He wore his old suit, even though the observer's gray one was much better and would have fitted him.

Similarly, the 'required' possessions and their treatment differed in areas of different rank, but this made the regulation of property use no less a group concern. In a high-rank area, a member of group 1 worked after school in a movie theater with the explicit aim of getting a car of the same model and year as that belonging to a high-status member of his group.

When the boys in the high-rank neighborhood planned a party, everyone was expected to chip in money equally. (Liquor, which was harder to come by, even with an illegal identification card and money, was shared, but the donor expected payment.) One member with less spending money than others tried on several occasions to get the members to gamble with him for cash. The members liked the game, but let him know their annoyance for trying to get *their* money in no uncertain terms. They began to give him the 'cold shoulder' when he appeared.

Individuals in groups with few cars available (5, 7, 8) gained enormously in standing by acquiring a car. Other members *expected* transportation from them as a matter of course.

Members of groups in middle- and high-rank areas would share cigarettes from a package, but not the same cigarette, nor a drink from the same bottle. Group 8 lived in a mixed ethnic neighborhood, somewhat more prosperous than several other low-rank neighborhoods, and its members all attended school. They once discussed their disdain for sharing a cigarette. The leader told of his great embarrassment on being stopped when on a date by a school mate who asked him for his cigarette butt.

In the other low-rank areas, where money and possessions are scarcer, a cigarette was routinely shared by passing it around, as were drinks and other consumables. In planning a party, every member was expected to contribute what he had, but was not usually excluded if he had nothing. On the contrary, the member who had more, especially if he were leader, contributed more. On several occasions, leaders in groups 2, 9, and 10 were observed to contribute or lend all of their cash to a common endeavor, even though they themselves needed new clothing.

Common practices in important activities

As the activities regularly engaged in by the groups varied, so did the areas in which behavior of members was normatively regulated. Those groups which engaged frequently in athletic activities had certain distinctive customs over and above the formal rules of the game (e.g. 'no foul shots permitted', 'no back-court rules', 'never criticize a fellow member's performance while in competition; save it').

In playing among themselves, fouling by a member usually brought forth strong reprimands from other members. However, leaders of athletically inclined groups (groups 3, 7, 8) were frequently observed to foul rather flagrantly in play with other members without being reprimanded.

For example, Roberto, the skillful athlete and leader of group 8, played very roughly against others in his own group – using elbows and hands in illegal ways. Yet, in competition with another team, he was the model of good sportsmanship. A boy in his group with lower standing reacted to in-group and intergroup competition in almost an opposite way. He was not overly rough in play with his fellow members, especially if he was playing against Roberto. But when the group was pitted against another team, he became very aggressive physically and verbally. In fact, in planning the line-up for one match, Roberto kept the boy dangling with the threat that he could not even go with them because 'you're too rough and you'll give us a bad reputation'. At the last minute, Roberto gave in and the boy went along, chastised but with hurt feelings. Not one member pointed out to

Roberto that he behaved in a similar fashion in in-group play. Instead, they urged the boy to 'reform' so he could go with them.

Fouling was considered all right in intergroup competition if one could get away with it. In instances in which members were scolded or removed from the game by leaders for fouling, it was because the referee caught them.

The most elaborate and most strictly enforced common practices concerned activities which would have been punished by adults if detected. The member of a high-rank group, drinking beer in a public place (where drinking was forbidden), was, for the time, screened from view by his fellows standing casually but strategically to cover him. In a low-rank area, the beer at a picnic was routinely covered with leaves and escape routes planned in the event of detection. Those groups whose members drank and hung around recreation centers (4, 5, 6, 7, 11) had customary modes and places for drinking which made their detection by the adult personnel less likely.

Groups which engaged in petty thievery often did so as a group. For example, the observer of group 3 was startled to find, after he had treated the whole group to cold drinks at a service station, that they had each managed to acquire at least one more bottle to drink after leaving. On a later occasion, he asked them not to repeat this performance while with him – to no avail. Getting more than paid for was a matter for ingenuity, and was considered a group joke.

In several groups (2, 4, 6, 9), stealing was not the incidental activity that it was in others. It was regarded as an acceptable and necessary means of getting needed possessions, or, more usually, cash.

Members of the aforementioned groups frequently engaged in theft when they were broke, usually selling articles other than clothing, and often using the money for group entertainment and treats. Such theft seldom involved more than two or three group members at a time. However, *its group reference is shown by the facts that other members were told about these events – with no fear of betrayal – and frequently enjoyed the benefits of the loot.* In these groups, theft was a permissible activity, its successful execution bringing admiration and praise from others.

In two of the groups whose members stole (4, 6), some of the boys had jobs paying about $20 or $30 a week. But they seldom had cash from their wages, which were turned over to their parents. This procedure was taken for granted by some of them as a necessity. But one boy, whose father was habitually unemployed, took the rent money he had been entrusted to pay and spent it on a big blowout for his group pals. He was found out, of course, but he said he would have done the same thing again, and his fellow members did not blame him. He stayed with one of them for several days afterward.

The fact that thefts of money, typewriters, tires, and the like involved only two or three members at a time reflects the boys' awareness that theft is a dangerous business in which too many members should not be involved at any one time. Without the element of sure legal prosecution, but with reference to agemate and adult reaction, participation in sexual adventure also usually involved only two or three boys at a time. A rape case occurred after observations were completed in group 11 involving three group members. Boys in group 1 would consult each other about a girl's reputation; but actual encounters with a 'loose' girl were usually alone or with one male companion. This precaution reflected the boys' efforts to protect their reputation among the 'nice' girls whom they wanted to date for school functions and private parties.

Girls frequently accompanied or attended the activities of groups 5 and 7, but the members lucky enough to attract a girl aimed at solitary dates. In low-rank areas, girls and group activities were more typically separate, except for dances, even though a few members of several groups (2, 4, 6) were married. Taking a girl out in group 9 involved consultations of at least two members, unless she was the one somewhat older woman in the neighborhood whom they all felt free to visit.

It was taken for granted in all groups that fellow members would not trespass on another's right to a girl, while he held that right, whether it included sexual relations or not. In any area, however, a girl known as promiscuous was fair play.

Bragging about sexual activities and information was proof of 'manliness' in all of these adolescent groups. It is notable that in groups 1, 4, 5, 6, 7, 9, and 2, the leaders were all considered successful with girls. The younger, late-maturing, or simply unattractive boy was considered not as manly. However, the conception of manliness in the groups composed of Spanish-speaking boys was coupled with the notion that a good group member must also *show* that he was not at the mercy of the whims of a woman. This concern doubtless reflects a cultural difference, at least in degree. While members of 'Anglo' groups bragged of their 'control' over girls, they were not constrained by other members for bringing girls into their group's activities, nor for having a date in preference to a group function.

The one instance of attempted fighting observed in a high-rank area occurred when a non-member had the audacity to visit a girl when she had a date with the leader. The leader was angry at the boy, not the girl. He proceeded to round up his friends, go to the offender's home, and shout challenges from the lawn. It will be recalled that fighting was prevented by the intervention of the offending boy's astonished father. Nevertheless, Sterling (the leader) was admired by his fellows for 'standing up for his rights' with the girl. This, too, is manliness.

The extended conversations about drinking and drunkenness were evidently also related to concepts of adult manliness. Members of group 7 (who were sixteen to nineteen years old) often engaged in feigned drunkenness, with or *without* alcohol, to the mutual hilarity of all. In fact, interest in having, acquiring and consuming alcohol was so frequent that it must be considered a valued substance common to these American boys. (The boys in group 8 were the only exceptions.)

To some investigators, this interest in drinking and drunkenness would be indicative of 'retreat'. However, both the actual circumstances of drinking and the bragging about drunken episodes point to their essentially social nature, tied to the role relationships of youth conceiving of themselves as near-adult males. The same generalization applies to observed instances of marijuana smoking and solvent sniffing. These practices were carried on by some but not all of the membership of some groups, at times when others drank beer and smoked tobacco, and in their presence. These observations, in our opinion, are difficult to reconcile with the classification of drug *usage* as a 'retreatist' type of activity, even though the end result of the activity is assuredly a detachment from reality. Addiction, on the other hand, seems to reduce group affiliations sharply, as several authors have found (e.g. Yablonsky, 1962). [. . .]

Norms for loyalty to the group

Negative sanctions applied to a member whose behavior varies beyond the bounds of acceptability are among the clearest evidence for the existence of group norms. In the foregoing illustrations, such sanctions were seen in the form of urgings, hazing, insulting or cold-shouldering the offender. However, the observers' reports reveal that sanctions more severe than these 'psychological' punishments were decidedly infrequent, confirming the findings of earlier investigators.

The bulk of conforming behavior reported by observers occurred *without external pressure* in the form of sanctions or threat of sanctions. On the other hand, the only severe sanctions observed were applied to members who evidenced disloyalty to the group in the presence of outsiders.

In one rather large group of fifteen boys (9), the leader discussed with his most trusted associates the need to 'weed out' certain individuals whom he suspected of talking to the police about group activities. Even when not police but only parents were involved, members knew that the worst thing they could do would be to talk with outsiders about their covert activities. Members of group 8, who were not under police watch and explicitly distinguished themselves as different from the 'tough gangs' in bordering areas, discussed at length the low character of a boy in the neighborhood (a nonmember) who had had the nerve to squeal to one of their fathers about their habit of smuggling cigarettes from his grocery store.

A boy in group 6 stole a typewriter with the companionship of two fellow members, and gave the police their names when he was caught. He was given a jail sentence. Although his companions were not, the entire membership agreed that a good beating awaited him when he was released.

A member of group 3 made the mistake of running away from his fellows when they were jumped by members of a hostile gang. The fact that the adversaries had knives, and that fright was an understandable reaction, carried no weight at all with group members. The boy was finally completely ostracized by the group. Members even succeeded in turning the girls in the neighborhood against him. The observer had some contacts with the boy afterward and reported that he was severely depressed, even despondent.

The 'proper' way to act in a dangerous situation was formulated by the leader of group 2: 'If you have to run, run like mad, but if one of your boys is caught by the opposition, then you have to stop and help him. If you don't, you're a punk.'

When the observer of a group in a middle-rank area of city A was riding with one of its members, they passed the car of another member. Through the window, a challenge to a drag race was hurled. Within a few blocks, the other car jumped the curb, smashing into a light post. The car in which the observer rode stopped. The driver rushed over to the other car to consult the accident victims, assuring the observer not to worry but to stay there. After a quick discussion, he came back and drove away, saying that the others were not hurt and had agreed that the policeman shortly to arrive would go easier if they were not present, since it would immediately involve the group in charges of drag racing on a main street. The code of loyalty had been observed and the decision made in terms of group maintenance.

Varying latitudes of acceptance, deviation and leadership

The foregoing discussion of normative regulation of behavior illustrates a pattern of findings supporting the following generalizations, to be examined in further research: *the latitude of acceptable behaviors, defined by the norms of a group, varies according to the importance of the activity to the members.* In matters incidental to the main activities of a group and to the motives bringing members together, considerable variation in behavior occurs without concerted measures by other members to alter it. Especially in matters affecting the identity and maintenance of the group, such as loyalty in the face of outside threat, the latitude of acceptability is restricted and its bounds are clear. In such matters, deviation from the latitude of acceptance calls forth stronger and more consensual sanctions, usually severe punishment or expulsion from the group.

Corresponding to the variations in the latitudes of acceptance in activities of different import to the group, the latitudes of acceptance for members of different standing in the group vary. In matters related to the maintenance of group activities and of loyalty, the leader is expected to be the exemplar. He is expected to contribute more, in the form of money, possessions or effort, to insuring the essentials for the activities the members enjoy most together. Especially in relationships with outsiders, which is one of the principal leadership functions, the latitude of acceptance is very narrow for the leader.

Thus, the leader of one of the most tightly knit groups (2) was chastised by his fellows for being so foolish as to carry a weapon with him under the seat of a car, for which he was picked up by the police. Unlike other members the leader endangers the identity and maintenance of the entire group by such behavior. In the description of group 3, we mentioned the continuing concern of members over their former leader, who inclined easily to fights with other groups. Their adventurous spirits were now fired with athletic competition, and they saw fights as potentially endangering their chances of playing, as well as getting them into serious difficulties with police.

In activities less significant to the group and *within* its bounds, however, the leader is frequently permitted much more deviation by other members. For example, he can commit fouls in games which would not be tolerated from others, and even strike another member for infractions of rules recognized by others.

These generalizations about latitude of acceptance and leader behavior are in line with the observations of other investigators of small groups (e.g. Homans, 1950). The concept *latitude of acceptance* is amenable to dimensional analysis of the observed phenomena, and to specification of the point at which deviations will be reacted to negatively by concerted actions of the members. In these terms, the generalizations may be summarized:

The more significant the activity for the identity and continued maintenance of the group and its central interests, the narrower the range of acceptable behaviors for all members, the latitude for the leader being narrowest. Conversely, the more incidental the activity to the foregoing concerns of the group, the broader the range of individual variation without the arousal of sanctions, the latitude for the leader being greatest.

Finally, our findings give striking testimony to the relative unimportance of coercion and pressure from other members in the normative regulation of behavior during the usual run of things in these adolescent groups. In terms of frequency, the bulk of observed conforming behavior occurred without punishment or threat of punishment. Conformity occurred, then, largely through the internal regulation of behavior by the individuals, for whom the group norms had become their own attitudes, expectations and ideals.

References
HOMANS, G. C. (1950), *The Human Group*, Harcourt, Brace & World.
YABLONSKY, L. (1962), *The Violent Gang*, Macmillan Co.

17 Peter M. Blau and W. Richard Scott

Processes of Communication in Formal Organizations

Excerpt from P. M. Blau and W. R. Scott, *Formal Organizations: A Comparative Approach*, Routledge & Kegan Paul, 1963, pp. 121–34.

Dysfunctions of hierarchical differentiation

The superiority of groups over individuals in certain kinds of task performance has been attributed primarily to three factors:

1. The sifting of suggestions in social interaction serves as an error-correction mechanism.
2. The social support furnished in interaction facilitates thinking.
3. The competition among members for respect mobilizes their energies for contributing to the task.

If our interpretation is correct, a comparison of groups that differ in these characteristics should reveal appropriate differences in performance. The best test of these explanatory hypotheses would be to introduce experimental differences in each of the three factors while controlling the remaining two and other relevant conditions. In the absence of such experimental evidence, we shall attempt to test our interpretations indirectly by examining social conditions that appear to inhibit these processes and noting the consequences for performance.

Hierarchical differentiation of status, particularly when formally established, appears to curtail these three group processes. First, explicit status distinctions tend to reduce social interaction and social support. A field study by Wessen of the personnel in a large general hospital found that social interaction typically followed status lines and was inhibited by status boundaries. Most social contacts of doctors were with other doctors, nurses primarily associated with other nurses, and the same was true for lower-status ward personnel (Wessen, 1958). An investigation by Kelley found that in experimentally created hierarchies feelings of friendliness across hierarchical boundaries declined when the upper-status individuals were insecure in their positions and the lower-status individuals had no chance of upward mobility (Kelley, 1951). Several studies report a tendency for lower-status group members to direct their friendship choices disproportionately to upper-status members (Hurwitz *et al.*, 1953, Sherif, 1951). Since upper-status members tend not to reciprocate but to direct their choices to others also high in status, lower-status members do not receive their share of the social support that is needed for stimulating thought and making suggestions.

Second, formally instituted status differences tend to undermine the process of competition for respect. In a *peer* group, a member's standing rests primarily on the respect of others, and this fact makes their respect and deference most important. But in the presence of formal distinctions of status, the respect of others is not the primary basis of a person's social standing, and competition for respect loses much, though not all, of its significance. Besides, status distinctions generally destroy the *laissez-faire* character of competition for respect. Members no longer seek to be respected by any and all, inasmuch as being respected by those of high status is of more significance than being respected by others of lower status. A field experiment conducted by Hurwitz and his colleagues provides some support for this interpretation (Hurwitz *et al.*, 1953). Participation in discussions at a conference on mental hygiene was found to be affected by the influence and the professional prestige of various members. Records of frequency of communication between conference members reveal that those of high prestige participated most in discussions, and that both low- and high-prestige persons directed most of their remarks to high-prestige persons. Liking choices were disproportionately often directed to high-status individuals, and there seemed to be more concern with receiving liking choices from high- than from low-status members. In short, participants appear to have competed primarily for being regarded and liked by the most prestigeful others. Seeking to win the approval of an elite has undoubtedly implications for conduct quite different from those of striving to earn the respect of most members of a group.

Third, status differences distort the error-correcting function of social interaction. It is not easy to oppose the judgement of a person with superior power or prestige, and most people will think twice before doing so. At the very least, they will want to be quite sure of their criticism before voicing it. In contrast, people do not usually hesitate to criticize the opinion of a person whom they do not respect. Indeed, lack of respect will incline them to find fault with proposals. Hence, there is a reluctance to criticize the suggestions offered by high-status members and a ready inclination to reject the suggestions and criticisms offered by low-status members. This interpretation gains support from an experiment in which Torrance observed the interaction during problem-solving sessions in three-man groups composed of Air Force personnel of different military ranks (1955). He found that the incorrect suggestions of high-status group members (crew captains) were disproportionately often accepted and the correct suggestions of low-status members (sergeant gunners) were disproportionately often rejected. The fact that status influences whose opinion carries most weight interferes with the detection of errors in group problem-solving.

There is, then, some indication that differentiation of hierarchical status in groups attenuates the very characteristics that have been hypothesized to be responsible for the superiority of groups over individuals in problem-solving. The interpretation implies, consequently, that the more pronounced the hierarchical differences in a group, the less effectively it will perform. There is some evidence in support of this inference. For example, in Torrance's experiment, permanent combat crews performed less well in solving problems than did temporary crews composed of similar personnel. Torrance accounts for this finding by explaining: 'In the temporary crews, the effects of status differences seems [sic] to have been diminished and all members less frequently fail to influence when they have the correct answer.' (p. 55). The famous studies on the effects of social climates inspired by Lewin and conducted by White and Lippitt also tend to support our prediction (1953; 1960). White and Lippitt conclude that groups of boys under 'democratic' leaders performed more 'efficiently' – if this term is defined to include member satisfaction as well as achievement of work goals – than those under autocratic leaders. The efficiency was especially evident in the groups' ability to work and cope with problems in the absence of the adult leader. Finally, several studies have reported that workers under authoritarian supervision do not perform as well as those whose supervisors minimize status distinctions by delegating work, encouraging discretion, and similar practices (Kahn and Katz, 1953; Argyle *et al.*, 1958). These studies suggest that, as was expected, a diminution of status differentials improves performance.

Functions of hierarchical structure

Research evidence, however, does not entirely support our expectation regarding the adverse effects of hierarchy on performance. Some studies have found groups with a status hierarchy to perform better than those with less differentiation of social status. Let us examine these studies and their implications for our theory. An experiment by Maier and Solem contrasts groups of five or six persons with and without an appointed discussion leader (1952). The task was solving mathematical problems. Groups with a leader proved to be superior in performance to those without one. An analysis of the interaction during the problem-solving sessions provides a clue for understanding this apparently negative case. Majority opinions on how to attack a problem tended to develop in these groups, and the majority often exerted pressures to suppress minority opinions, including correct suggestions. Discussion leaders, who acted as chairmen, saw to it that all members had an opportunity to express their views. The fact that persons in the minority had more opportunity to contribute to the correct solution in groups with a discussion leader than in those without seems to have been responsible for the superior performance of the former.

In this experiment, the social differentiation of a group into a majority and a minority created obstacles to the free flow of communication, just as hierarchical differentiation did in many other groups, and both forms of differentiation had adverse effects on problem-solving. The presence of a leader who removed obstacles to communication – those created by other aspects of group differentiation – improved the group's problem-solving abilities. This new information allows us to refine our theory by specifying why and under which conditions a status hierarchy interferes with performance. We have seen that the free flow of communication – in the form of criticisms, suggestions, manifestations of respect, and expressions of approval furnishing social support – furthers problem-solving. Hierarchical differentiation of status usually impedes the free flow of communication, and for this specific reason such differentiation tends to be detrimental for task performance. If leadership does not block but frees the flow of communication – as in the case of a discussion leader or procedural chairman in contrast to a dominant power – then leadership will further rather than hinder problem-solving.[1]

Another investigation permits further refinement of our interpretation. Heinicke and Bales studied developmental trends over four sessions of initially leaderless groups engaged in the discussion of a human-relations case (1953). The groups were instructed to arrive at a common solution. Status differences between members (measured by sociometric choices) crystallized in some groups but not in others, and the former were found to be more successful in reaching consensus on case problems. Why did the groups that established a status hierarchy perform the task more successfully? The reason may well be that the task was chiefly one of coordination. The criterion of success was not the quality of the recommendation made but whether the group could agree on a single recommendation. As we noted earlier when comparing the performance of individuals and groups, the free flow of suggestions and criticisms facilitates the sifting of ideas to find the single correct one, but this same process impedes coordination. Hierarchical differentiation of status, by curbing the free flow of ideas, facilitates the coordination of opinions to achieve consensus, just as the complete absence of communication (individual performance) facilitates coordination. In

1. This restatement may well also account for the finding in the White and Lippitt study that groups with 'democratic' leaders were more efficient than groups with 'laissez-faire' leaders. See the descriptions of these leadership styles in White and Lippitt (1953).

sum, groups are superior to individuals, and groups in which there is a free flow of communication are superior to groups in which differentiation impedes communication, in solving problems which call for a single correct or best answer; but individuals are superior to groups, and hierarchically differentiated groups are superior to undifferentiated groups, in performing tasks that primarily depend on efficient coordination.

A final group of studies reinforces the conclusion that hierarchical organization is important for coordination. These are experiments in which the communication network in a group is manipulated. Research by Leavitt (1951), based on earlier work by Bavelas (1950), imposed various communication networks on groups of five subjects. A variety of networks was used, but we shall consider only the two extremes of centralization. In the 'wheel' or 'X', a central person could communicate with all others, and they could communicate only with him. In the 'circle' or 'O', every person communicated with two neighbors. All subjects sat in separate cubicles and communicated in writing only. Each subject was given a sheet with five symbols on it and his task was to determine which one symbol was common to all the sheets. This is essentially a problem of coordination. Although there is a single correct solution, the difficulty is bringing the appropriate pieces of information together; once they are brought together, arriving at the answer is a trivial problem. The performance of wheel groups has been consistently found to be superior to that of circle groups. A centralized network of communication apparently contributes to effective coordination.

Later studies suggest that the crucial factor is not the formal network of communication but the group's ability to become hierarchically organized. The wheel imposes such hierarchical organization on a group, since the person in the central position naturally assumes the dominant role of coordinator. But if other types of groups are able to achieve status differentiation, then their performance becomes as good as that of the wheel groups. For example, Guetzkow and Simon (1955), using the same equipment and task as Bavelas and Leavitt, compared the performance of groups when members were linked by the wheel, the circle, and an all-channel network (all members can communicate with all others) (Mulder, 1960). Previous calculations had indicated that there were no significant differences between the three networks in terms of the time needed to accomplish the task *if* they were efficiently utilized; that is, any differences among the groups using the three networks was not due to the intrinsic limitations of a given network but rather to the use made of it. However, the difficulty of the organizational problem varied from network to network. The circle groups were expected to have the most difficult organizational problem, since they needed to establish relays for message passing as well as select one member to coordinate and distribute information. The wheel groups faced the least difficult organizational problems, since the network imposed a structure upon them. All-channel groups were considered intermediate, their problems being to eliminate excess channels and decide upon one person as coordinator. After a trial period, fifty-six groups were given twenty successive tasks with two-minute breaks between them during which members were allowed to discuss ways of improving their organization (also by an exchange of written messages). Using as a measure of efficiency the time needed to complete the task, wheel groups reached their maximum efficiency after only a few trials, all-channel groups were slower during early trials but most eventually performed as well as wheel groups, and circle groups generally did not reach optimum performance during the twenty trials. When and whether all-channel and circle groups achieved maximum efficiency depended on their success in developing a differentiated structure for communication.

In short, performance was negatively correlated with the difficulty of the organizational problems facing the groups. Among the groups of each type that did develop a hierarchical organization,[2] however, there were no significant differences in the efficiency with which they performed their tasks. A later publication analysed the messages sent by group members during the periods between trials and found that whether or not the all-channel or circle groups developed a hierarchical organization was related to the number of specific proposals made and promulgated in planning such organizational arrangements (Guetzkow and Dill, 1957).[3]

These experimental results strengthen our previous conclusions that hierarchical organization serves important functions for achieving coordination and that it does so specifically by restricting the free flow of communication. There is also some support for our hypothesis that the free flow of communication without hierarchical or other barriers is best suited for advancing new solutions to problems, including the ideas necessary to create a hierarchical organization where none exists. While hierarchically organized groups performed the coordination task better than groups not so organized, all-channel groups were more successful in developing an effective organization than were those groups where communication was restricted (circle groups).

2. All fifteen wheel groups, seventeen out of twenty all-channel groups, and only three of twenty-one circle groups developed hierarchies during the twenty trials.

3. Guetzkow and Dill also tested the hypothesis that circle groups would be more likely to achieve organization if they were permitted all-channel communication between trials. The results, however, were negative: the circle groups that were permitted inter-trial all-channel communication were slightly more likely to become organized than regular circle groups but the average performance of the two types of groups was similar because the performance of the unorganized groups among those with all-channel networks between trials was particularly low.

Field studies of communication in formal organizations

Consultation among peers

In turning from a discussion of controlled experiments to field studies concerned with communication, we are leaving behind the precision and safety of the laboratory. However, only by entering the field can we ascertain whether conclusions arrived at in the laboratory also hold for natural groups. One question is how accurately the experiment simulates the conditions it is supposed to represent, say, how well laboratory groups whose members are told they have similar interests reflect the salient aspects of solidarity in actual work groups. An even more fundamental problem is posed by the fact that experiments are designed to determine how a given factor in pure form and in the absence of variations in other conditions influences a second factor. Outside the laboratory, however, factors do not occur in pure form (there is no absolute vacuum, and neither is there completely unrestricted communication). Whether a condition occurs, or what effect it has if it does occur, is not independent of but contingent on other existing conditions. Field studies are needed to ascertain which social conditions typically occur together and which combinations of factors may be relevant for producing a given effect. Experiments are required to confirm the hypotheses derived from such field studies that a certain factor or set of factors actually has a certain effect. And field studies, in turn, must validate generalizations derived from experiments by showing that they apply outside the laboratory. The best approach, then, is to alternate between both methods; but in most areas of social research, experimentation is rarely used and, indeed, may not be feasible. Communication is one of the few subjects that have been investigated experimentally as well as in field studies and surveys, and this double-pronged approach lends it special significance.

As our first field study on communication, we undertook to analyse the interaction processes among colleagues in a federal law-enforcement agency (Blau, 1955, pp. 99–115). The main duty of the agents was to investigate business establishments in order to determine their compliance with two federal laws. The work was complex and involved a high degree of discretion. Agents not only had to know – or at least to know about – the many general regulations that governed their work, including legislative acts and amendments, administrative interpretations, and court decisions, but they also had to be able to gather and sift information from many sources on the firms investigated. The duty to detect possibly concealed violations as well as the complexity of the task required that agents be able to exercise discretion; uniform law enforcement, however, required that decisions conform strictly to legal principles. The control system in the organization was designed to meet this double requirement.

The operations of the agents were controlled through an evaluation of results achieved rather than by means of detailed operating rules. The agents enjoyed considerable freedom in deciding how to proceed – for example, nobody checked on how they spent their time either in or out of the office – but their results (decisions) had to conform strictly to the law. They knew that their work required rigid conformity to the law of the land since making exceptions, even for the sake of adhering to the intent of the law, could open a Pandora's box of legal loopholes. The importance of attaining correct results in strict conformity with the legal standards was emphasized by having cases reviewed by both the supervisors and a special review unit, and statistical records of performance also focused attention on results; for example, records were kept on the proportion of cases in which violations had been discovered. Errors of decision detected by either review and the quantitative performance record were given great weight in the periodic rating of agents by their supervisors.

Indications were that evaluation on the basis of results achieved rather than methods employed fostered disciplined responsibility among agents. Emphasis in an organization on conformity with operating procedures discourages the exercise of initiative and the willingness to assume responsibility. The federal-agency system, in contrast, permitted individual agents considerable freedom in their work but exerted constraints to make their final decisions conform to general legal principles. Not the road taken but the destination reached was the test of performance. This reward system promoted responsibility among agents in both senses of the term: it encouraged them to assume responsibility for their decisions and to exercise discretion, and it also held them accountable for making responsible decisions in conformity with all the relevant official standards.[4]

Because agents were free to arrive at their own decisions, their work satisfaction was high. The discretion they exercised made their jobs challenging and interesting. But such responsibility engendered anxieties over decision-making which interfered with the capacity to make correct decisions. If agents encountered problems in their work, they were expected to confer with their supervisors, who might in turn send them to a staff attorney for further advice. However, this official procedure did not and could not lessen the anxiety aroused by concern over the correctness of decisions. Since the supervisor's evaluation of their work was a major cause of this anxiety, agents could not relieve it by coming to him with their difficulties. In fact, agents were reluctant to go to a supervisor with their problems for fear that doing so would reveal their ignorance – or, at least, their inability to act independently – and thus have adverse effects on their ratings.

These obstacles to the use of official channels of communication led agents to satisfy their needs for advice and social support by consulting one

4. On the double meaning of 'responsibility', see Dimock (1959, pp. 218–19).

another. While the practice of turning to colleagues for advice was officially prohibited, it was tolerated, inasmuch as such operating rules were generally not strictly enforced. Consultation among peers appears to have had important consequences for the organization. This cooperative practice transformed an aggregate of individuals who merely had the same supervisor into a cohesive group. Moreover, it improved decision-making, not only by supplying information and advice when needed but also by reducing anxiety over decisions generally. The mere knowledge that one could ask a colleague for help when in difficulty decreased the anxiety engendered by the need to make complex decisions. Besides, the experience of being regularly asked by others for advice increased an agent's confidence in his own decisions. Hence, the decision-making ability of both participants was likely to benefit from consultations. By reducing anxiety and strengthening self-confidence, the pattern of unofficial consultation probably improved decisions even when no consultation took place. It should be noted that this conclusion is inferential. Although participation in consultation was associated with superior performance (Blau, 1955, pp. 106–7) it is impossible to tell whether this association actually indicates that participation improved performance or merely that competent agents were more apt to be drawn into consultation. The latter was undoubtedly the case, but the question is whether the former was also the case. To demonstrate that consultation affects decision-making would require an experimental or panel design.

Hierarchical status differences created obstacles to communication in this field situation, just as they did in laboratory experiments. Other field studies provide further support for the validity of this generalization. Argyris reports that supervisors in an industrial setting were very selective in the information they communicated to their superiors, tending to minimize problems, to emphasize successes, and to relay information detrimental to other supervisors whenever possible (1955, pp. 46–8). And research conducted by Blau in an employment agency indicates how operating directives became adjusted, redefined and amplified as they passed from the upper levels of the hierarchy to the lower (1955, pp. 21–8). Finally, a study by Zaleznik replicates the finding from the law-enforcement agency in a machine shop (1956, pp. 36–41). These manual workers were also reluctant to approach their supervisor with their problems and instead turned to their peers. In particular, workers focused their requests for help on one individual who was high in seniority and who appeared to function as an informal leader.

The dynamics of communication processes

A case study in which Shepard analyses the patterns of consultation in a university research organization provides some interesting contrasts and parallels (1954).[5] Most of the staff members of this engineering laboratory were recent university graduates who held temporary positions, which they looked upon primarily as a valuable opportunity to acquire good research experience – an advanced program of postgraduate training. Salaries were low compared with those engineers could command in industry. The staff was willing to sacrifice present income for experience and anticipated future earnings. Salaries were determined by the university, and superiors in the research organization had no control over them. Moreover, there was little chance for (and little interest in) promotion. Hence, employees were not dependent upon their superiors for receiving formal rewards – a situation quite different from that in most organizations.

We have seen that hierarchical dependence blocks the free flow of communications and, more specifically, disinclines staff members to discuss their problems with a superior for fear of revealing their ignorance to him. Where creativity is valued there is also the danger that free discussions will not occur even among peers, since each person will be concerned with 'getting credit' for his new ideas. Such communication barriers were not prevalent in this research organization: engineers readily discussed their problems with one another regardless of official rank.[6] Although he had no quantitative data it was Shepard's impression that this practice of freely talking problems over with colleagues stimulated ideas and improved research productivity. Indeed, these discussions seem to have served as a means for acquiring status and as an informal reward system. In the absence of formal rewards the prestige gained by demonstrating technical knowledge and solving complex problems provided an incentive for exerting effort. Moreover, the exchange of technical ideas in these discussions was a learning experience for all participants, which constituted another informal reward.

Let us contrast communication patterns in the university research group with those found in the federal law-enforcement agency. The free flow of consultations among colleagues probably improved performance in both organizations. Communications across hierarchical lines were more restricted in the law-enforcement agency than in the research organization – an expected consequence of the lesser hierarchical dependence in the latter. As we have seen, however, hierarchical dependence did not appear to impede consultation among colleagues in the federal agency. Perhaps advice would have been given less freely if the agents in the federal agency had received formal credit for having original ideas. But they obtained formal rewards

5. For a study that compares communication patterns in the administrative and the scientific sections of a large federal research bureau, see Weiss (1956).

6. There did appear to be some communication barriers between engineers and technicians (less highly trained employees). Shepard felt (1954, p. 461) that these stemmed from the difficulties of reciprocation: technicians could learn much from engineers but not engineers from technicians.

only for ideas that contributed to their own cases, not for all good ideas, such as those that might help solve the problems in a colleague's cases. In other words, federal agents were engaged in similar but not common work, and ideas were given official recognition only in relation to particular case problems. Since these agents, just as Shepard's engineers but for different reasons, could not gain formal rewards by withholding ideas from colleagues, the informal rewards they could gain from freely giving advice governed their conduct.

Shepard suggests that in the research organization, earning the respect of colleagues served as a substitute for formal rewards. But if the unofficial pattern of rewarding competence in problem-solving with high respect has the same function for performance as the official institution of rewarding such competence with good ratings and advancements, may the two not also have the same dysfunctions? If the informal status structure constitutes an effective incentive system, just as the formal status structure does, one would expect differences in informal status to impede communications, just as differences in formal status do. Fear of losing face is probably not much less inhibiting than fear of losing one's place. The study of the research organization provides no information on this matter, but the study of the federal agency does (Blau, 1955, pp. 106–10). The most competent agents were most often consulted, but most agents discussed the majority of their problems not with these experts but with others of lesser competence. Agents explained this preference by saying that they were reluctant to go regularly to other agents with whom they were not particularly friendly. Instead, they tended to establish partnerships for the purpose of mutual consultation.

Why did agents settle for advice which they knew to be not the best available? A person receives advice in exchange for paying respect. By repeatedly approaching another for advice, the questioner is implicitly acknowledging the superior competence of the adviser. The consultant earns respect, in exchange for which he must devote time and energy to helping colleagues with their problems. However, this system undergoes modifications that can be looked upon as resulting from marginal utility functions. The respect received for any single consultation declines as the number of consultations increases. A person seldom consulted will appreciate the respect for his judgement shown by a colleague who asks for his advice much more than the one often consulted. Correspondingly, the expenditure of time becomes increasingly difficult to bear as frequent consultations infringe more and more on the time a colleague needs for work on his own cases. Consequently, popular consultants find requests for advice less welcome than others, and may even become impatient and uncooperative when colleagues ask too frequently for their help. The cost of advice to the one who requests it changes in similar ways. Continually paying respect and giving deference to colleagues by asking for their help threatens the self-confidence of an agent and his standing among peers. If the cost of obtaining expert advice becomes too high for an agent, partly because he needs so much of it, he will seek to obtain advice of inferior quality at a cheaper price.

These processes promote the establishment of partnerships for mutual consultation, particularly among officials in frequent need of assistance. No deference is implied by asking the advice of a colleague who often asks one's own advice. In these partnerships, therefore, agents paid for advice not with deference, which they could ill afford, but with consulting time devoted to the partner's problems. This was a cheap price, since little demand was made on the consulting time of the less competent agent and he enjoyed being asked for advice. Inasmuch as the anxiety aroused by having to submit decisions to superiors for evaluation interfered with decision-making, agents could benefit from consulting a colleague whose competence was not superior to their own, for *his* decision-making ability on *their* cases was not impeded by such anxiety. Furthermore, the development of consulting partnerships enabled agents to make fewer demands on the time of the experts and thus to approach them more freely when faced with a particularly difficult problem.

Let us summarize the implications of this analysis. The formal status hierarchy in an organization creates obstacles to the free flow of communication. Specifically, dependence on superiors for formal rewards restricts consultation across hierarchical boundaries. Under special conditions, it may also discourage consultation among colleagues, but probably the more typical situation is that hierarchical obstacles to communication foster consultation among peers. The processes of consultation among peers give rise to an informal differentiation of status, because some members of the colleague group earn more respect as consultants than others. Such emerging distinctions of informal status also create obstacles to the free discussion of problems, just as formal status differences do. These obstacles may further redirect the flow of consultation, so that the highest frequency occurs between persons of equal informal as well as formal status. But even consultations among persons of equal competence probably improve the quality of performance, for anxiety interferes less with making decisions on a colleague's cases than with making decisions on one's own.

References

ARGYLE, M. *et al.* (1958), 'Supervisory methods related to productivity, absenteeism and labour turnover', *Hum. Rel.*, vol. 11, pp. 23–40.

ARGYRIS, C. (1953), *Executive Leadership*, Harper & Row.

BAVELAS, A. (1950), 'Communication patterns in task-oriented groups', *J. Acoust. Soc. Amer.*, vol. 22, pp. 725–30.

BLAU, P. M. (1955), The Dynamics of Bureaucracy, University of Chicago Press.

DIMOCK, M. E. (1959), *Administrative Vitality*, Harper & Row.

GUETZKOW, H., and DILL, W. R. (1957), 'Factors in organizational development of task-oriented groups', *Sociometry*, vol. 20, pp. 175–204.

GUETZKOW, H., and SIMON, H. A. (1955), 'The impact of certain communication nets upon organization and performance in task-oriented groups', *Management Sci.*, vol. 1, pp. 233–50.

HEINIECKE, C., and BALES, R. F. (1953), 'Developmental trends in the structure of small groups', *Sociometry*, vol. 16, pp. 7–38.

HURWITZ, J. I. *et al.* (1953), 'Some effects of power on the relations among group members', in D. Cartwright and A. Zander (eds.), *Group Dynamics*, Harper & Row.

KAHN, R. L., and KATZ, D. (1953), 'Leadership practices in relation to productivity and morale', in D. Cartwright and A. Zander (eds.), *Group Dynamics*, Harper & Row.

KELLEY, H. H. (1951), 'Communication in experimentally created hierarchies', *Human Rel.*, vol. 5, pp. 39–56.

LEAVITT, H. J. (1951), 'Some effects of certain communication patterns on group performance', *J. abnorm. soc. Psychol.*, vol. 46, pp. 38–50.

MAIER, N. R. F., and SOLEM, A. R. (1952), 'The contributions of a discussion leader to the quality of group thinking', *Hum. Rel.*, vol. 5, pp. 277–88.

MULDER, M. (1960), 'Communication structure, decision structure and group performance', *Sociometry*, vol. 23, pp. 1–14.

SHEPARD, H. A. (1954), 'The value system of a university research group', *Amer. Soc. Rev.*, vol. 19, pp. 456–62.

SHERIF, M. (1951), 'A preliminary experimental study of intergroup relations', in J. H. Rohrer and M. Sherif (eds.), *Social Psychology at the Crossroads*, Harper & Row.

TORRANCE, E. P. (1955), 'Some consequences of power differences on decision making in permanent and temporary three-man groups', in A. P. Hare *et al.* (eds.), *Small Groups*, Knopf.

WEISS, R. S. (1956), *Processes of Organization*, University of Michigan.

WESSEN, A. F. (1958), 'Hospital ideology and communication between ward personnel', in E. G. Jaco (ed.), *Patients, Physicians and Illness*, Free Press.

WHITE, R., and LIPPITT, R. (1953), 'Leader behavior and member reaction in three "social climates"', in D. Cartwright and A. Zander (eds.) *Group Dynamics*, Harper & Row.

WHITE, R., and LIPPITT, R. (1960), *Autocracy and Democracy*, Harper & Row.

ZALEZNIK, A. (1956), *Worker Satisfaction and Development*, Harvard University.

18 Edwin A. Fleishman and Edwin F. Harris

Patterns of Leadership Behavior related to Employee Grievances and Turnover

E. A. Fleishman and E. F. Harris, 'Patterns of leadership behavior related to employee grievances and turnover', *Personnel Psychology*, vol. 15, 1962, pp. 43–56.

This study investigates some relationships between the leader behavior of industrial supervisors and the behavior of their group members. It represents an extension of earlier studies carried out at the International Harvester Company, while the authors were with the Ohio State University Leadership Studies.

Briefly, these previous studies involved three primary phases which have been described elsewhere (Fleishman, 1951; 1953a; 1953b; 1953c; Fleishman, Harris and Burtt, 1955; Harris and Fleishman, 1955). In the initial phase, independent leadership patterns were defined and a variety of behavioral and attitude instruments were developed to measure them. This phase confirmed the usefulness of the constructs 'consideration' and 'structure' for describing leader behavior in industry.

Since the present study, as well as the previous work, focused on these two leadership patterns, it may be well to redefine them here:

Consideration includes behavior indicating mutual trust, respect, and a certain warmth and rapport between the supervisor and his group. This does not mean that this dimension reflects a superficial 'pat-on-the-back', 'first name calling' kind of human-relations behavior. This dimension appears to emphasize a deeper concern for group members' needs and includes such behavior as allowing subordinates more participation in decision making and encouraging more two-way communication.

Structure includes behavior in which the supervisor organizes and defines group activities and his relation to the group. Thus, he defines the role he expects each member to assume, assigns tasks, plans ahead, establishes ways of getting things done, and pushes for production. This dimension seems to emphasize overt attempts to achieve organizational goals.

Since the dimensions are independent, a supervisor may score high on both dimensions, low on both, or high on one and low on the other.

The second phase of the original Harvester research utilized measures of these patterns to evaluate changes in foreman-leadership attitudes and behavior resulting from a management-training program. The amount of change was evaluated at three different times – once while the foremen were still in the training setting, again after they had returned to the plant environment, and still later in a 'refresher' training course. The results showed that while still in the training situation there was a distinct increase in consideration and an unexpected decrease in structure attitudes. It was also found that leadership attitudes became more *dissimilar* rather than similar, despite the fact that all foremen had received the same training. Furthermore, when behavior and attitudes were evaluated back in the plant, the effects of the training largely disappeared. This pointed to the main finding, i.e. the overriding importance of the interaction of the training effects with certain aspects of the social setting in which the foremen had to operate in the plant. Most critical was the 'leadership climate' supplied by the behavior and attitudes of the foreman's own boss. This was more related to the foreman's own consideration and structure behavior than was the fact that he had or had not received the leadership training.

The third phase may be termed the 'criterion phase', in which the relationships between consideration and structure and indices of foremen proficiency were examined. One finding was that production supervisors rated high in 'proficiency' by plant management turned out to have leadership patterns high in structure and low in consideration. (This relationship was accentuated in departments scoring high on a third variable, 'perceived pressure of deadlines'.) On the other hand, this same pattern of high structure and low consideration was found to be related to high labor turnover, union grievances, worker absences and accidents, and low worker satisfaction. There was some indication that these relationships might differ in 'non-production' departments. An interesting sidelight was that foremen with low consideration *and* low structure were more often bypassed by subordinates in the informal organizational structure. In any case, it was evident that 'what is an effective supervisor' is a complex question, depending on the proficiency criterion emphasized, management values, type of work and other situational variables.

The present study examines some of the questions left unanswered by this previous work.

Purpose

The present study focused on two main questions. First, what is the *form* of the relationship between leader behavior and indices of group behavior? Is it linear or curvilinear? As far as we know, no one has really examined this question. Rephrased, this question asks if there are critical levels of consideration and/or structure beyond which it does or does not make a difference in group behavior? Is an 'average' amount of structure better than a great deal or no structure at all? Similarly, is there an optimum level of consideration above and below which worker grievances and/or turnover rise sharply?

The second question concerns the interaction effects of different combinations of Consideration and Structure. Significant correlations have been found between each of these patterns and such indices as rated proficiency, grievances, turnover, departmental reputation, subordinate satisfactions, etc. (e.g. Fleishman, Harris and Burtt, 1955; Halpin, 1954; Hemphill, 1955; Stogdill and Coons, 1957). These studies present some evidence that scoring low on both dimensions is not desirable. They also indicate that some balance of consideration and structure may be optimal for satisfying both proficiency and morale criteria. The present study is a more intensive examination of possible optimum combinations of consideration and structure.

The present study investigates the relationships between foreman behavior and two primary indices of group behavior: labor grievances and employee turnover. Both of these may be considered as partial criteria of group effectiveness.

Procedure
Leader behavior measures

The study was conducted in a motor truck manufacturing plant. Fifty-seven production foremen and their work groups took part in the study. They represented such work operations as stamping, assembly, body assembly, body paint, machinery and export. At least three workers, drawn randomly from each foreman's department, described the leader behavior of their foreman by means of the *Supervisory Behavior Description Questionnaire* (described elsewhere, Fleishman, 1953c; 1957). Each questionnaire was scored on consideration and structure, and a mean consideration score and a mean structure score was computed for each foreman. The correlation between consideration and structure among foremen in this plant was found to be 0·33. The correlation between these scales is usually around zero (Fleishman, 1957), but in this plant foremen who are high in structure are somewhat more likely to be seen as lower in consideration and vice versa. However, the relationship is not high.

Grievance measures

Grievances were defined in terms of the number presented in writing and placed in company files. No data on grievances which were settled at lower levels (hence, without their becoming matters of company record) were considered. The frequency of grievances was equated for each foreman's work group by dividing the record for that group by the number of workers in that group. The reliability of these records, computed by correlating the records for odd and even weeks over an eleven-month period and correcting by the Spearman-Brown formula, was 0·73. The entire eleven-month record (for each foreman's work group) was used in the present analysis.

Turnover measures

Turnover was figured as the number of workers who voluntarily left the employ of the company within the eleven-month period. Again, the records for each foreman's group were equated by dividing the number who resigned by the number of workers in his work group. The nature of the records did not permit an analysis of the reasons which each worker gave for leaving, and so all such terminations are included. The corrected odd-even weeks reliability for this period was 0·59.

The reliabilities for the grievance and turnover measures are for the foremen's work groups and not for the individual worker. In the case of turnover, this reliability is quite high when one considers that different workers are involved in each time period. (Once a worker leaves, of course, he cannot contribute to turnover again.) The findings of stable grievance and turnover rates among groups under the same foremen is an important finding in its own right. The correlation between grievances and turnover is 0·37. This indicates that, while high grievance work groups tend to have higher turnover, the relationship is not very high. Each index is worth considering as an independent aspect of group behavior.

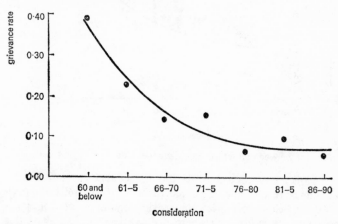

Figure 1 Relation between consideration and grievance rates

Results

Leader behavior and grievances

Figure 1 plots the average employee grievance rates for departments under foremen scoring at different levels of consideration. From the curve fitted to these points it can be seen clearly that the relationship between the foremen's behavior and grievances from their work groups is negative and curvilinear. For most of the range increased consideration goes with reduced grievance rates. However, increased consideration above a certain critical level (approximately 76 out of a possible 112) is not related to further decreases in grievances. Furthermore, the curve appears to be negatively accelerated. A given decrease in consideration just below the critical point (seventy-six) is related to a small increase in grievances, but, as consideration continues to drop, grievance rates rise sharply. Thus, a five-point drop on the consideration scale, just below a score of seventy-six, is related to a small grievance increase, but a five-point drop below sixty-one is related to a large rise in grievances. The correlation ratio (eta) represented by this curve is 0·51.

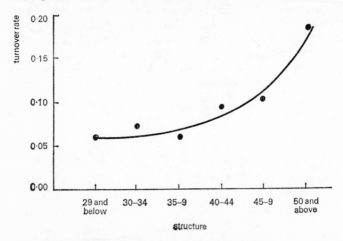

Figure 2 Relation between structure and grievance rates

Figure 2 plots grievances against the foremen's structure scores. Here a similar curvilinear relationship is observed. In this case the correlation is positive (eta = 0·71). Below a certain level (approximately thirty-six out of a possible eighty on our scale) structure is unrelated to grievances, but above this point increased structure goes with increased grievances. Again we see that a given increase in structure just above this critical level is accompanied by a small increase in grievances, but continued increases in structure are associated with increasingly disproportionately large increases in grievance rates.

Both curves are hyperbolic rather than parabolic in form. Thus, it appears that for neither consideration nor structure is there an 'optimum' point in the middle of the range below and above which grievances rise. Rather there seems to be a range within which increased consideration or decreased structure makes no difference. Of course, when one reaches these levels, grievances are already at a very low level and not much improvement can be expected. However, the important point is that this low grievance level is reached before one gets to the extremely high end of the consideration scale or to the extremely low end of the structure scale. It is also clear that extremely high structure and extremely low consideration are most related to high grievances.

Different combinations of consideration and structure related to grievances

The curves described establish that a general relationship exists between each of these leadership patterns and the frequency of employee grievances. But how do *different combinations* of consideration and structure relate to grievances? Some foremen score high on both dimensions, some score low on both, etc.

Figure 3 plots the relation between structure (low, medium and high) and grievances for groups of foremen who were either low, medium or high on consideration. The curves show that grievances occur most frequently among groups whose foremen are low in consideration, regardless of the

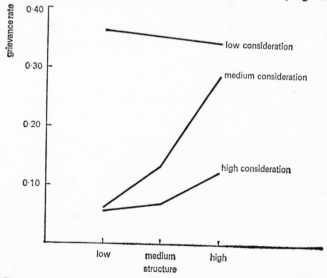

Figure 3 Combinations of consideration and structure related to grievances

Edwin A. Fleishman and Edwin F. Harris 265

amount of emphasis on structure. The most interesting finding relates to the curve for the high consideration foremen. This curve suggests that, for the high consideration foreman, structure could be increased without any appreciable increase in grievances. However, the reverse is not true; that is, foremen who were low in consideration could not reduce grievances by easing up on structure. For foremen average on consideration, grievances were lowest where structure was lowest and increased in an almost linear fashion as structure increased. These data show a definite interaction between consideration and structure. Apparently, high consideration can compensate for high structure. But low structure will not offset low consideration.

Before we speculate further about these relationships, let us examine the results with employee turnover.

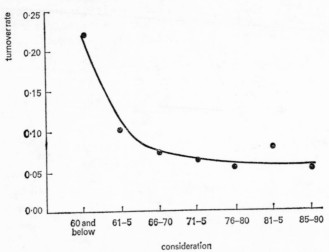

Figure 4 Relation between consideration and turnover rates

Leader behavior and turnover

Figures 4 and 5 plot the curves for the *Supervisory Behavior Description* scores of these foremen against the turnover criteria. Again, we see the curvilinear relationships. The correlation (eta) of consideration and turnover is 0·69; structure and turnover correlate 0·63. As in the case with grievances, below a certain critical level of consideration and above a certain level of structure, turnover goes up. There is, however, an interesting difference in that the critical levels differ from those related to grievances. The flat portions of each of these curves are more extended and the rise in turnover beyond the point of inflection is steeper. The implication of this is quite sensible and indicates that 'they gripe before they leave'. In other words, a given increase in structure (to approximately thirty-nine) or decrease in consideration (to sixty-six) may result in increased grievances, but not turnover. It takes higher structure and lower consideration before turnover occurs.

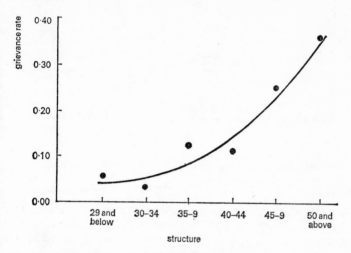

Figure 5 Relation between structure and turnover rates

Different combinations of consideration and structure related to turnover

Figure 6 plots the relation between structure (low, medium and high) and turnover for groups of foremen who were also either low, medium or high on consideration. As with grievances, the curves show that turnover is highest for the work groups whose foremen combine low consideration with high structure; however, the amount of consideration is the dominant factor. The curves show that turnover is highest among those work groups whose foremen are low in consideration, regardless of the amount of emphasis these same foremen show on structure. There is little distinction between the work groups of foremen who show medium and high consideration since both of these groups have low turnover among their workers. Furthermore, increased structure does not seem related to increased turnover in these two groups.[1]

1. This, of course, is consistent with our earlier finding that for increased turnover it takes a bigger drop in consideration and a bigger increase in structure to make a difference. Thus, our high and medium consideration groups separate for grievances, but overlap for turnover.

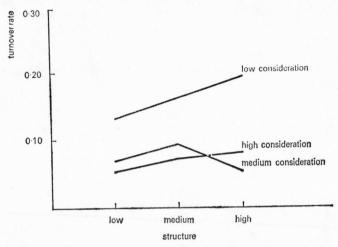

Figure 6 Combinations of consideration and structure related to turnover

Conclusions

This study indicates that there are significant relationships between the leader behavior of foremen and the labor grievances and employee turnover in their work groups. In general, low consideration and high structure go with high grievances and turnover.

There appear to be certain critical levels beyond which increased consideration or decreased structure have no effect on grievance or turnover rates. Similarly grievances and turnover are shown to increase most markedly at the extreme ends of the consideration (low end) and structure (high end) scales. Thus, the relationship is curvilinear, not linear, and hyperbolic, not parabolic.

The critical points at which increased structure and decreased consideration begin to relate to group behavior is not the same for grievances and turnover. Increases in turnover do not occur until lower on the consideration scale and higher on the structure scale, as compared with increases in grievances. For example, if consideration is steadily reduced, higher grievances appear before increased turnover occurs. It appears that there may be different 'threshold levels' of consideration and structure related to grievances and turnover.

Other principal findings concern the interaction effects found between different combinations of consideration and structure. Taken in combination, consideration is the dominant factor. For example, both grievances and turnover were highest in groups having low consideration foremen, regardless of the degree of structuring behavior shown by these same foremen.

Grievances and turnover were lowest for groups with foremen showing medium to high consideration together with low structure. However, one of the most important results is the finding that high consideration foremen could increase structure with very little increase in grievances and no increase in turnover. High consideration foremen had relatively low grievances and turnover, regardless of the amount of structuring engaged in.

Thus, with regard to grievances and turnover, leader behavior characterized by low consideration is more critical than behavior characterized by high structure. Apparently, foremen can compensate for high structure by increased consideration, but low consideration foremen cannot compensate by decreasing their structuring behavior.

One interpretation is that workers under foremen who establish a climate of mutual trust, rapport and tolerance for two-way communication with their work groups are more likely to accept higher levels of structure. This might be because they perceive this structure differently from employees in 'low-consideration' climates. Thus, under 'low-consideration' climates, high structure is seen as threatening and restrictive, but under 'high-consideration' climates this same structure is seen as supportive and helpful. A related interpretation is that foremen who establish such an atmosphere can more easily solve the problems resulting from high structure. Thus, *grievances* may be solved at this level before they get into the official records. Similarly, *turnover* may reflect escape from a problem situation which cannot be resolved in the absence of mutual trust and two-way communication. In support of this interpretation, we do have evidence that leaders high in consideration are also better at predicting subordinates' responses to problems (Fleishman and Salter, 1961).

One has to be careful in making cause and effect inferences here. A possible limitation is that our descriptions of foremen behavior came from the workers themselves. Those workers with many grievances may view their foremen as low in consideration simply because they have a lot of grievances. However, the descriptions of foreman behavior were obtained from workers drawn randomly from each foreman's group; the odds are against our receiving descriptions from very many workers contributing a disproportionate share of grievances. In the case of turnover, of course, our descriptions could not have been obtained from people who had left during the previous eleven months. Yet substantial correlations were obtained between foremen descriptions, supplied by currently employed workers, with the turnover rates of their work groups. Furthermore, we do have evidence that leader behavior over a year period tends to be quite stable. Test-retest correlations for consideration, as well as for structure, tend to be high even when different workers do the describing on the retest (Harris and Fleishman, 1955). Our present preference is to favor the interpretation that high turnover and grievances result, at least in part, from the leader behavior patterns described.

The non-linear relations between leader behavior and our criteria of effectiveness have more general implications for leadership research. For one thing, it points up the need for a more careful examination of the *form* of such relationships before computing correlation coefficients. Some previously obtained correlations with leadership variables may be underestimates because of linearity assumptions. Similarly, some previous negative or contradictory results may be 'explained' by the fact that (a) inappropriate coefficients were used or (b) these studies were dealing with only the flat portions of these curves. If, for example, all the foremen in our study had scored over seventy-six on consideration and under thirty-six on structure, we would have concluded that there was no relation between these leadership patterns and grievances and turnover. Perhaps in comparing one study with another, we need to specify the range of leader behavior involved in each study.

There is, of course, a need to explore similar relationships with other criteria. There is no assurance that similar curvilinear patterns and interaction effects will hold for other indices (e.g. group productivity). Even the direction of these relationships may vary with the criterion used. We have evidence (Fleishman, Harris and Burtt, 1955), for example, that consideration and structure may relate quite differently to another effectiveness criterion: management's perceptions of foremen proficiency. However, research along these lines may make it possible to specify the particular leadership patterns which most nearly 'optimize' these various effectiveness criteria in industrial organizations.

References

FLEISHMAN, E. A. (1951), '*Leadership Climate*' *and Supervisory Behavior*, Personnel Research Board, Ohio State University.

FLEISHMAN, E. A. (1953a), 'Leadership climate, human-relations training and supervisory behavior', *Personnel Psychol.*, vol. 6, pp. 205–22.

FLEISHMAN, E. A. (1953b), 'The description of supervisory behavior', *J. appl. Psychol.*, vol. 37, pp. 1–6.

FLEISHMAN, E. A. (1953c), 'The measurement of leadership attitudes in industry', *J. appl. Psychol.*, vol. 37, pp. 153–8.

FLEISHMAN, E. A. (1957), 'A leader behavior description for industry', in R. M. Stogdill and A. E. Coons (eds.), *Leader Behavior: Its Description and Measurement*, Bureau of Business Research.

FLEISHMAN, E. A., HARRIS, E. F., and BURTT, H. E. (1955), *Leadership and Supervision in Industry*, Bureau of Educational Research, Ohio State University.

FLEISHMAN, E. A., and SALTER, J. A. (1961), 'The relation between the leader's behavior and his empathy toward subordinates', *Advanced Management*, March, pp. 18–20.

HARRIS, E. F., and FLEISHMAN, E. A. (1955), 'Human-relations training and the stability of leadership patterns', *J. appl. Psychol.*, vol. 34, pp. 20–25.

HALPIN, A. W. (1954), 'The leadership behavior and combat performance of airplane commanders', *J. abnorm. soc. Psychol.*, vol. 44, pp. 19–22.

HEMPHILL, J. K. (1955), 'Leadership behavior associated with the administrative reputation of college departments', *J. educ. Psychol.*, vol. 96, pp, 385–401.

STOGDILL, R. M., and COONS, A. E. (eds.), (1957), *Leader Behavior: Its Description and Measurement*, Bureau of Business Research, Ohio State University.

19 F. E. Emery and E. L. Trist

Socio-Technical Systems

F. E. Emery and E. L. Trist, Socio-Technical Systems in C. W. Churchman, and M. Verhulst (eds.), *Management Sciences: Models and Techniques*, vol. 2, Pergamon, 1962, pp. 83-97.

The analysis of the characteristics of enterprises as systems would appear to have strategic significance for furthering our understanding of a great number of specific industrial problems. The more we know about these systems the more we are able to identify what is relevant to a particular problem and to detect problems that tend to be missed by the conventional framework of problem analysis.

The value of studying enterprises as systems has been demonstrated in the empirical studies of Blau (1955), Gouldner (1955), Jaques (1951), Selznick (1949) and Warner and Low (1947). Many of these studies have been informed by a broadly conceived concept of bureaucracy, derived from Weber and influenced by Parsons and Merton:

They have found their main business to be in the analysis of a specific bureaucracy as a complex social system, concerned less with the individual differences of the actors than with the situationally shaped roles they perform (Gouldner. 1955).

Granted the importance of system analysis there remains the important question of whether an enterprise should be construed as a 'closed' or an 'open system', i.e. relatively 'closed' or 'open' with respect to its external environment. Von Bertalanffy (1950) first introduced this general distinction in contrasting biological and physical phenomena. In the realm of social theory, however, there has been something of a tendency to continue thinking in terms of a 'closed' system, that is, to regard the enterprise as sufficiently independent to allow most of its problems to be analysed with reference to its internal structure and without reference to its external environment. Early exceptions were Rice and Trist (1952) in the field of labour turnover and Herbst (1954) in the analysis of social-flow systems. As a first step, closed-system thinking has been fruitful, in psychology and industrial sociology, in directing attention to the existence of structural similarities, relational determination and subordination of part to whole. However, it has tended to be misleading on problems of growth and the conditions for maintaining a 'steady state'. The formal physical models of 'closed systems' postulate that, as in the second law of thermodynamics, the inherent tendency of such systems is to grow toward maximum homogeneity of the parts and that a steady state can only be achieved by the cessation of all activity. In practice the system theorists in social science (and these include such key anthropologists as Radcliffe-Brown) refused to recognize these implications but instead, by the same token, did *'tend* to focus on the statics of social structure and to neglect the study of structural change' (Merton, 1949). In an attempt to overcome this bias, Merton suggested that 'the concept of dysfunction, which implies the concept of strain, stress and tension on the structural level, provides an analytical approach to the study of dynamics and change' (1949). This concept has been widely accepted by system theorists but while it draws attention to sources of imbalance within an organization it does not conceptually reflect the mutual permeation of an organization and its environment that is the cause of such imbalance. It still retains the limiting perspectives of 'closed system' theorizing. In the administrative field the same limitations may be seen in the otherwise invaluable contributions of Barnard (1948) and related writers.

The alternative conception of 'open systems' carries the logical implications that such systems may spontaneously re-organize toward states of greater heterogeneity and complexity and that they achieve a 'steady state' at a level where they can still do work. Enterprises appear to possess at least these characteristics of 'open systems'. They grow by processes of internal elaboration (Herbst, 1954) and manage to achieve a steady state while doing work, i.e. achieve a quasi-stationary equilibrium in which the enterprise as a whole remains constant, with a continuous 'throughput', despite a considerable range of external changes (Lewin, 1951; Rice and Trist, 1952).

The appropriateness of the concept of 'open system' can be settled, however, only by examining in some detail what is involved in an enterprise achieving a steady state. The continued existence of any enterprise presupposes some regular commerce in products or services with other enterprises, institutions and persons in its external social environment. If it is going to be useful to speak of steady states in an enterprise, they must be states in which this commerce is going on. The conditions for regularizing this commerce lie both within and without the enterprise. On the one hand this presupposes that an enterprise has at its immediate disposal the necessary material supports for its activities – a workplace, materials, tools and machines – and a work force able and willing to make the necessary modifications in the material 'throughput' or provide the requisite services. It must also be able, efficiently, to utilize its material supports and to organize the actions of its human agents in a rational and predictable manner. On the other hand, the regularity of commerce with the environment may be influenced by a broad range of independent external changes affecting markets for products and inputs of labour, materials and technology. If we examine the factors influencing the ability of an enterprise to maintain a steady state in the face of these broader environmental influences we find that:

1. The variation in the output markets that can be tolerated without structural change is a function of the flexibility of the technical productive apparatus – its ability to vary its rate, its end product or the mixture of its products. Variation in the output markets may itself be considerably reduced by the display of distinctive competence. Thus the output markets will be more attached to a given enterprise if it has, relative to other producers, a distinctive competence – a distinctive ability to deliver the right product to the right place at the right time.

2. The tolerable variation in the 'input' markets is likewise dependent upon the technological component. Thus some enterprises are enabled by their particular technical organization to tolerate considerable variation in the type and amount of labour they can recruit. Others can tolerate little.

The two significant features of this state of affairs are:

1. That there is no simple one-to-one relation between variations in inputs and outputs. Depending upon the technological system, different combinations of inputs may be handled to yield similar outputs and different 'product mixes' may be produced from similar inputs. As far as possible an enterprise will tend to do these things rather than make structural changes in its organization. It is one of the additional characteristics of 'open systems' that while they are in constant commerce with the environment they are selective and, within limits, self-regulating.

2. That the technological component, in converting inputs into outputs, plays a major role in determining the self-regulating properties of an enterprise. It functions as one of the major boundary conditions of the social system of the enterprise in this mediating between the ends of an enterprise and the external environment. Because of this the materials, machines and territory that go to making up the technological component are usually defined, in any modern society, as 'belonging' to an enterprise and excluded from similar control by other enterprises. They represent, as it were, an 'internalized environment'.

Thus the mediating boundary conditions must be represented amongst 'the open-system constants' (Von Bertalanffy, 1950) that define the conditions under which a steady state can be achieved. The technological component has been found to play a key mediating role and hence it follows that the open-system concept must be referred to the socio-technical system, not simply to the social system of an enterprise.

It might be justifiable to exclude the technological component from the system concept if it were true, as many writers imply, that it plays only a passive and intermittent role. However, it cannot be dismissed as simply a set of limits that exert an influence at the initial stage of building an enterprise and only at such subsequent times as these limits are overstepped. There is, on the contrary, an almost constant accommodation of stresses arising from changes in the external environment; the technological component not only sets limits upon what can be done, but also in the process of accommodation creates demands that must be reflected in the internal organization and ends of an enterprise.

Study of a productive system therefore requires detailed attention to both the technological and the social components. It is not possible to understand these systems in terms of some arbitrarily selected single aspect of the technology such as the repetitive nature of the work, the coerciveness of the assembly conveyor or the piecemeal nature of the task. However, this is what is usually attempted by students of the enterprise. In fact:

It has been fashionable of late, particularly in the 'human-relations' school, to assume that the actual job, its technology, and its mechanical and physical requirements are relatively unimportant compared to the social and psychological situation of men at work (Drucker, 1952).

Even when there has been a detailed study of the technology this has not been systematically related to the social system but been treated as background information (Warner and Low, 1947).

In our earliest study of production systems in coal mining it became apparent that

So close is the relationship between the various aspects that the social and the psychological can be understood only in terms of the detailed engineering facts and of the way the technological system as a whole behaves in the environment of the underground situation (Trist and Bamforth, 1951).

An analysis of a technological system in these terms can produce a systematic picture of the tasks and task interrelations required by a technological system. However, between these requirements and the social system there is not a strictly determined one-to-one relation but what is logically referred to as a correlative relation.

In a very simple operation such as manually moving and stacking railway sleepers ('ties') there may well be only a single suitable work relationship structure, namely, a cooperating pair with each man taking an end of the sleeper and lifting, supporting, walking and throwing in close coordination

F. E. Emery and E. L. Trist 275

with the other man. The ordinary production process is much more complex and there it is unusual to find that only one particular work relationship structure can be fitted to these tasks.

This element of choice and the mutual influence of technology and the social system may both be illustrated from our studies, made over several years, of work organization in British deep-seam coal mining. The following data are adapted from Trist and Murray (1948).

Thus Table I indicates the main features of two very different forms of organization that have both been operated economically within the same seam and with identical technology.

Table 1 Same technology, same coalseam, different social systems

	A conventional cutting long-wall mining system	A composite cutting long-wall mining system
Number of men	41	41
Number of completely segregated task groups	14	1
Mean job variation for members:		
Task groups worked with	1	5·5
Main tasks worked	1	3·6
Different shifts worked	2	2·9

The conventional system combines a complex formal structure with simple work roles: the composite system combines a simple formal structure with complex work roles. In the former the miner has a commitment to only a single part task and enters into only a very limited number of unvarying social relations that are sharply divided between those within his particular task group and those who are outside. With those 'outside' he shares no sense of belongingness and he recognizes no responsibility to them for the consequences of his actions. In the composite system the miner has a commitment to the whole group task and consequently finds himself drawn into a variety of tasks in cooperation with different members of the total group; he may be drawn into any task on the coal-face with any member of the total group.

That two such contrasting social systems can effectively operate the same technology is clear enough evidence that there exists an element of choice in designing a work organization.

However, it is not a matter of indifference which form of organization is selected. As has already been stated, the technological system sets certain requirements of its social system and the effectiveness of the total production system will depend upon the adequacy with which the social system is able to cope with these requirements. Although alternative social systems may survive in that they are both accepted as 'good enough' (Simon, 1957) this does not preclude the possibility that they may differ in effectiveness.

In this case the composite systems consistently showed a superiority over the conventional in terms of production and costs.

Table 2 **Production and costs for different forms of work organization with same technology**

	'Conventional'	'Composite'
Productive achievement[a]	78	95
Ancillary work at face (hrs per man-shift)	1·32	0·03
Average reinforcement of labour (percent of total face force)	6	
Percent of shifts with cycle lag	69	5
Number of consecutive weeks without losing a cycle	12	65

[a] Average percentage of coal won from each daily cut, corrected for differences in seam transport.

This superiority reflects, in the first instance, the more adequate coping in the composite system with the task requirements. The constantly changing underground conditions require that the already complex sequence of mining tasks undergo frequent changes in the relative magnitudes and even the order of these tasks. These conditions optimally require the internal flexibility possessed in varying degrees by the composite systems. It is difficult to meet variable task requirements with any organization built on a rigid division of labour. The only justification for a rigid division of labour is a technology which demands specialized non-substitute skills and which is, moreover, sufficiently superior, as a technology, to offset the losses due to rigidity. The conventional longwall cutting system has no such technical superiority over the composite to offset its relative rigidity – its characteristic inability to cope with changing conditions other than by increasing the stress placed on its members, sacrificing smooth cycle progress or drawing heavily upon the negligible labour reserves of the pit.

The superiority of the composite system does not rest alone in more adequate coping with the tasks. It also makes better provision to the personal requirements of the miners. Mutually supportive relations between task groups are the exception in the conventional system and the rule in the composite. In consequence, the conventional miner more frequently finds himself without support from his fellows when the strain or size of his task requires it. Crises are more likely to set him against his fellows and hence worsen the situation.

Similarly, the distribution of rewards and statuses in the conventional system reflects the relative bargaining power of different roles and task groups as much as any true differences in skill and effort. Under these conditions of disparity between effort and reward any demands for increased effort are likely to create undue stress.

The following table indicates the difference in stress experienced by miners in the two systems.

Table 3 Stress indices for different social systems

	'Conventional'	'Composite'
Absenteeism		
(Percent of possible shifts)		
Without reason	4·3	0·4
Sickness or other	8·9	4·6
Accidents	6·8	3·2
Total	20·0	8·2

These findings were replicated by experimental studies in textile mills in the radically different setting of Ahmedabad, India (Rice, 1958).

However, two possible sources of misunderstanding need to be considered:

1. Our findings do not suggest that work-group autonomy should be maximized in all productive settings. There is an optimum level of grouping which can be determined only by analysis of the requirements of the technological system. Neither does there appear to be any simple relation between level of mechanization and level of grouping. In one mining study we found that in moving from a hand-filling to a machine-filling technology, the appropriate organization shifted from an undifferentiated composite system to one based on a number of partially segregated task groups with more stable differences in internal statuses.

2. Nor does it appear that the basic psychological needs being met by grouping are workers' needs for friendship on the job, as is frequently postulated by advocates of better 'human relations' in industry. Grouping produces its main psychological effects when it leads to a system of work roles such that the workers are primarily related to each other by way of the requirements of task performance and task interdependence. When this task orientation is established the worker should find that he has an adequate range of mutually supportive roles (mutually supportive with respect to performance and to carrying stress that arises from the task). As the role

system becomes more mature and integrated, it becomes easier for a worker to understand and appreciate his relation to the group. Thus in the comparison of different composite mining groups it was found that the differences in productivity and in coping with stress were not primarily related to differences in the level of friendship in the groups. The critical prerequisites for a composite system are an adequate supply of the required special skills among members of the group and conditions for developing an appropriate system of roles. Where these prerequisites have not been fully met, the composite system has broken down or established itself at a less than optimum level. The development of friendship and particularly of mutual respect occurs in the composite systems but the friendship tends to be limited by the requirements of the system and not assume unlimited disruptive forms such as were observed in conventional systems and were reported by Adams (1953) to occur in certain types of bomber crews.

The textile studies (Rice, 1958) yielded the additional finding that *supervisory roles* are best designed on the basis of the same type of socio-technical analysis. It is not enough simply to allocate to the supervisor a list of responsibilities for specific tasks and perhaps insist upon a particular style of handling men. The supervisory roles arise from the need to control and coordinate an incomplete system of men-task relations. Supervisory responsibility for the specific parts of such a system is not easily reconcilable with responsibility for overall aspects. The supervisor who continually intervenes to do some part of the productive work may be proving his willingness to work but is also likely to be neglecting his main task of controlling and coordinating the system so that the operators are able to get on with their jobs with the least possible disturbance.

Definition of a supervisory role presupposes analysis of the system's requirements for control and coordination and provision of conditions that will enable the supervisor readily to perceive what is needed of him and to take appropriate measures. As his control will in large measure rest on his control of the boundary conditions of the system – those activities relating to a larger system – it will be desirable to create 'unified commands' so that the boundary conditions will be correspondingly easy to detect and manage. If the unified commands correspond to natural task groupings, it will also be possible to maximize the autonomous responsibility of the work group for internal control and coordination, thus freeing the supervisor for his primary task. A graphic illustration of the differences in a supervisory role following a socio-technical reorganization of an automatic loom shed (Rice, 1958) can be seen in the following two figures: Figure 1 representing the situation before and Figure 2 representing the situation after change.

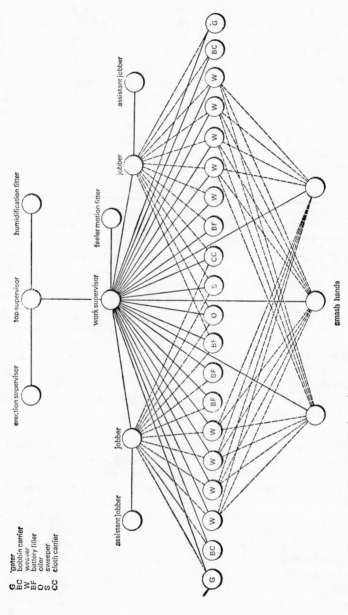

G   gater
BC   bobbin carrier
W   weaver
BF   battery filler
O   oiler
S   sweeper
CC   cloth carrier

erection supervisor   top supervisor   humidification fitter

assistant jobber   jobber   feeler motion fitter   work supervisor   jobber   assistant jobber

G BC W W W W W BF CC S O BF BF BF W W W W BC G

smash hands

Figure 1 Management hierarchy before change

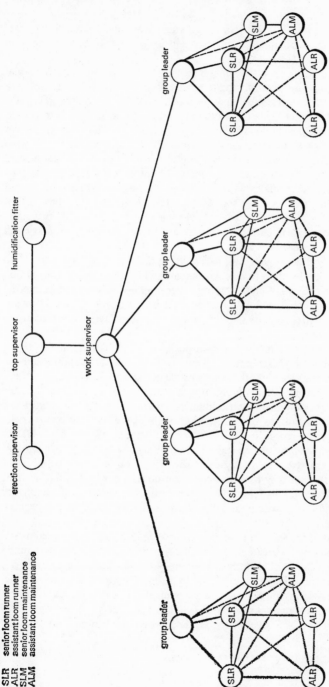

SLR   senior loom runner
ALR   assistant loom runner
SLM   senior loom maintenance
ALM   assistant loom maintenance

Figure 2 Management hierarchy after change

This reorganization was reflected in a significant and sustained improvement in mean percentage efficiency and a decrease in mean percentage damage.

The significance of the difference between these two organizational diagrams does not rest only in the relative simplicity of the latter (although this does reflect less confusion of responsibilities) but also in the emergence of clearly distinct areas of command which contain within themselves a relatively independent set of work roles together with the skills necessary to govern their task boundaries. In like manner the induction and training of new members was recognized as a boundary condition for the entire shed and located directly under shed management instead of being scattered throughout subordinate commands. Whereas the former organization had been maintained in a steady state only by the constant and arduous efforts of management, the new one proved to be inherently stable and self-correcting, and consequently freed management to give more time to their primary task and also to manage a third shift.

Similarly, the primary task in managing the enterprise as a whole is to relate the total system to its environment and is not in internal regulation *per se*. This does not mean that managers will not be involved in internal problems but that such involvement will be oriented consciously or unconsciously to certain assumptions about the external relations of the enterprise.

This contrasts with the common postulate of the structural–functional theories that 'the basic need of all empirical systems is the maintenance of the integrity and continuity of the system itself' (Selznick, 1948). It contrasts also with an important implication of this postulate, namely, that the primary task of management is 'continuous attention to the possibilities of encroachment and to the forestalling of threatened aggressions or deleterious consequences from the actions of others' (Selznick, 1948). In industry this represents the special and limiting case of a management that takes for granted a previously established definition of its primary task and assumes that all they have to do, or can do, is sit tight and defend their market position. This is, however, the common case in statutorily established bodies and it is on such bodies that recent studies of bureaucracy have been largely carried out.

In general the leadership of an enterprise must be willing to break down an old integrity or create profound discontinuity if such steps are required to take advantage of changes in technology and markets. The very survival of an enterprise may be threatened by its inability to face up to such demands, as for instance, switching the main effort from production of processed goods to marketing or from production of heavy industrial goods to consumer goods. Similarly, the leadership may need to pay 'continuous' attention to the possibilities of making their own encroachments rather than be obsessed with the possible encroachments of others.

Considering enterprises as 'open socio-technical systems' helps to provide a more realistic picture of how they are both influenced by and able to act back on their environment. It points in particular to the various ways in which enterprises are enabled by their structural and functional characteristics ('system constants') to cope with the 'lacks' and 'gluts' in their available environment. Unlike mechanical and other inanimate systems they possess the property of 'equi-finality'; they may achieve a steady state from differing initial conditions and in differing ways (Von Bertalanffy, 1950). Thus in coping by internal changes they are not limited to simple quantitative change and increased uniformity but may, and usually do, elaborate new structures and take on new functions. The cumulative effect of coping mainly by *internal* elaboration and differentiation is generally to make the system independent of an increasing range of the predictable fluctuations in its supplies and outlets. At the same time, however, this process ties down in specific ways more and more of its capital, skill and energies and renders it less able to cope with newly emergent and unpredicted changes that challenge the primary ends of the enterprise. This process has been traced out in a great many empirical studies of bureaucracies (Blau, 1955; Merton, 1949; Selznick, 1949).

However, there are available to an enterprise other aggressive strategies that seek to achieve a steady state by transforming the environment. Thus an enterprise has some possibilities for moving into new markets or inducing changes in the old; for choosing differently from amongst the range of personnel, resources and technologies offered by its environment or training and making new ones; and for developing new consumer needs or stimulating old ones.

Thus, arising from the nature of the enterprise as an open system, management is concerned with 'managing' both an internal system and an external environment. To regard an enterprise as a closed system and concentrate upon management of the 'internal enterprise' would be to expose the enterprise to the full impact of the vagaries of the environment.

If management is to control internal growth and development it must in the first instance control the 'boundary conditions' – the forms of exchange between the enterprise and its environment. As we have seen most enterprises are confronted with a multitude of actual and possible exchanges. If resources are not to be dissipated the management must select from the alternatives a course of action. The casual texture of competitive environments is such that it is extremely difficult to survive on a simple strategy of selecting the best from among the alternatives immediately offering. Some that offer immediate gain lead nowhere, others lead to greater loss; some alternatives that offer loss are avoidable, others are unavoidable if long run gains are to be made. The relative size of the immediate loss or gain is no sure guide as to what follows. Since also the actions of an enterprise can improve the alternatives that are presented to it, the optimum course is more likely to rest in selecting a strategic objective to be achieved in the long run. The strategic objective should be to place the enterprise in a position in its environment where it has some assured conditions for growth – unlike war the best position is not necessarily that of unchallenged monopoly. Achieving this position would be the *primary task* or overriding mission of the enterprise.

In selecting the primary task of an enterprise, it needs to be borne in mind that the relations with the environment may vary with (a) the productive efforts of the enterprise in meeting environmental requirements: (b) changes in the environment that may be induced by the enterprise and (c) changes independently taking place in the environment. These will be of differing importance for different enterprises and for the same enterprises at different times. Managerial control will usually be greatest if the primary task can be based on productive activity. If this is not possible, as in commerce, the primary task will give more control if it is based on marketing than simply on foreknowledge of the independent environmental changes. Managerial control will be further enhanced if the primary task, at whatever it is selected, is such as to enable the enterprise to achieve *vis-à-vis* its competitors, a *distinctive competence.* Conversely, in our experience, an enterprise which has long occupied a favoured position because of distinctive productive competence may have grave difficulty in recognizing when it is losing control owing to environmental changes beyond its control.

As Selznick (1957) has pointed out, an appropriately defined primary task offers stability and direction to an enterprise, protecting it from adventurism or costly drifting. These advantages, however, as he illustrates may be no more than potential unless the top management group of the organization achieves solidarity about the new primary task. If the vision of the task is locked up in a single man or is the subject of dissension in top management it will be subject to a great risk of distortion and susceptible to violent fluctuations. Similarly, the enterprise as a whole needs to be re-oriented and reintegrated about this primary task. Thus, if the primary task shifts from heavy industrial goods to durable consumer goods it would be necessary to ensure that there is a corresponding shift in values that are embedded in such sections as the sales force and designed department.

References

ADAMS, S. (1953), 'Status congruency as a variable in small-group performance', *Soc. Forces*, vol. 32, pp. 16–22.

BARNARD, C. I. (1948), *The Functions of the Executive*, Harvard University Press.

BERTALANFFY, L. V. (1950), 'The theory of open systems in physics and biology', *Science*, vol. 111, pp. 23–9.

BLAU, P. (1955), *The Dynamics of Bureaucracy*, University of Chicago Press.

DRUCKER, P. F. (1952), 'The employee society', *Amer. Sociol. Rev.*, vol. 58, pp. 358–63.

GOULDNER, A. W. (1955), *Patterns of Industrial Bureaucracy*, Routledge & Kegan Paul.

HERBST, P. G. (1954), 'The analysis of social flow systems', *Hum. Relat.*, vol. 7, pp. 327–36.

JAQUES, E. (1951), *The Changing Culture of a Factory*, Tavistock.

LEWIN, K. (1951), *Field Theory in Social Science*, Harper & Row.

MERTON, R. K. (1949), *Social Theory and Social Structure*, Free Press.

RICE, A. K. (1958), *Productivity and Social Organization: The Ahmedabad Experiment*, Tavistock.

RICE, A. K., and TRIST, E. L. (1952), 'Institutional and sub-institutional determinants of change in labour turnover (The Glacier Project – VIII)', *Hum. Relat.*, vol. 5, pp. 347–72.

SCHUTZENBERGER, M. P. (1954), 'A tentative classification of goal-seeking behaviors', *J. Ment, Sci.* vol. 100, pp. 97–102.

SELZNICK, P. (1948), 'Foundations of the theory of organization', *Amer. Sociol. Rev.*, vol. 13, pp. 25–35.

SELZNICK, P. (1949), *TVA and the Grass Roots*, University of California Press.

SELZNICK, P. (1957), *Leadership in Administration*, Harper & Row.

SIMON, H. A. (1957), *Models of Man*, Wiley.

TOLMAN, E. C., and BRUNSWIK, E. (1935), 'The organism and the causal texture of the environment', *Psychol. Rev.*, vol. 42, pp. 43–77.

TRIST, E. L., and BAMFORTH, K. W. (1951), 'Some social and psychological consequences of the longwall method of coal-getting', *Hum. Relat.*, vol. 4, pp. 3–38.

TRIST, E. L., and MURRAY, H. (1948), 'Work organization at the coal face: a comparative study of mining systems', *T.I.H.R.*

WARNER, W. L., and LOW, J. O. (1947), *The Social System of the Modern Factory*, Yale University Press.

Part Six
Personality and Social Interaction

It is obvious that individuals vary in their styles of social behaviour, but it is very difficult to account for their social performance in terms of conventional measures of personality. Traits like intelligence, extraversion and neuroticism have rather small correlations with behaviour in any specific situation, and the same individual behaves quite differently on different occasions. Better predictions can be made by taking account of the personalities of the other people present as well; Carment, Miles and Cervin (Reading 20) found that the *more* extraverted or the *more* intelligent of two people was the more persuasive and talked more. Another approach to the problem is to devise new dimensions which are relevant to particular areas of social behaviour. Singer (Reading 21) describes a study showing that measures of Machiavellianism have a startlingly high relationship with manipulation of college teachers by students. However, behaviour can also be predicted from knowledge of the situation; Moos (Reading 22) reports a study in which the variance in behaviour due to Persons, Situations and Persons × Situations is analysed. The large amount of variance due to P × S interaction shows that persons are not particularly consistent, and that conceptualizing persons in terms of general traits is not satisfactory. Similar results have been obtained in other studies, but there is still no generally accepted way of assessing and conceptualizing persons.

20 D. W. Carment, C. G. Miles and V. B. Cervin

Persuasiveness and Persuasibility as Related to Intelligence and Extraversion

D. W. Carment, C. G. Miles and V. B. Cervin, 'Persuasiveness and persuasibility as related to intelligence and extraversion', *British Journal of Social and Clinical Psychiatry*, vol. 4, 1965, pp. 1–7.

Introduction

The experiment reported here follows previous persuasion studies of Cervin (1957) and Carment (1961) in which they have examined the relationship of different levels of 'emotional responsiveness' and opinion strength to ascendant–submissive behaviour in two-person groups. In these investigations pairs of subjects were required to debate a topic on which they initially held opposed opinions with the purpose of arriving at a common statement of agreement, disagreement or compromise. Ascendant behaviour was assumed to be reflected by greater participation in the discussion and shorter latency of first statement, i.e. by greater persuasiveness, and greater resistance to change of opinion, i.e. lower persuasibility. It was the purpose of the present study to extend these investigations to include two other variables of importance in social interaction, intelligence and introversion–extraversion.

The relationship between intelligence and susceptibility to influence is not at all clear. Some previous studies have shown that, under certain conditions, persons of high intelligence were more influenced than those of lower intelligence (Hovland, Lumsdaine and Sheffield, 1949; Crutchfield, 1951) whereas others (Janis and Field, 1959) could find no relationship between intelligence and persuasibility. In the present context it seems reasonable to assume, as suggested by Skinner (1957), that intelligence can be considered to be related to the size of an individual's repertoire of arguments related to a given topic. It would be anticipated, therefore, that, other factors being equal, a subject of high intelligence when paired with a subject of low intelligence should speak first, speak the greatest proportion of the time and maintain his original position.

The personality variable introversion–extraversion has been described in detail by Eysenck (1957). In particular, he points out that the introvert is over-socialized, is less dependent on external circumstances, and that this makes him less susceptible to group pressure. On the other hand, the extravert, who does not have these internal controls, is not so independent of the social situation and therefore would become unduly responsive to group opinion, group standards and group approval. ... A direct consequence of this hypothesis would be the prediction that in experimental situations in which the perceptions or attitudes of the individual are opposed to group pressure ... introverts should be more likely to resist this pressure than extraverts (Eysenck, 1957, p. 214).

On these grounds it would be anticipated that introverts when paired with extraverts in a persuasion situation would tend not to change their opinion, i.e. show lower persuasibility.

On the other hand, in the manual accompanying the Maudsley Personality Inventory, developed to measure neuroticism and introversion–extraversion, Eysenck writes: '... extraversion, as opposed to introversion, refers to the out-going, uninhibited, sociable proclivities of a person' (Eysenck, 1959, p. 3). On the basis of this statement extraverts would be expected to speak first and speak the greatest proportion of the time when paired with introverts. If this is the case, the results of previous studies (Cervin, 1957; Carment, 1961) would suggest that extraverts would be more persuasive. This hypothesis is in direct contrast to the prediction derived from Eysenck (1957) above. This is because these previous investigations have been consistent in showing a high inverse correlation between amount of speaking and amount of opinion change. Subjects who speak the most tend not to change their opinions.

In the experiment reported here three different combinations of intelligence and introversion–extraversion are examined. In one group of pairs both members are of high intelligence and extraverted. In a second group, one member of each pair is of high intelligence and extraverted while his opponent is also of high intelligence but introverted. In a third group one member of each pair is of high intelligence and extraverted and opposed by a subject who is of low intelligence but also extraverted. Under the last two conditions evidence may be obtained to test our hypothesis of the relative contributions of intelligence and introversion–extraversion to the process of persuasion. The first one serves as a control condition under which we expect equal amounts of change, if any, in both subjects of the pairs.

Method
Subjects
Male and female students (average age 20·03 years) in an introductory psychology class at McMaster University were given the Shipley–Hartford scale as a measure of intelligence and Eysenck's E-scale, short form, as a measure of introversion–extraversion. High (H) score implies high intelligence or extraversion; low (L) score, low intelligence or introversion. Each subject in a pair is characterized by two scores; e.g. HL for high intelligence and introversion.

From this population ($N = 248$) forty-six high intelligence (mean score 18·25) and extraverted (mean score 10·45), thirty-three high intelligence (mean score 17·80) and introverted (mean score 3·0), and thirty-three low intelligence (mean score 12·16) and extraverted (mean score 10·13) subjects were selected.

High intelligence subjects were required to have scored sixteen or higher (the maximum possible score is 20) and low intelligence subjects to have scored fourteen or lower on the Shipley–Hartford Scale. Introverts had obtained five or less and extraverts nine or higher on the short E-scale. These subjects were then paired in two different orders so that effects of the main independent variables and of possible practice might be discerned. Matching on the variables was within one score point and a minimum of five points difference was maintained between all high and low scores.

The pairings were as follows:

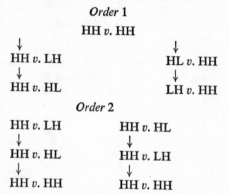

Order 1

HH *v.* HH

HH *v.* LH   HL *v.* HH

HH *v.* HL   LH *v.* HH

Order 2

HH *v.* LH   HH *v.* HL

HH *v.* HL   HH *v.* LH

HH *v.* HH   HH *v.* HH

In these tables HH stands for high intelligence-extraverted, HL for high intelligence-introverted, and LH for low intelligence-extraverted subjects. The arrows indicate the same subject.

It can be seen that the order of pairings is partially counterbalanced. However, upon analysis no effect attributable to practice was found and therefore all similar pairings, irrespective of order, were pooled to form three groups of pairs, HH *v.* HH, HH *v.* HL and HH *v.* LH.

The members of each pair were matched for sex, age, university year and opinion-strength (see below).

Procedure

These students had, at the time they filled out the personality and intelligence tests, indicated the nature and strength of their opinions on a number of discussion topics, chosen to have no undue emotional value (in particular, items of direct political and religious significance were omitted) but to be of some interest to them. For example, each had been asked to indicate whether he agreed or disagreed with items such as 'slipshod manufacture is characteristic of American products' and then to place a check on a three-point scale of opinion-strength ranging from 'of no concern to me whatsoever' through 'interested but not too concerned', to 'I feel very strongly about this issue'.

A topic had been selected on which the pair members had opposite opinions and the same opinion strength and they were then told:

In this experiment we are interested in observing people discussing various topics. You have indicated your opinions regarding a number of issues on this questionnaire which you answered in class. I would like you to discuss one of these issues with the purpose of arriving at a common statement of your opinions, that is, until you reach some conclusion such as a common statement on agreement, compromise or disagreement. (This order was alternated, with disagreement appearing first half the time.) You can talk as long as you want to. When you have reached a conclusion please put it into words that are acceptable to both of you, and then ring this bell. This will tell us that you have finished. I'll leave the room and in a few moments I'll knock on the window. This will be the signal for you to start talking. But it is very important that you do not talk until I knock. Do not say a word until then. Any question? (If necessary repeat instructions.)

I'll knock in a moment. Remember, don't talk.

Observers (one for each S in the pair) viewed the discussion through a one-way window and recorded the interaction on an Esterline–Angus event recorder.

They recorded:

1. The latency of the first response. This was the time from the signal to start until one or the other of the Ss began to speak.

2. The length of the speeches of each of the Ss.

3. Public statement of opinion change.

This was recorded at the conclusion of the discussion as change, compromise or no change by each observer independently. In making this judgement, the observer took into consideration the general tenor of the discussion and, in particular, the final common statement agreed upon by the two subjects together. Where the observers' decisions were not the same the tape recording of the discussion was played and a mutual decision reached. Observers were not aware of Ss personality scores at the time of observation.

The subjects were then seated at separate tables so that neither could see the other and they each then recorded their final opinion on the topic again.

It was made clear that this statement would be held in confidence and it is used as the fourth dependent measure – private statement of opinion change.

Results
Latency of first response

Table 1 shows the number of pairs in the HH *v.* HL and HH *v.* LH groups in

Table 1 **Latency of first response**

Groups of pairs	Number of pairs in which HH subject spoke first	Number of pairs in which other subject spoke first	Total
HH *v.* HL	26	7	33
HH *v.* LH	28	5	33
Total	54	12	66

which one or the other subject spoke first. Since the data are not independent two χ^2 are calculated. They indicate that when paired with HL subjects the HH subjects speak first significantly more often ($\chi^2 = 10\cdot93, p < 0\cdot01, 1df$) as is the case when they are paired with LH subjects ($\chi^2 = 16\cdot00, p < 0\cdot01, 1df$) thus supporting our hypotheses.

Amount of participation

Table 2 shows the number of pairs in which one or the other subject spoke

Table 2 **Participation differences**

Groups of pairs	Number of pairs in which HH subject spoke most of the time	Number of pairs in which other subject spoke most of the time	Total
HH *v.* HL	24	9	33
HH *v.* LH	23	10	33
Total	47	19	66

the greatest proportion of the time. It can be seen that when paired with either HL subjects or LH subjects the HH subjects speak the greatest proportion of the time ($\chi^2 = 6\cdot8, p < 0\cdot01$ and $\chi^2 = 5\cdot12, p < 0\cdot05, 1\ df$), thus supporting our hypotheses on this measure also.

Change of opinion

The data for both the public and private statements of opinion change are presented in Tables 3 and 4.

Table 3 **Frequency of opinion change**

Group of pairs		One-subject changes	Compromise and no change	Totals	X^2	p
HH v. HH	Public	3	20	} 23	{ 12·5	<0·01
	Private	4	19		9·8	<0·01
HH v. HL	Public	22	11	} 33	{ 3·66	<0·06
	Private	21	12		2·45	<0·12
HH v. LH	Public	22	11	} 33	{ 3·66	<0·06
	Private	18	15			

Table 4 **Frequency of opinion change**
(pairs in which one subject changes)

Pairs		HH subject changes	Other-subject changes	Total	X^2	p
HH v. HL	Public	0	22	22	22·0	<0·01
	Private	4	17	21	13·0	<0·01
HH v. LH	Public	3	19	22	11·6	<0·01
	Private	3	15	18	8·0	<0·01

The HH v. HH group is now included and among these pairs there were three pairs in which one subject publicly changed to agree with his opponent. A member of one additional pair indicated privately that he had changed to agree with his opponent. In the public data there were twelve cases of compromise and eight cases where no change of opinion took place (Ss agreed to disagree) and in the private data there were eleven compromises and eight cases of no opinion change. These data resulted in an χ^2 of 12·5 and 9·8 ($p < 0·01$, 1 df) respectively. In contrast, when the HH subjects were paired with HL subjects there were twenty-two cases of public change of opinion and twenty-one cases of opinion change in the private data. Publicly there were seven compromises and in four pairs there was no change whereas privately there were four compromises and in eight pairs no change of opinion was indicated. The public data results in a χ^2 of 3·66 ($p < 0·06$, 1 df), and the private data a χ^2 of 2·45 ($p < 0·12$, 1 df). When paired with LH subjects there were, again, twenty-two pairs in which there was a public change of opinion and eighteen pairs in which a subject privately recorded a change of opinion. Publicly there were seven compromises and in four cases no change of opinion took place. Privately there were four compromises and in eleven pairs no change of opinion occurred. The difference in the public data is significant ($\chi^2 = 3·66$, $p < 0·06$, 1 df), whereas the private data is not, although it is in the appropriate direction.

Among the group of pairs in which one subject changed the tendency is clearly for HH subjects not to change their opinions either publicly or privately (Table 4). These results support our hypotheses.

It should be noted that all significance levels are based on a two-tail test. Since the results are in the predicted direction, a one-tail test would be appropriate and the significance levels increased accordingly.

Discussion

In this experiment two measures of persuasiveness or dominance have been obtained. The tendency to speak first and to speak the greatest proportion of the time; and one of persuasibility, i.e. tendency to change or not to change opinion when placed in a persuasion situation which requires arguing a topic with an individual who holds an opposing opinion. It is clear from the data that if two extraverted individuals who differ in intelligence are paired, then the more intelligent individual will be more persuasive and less persuasible in terms of these three measures. On the other hand, it is also apparent that if two high intelligent subjects, one extraverted and the other introverted, are placed in this situation then the extraverted subject will be more persuasive.

Of particular interest are the data concerning opinion change. First, when the subjects in a pair are matched for high intelligence and extraversion, the most likely outcome is either a compromise or no change. This finding is in line with the results of previous studies in this area in which subjects were also matched on pertinent variables (Cervin, 1957; Carment, 1961). Secondly, the finding that high intelligent subjects are less likely to modify their opinions than their less intelligent opponents is of some interest in view of the rather equivocal findings of previous research (see Blake and Mouton, 1961).

The reasons for these different outcomes have not been determined, but one factor to note is that the semi-free discussion technique of the present study differs considerably from the methods used in earlier investigations. A further hypothesis to investigate would be that intelligent subjects who are already familiar with the topic should be less persuasible than intelligent subjects unfamiliar with the argument at the time of debate.

It should also be pointed out that our results were obtained using subjects drawn from a relatively homogeneous population and among whom intellectual differences were not large.

It was also found that high intelligence introverts are more likely to be persuaded than are intelligent extraverts. This is directly opposed to Eysenck's contention that extraverts are more susceptible to social influence than are introverts. Yet it may well be in line with his hypothesis (supported by the experiments of Franks, 1957, and Willett, 1960) that introverts condition more rapidly than extraverts. With change of opinion occurring as a result of the punishing and reinforcing responses emitted by each member of the pair, it may be that extraverts cannot learn a new response as rapidly as introverts, or because of the lower verbal output of introverts the extraverts are not subjected to the reinforcing and punishing verbal bombardment that introverts receive. Obviously many important questions remain to be answered in this regard but it should be emphasized that while not all introverts changed their opinions towards those held by their extraverted opponent, not a single extravert publicly changed to agree with his introverted opponent, and only four did so privately.

Not unexpectedly there was less admission to opinion change privately than publicly. But the private data is sufficiently similar to the public data to indicate that the changes observed were more than just superficial verbal compliance and that the subjects did not generally take advantage of this privacy to revert to their original position.

References

BLAKE, R. R., and MOUTON, J. S. (1961), 'The experimental investigation of interpersonal influence', in A. D. Biderman and H. Zimmer (eds.), *The Manipulation of Human Behavior*, Wiley.

CARMENT, D. W. (1961), 'Ascendant-submissive behavior in pairs of human subjects as a function of their emotional responsiveness and opinion-strength', *Canad. J. Psychol.*, vol. 15, pp. 45–51.

CERVIN, V. B. (1957), 'Relationship of ascendant-submissive behavior in dyadic groups of human subjects to their emotional responsiveness', *J. abnorm. soc. Psychol.*, vol. 54, pp. 241–9.

CRUTCHFIELD, R. S. (1951), 'Assessment of persons through a quasi group interaction technique', *J. abnorm. soc. Psychol.*, vol. 46, pp. 577–88.

EYSENCK, H. J. (1957), *Dynamics of Anxiety and Hysteria*, Routledge & Kegan Paul.

EYSENCK, H J. (1959), *Manual, Maudsley Personality Inventory*, University of London Press.

FRANKS, C. M. (1957), 'Personality factors and rate of conditioning', *Brit. J. Psychol.*, vol. 48, pp. 119–26.

HOVLAND, C. I., LUMSDAINE, A. S., and SHEFFIELD, F. D. (1949), *Experiments on Mass Communication*, Princeton University Press.

JANIS, I. L., and FIELD, P. B. (1959), 'Sex differences and personality factors related to persuasibility', in C. I. Hovland and I. L. Janis (eds.), *Personality and Persuasibility*, Yale University Press.

SKINNER, B. F. (1957), *Verbal Behavior*, Appleton-Century-Crofts.

WILLETT, R. A. (1960), 'Conditioning, associated measures, and personality', in H. J. Eysenck (ed.), *Experiments in Personality*, Routledge & Kegan Paul.

21 Jerome E. Singer

The Use of Manipulative Strategies:
Machiavellianism and Attractiveness

J. E. Singer, 'The use of manipulative strategies: Machiavellianism and attractiveness', *Sociometry*, vol. 27, 1964, pp. 128–50.

It is not a novel statement to assert that human beings, or any other organisms, for that matter, survive by manipulating their environment. If 'manipulate' is defined in its broad sense, then almost all of psychology as well as its sister biological and social sciences have been absorbed in the study of the means, effects and results of environmental manipulation. Yet manipulate has a much narrower sense with overtones of illegal power, immorality, and a conscienceless puppet-like working of other people. Even in this narrower sense, manipulation has long fascinated scholars.

Although these questions have held as much fascination for psychologists as for others, only recently have psychologists turned specifically to ascertaining whether conniving, manipulating strategies do in fact exist as personality syndromes, and, if they do, whether they can be validly measured. As a result of the work of Christie and his associates (1962), some answers are emerging. Using *The Prince* as a prime example of manipulatory tactics, they have developed a scale to measure Machiavellian attitudes. The *Mach V* form of the scale consists of twenty triads of items, and enables the investigator to derive independently both a score representing Machiavellian attitudes and a social desirability score, for each subject. Both scores can range from zero to a high of twenty. A number of studies by Christie (1962; Christie and Budner, 1959) and others (Exline *et al.*, 1961; Jones and Daugherty, 1959) have shown not only that the scale is reliable and consistent, but equally as important, that people who score high on the scale do behave in a more Machiavellian fashion than those who score low.

The question on which we will focus our attention is whether or not Machiavellian attitudes are effective in the collegiate world of the entering Freshman. Undergraduate folklore conveys the supposition that some students succeed by adroit manipulation of interpersonal relationships. The object of their machinations is, of course, higher grades. Investigators have long been able to show that tests of academic aptitudes and abilities do not correlate highly with grades. The search for non-academically oriented abilities or traits which would help to reduce the unexplained grade variance has included need for achievement (Chahbazi, 1960), anxiety (Phillips, Hindsman, and McGuire, 1960), 'dogmatic' attitudes (Ehrlich, 1961), and, in the study by Schachter to which we shall return, birth order in the family (1963). It is plausible to expect that manipulative ability (Machiavellian tendencies) would be as important a determinant of a high grade point average as need for achievement. [. . .][1]

The second Machiavellian study
Procedure and samples

In the fall of 1962, with the assistance of Mr Bruce Carrier, we gave approximately one-fourth of the freshmen entering Penn State the *Mach V* scale as part of their battery of tests during orientation week. Routinely included in this battery were verbal and quantitative ability tests, different from those used in our previous research. They were the standard admission and placement tests at Penn State, a locally constructed series of scales called the Moore–Castore tests. These tests consist of four parts: vocabulary, paragraph reading, arithmetic and algebra subtests; plus a four-part total score obtained by summing all subtests.

Nine hundred and fifty students, 573 males and 377 females, were tested during their orientation week. Although this sample male–female ratio is about the same as the all-university ratio, it was decided to secure additional female respondents. Consequently, during the first three weeks of the Fall Term of 1962, eighty-four freshmen girls recruited from introductory psychology classes or from dormitories were administered the *Mach V* scale and biographical face sheet. Since the augmented sample means on all variables were no different from those of the female students tested during the orientation week, the two groups were merged. The students in the augmented sample had taken the Moore–Castore ability tests during the orientation week, as had the regular group.

It was possible to get Moore–Castore results for only twenty-two of the 112 subjects in our first study and correlations between the appropriate parts of these and the ETS tests were computed. For the vocabulary test the correlation was $+ 0.82$; for the arithmetic test, $+ 0.86$. Both correlations are significant; they are quite as high as could be expected. The battery of tests was administered in September of 1962; and in December of that year at the close of the Fall Term, grade point averages were obtained for as many subjects as possible.

1. The first Machiavellian study is omitted. [Ed.]

Only first term freshmen had been used, in an effort to eliminate selective bias. If Machiavellian tendencies contribute to success as measured by grades, seniors might include a survival population of only the high *Mach* scorers and/or the very bright. To the extent that the admission of students is less selective than their continuance, the entering freshmen should be more heterogeneous in abilities than any other group of students. However, there were some losses among these freshmen, and complete sets of data could be obtained for only 994 subjects. The remaining forty subjects (less than 5 per cent of our original sample) were dropped for four reasons: although they took the freshman orientation tests, they never enrolled; they dropped out or withdrew from school before the completion of their first term; they took the tests both during orientation week and as part of the augmented sample; or they made errors in filling out the Machiavellian scale forms or the Moore–Castore forms. The surviving sample of 450 females and 544 males was large enough so that the mean scores on each of the variables could be analysed by birth order and size of family.

Results

The Moore–Castore results are highly intercorrelated, and for simplicity of exposition only the four-part total scores will be discussed. [. . .] There are some interesting results. Christie reports that males have consistently scored higher than females on the *Mach V*, but we find no such trend in our sample. Females have higher ability scores and higher grade point averages than males. As expected, the female superiority on the ability tests was due to higher verbal ability; the males demonstrated superior quantitative abilities. Birth-order effects are obscure, but later-borns are somewhat more Machiavellian, have slightly lower ability scores and lower grades. The ability results are in accord with the previously mentioned findings of Schachter. All of the significant ability differences relating to birth order or family size are with respect to verbal abilities; there were no subgroup differences in quantitative abilities.

[. . .] A large number of the correlations are significant for the total sample, but the percentage of variance they explain is not nearly so large as in our first study. For females, once again, there is no consistent correlation between Machiavellianism and grade point average. For males, however, this correlation coefficient is significant in a large proportion of the subgroups and can be fairly reliably estimated at between $+ 0.25$ and $+ 0.35$. This value, while not very large, is quite stable. The first-born and later-born differences, although not as dramatic as in the first study, are significant and indicate that manipulative strategy correlates with GPA more highly for later-borns than for first-borns.

Similar tabulations were made for the correlation of *Mach* scores by social desirability scores and for grade point average by ability scores.[2] Abilities correlate with grade point averages, although, in general, they do not correlate with Machiavellian attitudes.[3] Of further interest is the fact that in almost every subgroup, there is a significant inverse correlation between *Mach* and social desirability scores. These correlations, as large as -0.35 for first-born females, are in partial contradiction to results reported by Christie.

The ordinal position and family-size breakdowns are of interest, for first-born and only children are overrepresented,[4] as in Schachter's samples. A close scrutiny of the correlations reveals weak ordinal position and family size effects for males. The more later-born the sample or the larger the family, the greater is the correlation between *Mach* score and grade point average. These trends are mitigated by two factors: some of the subsamples have too few cases for reliable estimates and, more interestingly, the subsamples of unknown birth order and family size show large negative correlations. Unknown birth order or family-size classifications may be assigned to subjects for any of several reasons – if they are twins, adopted, foster children, or if they fill out the forms incorrectly. In any event, those who do not fit the usual classifications do not respond in the usual fashion.

The key, as in the first study, lies in the table of partial correlations. The correlations of Machiavellian scores with grade-point averages for the female subsamples are not of sufficient magnitude for useful partial *rs*. The total sample does show some significant correlations, but since these are

2. Copies of the tables of means for abilities, grade-point averages, social desirability scores, and their correlations with Machiavellianism and each other have been deposited as Document number 7925 with the ADI Auxiliary Publications Project, Photoduplication Service, Library of Congress, Washington 25, D.C. A copy may be secured by citing the Document number and remitting $1.25 for photoprints, or $1.25 for 35mm. microfilm. Advance payment is required. Make checks or money orders payable to: Chief Photoduplication Service, Library of Congress.

3. The lack of correlation between abilities and attitudes indicates that the Machiavellian scale is not just an alternative form of an intelligence test. The insignificant Machiavellianism-abilities correlations could be the result of an artifact: the bright Machiavellians see through the questionnaire and falsely answer in a non-Machiavellian socially approved manner. If this were true, a non-linear, inverted U-relationship would be expected between the variables. Examination of their scattergram revealed no such trend.

4. This was determined by examining the distribution of ordinal positions within each family size. For example, of those students who come from families with three children (size 3), chance would have one-third first-born, one-third second-born and one-third third-born. Expectancies can be determined in similar fashion for the other family sizes. To what extent there are more first-borns and fewer later-borns than expected by chance can be assessed by comparing the actual distribution with the chance expectancies. The chi square of the comparison is 25·88, which with thirteen degrees of freedom is significant at the 0·02 level.

almost entirely a function of the correlations of the male subsample, data will be presented for the male group only. Two sets of partial correlation were derived. One set was obtained from the multiple regression equations predicting grade point average from six independent predictor variables: Machiavellian score, social desirability score, and the four individual ability scores from the Moore–Castore battery. The magnitude of the partial correlation coefficients (top half of Table 1) is not very great. For the total sample it is $+ 0.23$. The table reports an r for each of fifteen groups identified by family size and birth order. The partial correlation coefficient of *Mach* score and grades is greater than the partial correlation of any one of the four ability test predictors with grades for eight of the fifteen known birth order and family size groups ($p < 0.005$, binomial). Machiavellian scale scores do not account for a large percentage of the variance; nevertheless, they are the largest single contributor.

The second half of Table 1 shows these partial correlations between Machiavellian score and grade point average computed in the same manner but with different input. These were obtained from multiple regression equations in which only three predictor variables were used: *Mach* score, social desirability score, and total four-part Moore–Castore score. Under these circumstances the *Mach*-grade point average partial correlations are slightly greater than those obtained by the first method, although not of the magnitude of the first study ($r = + 0.39$); they are significant in most of the cases for which both birth order and family size are known. Even in the subsamples of small size, although the correlations are insignificant, they are of the same magnitude as the others. Indeed, considering the pilot work and the first study, the results confirm that there is a highly reliable relationship between the manipulative skills and the ability of subjects to obtain good grades in college. As before, while the differences are not as pronounced, there is evidence to show that later-born males are more effective in the use of their manipulative strategies than are first-born (p, first-born correlation of 0.17 v. later-born correlation of 0.33, < 0.001).

Discussion

There is one interpretative problem presented by the results: first-born males have as high a mean Machiavellian score as later-born, yet they have consistently lower Machiavellian-grade point average correlations. The explanation can lie in a distinction between the possession of a belief and the ability to utilize it. First-borns and later-borns do not differ in the extent to which they endorse Machiavellian attitudes, and if the scale is as valid as has been reported, they should not differ in the extent to which they attempt manipulative strategies. We suggest that higher partial correlations on the part of the later-borns compared with first-borns shows the differential

Table 1 Correlations of Machiavellian scores with grade-point averages, male sample

Ordinal position	Family size						Ordinal position totals	Total later-born
	One	Two	Three	Four	Five and larger	Unknown		
	(Social desirability and four Moore–Castore subtests held constant)							
First-born	0·234 N = 66	0·196 N = 98	0·182 N = 61	0·266 N = 25	0·220 N = 13	−1·000** N = 6	0·168** N = 269	
Second-born		0·236* N = 85	0·463** N = 54	0·367 N = 17	0·375 N = 11		0·275** N = 167	0·328** N = 256
Third-born			0·480** N = 31	0·779** N = 15	1·000** N = 3		0·502** N = 49	
Fourth-born				0·294 N = 21	−1·000** N = 6		0·201 N = 27	
Fifth and later-born					0·312 N = 10		0·312 N = 10	
Unknown						−1·000** N = 3	−1·000** N = 3	
Later-born Unknown						−0·336 N = 19	−0·336 N = 19	
Family size totals	0·234 N = 66	0·200** N = 183	0·329** N = 146	0·421** N = 78	0·130 N = 43	−0·275 N = 28	0·232** N = 544	

	(Social desirability and total Moore–Castore scores held constant)							
First-born	0·252* N = 66	0·192 N = 98	0·118 N = 61	0·291 N = 25	0·081 N = 13	−0·680 N = 6	0·157* N = 269	0·331** N = 256
Second-born		0·237* N = 85	0·451* N = 54	0·264 N = 17	0·359 N = 11		0·284** N = 167	
Third-born			0·558** N = 31	0·515* N = 15	1·000** N = 3		0·508** N = 49	
Fourth-born				0·462* N = 21	−0·984** N = 6		0·317 N = 27	
Fifth and later-born					0·394 N = 10		0·394 N = 10	
Unknown later-born						−1·000** N = 3	−1·000** N = 3	
Unknown						−0·313 N = 19	−0·313 N = 19	
Family size totals	0·252* N = 66	0·197** N = 183	0·310** N = 146	0·369** N = 78	0·111 N = 43	−0·289 N = 28	0·221** N = 544	

*$p < 0.05$, two-tailed.   **$p < 0.01$, two-tailed.

efficacy of putting beliefs into practice. First-born males may desire to be confidence men or bunco artists as much as later-borns; they just do not have the same skills. This conclusion seems reasonable in light of much of the evidence in other differences between first- and later-borns. First-borns are more influenceable (Ehrlich, 1958). First-borns get more anxious (Schachter, 1959), and affiliate more (Wrightsman, 1960). First-borns are more dependent than later-borns for evaluation of opinions (Radloff, 1961), and in college dormitory rooming situations, first-borns are more susceptible to roommate influence while later-borns exert more influence over roommates (Hall and Willerman, 1963). The whole body of evidence pertaining to ordinal position suggests that first-borns are much more dependent on other people, care much more about social correctness, and are more anxious than later-borns. All of these characteristics would weigh heavily against the successful manipulation of others' attitudes, opinions and behaviors.

Christie, in a personal communication, has provided some evidence for the plausibility of this explanation. His factor analysis of an NORC national sample of 1482 cases revealed the existence of two separate Machiavellian factors. One related to an orientation or attitude component, the other to a 'set of tactics' component. It is a testable speculation that later-borns load on both factors, while first-borns load only on the attitudinal one.[5]

Feminine attractiveness and manipulation

Basic considerations

One question is immediately suggested by the results. For male students, there is a positive relationship between Machiavellian skills and high grade averages. Since no such relationships exist for the female population, do there exist any qualities, traits or strategies by which females manipulate their environment? This same question was raised by the results of the first study. The most plausible suggestion was that females also manipulate, using strategies of attractiveness and appearance rather than deceit and management. Simply stated, the more attractive the females, the more likely their success in college.

The female students did not differ from the males on the Machiavellian scale. Even though they hold manipulative attitudes as strongly as do males, there are many sociocultural factors which would mitigate against either

5. For a case study of a belief–skill discrepancy one need only look at a biography of Niccolo Machiavelli, certainly the archetype of those who subscribe to the 'Prince's' philosophy. He was twice exiled from Florence and died out of favor. Although nominally the second of four children, since, as Muir speculates, '... there was an elder (brother) Totto, of whom very little is known ... presumably Totto died young ...,' Machiavelli's ordinal position is indeterminant (cf. Muir, 1936, p. 17).

expressing the attitudes behaviorally or becoming adept at their direct use. Some support for this interpretation can be derived from a comparison of the male and female social desirability scores. The girls reported higher social desirability means than did the boys. The female mean is 14·87, the male mean is 14·24. The difference between them is significant at better than the 0·001 level (t = 3·94). In addition, the correlations between Machiavellianism and social desirability are negative and follow the hypothesized sex and birth-order effects. For first-born females the coefficient is −0·35; for later-borns it is −0·23. The corresponding values in the male sample are −0·28 and −0·22. Uesugi and Vinacke analysed the behavior of males and females in a game playing situation. They report that the strategies of male players are 'exploitative' while the strategies of the female players are 'accommodative' (1963). This distinction is analogous to the one we are suggesting: the males' use of Machiavellian tactics is 'exploitative'; the females' use of attractiveness is 'accommodative'. This is all the more reason to suspect that female manipulative strategies are expressed in other, more socially acceptable ways, e.g. capitalizing on good looks.

Pilot studies

Several pilot studies were included in the first study in order to explore this hypothesis. Two measures of female attractiveness were secured. While the students were taking their weekly quizzes in an introductory psychology class, various instructors, acting as proctors, made ratings of the girls' attractiveness on blank seating charts. The attractiveness ratings of the freshmen made by five different instructors were averaged and treated by multiple regression analysis, together with the available ability test scores and grade-point averages. For some freshmen there were photographs available which were duplicates of those on their student matriculation cards. These photographs, first cousins to passport photos, do not quite accurately represent the subjects, and show only heads and shoulders. Hence the ratings should not be as consistent or as reliable as the in-class 'live body' ratings, and any pattern of relationships with 'picture' attractiveness would tend to be conservative. Nevertheless, for both groups of subjects, the results showed a consistent trend. For the later-borns among the girls there was no ostensible relationship between rated attractiveness and grade point average, with abilities partialed out ('live-body' ratings, $r = 0·16$, $N = 21$; photographs, $r = +0·11$, $N = 10$). However, for first-borns, this correlation was positive. In the first case with 'live-body' ratings it was $+0·21$; in the second case, with the photographs, it was $+0·32$. The sample sizes of eighteen and fourteen, respectively, were so small as almost to preclude significant correlations, and there was not enough overlap between the two samples so that a correlation between 'live-body' attractiveness and picture attractiveness could be obtained. But the results were suggestive and a more definitive investigation was undertaken.

Procedure and sample

In the second study it was possible to secure matriculation card photos for 192 of the 450 freshmen girls in the sample. These photographic negatives were enlarged to $2\frac{1}{4}$ inches by $3\frac{1}{4}$ inches, were trimmed so that all identifying material was removed, were mounted on white index cards, and were then distributed for judgements of attractiveness. Since we are talking about the correlation of judged or rated attractiveness with grade-point average, the appropriate group of judges or raters should be drawn from the population of college instructors who assign trades. In order to tap this population of raters, the 192 pictures were randomly divided into eight sets of twenty-four pictures each. Each of the eight sets was rated by a faculty member at the Pennsylvania State University. The ratings themselves were a forced rectangular distribution; the raters were instructed to separate their set of twenty-four pictures into six piles of four each from 'most attractive' to 'least attractive'. Those in the 'most attractive' pile were given a score of six, those in the 'least attractive' pile a score of one. After the first eight judges had rated a set of twenty-four pictures the 192 pictures were recombined and were then randomly separated into another eight sets and a second group of eight judges rated the pictures. By repeating this procedure, it was possible to utilize forty different faculty members as judges, with each picture being rated five times.

Although not selected on a random basis, the judges formed a heterogeneous group. Almost the entire psychology department was utilized as well as a number of people from the departments of English, Romance Languages, history, political science, business administration, physics, computer science and education, both elementary and secondary. In academic rank they ranged from temporary instructors to department chairmen. The forced distribution procedure was used since pilot testing from the first study had indicated that when 'free' ratings were used, the rather bleak visages presented by the pictures tended to shift the entire distribution toward the unattractive ranks. This procedure also controlled for the possible effects of different judges using different scales of attractiveness or category widths.[6]

6. The ratings by the judges showed a good deal of consistency. Since no two judges saw the same group of twenty-four pictures, consistency of judgement could not be assessed by standard techniques of concordance, but was tested as follows. Each picture was rated by five judges; therefore each picture has both a mean rating and a standard deviation around this mean. Since the ratings for each picture could vary from one

Results

The obtained ratings were combined with the Moore–Castore scores and the grade point averages and a correlation analysis was made. The total sample correlation between attractiveness and grade-point average is reported in Table 2. The trend is similar to that reported for the males

Table 2 **Correlations of attractiveness with grade-point average**

Type of measure	Total sample (N = 192)	First-borns (N = 92)	Later-borns (N = 89)	Unknown birth-order (N = 11)
Zero order correlations	0·189*	0·401**	0·005	0·264
Partial correlations with Machiavellian score, social desirability score and four Moore–Castore subtests held constant	0·176*	0·373**	−0·004	0·205
Partial correlations with Machiavellian score, social desirability score and total Moore–Castore score held constant	0·173*	0·367**	−0·036	0·001
Mean attractiveness	3·50[a]	3·42	3·58	3·53
Standard deviation	1·24	1·24	1·22	1·28

* $p < 0.05$, two-tailed. ** $p < 0.01$, two-tailed.

[a] The forced distribution rating procedure arithmetically determined a grand mean of 3·50, with 6 = most attractive; 1 = least attractive.

(Machiavellian attitudes only), but with birth order effects inverted. It is significant for first-borns and insignificant for later-borns. The unknowns yield a value, which because of the small sample size cannot easily be interpreted.

The partial correlations of attractiveness and grade point average are also shown in the table with the Moore–Castore ability scores partialed out in two ways, one utilizing all four ability subtest scores and the other using the total four-part score. In both cases Machiavellian and social desirability scores were also held constant. The partial correlations show the same patterns as the raw correlations. There is a significant relationship between

---

to six for each of five judges, it is possible to construct the random sampling distribution of these standard deviations. This theoretical distribution can be compared with the distribution of picture standard deviations obtained in this study. Consistency of judgement can be inferred if the obtained standard deviations were smaller than those expected by random sampling. This comparison was made via a *chi square* test with eight degrees of freedom. The obtained chi square of 27·14 was significant at greater than the 0·001 level and, the ratings were in the direction indicating greater consistency.

attractiveness, as judged by faculty members, and grade point average for first-born females, but not for later-borns.[7]

Discussion

In order to explain the males' success in using Machiavellian attitudes, we could assume that faculty members are indeed manipulatable. This manipulatability, however, may simply mean that faculty members are willing to give the student the benefit of the doubt; that they are concerned and humanitarian; that they would rather make the positive error of passing an unworthy student rather than make a negative error of failing a deserving one. But the same explanation cannot be easily extended to the attractiveness-grade-point correlations. Furthermore, the freshman class at Penn State is approximately 4000 students in size and most of the freshmen girls, for many of their courses, attended classes in sections as large as 300–400 students. The grade-point averages were achieved in courses where it is highly unlikely that they could have been singled out by the instructor for special treatment. A possible explanation is simply that attractive girls get the benefit of the doubt in grades. This would require two assumptions. First, faculty give the benefit of the doubt when grading to those whose names and faces they associate and remember. Second, there are none so likely to have their names and faces remembered as the attractive girls in the class. Although we have no evidence directly relating to this point, many of our colleagues acknowledge that they can recall the names of the pretty girls in their classes. [. . .]

Exhibiting behavior and ordinal position

The findings for girls would be explained if first-born girls more often make themselves known to instructors and provide their professors with greater opportunity to see them and learn their names. In an effort to test this supposition, two related studies were carried out. Questionnaires were administered in two psychology classes: one introductory course and one course in developmental psychology. A total of 161 girls filled in the questionnaires. Several questions were asked concerning students' classroom behavior, and the answers of the female students to questions dealing with

7. A serendipitous aspect of the attractiveness rating is that they can be used to test, many ancillary hypotheses. When the ratings of the girls wearing spectacles ($\overline{X} = 2\cdot21$ $N = 27$) were compared with those not wearing them ($\overline{X} = 3\cdot72, N = 165$), a t of $7\cdot09$, significant at greater than the $0\cdot001$ level, was obtained. While a literalist might interpret this as the predilection of academicians for unadorned female faces, we prefer to regard it as inferential evidence for Mrs Parker's famous dictum. Miss Loos's hair color preference prediction is also supported, though not as dramatically. For blondes ($N = 39$), the mean attractiveness rating is $3\cdot87$; for the remainder of the sample ($N = 153$), it was $3\cdot41$. The difference yields a t of $2\cdot09$, significant at the $0\cdot05$ level.

Table 3 Questionnaire reports of 'exhibiting' behavior

Question	First-borns N = 87	Later-borns N = 65	Unknown birth-order N = 9
'If something were not clear to you concerning a course, how likely would it be for you to see your instructor during his office hours?'[a]	$\bar{x} = 1\cdot64$ s = 0·47 First v. Later-born 0·02>p>0·01	$\bar{x} = 1\cdot90$ s = 0·79 t = 2·60	$\bar{x} = 1\cdot56$
'How likely are you to sit in the front of the room for a class lecture?'[a]	$\bar{x} = 1\cdot61$ s = 0·84 First v. Later-born 0·05>p>0·02	$\bar{x} = 2\cdot01$ s = 0·73 t = 2·00	$\bar{x} = 1\cdot56$
'How likely are you to go up to an instructor after class to ask questions?'[a]	$\bar{x} = 1\cdot67$ s = 0·89 First v. Later-born 0·10>p>0·05	$\bar{x} = 2\cdot09$ s = 0·89 t = 1·67	$\bar{x} = 2\cdot22$

[a] 1 = very likely; 2 = somewhat likely; 3 = not too likely; 4 = not at all likely

'exhibiting' behavior were tabulated. Table 3 reports the results for three questions: whether the students sat in the front of the room, whether they came to see the instructor after the class, and whether they saw the instructor during his office hours. When the results for the ordinal position subsamples on each of these three questions are compared, in all three cases first-borns are more likely to 'exhibit'. They tend to sit in the front of the room, to come up after class, and to see the instructor during his office hours. These results, however, are students' self reports, and may just represent consistent response biases on the part of subjects and not their actual behavior. Therefore, for one introductory psychology course, records were kept on which students did in fact come up after class; which students did see the instructor in his office; and, through an analysis of a class-seating chart (seats chosen voluntarily by the students), a tabulation and comparison was made between the seating preferences of the first-born and later-born females. Table 4 presents these results, and it can be seen that they correspond

Table 4 'Exhibiting' behavior in the classroom

	First-born [a] (N = 18)	Later-born (N = 15)
Front half of the classroom	12	4
Rear half of the classroom	6	11
P (Fisher exact test) = 0·002		
Asked questions after class	6	1
Did not ask questions after class	12	14
P (Fisher exact test) = 0·065)		

[a] Data from three girls whose birth order could not be determined were removed from the analysis.

with those obtained from the questionnaire. The analysis shows that in two cases females who are first-born are more likely to engage in behaviors which make them more visible and which bring them into more frequent contact with instructors. In the third case, since only three female students made office-hour appointments, no analysis was possible. These findings, together with our original explanation, could account for both the correlation and its differential manifestation by first-borns and later-borns.

Personal knowledge and social norms of attractiveness

The second question is a more difficult one to answer, for there are problems raised in the attempts to assess the extent to which attractiveness is used in a manipulatory fashion by undergraduate females. If it could be shown that the first-borns – for whom the correlation between attractiveness and grades is strongest – were somehow more cognizant and socially concerned about their looks, this finding would establish one of the prerequisites for an attractiveness–manipulation interpretation. In an attempt to secure such evidence a study was conducted by Singer and Lamb (1963) which sought evidence on two hypotheses: that first-borns are more socially concerned about their figures; and that they are more knowledgeable concerning their figures.

Procedure and sample

Volunteer female subjects were recruited from introductory psychology sections to take part in a series of tests. They were told that the tests were part of a psychomedical survey which was being conducted in several universities to secure norms on the health and health-related characteristics of college students. The girls filled in a 'medical record' containing a series of dummy items for credance, interspersed with critical questions. The latter asked girls to estimate their own body measurements and to specify what they regarded as the ideal set of body measurements. Following the completion of the questionnaire they were then actually measured, so that for each girl there are three sets of measurements: self-estimated, ideal and actual.

There were two conditions in the experiment. In one the girls did not know that they were to be measured until after they had completed the questionnaire, and in the other, girls were repeatedly instructed before filling in their estimated and ideal dimensions that they were to be measured afterward. These conditions will be referred to as the *unaware* and the *aware*, respectively. Eight dimensions were used. Five are those conventionally used in descriptions of the female figure: height, weight, bust, waist, and hips; as a control three irrelevant dimensions were included: neck, ankle, and wrist size. This procedure is similar to that used by Jourard and Secord (1955).

Consistently, when actual size is compared to estimated size, girls underestimate their hips, their waists, their weights and their necks, wrists and ankles; estimates for height and bust are sometimes too large and sometimes too small. However, even for these two measurements, the direction of deviation can be predicted, for in most of the cases the direction of the error was toward the ideal measurement reported by the subject. For each measurement on each subject a deviation score consisting of estimated size minus actual size was computed. This was scored positively if it were in the direction toward ideal size, and was given a negative sign if in the direction away from ideal size.

Results

Table 5 reports the results for all eight measurements for both the aware and unaware samples, separated by birth order. On seven of the eight measures in the unaware sample, first-borns have larger discrepancy scores than laterborns. This difference is significant at the 0·035 level by the binominal test. For the unaware sample then, these results suggest that with respect to the socially relevant measures of bodily attractiveness, good looks or physique, first-borns tend to distort more toward an ideal size.

On the other hand, in the aware sample a different picture emerges. If the first-borns are again compared with the later-borns, first-borns now show less distortion (again, $p = 0·035$). Under conditions when girls knew they were to be measured, first-borns were able to display greater accuracy in estimating their bodily measurements than were later-borns. This curious interaction of accuracy of body-size estimation and knowledge of subsequent measurement leads to the conclusion that first-borns are on one hand more knowledgeable about their body sizes and on the other hand, that they are more likely to distort their own image toward the ideal.

A comparison of the standard deviations in both the aware and unaware conditions reveals more agreement about ideal size than about either estimated or actual dimensions. This agreement with respect to ideal size leads to the inference of a cultural stereotype of good female form toward which the first-born distort their own bodily measurements. Table 5 also shows that when the mean ideal size for each of the eight measurements is computed for the entire sample, the standard deviations about these ideal sizes reported by first-borns are smaller than those reported by the later-borns for seven out of eight measurements ($p = 0·035$).

Discussion

Three conclusions emerge: that first-borns are more knowledgeable about the norm, that they have more accurate information concerning their own body size, and that they tend to distort their body size more toward the norm

Table 5 Mean distortion of estimated body measurements toward ideal measurements

Condition and birth-order	Height (inches)	Weight (pounds)	Bust (inches)	Waist (inches)	Hips (inches)	Neck (inches)	Wrist (inches)	Ankle (inches)
Mean distortion								
Unaware								
First-borns N = 27	0·167	2·120	0·306	1·029	1·227	0·421	0·634	0·949
Later-borns N = 22	0·091	1·838	0·230	1·163	0·432	0·148	0·511	0·830
Aware								
First-borns N = 25	0·020	0·830	0·620	0·910	0·395	0·320	0·071	0·052
Later-borns N = 19	0·132	1·092	0·040	1·053	0·942	0·809	0·111	0·238
Mean ideal measurement								
First-born Standard Deviations N = 52	1·13	7·17	1·43	1·28	1·38	2·71	1·19	1·81
Later-born Standard Deviations N = 41	1·42	7·30	1·69	1·18	2·48	2·77	1·28	2·05
Total sample N = 93	65·18	120·57	35·14	22·55	35·14	11·39	5·68	7·22

when reporting it. These findings support precisely the notion that the first-born attractiveness-grade point average correlation is not merely the result of fortuitous grading or differential remembering by instructors, but that it reflects, in part, a manipulative strategy using physique rather than Machiavellian procedures as the main tactic.

In order to document this supposition fully, further evidence is required. There should be an attractiveness gradient of classroom seating for first-born girls – the attractive ones toward the front, the unattractive ones toward the back. No such gradient would be expected for later-born girls. We would also predict that the first-born girls who ask questions after class would be more attractive than those who do not. Unfortunately, we do not have the data necessary to evaluate these hypotheses. [. . .]

Summary and conclusions

In summary, let us recapitulate the evidence we have obtained for the efficacy and utility of manipulative strategies.

1. A pilot study revealed a partial correlation for a combined male and female sample of $+0.23$ between Machiavellian scale scores and grade point averages, with verbal and mathematical abilities controlled.

2. A study based on a sample of 112 students revealed that this partial correlation could be replicated for males ($r = +0.39$), but not for females ($r = +0.20$). Within the male sample, the correlation was more marked for later-borns than for first-borns.

3. A sample of 994 freshmen revealed the same partial correlation (about $+0.25$) between Machiavellianism and grades for the male sample, and, again, the relationship was more pronounced for later-born males than for first-borns.

4. Two pilot studies showed positive, but not significant, partial correlations between girls' attractiveness and their grade point averages for first-borns, and slightly negative or zero correlations for later-borns.

5. The correlation of attractiveness-to-faculty ratings and grades (with abilities, Machiavellianism, and social desirability held constant) obtained from the data on 192 freshman girls was equal to $+0.37$ for first-borns and -0.04 for later-borns.

6. Both behaviorally and by self report, it was shown that first-born girls tend to sit in front of the class, see the instructor after class, and visit the instructor in his office more often than do later-born girls.

7. In support of an interpretation of manipulative intent, it was demonstrated that first-borns have more accurate information about their bodily measurement; that they are more accurate in stating the norms of the ideal

female figure, and that they are more likely to distort their measurement toward the ideal norms than are later-borns.

8. Evidence has been collected which demonstrates that later-born girls neither study less nor date more than first-borns.

In some respects the results are not at all surprising. The suggestion that men live by their brains and women by their bodies was made as far back as Genesis. Although not astoundly new, the implications are rather frightening. The documentation of the utility of manipulative skills was obtained from a population of freshmen in a university setting, with a criterion of academic success. The results imply that the poor college professor is a rather put-upon creature, hoodwinked by the male students (later-born) and enticed by the female students (first-born) as he goes about his academic and personal responsibilities. He is seemingly caught in a maelstrom of student intrigue and machination. The picture is bleak. In defence we can only offer the consolation that when twenty-two male members of the faculty at the Pennsylvania State University were administered the Machiavellian scale, their mean score was 10·44. When compared with the total sample values from the 994 subject study, the faculty appear significantly more manipulative than the students ($t = 2·43$, $p > 0·02$). It is hoped that the academicians are fighting strategem with strategem.

References

CHAHBAZI, P. (1960), 'Use of projective tests in predicting college achievement', *Educ. Psychol. Measurement*, vol. 20, pp. 839–42.

CHRISTIE, R. (1962), 'Impersonal interpersonal orientations and behavior', Columbia University mimeograph.

CHRISTIE, R., and BUDNER, S. (1959), 'Medical school climates and Machiavellian orientations of students', Columbia University mimeograph.

EHRLICH, D. (1958), *Determinants of Verbal Commonality and Influenceability*, University of Minnesota, unpublished.

EHRLICH, H. J. (1961), 'Dogmatism and learning', *J. abnorm. soc. Psychol.*, vol. 60, pp. 148–9.

EXLINE, R., THIBAUT, J., BRANNON, C., and GUMPERT, P. (1961), 'Visual interaction in relation to Machiavellianism and an unethical act', *Amer. Psychol.*, vol. 16, p. 396.

HALL, R. L., and WILLERMAN, W. (1963), 'The educational influence of dormitory roommates', *Sociometry*, vol. 26, pp. 294–318.

JONES, E. E., and DAUGHERTY, B. N. (1959), 'Political orientation', *J. abnorm. soc. Psychol.*, vol. 59, pp. 340–49.

JOURARD, S. M., and SECORD, P. F. (1955), 'Body cathexis and the ideal female figure', *J. abnorm. soc. Psychol.*, vol. 50, pp, 243–6.

MUIR, D. E. (1936), *Machiavelli and His Times*, Heinemann.

PHILLIPS, B. N., HINDSMAN, E., and McGUIRE, C. (1960), 'Factors associated with anxiety and their relation to school achievement of adolescents', *Psychol. Reports*, vol. 7, pp. 365–72.

RADLOFF, R. W. (1961), 'Opinion evaluation and affiliation', *J. abnorm. soc. Psychol.* vol. 62, pp. 578–85.

SCHACHTER, S. (1959), *The Psychology of Affiliation*, Stanford University Press.

SCHACHTER, S. (1963), 'Birth order, eminence and higher education', *Amer. soc. Rev.*, vol. 28, pp. 757–68.

SINGER, J. E., and LAMB, P. F. (1963), 'Social concern, body size and birth order', *Pennsylvania State University*, mimeograph.

UESUGI, T. K., and VINACKE, W. E. (1963), 'Strategy in a feminine game', *Sociometry*, vol. 26, pp. 75–88.

WRIGHTSMAN, L. S. Jr (1960), 'Effects of waiting with others on changes in level of felt anxiety', *J. abnorm. soc. Psychol.*, vol. 61, pp. 216–22.

22 Rudolf H. Moos

Sources of Variance in Responses to Questionnaires
and in Behavior

R. H. Moos, 'Sources of variance in responses to questionnaires and in behavior',
Journal of Abnormal Psychology, vol. 74, 1969, pp. 405-12.

Several recent studies have demonstrated that persons, settings and Person × Setting interactions each account for statistically significant and important proportions of the total variance in responses to different questionnaires and in inferential ratings of behavior. The relative amounts of variance accounted for by different sources of variance vary importantly, depending upon the particular sample of persons and settings chosen for the study; however, it is generally true that the variance accounted for by the interaction between settings and persons is greater, sometimes substantially greater, than the variance accounted for by either persons or settings alone.

For example, Endler, Hunt and Rosenstein (1962) and Endler and Hunt (1967) found that persons, settings, and Person × Setting interactions each contributed significantly to behavioral variance in both anxiety and hostility. Raush, Dittman and Taylor (1959) and Raush, Farbman and Llewellyn (1960), studying hyperaggressive and control children in a psychiatric ward milieu, found that interactions between child and setting were far more important in accounting for behavior than was either the child or the setting alone.

In a series of earlier studies (Moos, 1967; 1968b; Moos and Daniels, 1967), patient and staff responses to a number of different psychiatric ward subsettings, for example, individual therapy, group therapy and community meeting, were analysed for each of five different sets of adjectives reflecting trust, extroversion, security, involvement and sociability. The results indicated that consistent individual differences among patients accounted for between 24 per cent and 40 per cent of the total variance; consistent setting differences always accounted for less than 5 per cent of the total variance; and the Patients × Settings interaction effect, with only one exception, accounted for a significant percentage of the total variance (between 17 per cent and 26 per cent). Results for staff were generally similar, except that consistent differences among individuals accounted for less variance than setting differences.

For example, one group of patients was more trusting in settings in which only one other person was present than in settings in which several others were present, whereas the results for a second group of patients were exactly the reverse. These findings need to be replicated using different samples for responses, persons and settings. They are of particular importance for both the assessment and prediction of behavior and for the planning of maximally therapeutic environments, since they suggest that different types of settings may be maximally beneficial to different types of patients, and that psychological assessment procedures must systematically sample both persons and settings in order to predict behavior accurately.

The extent to which these results would be replicated if the data used were observations of actual behavior in different settings is important. Setting and Person × Setting interactions might account for consistently greater or consistently less of the total variance when actual behavior is observed than when questionnaire responses are obtained. The extent to which the proportions of variance accounted for by different sources of variance change depending upon the particular time at which the sample is studied is also important. Does the percentage of variance attributable to persons or settings change with increasing familiarity with the environment and/or with successful psychiatric treatment?

Purpose

There were three major purposes for the present study: (a) to replicate earlier findings (Moos, 1968b) indicating that for psychiatric patients, differences among persons and Person × Setting interactions account for much larger proportions of variance than setting differences; (b) to compare the percentages of variance accounted for by different sources of variance in questionnaire responses and in actual behavior; (c) to estimate the direction and extent to which the percentages of variance attributable to different sources of variance change with increasing familiarization with the environment and/or change in psychiatric status.

Method

Settings and subjects

The research was conducted on an open-door, thirty-patient psychiatric ward located in a large Veterans' Administration Hospital. This was a mixed ward with approximately eighteen male and twelve female patients at any one time. The treatment was based upon patient responsibility, decision making and self-regulation within the framework of the ward community. There was a maximum emphasis on active coping with the milieu, on behavior change, and on the process of making practical plans for release, for example, obtaining a job, handling financial crises, and reconstituting family relationships. Open communication between staff and patients and active patient participation were strongly encouraged.

During the study, community meetings and small-group therapy were each held two days a week. Individual therapy was formally arranged for the majority of the patients; for some of these, it was centered around frequent but brief contacts. The remainder of the treatment program consisted of recreational activities and various hospital workshop and industrial work assignments.

The patients who were initially admitted to the ward essentially constituted a representative sample of male and female veterans with diagnoses of neuropsychiatric disorders; that is, there were no specific criteria which were applied for admission to the ward.

Each of sixteen patients (eight male, eight female) was selected on the basis of several criteria: (a) their conversation had to be easily understandable; (b) they had to be able to cooperate in wearing a wireless radio transmitter, and also to be willing to answer a questionnaire about their reactions in each setting; (c) they had to be on the ward long enough for systematic behavioral change to occur. The average age of the patients was 38·8 years ($SD = 7·1$), and their average education was 13·4 years ($SD = 1·1$). The median length of hospitalization was approximately three months and the number of previous hospitalizations ranged from none to five. Eight of the patients carried a primary diagnosis of neurosis; seven carried a primary diagnosis of schizophrenia, and one carried a primary diagnosis of character disorder.

Procedure

The research was completed as a part of a larger project studying the behavior of psychiatric patients by the use of behavior observers and a miniature wireless radio transmitter. The plans for the use of the radio transmitter were discussed in both staff and patient–staff meetings, and the patients participated in putting up television antennae around the ward including bedrooms, dayroom, visitors' room, dining room, etc.

The sixteen Ss were each observed twice in each of six different ward subsettings. These subsettings were (a) an intake meeting (or discharge-planning meeting), in which the entire ward staff observed the patient being interviewed by one of the resident psychiatrists; (b) an individual therapy session; (c) a group-therapy session in which the patient was a member of a group of approximately eight patients; (d) a community meeting in which all patients and staff participated; (e) lunch time, which occurred in a dining room on the ward; and (f) free time, which was unscheduled time on the ward during which the patient was free to engage in any activity he chose.

These six settings constituted a representative sample of regularly scheduled ward activities in which all patients participated.

The initial set of observations occurred during the first and second weeks of hospitalization. A second set of observations was made on twelve of these patients approximately three months later, the week before the patient had improved enough to leave the hospital. Four of the patients could not be observed a second time, either because they had left the hospital against medical advice or because they had to be discharged without adequate prior warning.

Three sets of observations were obtained on each patient in each setting: (a) questionnaire responses relevant to how patients were feeling; (b) behavioral observations of what patients were actually doing; and (c) recordings of what patients were saying. Only the results of the first two sets of observations are discussed in this report.

Patients were given a questionnaire immediately after their participation in each of the six settings. This questionnaire consisted of nine dimensions measured by three items each, on each of which patients rated their experience on a 1–5 scale. Four affect dimensions were measured, for example, anxiety (uneasy, fearful, anxious), depression (sad, lonely, blue), vigor (lively, active, energetic), pleasantness (pleased, lighthearted, elated). Two of the dimensions measured the perceived worth (worthwhile, important to me, glad I went) and the perceived therapeutic benefit of the setting (made me feel better, helped me gain self-confidence, helped me get well). The other three dimensions measured affiliation (I worked closely with others, people were friendly to me, I was included), participation (I worked hard, I was active, I talked freely and openly), and leadership (I was needed, I played an important part, I helped decide what to do).

The items for the first four dimensions were taken partially from the Nowlis (1965) Mood Adjective Check List and partially from other items used in the earlier study (Moos, 1968b). The items for the other five dimensions were directly related to Barker and Gump's (1964) notions of the possible effects of different types of behavior settings.

Each of the patients was also actually observed in each setting. These behavior observations were made by two Os. The Ss knew that they would be observed by one of these Os during the time they had the microphone on. The Os, who had spent several months on the ward and were integrated with the staff and familiar to all the patients, had been trained to categorize and note patient behavior in terms of sixteen relatively simple behavior categories, for example, smiling, talking, arm movement, etc., taken from those used by Zinner (1963). During the intake and community-meeting settings, O sat in the same room as Ss and staff, and during the group-therapy and individual-therapy settings O sat behind a one-way vision screen. During the lunch and free-time settings O followed the patient around as un-obtrusively as possible.

In order to estimate the effects of these observations, Ss were observed both with and without the microphone on in both community meeting and group therapy. Results indicated that the average effects of wearing and being observed with the wireless radio transmitter microphone were very small, and that the differences that did occur suggested a slight increase in purposeful and a slight decrease in purposeless activity while wearing the transmitter. These results, which are similar to those of other studies in showing that observational effects may be quite small, are more fully discussed in another paper (Moos, 1968a).

Results

The reliability of the behavioral observations was established by having the two behavior Os observe and rate for sixteen reliability sessions after a period of initial training. The task was to note the occurrence of each coded behavior during each minute of a twenty-minute observation session. The reliability correlations were very acceptable, ranging from a low of 0·77 to a high of 0·99.

The data were analysed by using an analysis of variance design. Separate analyses of variance were calculated for each of the nine questionnaire scales and each of eight behavior categories in each of the two sets of observations. With this technique it is possible to specify, for each of the questionnaire and behavior dimensions, the proportion of the total variance which is accounted for by persons, by settings, and by their interaction.

The percentages of variance accounted for by each source of variance were calculated for these random-effects analysis of variance models using the rationale and equations given by Gleser, Cronbach and Rajaratnam (1965) and Endler (1966). These authors have pointed out that the analysis of variance technique can be used to estimate the relative magnitude of each individual component of variance, expressed as a percentage of the sum of the different variance components. The general logic of this technique involves breaking the expected mean squares into their various variance components and solving separately for each component.

Tables 1 and 2 give the percentages of variance accounted for by different sources of variance in the questionnaire scales for the first and second sets of observations. Consistent person differences accounted for between 0 and 45 per cent, consistent differences between settings for between 0 and 18 per cent, and the interactions between persons and settings for between 9 and 38 per cent of the total variance. Differences between adjectives, Adjective × Person, and Adjective × Setting interactions generally accounted for less than 10 per cent of the total variance.

Table 1 **Percentages of variance accounted for by different sources of variance in questionnaire scales – first observations**

Scale	Source						
	A	P	S	A×I	A×S	P×S	A×P×S
Anxiety	5·6	25·4	7·4	8·3	1·4	20·8	31·0
Depression	0·0	26·7	0·0	4·0	0·5	29·2	39·0
Vigor	2·0	25·0	5·0	5·0	1·9	29·2	32·1
Pleasantness	12·8	12·8	1·5	6·7	3·8	15·0	47·4
Worth	0·0	21·0	0·0	0·9	3·5	24·6	51·7
Therapeutic benefit	0·3	13·0	3·0	4·1	0·9	37·9	40·8
Participation	0·0	5·3	10·5	19·4	3·7	19·7	41·6
Affiliation	0·0	18·0	4·6	15·8	2·2	9·2	51·0
Leadership	1·2	11·5	0·8	10·5	1·6	24·4	50·0

Note *A* = adjectives, *P* = person, *S* = setting.

Table 2 **Percentages of variance accounted for by different sources of variance in questionnaire scales – second observations**

Scale	Source						
	A	P	S	A×P	A×S	P×S	A×P×S
Anxiety	5·2	25·3	11·0	4·5	1·9	16·2	35·7
Depression	0·0	45·1	0·0	3·3	1·6	17·2	32·0
Vigor	7·3	10·6	7·3	4·1	3·3	34·9	32·5
Pleasantness	13·3	9·7	4·4	11·5	0·0	15·0	45·1
Worth	0·0	22·2	3·3	0·2	3·1	24·5	47·5
Therapeutic benefit	1·0	26·8	9·8	1·6	0·0	32·4	29·5
Participation	15·0	6·6	17·8	9·2	2·3	18·9	30·2
Affiliation	4·0	9·7	5·2	9·1	0·0	18·4	53·9
Leadership	4·2	0·1	9·9	17·2	2·2	23·3	43·1

In both sets of observations the variance accounted for by Person × Setting interactions was greater than the variance accounted for by settings for all nine dimensions, and was approximately the same as the variance accounted for by persons. Also, the proportion of variance accounted for by persons was consistently greater than the proportion accounted for by settings. The amount of variance accounted for by settings increased from the initial to the final set of observations for eight of the nine response dimensions, whereas the changes for person differences and Person × Setting interactions showed no consistent patterns.

Tables 3 and 4 show the percentages of variance accounted for by different sources of variance for the first and second set of behavior observations. The sixteen behaviors had been classified into four categories on the basis

Table 3 **Percentages of variance accounted for by different sources of variance in behavior categories – first observations**

| Category | Source | | | |
	Persons	Settings	$P \times S$	Within
Hand and arm movement	16·8	11·9	31·9	39·4
Foot and leg movement	27·4	10·0	26·7	35·9
Scratch, pick, rub	30·7	13·1	24·5	31·6
General movement and shifting	17·3	1·4	47·1	34·1
Nod yes	4·2	42·9	33·5	19·4
Smile	35·3	3·6	35·4	25·6
Talk	10·5	68·3	13·9	7·4
Smoke	41·9	7·1	20·7	30·2

Table 4 **Percentages of variance accounted for by different sources of variance in behavior categories – second observations**

| Category | Source | | | |
	Persons	Settings	$P \times S$	Within
Hand and arm movement	17·2	13·8	29·6	39·3
Foot and leg movement	27·3	13·0	31·2	28·6
Scratch, pick, rub	26·3	18·2	27·6	27·9
General movement and shifting	23·1	4·4	48·2	24·3
Nod yes	4·6	56·5	21·3	18·5
Smile	33·4	8·3	36·1	22·3
Talk	7·4	60·1	19·9	12·5
Smoke	36·5	12·2	10·2	41·1

of their intercorrelations, and the eight behaviors shown in Table 3 represent the behaviors in each category which showed the most frequent occurrence. The behaviors of hand and arm movement; foot and leg movement; scratching, picking or rubbing; nodding yes; and general movement and shifting fell into the general movement category; smiling fell into a category called expressiveness; and smoking and talking each fell into separate categories.

The percentage of variance accounted for by different sources of variance varied greatly depending upon the particular behavior being considered. Talking and nodding yes were more a function of the setting than of the person, although the Person × Setting interactions were substantial, especially for nodding yes. The other six behaviors showed generally similar results, in that the variance accounted for by persons and by Person × Setting interactions were both always greater than that accounted for by settings. The variance accounted for by Person × Setting interactions generally tended to be as great as, or somewhat greater than, that accounted for by consistent person differences.

The findings indicate that there is much greater variation in the proportion of variance attributable to different sources of variance in actual behavior than in responses to questionnaires, especially in the proportion of variance attributable to settings, which varied from 1 to 68 per cent. Most of the variance in talking was related to setting differences; that is, persons consistently tended to talk more in some settings than in others. On the other hand, most of the variance in smoking was related to person differences; that is, some people consistently smoked more than others. Furthermore, the amount of Person × Setting interaction variance was consistently high, indicating that, for example, some persons tended to smile more in Setting A than in Setting B, whereas other persons showed just the reverse tendency.

The changes from the initial to the final set of observations were very similar to those for the questionnaire responses. The variance attributable to settings showed an increase for seven of the eight behaviors (all except talking, which initially showed an extremely high setting variance), whereas the variance attributable to persons and to Person × Setting interactions showed no consistent changes.

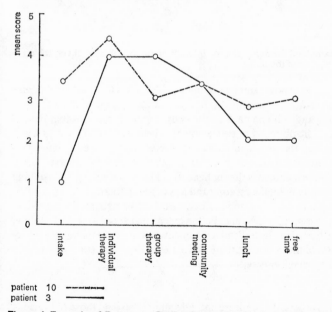

patient 10 ————
patient 3 —————

Figure 1 Example of Person × Setting interaction for the variable of therapeutic benefit of setting

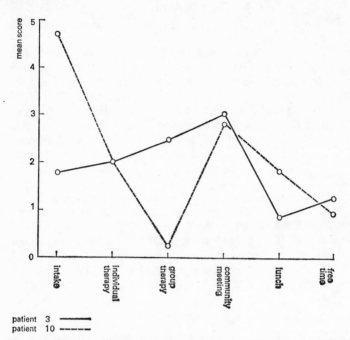

patient 3 ──────
patient 10 ──────

Figure 2 Example of Person X Setting interaction for the variable of scratching and rubbing parts of the body

Figures 1 and 2 show examples of interaction effects for the questionnaire variable of therapeutic benefit and the behavioral variable of the frequency of scratching and rubbing parts of the body. Figure 1 indicates that patient 10 stated that he obtained more treatment benefit from intake meeting and less from group therapy than patient 3, whereas there were no differences between these two patients in either individual therapy or community meeting. Figure 2 indicates that patient 10 did more scratching and rubbing parts of his body in intake meeting and less in group therapy than patient 3, whereas there were no differences between the two patients in individual therapy or community meeting. To the extent that scratching and rubbing parts of the body may be indicative of anxiety, an O would make very different estimates of the anxiety of these two patients, depending upon the setting in which they were observed.

Discussion

These results essentially replicate and substantially extend those of previous studies. The questionnaire results for the two sets of observations were very similar to those obtained in an earlier study (Moos, 1968b), despite a different patient sample, the use of a different psychiatric ward, the sampling of different settings and the measurement of different response dimensions.

The results also indicate that persons, settings and Person × Setting interactions generally account for significant and important proportions of the total variance in behavior. These findings are consistent with those of Dittman (1963) and Ekman (1965), who have previously discussed the important influence of situational factors on non-verbal behavior, and Zinner (1963), who recorded observations of fifty-six specific behaviors on ninety airmen in basic training in thirty different real-life settings and found that there were dependencies between settings and behaviors; for example, there were settings that either facilitated or inhibited smoking and talking to varying degrees.

The proportion of variance accounted for by different sources both in responses to questionnaires and in behavior were remarkably constant in the two sets of observations, except that the variance attributable to setting differences generally increased over time. These findings probably indicate that settings tend more consistently to elicit particular behaviors as persons become more familiar with the general milieu. As the twelve patients tested the second time had all improved in psychiatric condition, this change may be related to changes in psychiatric status. The current data do not allow a test between these alternative explanations, since psychiatric improvement and increasing familiarization with the milieu are confounded.

These findings replicate those of Raush, Dittman and Taylor (1959, Raush, Farbman and Llewellyn, 1960) in indicating that situational factors (setting differences) may play a more potent role in behavior after treatment and/or experience with the general milieu. The two studies were so different (age of Ss, length of time between initial and final observations, range of settings, types of response dimensions studied, etc.) that these similarities indicate that the replicated findings may be highly general.

On the other hand, the specific sample of settings, persons and response indicators used may affect importantly the relative proportions attributable to different sources of variance. For example, the results for the variable of anxiety were generally similar to those that Endler, Hunt and Rosenstein (1962) obtained for their anxious questionnaires; however, the percentage of variance accounted for by modes of response (adjective differences) was less, whereas the percentages of variance accounted for by consistent individual differences were greater in this study. The former difference is probably due to the fact that Endler *et al.* sampled a wider range of anxiety indicators, whereas the latter difference may be due to the fact that psychiatric patients are generally high-anxiety individuals and, as such, would be expected to be more consistently anxious across settings than college student Ss.

Moos and Clemes (1967) studied the amount of actual talking (by word count) of therapists in different individual therapy settings, and found that 18·5 per cent of the variance was attributable to setting differences. This indicates that the variance related to settings is still statistically significant, even when all the settings sampled are similar; however, the actual proportion attributable to settings may decrease markedly when the range of settings is curtailed.

Further studies need to explore systematically these effects by experimentally or statistically (through Monte Carlo methods) sampling different populations of persons, settings and response indicators. The degree of variation in the proportion of variance accounted for by different sources of variance clearly is much greater than has been assumed heretofore. This is particularly important since the percentage of variance accounted for by consistent differences between individuals is related to the upper limit of the validity of predictions. If 9 per cent of the total variance is accounted for by consistent individual differences, then the upper limit of validity is 0·3; if 16 per cent of the variance is accounted for, then the upper limit is 0·4; and if 25 per cent of the variance is accounted for then the validity may go as high as 0·5; etc. Thus, no predictions made from individual differences on the nine questionnaire response dimensions for the initial set of observations could have a validity better than 0·5. Predictions made from the behavior categories could be somewhat better, and might be as high as 0·6 for the category of smoking.

The general implications of these results for the measurement and prediction of behavior and for the planning of therapeutic milieus have been more fully discussed in an earlier paper (Moos, 1968b). It is perfectly clear that as long as there are large percentages of variance which are due to Person × Setting interactions, the particular behavioral potential of the person–setting unit must be more fully studied. The most important aspects of this research area are that the percentages of variance accounted for by different sources of variance determine the extent of validity possible with the use of standard questionnaire and interview or rating measures of personality, and that different psychiatric ward subsettings may be differentially beneficial to different patient groups.

References

BARKER, R. G., and GUMP, P. V. (1964), *Big School, Small School*, Stanford University Press.

DITTMAN, A. T. (1963), 'Patterns of body movement', paper presented at the meeting of the American Psychological Association, Philadelphia.

EKMAN, P. (1965), 'Communication through non-verbal behavior: a source of information about an interpersonal relationship' in S. S. Tomkins and C. E. Izard (eds.), *Affect, Cognition and Personality*, Springer.

ENDLER, N. S. (1966), 'Estimating variance components from mean squares for random and mixed effects analysis of variance models', *Percept. Motor Skills*, vol. 22, pp. 559–70.

ENDLER, N. S., and HUNT, J. McV. (1967), 'S-R inventories of hostility and comparisons of the proportions of variance from persons, responses and situations for hostility and anxiousness', unpublished manuscript, University of Illinois.

ENDLER, N. S., HUNT, J. McV., and ROSENSTEIN, A. J. (1962), 'An S-R inventory of anxiousness', *Psychol. Mono.*, vol. 76 (17, Whole No. 536).

GLESER, G. C., CRONBACH, L. J., and RAJARATNAM, N. (1965), 'Generalizability of scores influenced by multiple sources of variance', *Psychometrika*, vol. 30, pp. 395–418.

MOOS, R. (1967), 'Differential effects of ward settings on psychiatric patients', *J. nerv. ment. Dis.*, vol. 145, pp. 272–83.

MOOS, R. (1968a), 'Behavioral effects of being observed: reactions to a wireless radio transmitter', *J. consult. clin. Psychol.*, vol. 32, pp. 383–8.

MOOS, R. (1968b), 'Situational analysis of a therapeutic community mileu', *J. abnorm. Psychol.*, vol. 73, pp. 49–61.

MOOS, R., and CLEMES, S. (1967), 'Multivariate study of the patient-therapist system', *J. consult. Psychol.*, vol. 31, pp. 119–30.

MOOS, R., and DANIELS, D. (1967), 'Differential effects of ward settings on psychiatric staff', *Archives of General Psychiatry*, vol. 17, pp. 75–83.

NOWLIS, V. (1965), 'Research with the mood adjective check list', in S. S. Tomkins and C. E. Izard (eds.), *Affect, Cognition and Personality*, Springer.

RAUSH, H. L., DITTMAN, A. T., and TAYLOR, T. T. (1959), 'Person, setting and change in social interaction', *Hum. Rel.*, vol. 12, pp. 361–78.

RAUSH, H. L., FARBMAN, I., and LLEWELLYN, L. G. (1960), 'Person, setting and change in social interaction: II, a normal control study', *Hum. Rel.*, vol. 13, pp. 305–32.

WINER, C. J. (1962), *Statistical Principles in Experimental Design*, McGraw-Hill.

ZINNER, L. (1963), 'The consistency of human behavior in various situations: a methodological application of functional ecological psychology', Unpublished doctoral dissertation, University of Houston.

Part Seven
The Self and Social Interaction

In order to understand a number of aspects of social performance it is necessary to postulate a self-image. This is a cognitive structure, arising out of past experience, which directs behaviour and may be regarded as a central mechanism in the personality.

One of the main origins of the self-image is the reaction of others. Videbeck (Reading 23) reports one of the few studies to have given an experimental demonstration of this effect. There are a number of other sources of the self-image such as comparison with others and experience of playing various roles. During late adolescence there are mounting pressures to arrive at an integrated ego identity, as Erikson (1956) suggested on the basis of clinical studies. Erikson's ideas about the various forms the self-image can take at this stage were largely confirmed in a more systematic investigation by Marcia (Reading 24). However, the self-system is not active all the time, but is particularly active when a person is being assessed, appearing in public, and so on. Goffman (1956) suggested that embarrassment was brought about by the exposure of a false self-image which has been presented. This theory has been tested by Gross and Stone (Reading 25) who analysed a large number of instances of embarrassment.

References

ERIKSON, E. H. (1956), 'The problem of ego identity', *Amer. J. Psychoanal.*, vol. 4, pp. 56–121.
GOFFMAN, E. (1956), 'Embarrassment and social organization', *Amer. J. Sociol.*, vol. 62, pp. 264–71.

23 Richard Videbeck

Self-Conception and the Reactions of Others

R. Videbeck, 'Self-conception and the reactions of others', *Sociometry*, vol. 23, 1960, pp: 351–9

The view that one's self-conception is learned from the reactions of other individuals to him has achieved wide acceptance in social psychology today, but its implications have not been much exploited empirically. Helper (1955), Manis (1955) and Miyamoto and Dornbusch (1956) report findings which show that an individual's self-ratings are significantly correlated with the ratings of him made by his associates. Their work on the social origins of the self is lodged in Cooley's formulation of the 'looking-glass self' (1902) and in Mead's conception of the self as an organization of socially derived and symbolically represented self-identification (1934). Helper, Manis and other investigators make inferences from their findings about the tenability of this general view, but they do not demonstrate that 'other's reactions' are necessary antecedent conditions to self-ratings. It is the purpose of the study reported in this paper to test the hypothesis in a more direct fashion, by experimentally varying the reactions of others and observing subsequent changes in self-ratings.

Self-conception is a term used to refer to a person's organization of his self attitudes. Operationally, it is frequently defined as a set of interrelated self-ratings, usually upon bipolar scales using some personal or behavioral quality as the referent of the scale. It is possible to distinguish between *ideal-self* ratings, i.e. the degree of the attribute implied in the scale which the person would like to possess, and *actual-self* ratings, i.e. the extent to which, in the person's own opinion, he currently possesses the specified scale attribute. This report is concerned only with changes in the latter self-ratings. As used here, actual-self ratings are defined as *reinforced* scale responses. It is assumed that the person's choice of one scale point over the alternative points on the scale reflects the fact that informational cues have been supplied to the individual which 'verify or validate' the selected scale point as being correct. According to the hypothesis, the principal source of such cues lies in the reactions of other people to the individual. Commonly, in the course of social interaction, other persons will express some degree of approval or disapproval of the individual or his behavior. The expressed degree of approval or disapproval is such a cue. In so far as these expressions represent reward or punishment for the individual, the other's reactions reinforce a particular self-rating response. The response which is reinforced by such reaction is the choice of that point on the rating scale which corresponds to the degree of approval or disapproval inferred from the reaction. In simple outline, if a person is told that he is doing something very well, he will be *more likely* to rate himself as being more capable of doing that something or possessing the qualities related to doing it, than if he had been told he was doing it poorly.

The extent to which another can effectively reinforce an individual's self-rating response on a specific scale will depend on a number of factors, of which only four are considered here. First, it will depend upon the *number of times* the other consistently approves or disapproves of the individual with reference to the specific qualities of the scale referent. Secondly, it will depend upon *how appropriate or qualified the other is*, in the opinion of the individual, to show approval or disapproval. Thirdly, it will depend upon how *strongly motivated* the individual is with reference to the attribute of the scale, i.e. how strongly he strives to attain some ideal-self point on the scale. Fourth, the effectiveness of another's reaction in reinforcing the individual's self-rating response will vary with the *intensity* with which the approval or disapproval is expressed, i.e. the other's apparent confidence and conviction of his expression. If these four conditions are held constant at a level sufficient to insure reinforcement of an individual's self-ratings, two hypotheses about the effects of another's reaction can be stated:

1. If another person reacts approvingly toward the individual with reference to some specified attribute, then the subject will change his actual-self rating, re that attribute, to a point closer to his ideal-self rating; but if the other reacts disapprovingly, then the subject will change his actual-self rating to a point farther away from his ideal-self rating.

2. If disapproving reactions do not substantively differ from approving reactions except for the element of negation, then there will be no difference in absolute amounts of change in self-ratings between subjects reacted to approvingly and disapprovingly, with reference to a given attribute.

Defining self-conceptions as organizations of interrelated sets of self-ratings may be interpreted to mean that in some way changes in one scale, measuring self-ratings, will lead to changes in the self-ratings upon other scales. If the attribute of a scale is viewed as a stimulus pattern, then by the principle of stimulus generalization it can be hypothesized that:

3. If another person reacts approvingly or disapprovingly to the qualities of an individual referred to in one scale, and if as a result the individual changes his self-rating on that scale, he will also change his self-ratings on other

scales to the extent that the attributes of these other scales are functionally similar to the evaluated attribute.

Method

To test the hypotheses, a 2 by 3 design was employed, with two variations in the evaluative reactions of another, and three variations of similarity between rating-scale attributes. The three dependent variables, corresponding to the three hypotheses, are (a) the direction of change, (b) the amount of change, and (c) the spread of change of self-rating responses.

Thirty subjects, who had been rated superior by their instructors, were chosen from introductory speech classes. They were told that they would participate in an experiment to determine whether men or women were better in certain forms of oral communication. In the experimental session each read six poems. After the subject had read each poem, a person, who had been introduced as a visiting speech expert, evaluated the subject's reading performance. The subjects had been randomly assigned to one of the two 'evaluative treatments'. Regardless of the objective quality of their performance, half the subjects received approving reactions and half received disapproving reactions. The evaluative reactions were standardized, prepared statements which the 'experts' read as if they were their own comments.

Before and after the experimental session, each subject rated himself on twenty-four items, each of which began with the prefatory phrase: 'If you were required to, how adequately could you. . . .' A nine-point scale was used with 'extremely adequate' and 'extremely inadequate' defining the poles of the scale. Sixteen of the items dealt with aspects of oral interpretive reading in which all of the subjects had had equal and extensive training in their speech course. Eight of these items specifically dealt with (a) conveying meaning and emotional tone and (b) voice control in oral reading. These items constituted the *criticized scale*, since the reactions of the 'expert' were exclusively confined to the referents of these eight items. The other eight items constituted a scale which is called the *related scale*, because they are substantively similar to the items of the criticized scale, but were not reacted to by the expert. The remaining eight items dealt with oral communication in general social situations, such as leading a discussion group, engaging a stranger in conversation, etc. This scale is called the *unrelated scale*, to indicate that it is substantively less similar to the criticized scale than is the related scale.

After the second administration of the scales, the subjects were given a full explanation of what had transpired and the purposes of the study. The experiment lasted somewhat less than an hour for each subject.

In the above design the four factors relating to effectiveness for reinforcing an individual's self-rating were held constant. To illustrate, each subject entered the experiment with approximately the same level of rated competence and training and each subject received six reactions, hence the first factor (number of consistent reactions) was constant for all subjects. With regard to the second factor (qualification of other to evaluate) all subjects reported in the post-experimental interview that they thought their critic was an expert. According to the estimates of their speech instructors, all subjects were above the average of their classes in interest in the subject matter and in their aspirations for quality of oral reading performance, thus all subjects were similar in general motivational level. As for the fourth factor, the assistants who served as 'experts' had been trained to read both the approving and disapproving evaluations with the same intensity of expression. The standardized reactions were identical in wording for all subjects, except for evaluative terms, such as good–poor, succeeded in–failed to, etc. Thus, in terms of scale values, it was assumed that the approving reaction conveyed approval to the same degree as the disapproving reaction conveyed disapproval.

Findings

The initial differences between the approval and disapproval treatments for each scale are small and could have occurred more than nine times out of ten by chance (Table 1, row B, cols. 7–9). Therefore, any observed difference between the experimental groups in their after-ratings cannot be attributed to initial differences. Furthermore, the consistently high correlation between before and after ratings for all scales (Table 1, row F) suggest that the rating scales are reliable as used in this experiment, and thus any significant differences in means between the two ratings can be attributed to the experimental conditions.

Hypothesis 1 – Direction of change

Considering only changes in the criticized-scale scores, the mean change for subjects under the approval treatment are positive, and negative for disapproval subjects (Table 1, row D, cols. 1 and 4). An analysis of each subject's change reveals that thirteen of the fifteen approval subjects and fourteen of the fifteen disapproval subjects changed in the predicted direction. On the basis of these findings, the hypothesis that a person will rate himself closer to his ideal-self rating if he receives approval and farther away from it if he receives disapproval is considered tenable.

Hypothesis 2 – Absolute amounts of change

If this hypothesis is acceptable, then differences between treatments in mean absolute amounts of change will not be significant at the 0·01 level for criticized-scale scores. The results (Table 1, row D, cols. 1, 4 and 7) reveal

Table 1 Changes in self-rating, after approval or disapproval, by relation of rating scale to content of criticism

| | Approval treatment | | | Disapproval treatment | | | Significance of difference between treatment means (one-tailed 't' test for uncorrelated means) | | |
	(1) Criticized scale	(2) Related scale	(3) Unrelated scale	(4) Criticized scale	(5) Related scale	(6) Unrelated scale	(7) Criticized scale	(8) Related scale	(9) Unrelated scale
A. Ideal-Self Rating	2·16	2·21	2·32	2·09	2·26	2·22	ns	ns	ns
B. Actual-Self Rating: 'Before' Mean Score	3·99	3·78	3·66	3·86	3·95	3·70	>0·90	>0·90	>0·90
C. Actual-Self Rating: 'After' Mean Score	3·50	3·53	3·54	5·16	4·47	3·79	<0·01	<0·01	ns
D. Change: Difference between 'Before' and 'After' Mean Scores (in scale units)	+0·49	+0·25	+0·12	-1·30	-0·52	-0·09	<0·01	<0·05	ns
E. Level of significance of difference between 'Before' and 'After' Mean Scores (one-tailed 't' test for correlated means)	ns	ns	ns	>0·01	ns	ns			
F. Correlation between 'Before' and 'After' Scale Scores (Pearson product-moment correlation coefficients)	0·873*	0·927*	0·742*	0·807*	0·828*	0·597**			

* Significant at 0·01 level.
** Significant at 0·05 level.

that, disregarding signs, the difference is significant and the disapproval mean is two and a half times greater than the approval mean. This difference may be due to one of several factors. First, the degrees of approval and disapproval implied in the reactions of the other may not have been equal, as was initially assumed. Secondly, the observed difference may be an artifact of limitations imposed on the self-rating response by the scale. Thirdly, it is possible that approving and disapproving reactions lead to differential psychological effects, thereby producing differences in rating responses.

The assumption of equality of degrees of approval and disapproval was tested after the experiment by asking nine speech students to rate the reactions *qua* reactions for the amount of approval and disapproval implicit in them. These students, not used as experimental subjects, were asked first to read the approving reactions and then indicate how adequately they felt the person who received the reaction had performed. This was then repeated for the disapproval reactions. The mean rating assigned to the approval reactions was 1·89 or 3·11 scale units from the scale mid-point '5', and for disapproving reactions the mean rating was 7·91 or 2·91 scale units from the mid-point. By 't' test, the difference between the mean distances from the midpoint was not significant at the 0·01 level for eight degrees of freedom. On the basis of this post-experimental evidence, the assumption of 'objective' equality of degrees of approval and disapproval would appear to be tenable and not likely to account for the observed differences in absolute amounts of change between treatments.

A second factor which might account for the observed difference may be the relatively greater maximum amount of change possible for disapproval subjects. The maximum amount possible for subjects receiving approving reactions was 2·99 scale units, i.e. the scale distance from their initial mean to the 'approval' extreme of the scale. For disapproval subjects, the maximum amount possible was 5·14 scale units. When the observed amounts of change are expressed in terms of their appropriate maximums, the disapproval subjects still changed relatively more than did the approval subjects: 0·253 *v.* 0·167 of their respective maximum. All evidence considered, the hypothesis is not acceptable.

Since the correlation between the before and after ratings for both treatments is significant, the observed amounts of change must be seen as a product of the experimental conditions. In like manner, the observed differences between treatments must also be seen as the result of some systematic variation between the treatments. In part, the reaction of the other serves as an informational cue, i.e. tells the subject where the other judges him to be on the rating scale. For example, according to the ratings given the reactions by the nine speech subjects, the subjects receiving the approval treatment were in effect 'told' by the other that they had performed in a 'decidedly adequate' fashion, and the disapproval subjects that they had performed 'decidedly inadequately'. For the approval subjects, the 'expert's' reactions tend generally to confirm the self-ratings derived from their experiences in the speech class and hence changed their self-rating only slightly. However, the disapproval subjects were confronted with an appraisal of their performance which was at variance with what they had become accustomed to receiving from their speech instructor, necessitating a revision of their self-estimates. According to the 'adaptation level' principle, each subject enters the experimental situation with a self-estimate which reflects past experiences tempered by the unfamiliar experimental setting. Successive self ratings will in turn be joint products of the initial self ratings and the subsequent stimuli, i.e. the reactions of the 'expert'. Following the adaptation-level interpretation, shifts between before and after ratings should be proportional to the *interval* between the initially anchored scale point (i.e. the before rating), and the 'objective' scale point of the intervening stimuli. Since the 'objective' scale point of the other's reactions is constant within treatments, the 'adaptation level' interpretation of the observed changes of self ratings can be tested by correlating the initial self ratings with the absolute amount of change between self ratings. For approval subjects, the correlation coefficient is 0·018 and for disapproval subjects it is 0·863. The latter coefficient tends to support this interpretation; the higher the initial self rating the greater the amount of change resulting from disapproving reactions. The nearly zero coefficient associated with the approval treatment is not surprising, in view of the fact that the difference between the before and after mean ratings was quantitatively small and statistically not significant.

Hypothesis 3 – Spread of change between scales

This hypothesis will be deemed acceptable if, within treatments, the amount of change for the related scale is *less* than the amount of change for the criticized scale but *more* than the change associated with the unrelated scale. The evidence (Table 1, row D; Figure 1) tends to support the hypothesis.

The findings suggest that the reactions of others tend to have generalized effects upon self ratings, but the degree of generalization diminishes as the scales become functionally dissimilar. When the data are presented in graphic form, as in Figure 1, it can be seen that the gradient of change for the disapproval treatment is steeper than the gradient for the approval treatment. No doubt this difference in steepness is due in part to marked differences in change in criticized-scale scores; however, it does not explain why both gradients converge at the unrelated scale. Heider's concept 'cognitive balance' (1946) offers a possible explanation. When a subject is confronted with information which contradicts previously acquired information, and the information cannot readily be ignored or refuted, then the individual will incorporate the new information into his existing cognitive organization in such a way as to produce the least amount of change. Since the reactions of the other presented confirming information to the approval subjects, there is no need of isolating the other's evaluation within their total conception of themselves. The effects of negative reactions, on the other hand, seem to lead to greater discrimination between attributes of one's self-conception.

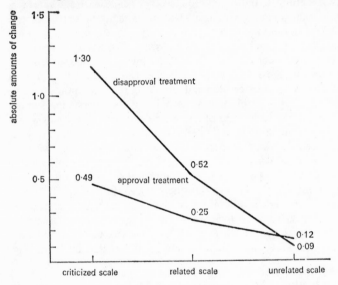

Figure 1

Furthermore, it is interesting to note that the relative rates of change between adjacent scales is almost identical for both treatments. For example, when the difference between the amount of change associated with the criticized scale and for the related scale is expressed as a proportion of the total amount of change between the criticized and unrelated scales, there is no difference between treatments, the percentages being 64 per cent for the approval treatment and 65 per cent for the disapproval treatment. This constant, relative rate of change suggests that the adaptation level concept applies not only to the criticized scale but equally well to functionally similar scales.

Summary

The findings of this study tend to support the general view that self-conceptions are learned, and that the evaluative reactions of others play a significant part in the learning process. Observed differential effects of approval and disapproval treatments were interpreted to be a function of an interaction between the subject's initially anchored self rating and the objective scale value of the approval or disapproval implied in the other's reaction. The findings also tend to support the hypothesis that one's self conception is an organization of discrete self ratings which are unitized by the principle of stimulus generalization. These findings and interpretations are qualified by the fact that the number of reactions of others, the consistency of reactions within treatments, the qualifications of the other to evaluate, and the subjects' motivation were held constant.

References

COOLEY, C. H. (1902), *Human Nature and the Social Order*, Scribners.

HEIDER, F. (1946), 'Attitudes and cognitive organization', *J. Psychol.*, vol. 21, pp. 107–12.

HELPER, M. (1955), 'Learning theory and the self concept', *J. abnorm. soc. Psychol.*, vol. 51, pp. 184–94.

MANIS, M. (1955), 'Social interaction and the self concept', *J. abnorm. soc. Psychol.*, vol. 51, pp. 362–70.

MEAD, G. H. (1934), *Mind, Self, and Society*, C. W. Morris (ed.), University of Chicago Press.

MIYAMOTO, S. F., and DORNBUSCH, S. M. (1956), 'A test of interactionist hypotheses of self-conception', *Amer. J. Sociol.*, vol. 61, pp. 399–403.

24 James E. Marcia

Ego-Identity Status: Relationship to Change in Self-Esteem, General Maladjustment, and Authoritarianism

J. E. Marcia, 'Ego-identity status: relationship to change in self-esteem, "general maladjustment", and authoritarianism', *Journal of Personality*, vol. 35, 1967, pp. 118–33.

Faced with the imminence of adult tasks (e.g. getting a job, becoming a citizen, planning marriage) in which he must now become one of the 'givers' rather than the 'given', the late adolescent is seen by Erikson (1956) as dealing with an identity crisis. He may resolve this crisis either by the achievement of ego identity, based on a sense of personal continuity with the past and future, or by continuing in an identity diffuse state, in which commitments to both past and future are vague or non-existent. The achievement of ego identity requires the individual to relinquish his claims to infantile sources of gratification and to renounce lingering infantile fantasies of omnipotence. In short, he must choose among alternatives and make a subsequent commitment to the alternative chosen.

Two crucial areas in which the adolescent must make such commitments are occupation and ideology. With respect to the importance of occupational commitment, Erikson, in speaking of identity diffusion, says: 'In most instances, however, it is the inability to settle on an occupational identity which disturbs individual young people' (1963, p. 262). In reference to ideology, Erikson states:

we will tentatively view it here and discuss it later – *as a necessity for the growing ego* which is involved in the succession of generations, and in adolescence is committed to some new synthesis of past and future; a synthesis which must include but transcend the past, even as identity does (1956, p. 97).

The variable of commitment, however, cannot be the sole criterion for ego identity. The individual about to become a Methodist, Republican farmer like his Methodist, Republican farmer father, with little or no thought in the matter, certainly cannot be said to have 'achieved' an identity, in spite of his commitment. The integrating, synthesizing activity of which Erikson speaks seems not to have taken place. Hence, another criterion for the achievement of ego identity, in addition to commitment, is necessary: crisis. Crisis refers to times during adolescence when the individual seems to be actively involved in choosing among alternative occupations and beliefs.

Commitment refers to an occupation of personal investment the individual expresses in an occupation or belief.

In this recent approach to ego identity (Marcia, 1966), an individual is placed into one of four 'identity statuses'; these are individual styles of coping with the identity crisis. Presence or absence of crisis and extent of commitment in the two areas of occupation and ideology serve to define the statuses. The *identity achievement* status has experienced a crisis period and is committed to an occupation and ideology. The *moratorium* status refers to those individuals currently engaged in decision making with commitments vague. Individuals in the *foreclosure* status are similar to the illustration given above; they seem to have experienced no crisis, yet have firm, often parentally determined commitments. The *identity diffusion* status has no apparent commitments. Moratoriums, in contrast to identity diffusions, are characterized by the presence of struggle and attempts to make commitments. Foreclosures are distinguished from identity achievement individuals by the lack of any crisis period in the former.

A continuum of ego identity based upon the proximity of an individual to identity achievement is assumed to underly the statuses. Some empirical support for the continuum in the form of scores on a measure of 'overall ego identity' was provided in a previous study by Marcia (1966) (see Figure 1, p. 351). The relationship between the identity statuses and the continuum of ego identity may be explained as follows. A moratorium S, by virtue of his active concern with psychosocial issues, is probably closer to identity achievement than a foreclosure S who may be somewhat solidified in a position of close parental identification that makes movement difficult. Identity diffusion Ss lack even the appearance of identity achievement often found in foreclosures. However, at any time, Ss may move from one status to another, except that once the foreclosure position is left behind (i.e. a crisis has been experienced), it is no longer an option. An identity-diffuse person, for example, would not necessarily be expected to remain in this status. A likely progression would be from diffusion through moratorium to identity achievement. By the same token, ego identity is not achieved once and for all. Severe environmental shifts might precipitate a diffuse state, although this would be less likely to happen to an individual who had once achieved an identity than to, say, a foreclosure individual.

Identity statuses are established by means of a thirty-minute semi-structured interview. All interviews follow the same outline, although deviations from the standard form are permitted in order to explore some areas more thoroughly. In most cases, the criteria for ending an interview involve the completion of the prescribed questions as well as some feeling of certainty on the interviewer's part that the individual has provided enough information to be categorized. Interviews are tape recorded and then re-played for judging; hence, each interview is heard at least twice.

A scoring manual (Marcia, 1964) has been constructed using both theoretical and empirical criteria. Each S is evaluated in terms of presence or absence of crisis as well as degree of commitment for occupation and ideology (divided into religion and politics). The interview judge familiarizes himself with the descriptions of the statuses provided in the manual and sorts each interview into that pattern which it most closely resembles. Examples of interview questions are reported in a recent article by Marcia (1966).

Interjudge reliability has been established on two separate samples of Ss at two different colleges. The first investigation (Marcia, 1964) used two judges rating twenty randomly selected Ss and obtained 70 per cent agreement on the identity statuses. The second investigation (Marcia, 1966), using a scoring manual revised on the basis of the previous study, employed three judges, one of whom was untrained, rating twenty randomly selected Ss. There was 75 per cent agreement obtained in this study. Considering the complexity of the variables, this degree of agreement was thought to be satisfactory.

Two previous studies have been conducted investigating the validity of the identity statuses. The first (Marcia, 1964) dealt with the development of a scoring manual for the interviews, establishment of interjudge reliability, and investigation of concurrent validity. The second study (Marcia, 1966) explored the relationship between the identity statuses and performance on a stressful concept-attainment task, level of aspiration patterns, change in self-esteem following positive or negative task feedback, and authoritarianism. Identity achievement Ss showed superior performance on the stressful concept-attainment task; moratorium Ss performed similarly to identity achievement Ss (with the exception of being significantly more variable on the concept-attainment task); foreclosure Ss endorsed authoritarian values, set goals unrealistically high, and had considerable difficulty on the stressful concept-attainment task; identity diffusion Ss were similar on some measures to foreclosure Ss.

A major variable in this previous study that failed to distinguish among statuses was change in a self-esteem measure following positive or negative personality-relevant information. This failure was attributed to unreliability in the self-esteem measure engendered by the two-month span between its first and second administrations. One aim of the present study was to pursue further this hypothesis by employing disguised parallel forms of the self-esteem scale with less than an hour between the 'before' and 'after'. administrations, as well as to maximize chances for observing change by employing a second, 'obvious' self-esteem measure. The hypothesis is that Ss high in identity status (identity achievement and moratorium) will be less vulnerable (i.e. change less) in the face of self-esteem manipulation than Ss low in identity status (foreclosure and identity diffusion).

Although each of the identity statuses was conceptualized as having unique characteristics, Bugelski[1] has suggested that they may actually represent a continuum of maladjustment or psychopathology, ranging from identity achievement to identity diffusion. A second aim of the present study was to investigate this hypothesis by comparing the statuses on the Welsh Anxiety Scale (Welsh, 1956).

The precise construct measured by the WAS is somewhat in question. However, some direction is provided by Block's (1965) recent factor-analytic study on the MMPI. He extracted two main factors after having balanced items to control for response sets. Of the most pervasive factor, Alpha, he says:

The first factor . . . is defined at its negative end by a cluster of scales purporting to reflect a neurotic and maladaptive character structure (e.g. Pt, Sc, Pn[2]) and at the other end by scales, led by Edwards's Social Desirability measure, which relate to a more self-satisfied and culturally valued adjustive mode (e.g. Lp, Sp, St, Ie). . . . For Edwards, Alpha is the Social-Desirability dimension; for Welsh, the preferred label for the dimension (reversed) is Anxiety (pp. 50–51).

For Block, the preferred label is 'ego resiliency'. Regardless of these questions, it can be said that within an essentially normal population such as we are dealing with in this study, the higher one scores on the WAS, in general, the more adjusted one should appear. 'Should appear' is not to be taken lightly: 'All of these scales are susceptible to deliberate feigning attempts or attempts to deny actually existing personal frailties' (Block, 1965, p. 112). If the hypothesis of an underlying dimension of apparent maladjustment characterizes the identity statuses, there should be a significant negative relationship between WAS scores and the identity statuses dichotomized into high and low groups.

A third purpose of this study was to replicate previous findings concerning the foreclosure status' Ss scoring significantly higher on the F Scale.

Method
Subjects

Ss were seventy-two males enrolled in introductory psychology courses at the State University of New York at Buffalo, fulfilling the requirement of participating in experiments for course credit.

1. B. R. Bugelski, personal communication, 1964.
2. The Pn scale and the WAS are, in Block's words, 'functionally equivalent'.

Confederate experimenters

In order to minimize intercommunication as well as E bias effects (Rosenthal, 1964), the study employed twenty-five confederate Es who administered the stressful concept-attainment task in one four-hour period to all Ss.

Measures of variables

Identity status. Identity status was determined by means of the thirty-minute semistructure interview previously described. Approximately half of the Ss were interviewed by the author and half by a research assistant. Identity statuses were judged by the author. Although a few Ss were not easily classifiable the author based his decision on the predominant 'tone' of the interview. No S was dropped because he was difficult to classify. Hence, any significant findings were obtained in spite of not using 'pure types' and in spite of the variance contributed by the twenty-five confederate Es.

Change in self-esteem. Two measures were used to assess change in self-esteem of the identity statuses. A disguised measure consisted of questionnaire items developed by deCharms and Rosenbaum (1960) which tapped feelings of self-confidence and worthiness. This measure (SEQ) was divided into equivalent halves by means of an item analysis. Disguise was achieved by embedding each half in either the Welsh Anxiety Scale or the authoritarian measure. A more obvious measure of self-esteem involved two simple thermometer-like scales on which the S indicated his estimate of his IQ (85–150) and his self-confidence (0–50). These scales were administered immediately prior to a concept-attainment task and again following positive or negative task feedback.

The feedback given each S concerned his performance on the concept-attainment task which he had been told was related to intelligence and academic success. The E appeared to score the test and then informed the S that he had performed five of the seven problems either better or worse than the national norms. Taking this information into considertion, the S then reestimated his IQ and self-confidence on the same scale he had previously marked. Positive or negative task feedback was assigned to Ss by the author before they were tested by the confederate Es. An alphabetical list of Ss was made and every other one was assigned either positive or negative feedback; thirty-six were to receive positive feedback and thirty-six to receive negative feedback. Through E error, thirty-eight actually received positive and thirty-four got negative. Type of feedback to be given was communicated to the confederate E by the way in which the S's name appeared on the CAT scoring sheet; underlining signified positive information; no underlining indicated negative.

The concept-attainment task (CAT) used was that developed by Bruner,

Goodnow and Austin (1956) and modified by Weick (1964). Administration of the CAT was similar to the procedure described by Marcia (1966) except that the unusually large number of confederate Es, together with time limitations, prohibited the most effective imposition of the stress conditions of evaluation apprehension and oversolicitousness. Hence, the CAT administration was not considered as an attempt at replication of previous findings.

Authoritarianism and anxiety. Authoritarianism was measured by means of the authoritarian submission and conventionality subcluster of the California F Scale (Adorno, Frenkel-Brunswik, Levinson and Sanford, 1950). Anxiety or general maladjustment was measured by the Welsh Anxiety Scale (WAS) (Welsh, 1956). Both questionnaires had embedded self-esteem items.

Procedure

The experimental procedure followed this sequence:
1. Each S was interviewed to determine his identity status.
2. On the day of the experiment, a S went through the following conditions: (a) Completion of the combined WAS–SEQ questionnaire in a group setting. (b) Completion of the IQ–self-confidence rating scale in the presence of the confederate E. (c) Performance of the CAT. (d) Reevaluation of IQ–self-confidence ratings following positive or negative task feedback in the presence of the confederate E. (e) Completion of the combined F–SEQ questionnaire in a group setting. (f) 'Debriefing' about the deceptive task feedback as S left the building.

Results
Self-esteem change

Change in self-esteem may be looked at in two ways: amount and direction of change as a function of positive or negative information, and overall change regardless of characteristics of information.

Self-esteem change as a function of type of information. Amount of change as a function of positive or negative information was not found to differ significantly among the identity statuses. That is, no status appeared to be differentially affected by positive or negative information.

Analysis of direction of self-esteem change as a function of type of information should answer the following questions. Was the information, as a treatment condition, generally effective? Was the information more effective for some statuses than for others? Table 1 presents the direction of change on both the obvious and disguised self-esteem measures as a function of positive or negative information. Data in this table were analysed by means of tetrachoric correlation and chi-square.

Table 1a Direction of self-esteem change as a function of positive or negative information

Information	Direction of change	Identity achievement (A) Obvious	Disguised	Moratorium (B) Obvious	Disguised	Foreclosure (C) Obvious	Disguised	Identity diffusion (D) Obvious	Disguised
Positive	Positive	5	5	6	7	8	8	3	2
Positive	Negative	2	1	2	2	3	6	4	4
Negative	Negative	3	5	6	8	8	5	6	3
Negative	Positive	0	4	1	4	1	3	0	5
Positive	Zero	2	0	2	0	0	0	0	0
Negative	Zero	3	0	4	0	2	0	1	0

Table 1b **Direction of change, obvious condition**

Type of information	Direction of change			Zero change	
	Positive	Negative		A+B	C+D
Positive	11	22	Zero	11	3
Negative	23	2	More than zero	25	33
	$r_{tet} = 0.91$****			$\eta^2 = 5.67$**	

** $p < 0.02$.
**** $p < 0.0001$.

Table 1c **Direction of change, disguised condition**

Type of information	Direction change		A+B		A+C	
	Positive	Negative	Positive	Negative	Positive	Negative
Positive	16	22	8	12	8	10
Negative	13	22	3	13	10	8
	$r_{tet} = -0.08$		$r_{tet} = -0.40$*		$r_{tet} = -0.20$	

* $p < 0.05$.

A tetrachoric r of 0·91 between direction of information and direction of change in the obvious measure indicates a general effectiveness of the treatment condition, positive information yielding positive change, negative information yielding negative change. The tetrachoric rs between direction of information and direction of change for identity achievement plus moratorium and for foreclosure plus identity diffusion of 0·92 and 0·93, respectively, indicate no differential effect among the identity statuses in terms of direction on this variable.

The most interesting directional findings in the obvious measure of self-esteem change involved 'zero change'. Significantly more Ss in the high ego identity statuses showed zero change (i.e. greater resistance to self-esteem manipulation) than in the low ego identity statuses ($\chi^2 = 5.67$, $df = 1$, $p < 0.02$).

Change in the disguised self-esteem measure is more complex than in the obvious measure. The tetrachoric r between direction of information and direction of change was − 0·08, indicating no overall directional effectiveness of the treatment condition. However, when the data were analysed separately for the statuses, the tetrachoric r for identity achievement plus moratorium was − 0·40; for foreclosure plus identity diffusion it was 0·20. While this indicates a slight tendency for those Ss higher in ego identity to change in a direction opposite to the information, the most important finding lies in the significance of difference between the two correlations ($z = 2\cdot52, p = 0\cdot012$). Again, it is those Ss lower in ego identity who tend to change more consistently in the direction of the information.

Self-esteem change independent of direction of information. The most important question with respect to self-esteem change is the overall amount of change produced by the personality-relevant information. Differences among the identity statuses with respect to change in both the obvious and disguised self-esteem measures were investigated by means of Kruskal-Wallis one-way analysis of variance and Mann-Whitney Us. (The change scores for the IQ–self-confidence measures were converted to z scores, combined, and then ranked.) The results of this analysis are presented in Table 2.

Table 2 **Differences among identity statuses in self-esteem change on both disguised and obvious measures**

	Identity achievement	Moratorium	Foreclosure	Identity diffusion
N	15	21	22	14
R (obvious)	31·57	33·17	43·23	37·68
R (disguised)	31·53	32·62	39·50	45·29

H (obvious) = 20·37, $df = 3, p < 0\cdot001$; H (disguised) = 13.60, $df = 3, p < 0\cdot01$.

The statuses differed significantly in self-esteem changes on both the obvious and disguised measures, with those Ss high in ego identity changing less than those low in ego identity (obvious: $U = 792, z = 1\cdot63, p = 0\cdot052$ [one-tailed]; disguised: $U = 804, z = 1\cdot78, p = 0\cdot038$ [one-tailed]).[3]

Looking at the foreclosure and identity-diffusion statuses alone, an interesting supplementary finding was that foreclosure Ss changed significantly more than identity diffusion Ss on the obvious measure ($U = 233, z = 3\cdot11, p = 0\cdot002$),[4] yet these groups were not significantly different on the disguised measure ($U = 146\cdot5, z = 0\cdot24$, n.s.). In addition, foreclosure Ss changed somewhat more in self-esteem on the obvious measure than on the disguised measure ($U = 273, z = 1\cdot82, p = 0\cdot070$); and identity-diffusion Ss changed somewhat more on the disguised measure than on the obvious measure ($U = 147, z = 193, p = 0\cdot054$).

Anxiety

The point biserial correlation between Welsh Anxiety Scale (WAS) scores and the identity statuses, dichotomized into high (identity achievement plus

3. No significant differences among statuses in their initial SEQ scores or IQ–self-confidence ratings were found.
4. All significance levels in this paragraph are two-tailed.

moratorium) and low (foreclosure plus identity diffusion) groups, was 0·24 ($df = 72$, $p < 0·05$). This barely significant correlation was in the opposite direction from the hypothesized continuum of maladjustment. In fact, the highest and lowest identity statuses fall in the middle of a continuum of WAS scores.

Table 3a **Differences among identity statuses in Welsh Anxiety Scale scores: identity status**

Identity status	N	MS	SD
Identity achievement (A)	15	45·42	10·89
Moratorium (B)	21	56·10	15·90
Foreclosure (C)	22	41·32	14·26
Identity diffusion (D)	14	48·36	15·74

Table 3b **Differences among identity statuses in WAS scores: groups compared**

Comparisons	t	Comparisons	t
A v. B	2·18*	B v. A+C+D	3·02***
A v. C	n.s.	C v. A+B+D	2·42**
A v. D	n.s,	D v. A+B+C	n.s.
B v. C	10·26****	A+B v. C+D	2·11*
B v. D	1·38	A+C v. B+D	2·83***
C v. D	1·48	A+D v. B+C	n.s.
A v. B+C+D	n.s.		

Note: All significance levels in this table are by two-tailed test.
*$p < 0·05$.
**$p < 0·02$
***$p < 0·01$.
****$p < 0·001$.

Differences among the statuses in WAS scores were investigated by means of a one-way analysis of variance and t tests between groups. These data are presented in Table 3.

The groups differed significantly in WAS scores ($F = 7·26$, $df = 3/68$, $p < 0·0005$) with most of the variance accounted for by the moratorium status. Comparisons not involving this group were not significant. Also of interest is the tendency for foreclosure Ss to appear lowest on this measure. These findings further refute the hypothesis that the statuses constitute continuum of maladjustment or psychopathology.

Authoritarianism

Differences among the identity statuses in F scores were analysed by means of one-way analysis of variance and *t* tests. These results are found in Table 4.

As hypothesized, foreclosure Ss were significantly higher in their endorse-

Table 4 **Differences among the identity statuses in F scores**

	Identity achievement	Moratorium	Foreclosure	Identity diffusion
N	15	21	22	14
SD	6·43	7·82	7·39	4·43
MS	31·80	28·95	37·05	29·29

$F = 5·76$, $df = 3/68$, $p < 0·005$; *Foreclosure* v. *other statuses combined*: $t = 3·98$, $df = 70$, $p < 0·0005$ (one-tailed).

ment of authoritarian values than other statuses. This finding constitutes a replication of previous results (Marcia, 1966).

Discussion

Figure 1 summarizes the findings to date with respect to the identity statuses. The measures of overall ego identity, concept-attainment, task performance, and level of aspiration are those obtained in a previous study (Marcia, 1966).

The finding in the present study, that identity achievement and moratorium Ss are less vulnerable to self-esteem manipulation than Ss in foreclosure and identity diffusion statuses, is consistent both with Gruen's (1960) finding that ego identity Ss accept false personality sketches of themselves less than identity diffusion Ss, and with the theoretical description of Ss who have achieved an identity as having developed an internal, as opposed to external, locus of self-definition (Marcia, 1964).

The non-hypothesized, yet theoretically consistent, finding of differences (albeit, low level) between foreclosure and identity diffusion Ss on obvious *v.* disguised self-esteem change measures suggests that perhaps when given a structured, face-to-face encounter with an authority figure, foreclosures easily acquiesce to the situational demands and exhibit change, while identity diffusions present a facade of self-consistency. However, in a group situation with the measure disguised, the pull to change is not so great for the foreclosures, nor is actual change so easy to deny for the identity diffusions, and the differences between these two decrease. This explanation also may account for the significant changes from the obvious to the disguised measures found within each group. This finding, suggestive only pending further experimentation, does indicate support for the statuses as distinctive groupings.

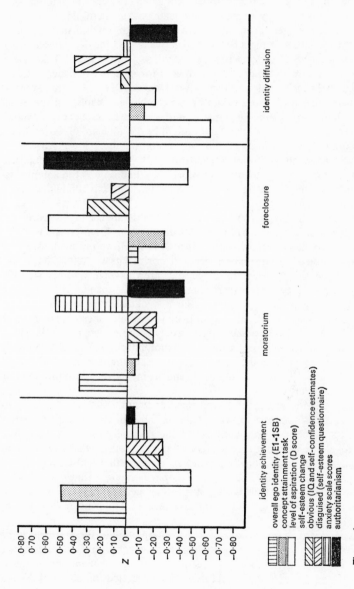

identity achievement
moratorium
foreclosure
identity diffusion

overall ego identity (E1-1SB)
concept attainment task
level of aspiration (D score)
self-esteem change
obvious (IQ and self-confidence estimates)
disguised (self-esteem questionnaire)
anxiety scale scores
authoritarianism

Z

0·80
0·70
0·60
0·50
0·40
0·30
0·20
0·10
0
-0·10
-0·20
-0·30
-0·40
-0·50
-0·60
-0·70
-0·80

Figure 1

The finding of no significant differences among the statuses in initial self-esteem measures may appear theoretically inconsistent. However, this apparent inconsistency depends upon a certain degree of faith in the validity of the tests' labels. It might be less speculative to describe the variable being measured as a S's 'tendency to say good things about himself'. Taking this view, together with the previous finding of foreclosure Ss' tendency to set inordinately high goals for themselves (Marcia, 1966), one might have predicted that foreclosure would obtain the highest scores. On the other hand, there would still be the question of identity achievement Ss' 'valid' high self-esteem. Still another factor might be the influence of the tendency of moratorium Ss to introspect, thus, perhaps, obtaining lower self-esteem scores than identity diffusion Ss even though the former are conceptualized as being higher in ego identity. In short, the situation was too complex to hypothesize differences on this variable and the failure to obtain them does little damage to the theory.

Another initially puzzling finding might be the higher WAS scores for moratoriums. Block (1965) leaves little doubt about his impressions of the maladaptive nature of low Alphas (high WAS). However, one must recall the definition of moratoriums as being 'in crisis'. The world for them is not, currently, a highly predictable place; they are vitally engaged in a struggle to make it so; they report experiencing more anxiety than do Ss in any other status. Although one might expect identity diffusion Ss to score equally high on this measure, the identity diffusion Ss within our essentially normal population do not experience much anxiety because there is little in which they are invested. As they begin to care more, probably one of two things happens: they move to the moratorium status, or they become so disturbed that they are diagnosed schizophrenic and are moved out of the range of our sample population.

The low WAS scores for the foreclosures do not present much of a problem. These Ss' tendency to say socially desirable things about themselves is understandable not only in terms of the status definition as essentially approval-oriented, but also in light of the previously cited experimental findings (viz., unrealistically high levels of aspiration and extent of self-esteem change in the presence of an authority figure). That their 'adjustment' is rather superficial is suggested by their generally shifting self-esteem and their difficulty in the stressful concept-attainment task (Marcia, 1966).

Whatever the complexities of WAS interpretation, Block's concept of 'ego resiliency', particularly since it is based on behavioral measures rather than on purely item-labeling procedures, is too valuable and too pertinent to ego identity not to explore it further. His suggested combining of the ego resiliency measure with L and K scale measures to separate out 'plusgetters' should distinguish very nicely between identity achievement and foreclosure Ss.

Returning to the point concerning a continuum of maladjustment underlying the statuses, the only continuum observed thus far is overall ego identity. Besides, any continuum approach overlooks the main contribution of the identity statuses: a method of describing individual modes of coping with the identity crisis.

The foreclosure Ss' endorsement of authoritarian values, a replication of previous findings, is consistent with the description of them as becoming their parents' alter egos (Marcia, 1966). Although this replicated finding may appear somewhat trivial in view of its obviousness, the identity statuses are new constructs, and, in this stage of nomological net construction, their province is both established and enlarged by tying them to older, more thoroughly researched constructs.

Some directions for further research on the identity statuses, in addition to the investigation of Block's ego resiliency concept, are: development of a questionnaire form to replace the lengthy interview; investigation of cognitive styles characteristic of the statuses; exploration of antecedent conditions to ego identity in the form of parent variables; and development of psychosocial criteria for ego identity in women.

Summary

Additional validational evidence for the ego identity statuses – four styles of coping with the identity crisis – was established. Ss, seventy-two college males, were interviewed to determine identity status, exposed to a self-esteem manipulation condition, and administered both the Welsh Anxiety Scale and an authoritarianism measure. Ss low in ego identity changed more in self-esteem and more in a direction consistent with the manipulated information than Ss high in ego identity. There was also some evidence for differential change between the two low ego identity statuses on obvious v. disguised measures of self-esteem change. Welsh Anxiety Scale scores did not indicate a continuum of general maladjustment for the statuses. The 'in crisis' status scored highest on this measure; the status characterized by adherence to parental wishes was lowest. This latter group also obtained significantly high F-scale scores, a replication of previous findings. A figure summarizing current empirical evidence supporting the identity statuses is provided.

References

ADORNO, T. W., FRENKEL-BRUNSWIK, E., LEVINSON, D. J., and SANFORD, R. N. (1950), *The Authoritarian Personality*, Harper & Row.
BLOCK, J. (1965), *The Challenge of Response Sets: Unconfounding Meaning Acquiescence, and Social Desirability in the MMPI*, Appleton-Century-Crofts.

BRUNER, J. S., GOODNOW, I. J., and AUSTIN, G. A. (1956), *A Study of Thinking*, Wiley.

DE CHARMS, R., and ROSENBAUM, M. E. (1960), 'Status variables and matching behavior', *J. Pers.*, vol. 28, pp. 492–502.

ERIKSON, E. H. (1963), *Childhood and Society*, Norton.

ERIKSON, E. H. (1956), 'The problem of ego identity', *Amer. J. Psychoanal.* vol. 4, pp. 56–121.

GRUEN, W. (1960), 'Rejection of false information about oneself as an indication of ego identity', *J. consult Psychol*, vol. 24, pp. 231–3.

MARCIA, J. E. (1964), 'Determination and construct validity of ego-identity status', Unpublished doctoral dissertation, Ohio State University.

MARCIA, J. E. (1966), 'Development and validation of ego-identity status', *J. pers. soc. Psychol.*, vol. 3, pp. 551–9.

ROSENTHAL, R. (1964), 'Experimenter outcome-orientation and the results of the psychological experiment', *Psychol. Bull.*, vol. 61, pp. 405–12.

WEICK, K. E. (1964), 'Reduction of cognitive dissonance through task enhancement and effort expenditure', *J. abnorm. soc. Psychol.*, vol. 68, pp. 533–9.

WELSH, G. S. (1956), 'Factor dimensions A and B', in G. S. Welsh and W. G. Dahlstrom (eds.), *Basic Readings on the MMPI in Psychology and Medicine*, University of Minnesota Press.

25 Edward Gross and Gregor P. Stone

Embarrassment and the Analysis of Role Requirements

E. Gross and G. P. Stone, 'Embarrassment and the analysis of role requirements', *American Journal of Sociology*, vol. 70, 1964, pp. 1–15.

Embarrassment and the analysis of role requirements

Embarrassment exaggerates the core dimensions of social transactions, bringing them to the eye of the observer in an almost naked state. Embarrassment occurs whenever some *central* assumption in a transaction has been *unexpectedly* and unqualifiedly discredited for at least one participant. The result is that he is incapacitated for continued role performance. Moreover, embarrassment is infectious. It may spread out, incapacitating others not previously incapacitated. It is destructive dis-ease. In the wreckage left by embarrassment lie the broken foundations of social transactions. By examining such ruins, the investigator can reconstruct the architecture they represent.

To explore this idea, recollections of embarrassment were expressly solicited from two groups of subjects: (1) approximately 800 students enrolled in introductory sociology courses; and (2) about eighty students enrolled in an evening extension class. Not solicited, but gratefully received, were many examples volunteered by colleagues and friends who had heard of our interest in the subject. Finally we drew upon many recollections of embarrassment we had experienced ourselves. Through these means at least one thousand specimens of embarrassment were secured.

We found that embarrassments frequently occurred in situations requiring continuous and coordinated role performance – speeches, ceremonies, processions or working concerts. In such situations embarrassment is particularly noticeable because it is so devastating. Forgetting one's lines, forgetting the wedding ring, stumbling in a cafeteria line, or handing a colleague the wrong tool, when these things occur without qualification, bring the performance to an obviously premature and unexpected halt. At the same time, manifestations of the embarrassment – blushing, fumbling, stuttering, sweating[1] – coerce awareness of the social damage and the need for immediate repair. In some instances, the damage may be potentially so great that embarrassment cannot be allowed to spread among the role per-

1. Erving Goffman (1956) describes these manifestations vividly.

formers. The incapacity may be qualified, totally ignored, or pretended out of existence.[2] For example, a minister, noting the best man's frantic search for an absent wedding ring, whispers to him to ignore it, and all conspire to continue the drama with an imaginary ring. Such rescues are not always possible. Hence we suggest that every enduring social relation will provide means of preventing embarrassment, so that the entire transaction will not collapse when embarrassment occurs. A second general observation would take into account that some stages in the life cycle, for example, adolescence in our society, generate more frequent embarrassments than others. These are points to which we shall return.

To get at the content of embarrassment, we classified the instances in categories that remained as close to the specimens as possible. A total of seventy-four such categories were developed, some of which were forced choices between friends, public mistakes, exposure of false front, being caught in a cover story, misnaming, forgetting names, slips of the tongue, body exposure, invasions of others' back regions, uncontrollable laughter, drunkenness in the presence of sobriety (or vice versa), loss of visceral control, and the sudden recognition of wounds or other stigmata. Further inspection of these categories disclosed that most could be included in three general areas: (1) inappropriate identity; (2) loss of poise; (3) disturbance of the assumptions persons make about one another in social transactions.

Since embarrassment always incapacitates persons for role performance (to embarrass is, literally, to bar or stop), a close analysis of the conditions under which it occurs is especially fruitful in the revelation of the requirements *necessary* for role-playing, role-taking, role-making, and role-performance in general. These role requirements are thus seen to include the establishment of identity, poise, and valid assumptions about one another among all the parties of a social transaction. We turn now to the analysis of those role requirements.

Identity and poise

In every social transaction, selves must be established, defined, and accepted by the parties. Every person in the company of others is, in a sense, obligated to bring his best self forward to meet the selves of others also presumably best fitted to the occasion. When one is 'not himself' in the presence of others who expect him to be just that, as in cases where his mood carries him away either by spontaneous seizure (uncontrollable laughter or tears) or by induced seizure (drunkenness), embarrassment ensues. Similarly, when one is 'shown up' to other parties to the transaction by the exposure of unacceptable moral qualifications or inappropriate motives, embarrassment

2. A more general discussion of this phenomenon under the rubric civil inattention is provided in Goffman (1963a, pp. 83–8).

sets in all around. However, the concept, self, is a rather gross concept, and we wish to single out two phases that frequently provided focal points for embarrassment – identity and poise.

Identity

Identity is the substantive dimension of the self.

Almost all writers using the term imply that identity establishes what and where the person is in social terms. It is not a substitute word for 'self'. Instead, when one has identity, he is *situated* – that is, cast in the shape of a social object by the acknowledgement of his participation or membership in social relations. One's identity is established when others *place* him as a social object by assigning the same words of identity that he appropriates for himself or *announces*. It is in the coincidence of placements and announcements that identity becomes a meaning of the self (Stone, 1962, p. 93).

Moreover, as we have already pointed out, identity stands at the base of role. When inappropriate identities are established or appropriate identities are lost, role performance is impossible.

If identity *locates* the person in social terms, it follows that locations or spaces emerge as symbols of identity, since social relations are spatially distributed. Moreover, as Goffman has remarked (1959, p. 25), there must be a certain coherence between one's personal appearance and the setting in which he appears. Otherwise embarrassment may ensue with the resulting incapacitation for role performance. Sexual identity is pervasively established by personal appearance, and a frequent source of embarrassment among our subjects was the presence of one sex in a setting reserved for the other. Both men and women reported inadvertent invasions of spaces set aside for the other sex with consequent embarrassment and humiliation. The implication of such inadvertent invasions is, of course, that one literally does not know where one is, that one literally has no identity in the situation, or that the identity one is putting forward is so absurd as to render the proposed role performance totally irrelevant. Everyone is embarrassed, and such manifestations as, for example, cries and screams, heighten the dis-ease. In such situations, laughter cannot be enjoined to reduce the seriousness of the unexpected collapse of the encounter, and only flight can insure that one will not be buried in the wreckage.

To establish *what* he is in social terms, each person assembles a set of apparent symbols which he carries about as he moves from transaction to transaction. Such symbols include the shaping of the hair, painting of the face, clothing, cards of identity, other contents of wallets and purses, and sundry additional marks and ornaments. The items in the set must cohere, and the set must be complete. Taken together, these apparent symbols have been called *identity documents* (Goffman, 1963b, pp. 59–63),[3] in that they enable others to validate announced identities. Embarrassment often resulted when our subjects made personal appearances with either invalid or incomplete identity documents. It was embarrassing for many, for example, to announce their identities as customers at restaurants or stores, perform the customer role and then, when the crucial validation of this identity was requested – the payoff – to discover that the wallet had been left at home.

Because the social participation of men in American society is relatively more frequently caught up in the central structures, for example, the structure of work, than is the social participation of women who are relatively more immersed in interpersonal relations, the identities put forward by men are often *titles*; by women, often *names*. Except for very unusual titles, such identities are shared, and their presentation has the consequence of bringing people together. Names, on the other hand, mark people off from one another. So it is that a frequent source of embarrassment for women in our society occurs when they appear together in precisely the same dress. Their identity documents are invalidated. The embarrassment may be minimized, however, if the space in which they make their personal appearance is large enough. In one instance, both women met the situation by spending an entire evening on different sides of the ballroom in which their embarrassing confrontation occurred, attempting to secure validation from social circles with minimal intersection, or, at least, where intersection was temporally attenuated. Men, on the other hand, will be embarrassed if their clothing does not resemble the dress of the other men present in public and official encounters. Except for 'the old school tie', their neckties seem to serve as numbers on a uniform, marking each man off from every other. Out of uniform, their structural membership cannot be visibly established, and role performance is rendered extremely difficult, if not impossible.

Not only are identities undocumented, they are also misplaced, as in misnaming or forgetting, or other incomplete placements. One relatively frequent source of embarrassment we categorized as 'damaging someone's personal representation'. This included cases of ethnically colored sneers in the presence of one who, in fact, belonged to the deprecated ethnic group but did not put that identity forward, or behind-the-back slurs about a woman who turned out to be the listener's wife. The victim of such misplacement, however inadvertent, will find it difficult to continue the transaction or to present the relevant identity to the perpetrators of the embarrassment in the future. The awkwardness is reflexive. Those who are responsible for the misplacement will experience the same difficulties and dis-ease.

Other sources of embarrassment anchored in identity suggest a basic

3. Goffman confines the concept to personal identity, but his own discussion extends it to include matters of social identity.

characteristic of all human transactions, which, as Strauss puts it, are 'carried on in thickly peopled and complexly imaged contexts' (1959, p. 57). One always brings to transactions more identities than are necessary for his role performance. As a consequence, two or more roles are usually performed at once by each participant.[4]

If we designate the relevant roles in transactions as *dominant roles* then we may note that *adjunct roles* – a type of side involvement, as Goffman would have it, or better, a type of side *activity* – are usually performed in parallel with dominant role performance. Specifically, a lecturer may smoke cigarettes or a pipe while carrying out the dominant performance, or one may carry on a heated conversation with a passenger while operating a motor vehicle. Moreover, symbols of *reserve identities* are often carried into social transactions. Ordinarily, they are concealed, as when a court judge wears his golfing clothes beneath his robes. Finally, symbols of abandoned or *relict identities* may persist in settings where they have no relevance for dominant role performances.[5] For example, photographs of the performer as an infant may be thrust into a transaction by a doting mother or wife, or one's newly constituted household may still contain the symbols of a previous marriage.

In these respects, the probability of avoiding embarrassment is a function of at least two factors: (1) the extent to which adjunct roles, reserve identities and relict identities are not incongruent with the dominant role performance, and (2) the allocation of prime attention to the dominant role performance so that less attention is directed toward adjunct role performance, reserve identities, and relict identities. Thus the professor risks embarrassment should the performance of his sex role appear to be the main activity in transactions with female students where the professorial role is dominant – for example, if the student pulls her skirt over her knees with clearly more force than necessary. The judge may not enter the courtroom in a golf cap, nor may the husband dwell on the symbols of a past marriage in the presence of a new wife while entertaining guests in his home. Similarly, should adjunct role performance prove inept, as when the smoking lecturer ignites the contents of a wastebasket or the argumentative driver fails to observe the car in front in time to avert a collision attention is diverted from the dominant role performance. Even without the golf cap, should the judge's robe be caught so that his golfing attire is suddenly revealed in the courtroom, the transactions of the court will be disturbed. Fetishistic devotion to the sym-

4. This observation and the ensuring discussion constitute a contribution to and extension of present perspectives on role conflict. Most discussions conceive of such conflict as internalized contradictory obligations. They do not consider simultaneous multiple-role performance. An exception is Everett C. Hughes's discussion of the Negro physician innocently summoned to attend a prejudiced emergency case (1945).

5. This phenomenon provides the main theme and source of horror and mystery in Daphne du Maurier's now classic *Rebecca*.

bols of relict identities by bereaved persons is embarrassing even to well-meaning visitors.

However, the matter of avoiding incongruence and allocating attention appropriately among the several identities a performer brings to a transaction verges very closely on matters of poise, as we shall see. Matters of poise converge on the necessity of controlling representations of the self, and identity-symbols are important self-representations.

Personal poise

Presentation of the self in social transactions extends considerably beyond making the appropriate personal appearance. It includes the presentation of an entire situation. Components of situations, however, are often representations of self, and in this sense self and situation are two sides of the same coin. Personal poise refers to the performer's control over self and situation, and whatever disturbs that control, depriving the transaction, as we have said before, of any relevant future, is incapacitating and consequently embarrassing.

Loss of poise was a major dimension in our scrutiny of embarrassment, and its analysis can do much to shed light on the components of social situations – a necessary task, because the concept, 'situation', is quite difficult to specify and operationalize. Working from the outside in, so to speak, we wish to single out five[6] elements of self and situation with reference to which loss of control gave rise to considerable embarrassment.

First, *spaces* must be so arranged and maintained that they are role-enabling. This is sometimes difficult to control, since people appear in spaces that belong to others, over which they exercise no authority and for which they are not responsible. Students, invited to faculty parties where faculty members behave like faculty members, will 'tighten up' to the extent that the students' role performance is seriously impeded. To avoid embarrassment, people will go to great lengths to insure their appearance in appropriate places, and to some to be deprived of access to a particular setting is to limit performance drastically.

Spaces are often fixed in location and have boundaries. As such they may partake of the character of territories or domains: a particular person (or persons) is 'in command' (it is 'his' domain) and most familiar with it, and the territory is in continual danger of being invaded (deliberately or inadvertently). Embarrassments were reported for both of these features of space. Being 'in command' and familiar with an area means knowing where the back regions are and having the right of access to them. The host at a

6. The five components to be discussed – spaces, props, equipment, clothing and the body – are not offered as an exhaustive list. We have been able to distinguish close to forty such elements.

party in his own home, however much he may be vanishing (Riesman, Potter and Watson, 1960), is at least the person in whose territory the gathering takes place. Should a guest spill food on his clothes, he has no choice but to suffer embarrassment for the remainder of the party. The host, by contrast, can retire to his bedroom and change his clothes quickly, often before the momentary loss of poise becomes known. A striking case of the man 'in command' of a territory is the person delivering a speech to a fixed audience in a closed room. In being presented to the audience, he may even be told, 'The floor is yours.' To underline his exclusive domain, the speaker may wait until waiters clear the last table of cups and saucers and the doors are closed. In such a setting, where the audience is not free to leave, the speaker is now in great danger of embarrassing his audience unless his speech is such that the audience is not let down. Should he show lack of poise, the audience will feel embarrassed for him, yet be unable to escape, for that would further embarrass him. Hence they will suffer silently, hoping for a short speech.

In a situation reported to us, the discussant at a professional meeting was able to save the situation. The speaker was a man of national reputation – one of the pillars of his discipline. To everyone's dismay and embarrassment, he proceeded to give a pedestrian address of the caliber of an undergraduate term essay. Everyone hoped the discussant would save them, and he did. His tactic was to make clear to the audience that the identity presented by the speaker was not his real identity. This result he accomplished by reminding the audience of the major contributions of the speaker, by claiming the paper presented must be interpreted as evidence that the speaker was still productive, and that all could expect even more important contributions in the future. When the audience thundered applause, they were not simply expressing their agreement with the discussant's appraisal of the speaker: they were also thanking him for saving them all from embarrassment by putting the speaker back in command of the territory.

We have already touched upon problems presented by invasions of spaces, and little more need be said. Persons lose poise when they discover they are in places forbidden to them, for the proscription itself means they have no identity there and hence cannot act. They can do little except withdraw quickly. It is interesting that children are continually invading the territories of others – who can control the course of a sharply hit baseball? – and part of the process of socialization consists of indications of the importance of boundaries. Whether territories are crescive or contrived affects the possibility of invasion. When they are contrived and boundaries are marked, the invader knows he has crossed the boundary and is embarrassed if caught. With crescive territories inadvertent invasions occur, as when a tourist reports discovery of a 'quaint' area of the city only to be met with the sly smiles of those who know that the area is the local prostitution region.

Such considerations raise questions concerning both how boundaries are defined and how boundary violations may be prevented. Walls provide physical limits, but do not necessarily prevent communications from passing through (Goffman, 1963a, pp. 151–2). Hence walls work best when there is also tacit agreement to ignore audible communication on the other side of the wall. Embarrassment frequently occurs when persons on one side of the wall learn that intimate matters have been communicated to persons on the other side. A common protective device is for the captive listeners to become very quiet so that their receipt of the communication will not be discovered by the unsuspecting intimates. When no physical boundaries are present, a group gathered in one section of a room may have developed a common mood which is bounded by a certain space that defines the limits of their engagement to one another. The entry of someone new may be followed by an embarrassed hush. It is not necessary that the group should have been talking about that person. Rather, since moods take time to build up, it will take time for the newcomer to 'get with it' and it may not be worth the group's trouble to 'fill him in'. However unintentionally, he has destroyed a mood that took some effort to build up and he will suffer for it, if only by being stared at or by an obvious change of subject. In some cases, when the mood is partially sustained by alcohol, one can prepare the newcomer immediately for the mood by loud shouts that the group is 'three drinks ahead' of him and by thrusting a drink into his hand without delay. So, too, a function of foyers, halls, anterooms, and other buffer zones or decompression chambers around settings is to prepare such newcomers and hence reduce the likelihood of their embarrassing both themselves and those inside.

Spaces, then, include bounded areas within which transactions go on. The boundaries may be more or less sharply defined, that is, walled in or marked off by the distances that separate one encounter from another. Overstepping the bounds is a source of embarrassment, signaling a loss of poise. Consequently, the boundaries are usually controlled and patrolled and come to represent the selves of those who are authorized to cross them.

A second component of self and situation that must be controlled to maintain poise is here designated *props*. Props are arranged around settings in an orderly manner commonly called decor. Ordinarily they are not moved about during a transaction, except as emergencies arise, to facilitate the movement of people about the setting and to protect the props from damage. In some cases, their adherence to settings is guaranteed by law. Wall-to-wall carpeting, mirrors attached to walls, and curtain fixtures, for example, may not be removed from houses, even though ownership of such domestic settings may change hands. The arrangement of less adhesive props within a setting may mark off or suggest (as in the case of 'room dividers') smaller subsettings facilitating the division of large assemblies into more intimate circles. Moreover, although props are ordinarily not moved about *during* transactions, they are typically rearranged or replaced between major changes of scene, marking off changes in life situations.[7]

Perhaps just because of their intimate connection with the life situations of those who control them,[8] loss of control over props is a more frequent (though usually milder) source of embarrassment than the violation of boundaries. When one stumbles over his own furniture or slips on his own throw rug, doubt may be cast on the extent to which such props represent, in fact, the self and situation of the person or team members who have arranged them. Gifts of props are frequently embarrassing to the recipients. Thus an artist (or would-be artist) may foist a painting on a friend without recognizing that the painting is contrary to the recipient's aesthetic taste. Moreover, the artist may expect that his work will be given a prominent display commensurate with his investment. A conflict is immediately established between loyalty to the artist-friend and loyalty to the recipient's self. A way out is to include the prop in question only in those situations where the donor is present, but this may become tedious, depending on the frequency and scheduling of visiting. A classic case is the wealthy relative's gift of a self-photograph, which must be dragged out of the closet for display when the relative visits.

Clashing differences in domestic décor will usually terminate or restrict house-to-house visiting. Because of this, many wartime friendships have been abruptly ended shortly after the cessation of hostilities and demobilization. In a common military setting, servicemen would meet and become close friends, sometimes building up life-and-death obligations to one another. They would eagerly anticipate extending their hard-won intimacy into the workaday world of peacetime. Then, when they met in one or the other's home, the glaring incompatibility in décor would silently signal an incompatibility in life situation. Such embarrassing confrontations would be covered over with empty promises and futile vows to meet again, and the former friends would part as embarrassed strangers. If incompatibilities in décor can bring about the estrangement of friends who owe their lives to one

7. David Riesman and Howard Roseborough, in a discussion of family careers, indicate the linkage between the rearrangement of props and the rearrangement of life situations: 'One of our Kansas City respondents, whose existence had been wrapped up in her daughters' social life, when asked what she did when the daughters married and moved away, said that she slept more – and redecorated the living room. Still another became more active in church work – and redecorated the vestry' (1955, p. 14).

8. Striking examples are provided by Zorbaugh (1926, pp. 103–4; and in *Anonymous*, 1962, pp. 46–8).

another, we can see how props and their arrangement become powerful guaranties of the exclusiveness of social circles and status strata.

Much of our earlier discussion of adjunct roles reserve identities and relict identities applies to props. The porcelain dinnerware may always be kept visibly in reserve for special guests, and this very fact may be embarrassing to some dinner guests who are reminded that they are not so special after all, while, for other guests, anything but the everyday props would be embarrassing. Relict props also present a potential for embarrassment, persisting as they do when one's new life-situation has made them obsolete. The table at which a woman used to sit while dining with a former husband is obviously still quite serviceable, but it is probably best to buy another.

Third, every social transaction requires the manipulation of *equipment*. If props are ordinarily stationary during encounters, equipment is typically moved about, handled, or touched.[9] Equipment can range from words to physical objects, and a loss of control over such equipment is a frequent source of embarrassment. Here are included slips of the tongue, sudden dumbness when speech is called for, stalling cars in traffic, dropping bowling balls, spilling food and tool failures. Equipment appearances that cast doubt on the adequacy of control are illustrated by the clanking motor, the match burning down to the fingers, tarnished silverware or rusty work tools. Equipment sometimes extends beyond what is actually handled in the transaction to include the stage props. Indeed, items of equipment in disuse, reserve equipment, often become props – the Cadillac in the driveway or the silver service on the shelf – and there is a point at which the objects used or scheduled for use in a situation are both equipment and props. At one instant, the items of a table setting lie immobile as props; at the next, they are taken up and transformed into equipment. The close linkage of equipment and props may be responsible for the fact that *embarrassment* at times not only *infects* the participants in the transaction but the *objects* as well. For example, at a formal dinner, a speaker was discovered with his fly zipper

9. Whether objects in a situation are meant to be moved, manipulated or taken up provides an important differentiating dimension between equipment on the one hand and props (as well as clothing, to be discussed shortly) on the other. Equipment is meant to be moved, manipulated, or taken up *during* a social transaction whereas clothing and props are expected to remain unchanged during a social transaction but will be moved, manipulated, or taken up *between* social transactions. To change props, as in burning the portrait of an old girl friend (or to change clothes, as in taking off a necktie), signals a change in the situation. The special case of the strip-tease dancer is no exception, for her act transforms clothes into equipment. The reference above to the 'stickiness' of props may now be seen as another way of describing the fact that they are not moved, manipulated, or taken up during transactions, but remain unchanged for the course of the transaction. Clothing is equally sticky but the object to which it sticks differs. Clothing sticks to the body; props stick to the settings.

undone. On being informed of this embarrassing oversight after he was re-seated, he proceeded to make the requisite adjustments, unknowingly catching the table cloth in his trousers. When obliged to rise again at the close of the proceedings, he took the stage props with him and of course scattered the dinner tools about the setting in such a way that others were forced to doubt his control. His poise was lost in the situation.

Just as props may be adjunct to the dominant role performance, held in reserve, or relict, so may equipment. Indeed, as we have said, reserve equipment is often an important part of décor.

Fourth, *clothing* must be maintained, controlled and coherently arranged. Its very appearance must communicate this. Torn clothing, frayed cuffs, stained neck-ties and unpolished shoes are felt as embarrassing in situations where they are expected to be untorn, neat, clean and polished. Clothing is of special importance since, as William James observed (1892, pp. 177-8), it is as much a part of the self as the body – a part of what he called the 'material me'. Moreover, since it is so close to the body, it conveys the impression of body maintenance, paradoxically, by concealing body-maintenance activities.[10] Hence, the double wrap – outer clothes and under-clothes. Underclothes bear the marks of body maintenance and tonic state, and their unexpected exposure is a frequent source of embarrassment. The broken brassiere strap sometimes produces a shift in appearance that few women (or men, for that matter) will fail to perceive as embarrassing.

Fifth, the *body* must always be in a state of readiness to act, and its appearance must make this clear. Hence any evidence of unreadiness or clumsiness is embarrassing. Examples include loss of whole body control (stumbling, trembling or fainting), loss of visceral control (flatulence, involuntary urination or drooling), and the communication of other 'signs of the animal'. The actress who is photographed from her 'bad side' loses poise, for it shakes the foundation on which her fame rests. So does the person who is embarrassed about pimples, warts or missing limbs, as well as those embarrassed in his presence.

Ordinarily, persons will avoid recognizing such stigmata, turn their eyes away, and pretend them out of existence, but on occasion stigmata will obtrude upon the situation causing embarrassment all around. A case in point was a minor flirtation reported by one of our students. Seated in a library a short distance from a beautiful girl, the student began the requisite gestural invitation to a more intimate conversation. The girl turned, smiling, to acknowledge the bid, revealing an amputated left arm. Our student's gestural line was brought to a crashing halt. Embarrassed, he abandoned

10. A complete exposition of the body-maintenance function of clothing is set forth in an advertisement for Jockey briefs, entitled: 'A frank discussion: what wives should know about male support', *Good Housekeeping*, May, 1963, p. 237.

the role he was building even before the foundation was laid, pretending that his inviting gestures were directed toward some imaginary audience suggested by his reading. Such stigmata publicize body-maintenance activities, and, when they are established in social transactions, interfere with role performances. The pimples on the face of the job applicant cast doubt on his maturity, and, consequently, on his qualifications for any job requiring such maturity.

All this is to say that self and situation must be in a perpetual condition of poise or readiness, adequately maintained, and in good repair. Such maintenance and the keeping of self in a state of good repair obviously require energy and time. While engaged in maintenance or repair, the person is, for that time, unable to play the role. Hence we may expect that persons will, in order to avoid casting doubt on their ability to play a role, deliberately play down or conceal maintenance and repair activity. Speakers know that spontaneity cannot be left to chance but must be prepared for, even rehearsed. Yet, obviously information on the amount of preparation it took to be spontaneous would destroy the audience's belief in the spontaneity. Outer clothes require underclothes, as social life requires an underlife (which is, of course, also social).[11]

Maintenance of confidence

When identities have been validated and persons poised, interaction may begin. Its continuation, however, requires that a scaffolding be erected and that attention be given to preventing this scaffolding from collapsing. The scaffold develops as the relationship becomes stabilized. In time persons come to expect that the way they place the other is the way the others announces himself, and that poise will continue to be maintained. Persons now begin to count on these expectations and to have confidence in them. But at any time they may be violated. It was such violations of confidence that made up the greatest single source of embarrassment in our examples. Perhaps this is only an acknowledgement that the parties to every transaction must always maintain themselves *in role* to permit the requisite role-taking, or that identity-switching ought not be accomplished so abruptly

11. Consider the fact that the physician often needs time and opportunity to consult medical books and colleagues before he can render an authoritative medical diagnosis. A structural assurance is provided by his having been taught to make diagnoses slowly. Through time thus gained, he takes advantage of informal encounters with colleagues and spare moments between patients when he can consult medical books. A direct revelation of his need for such aids and his rather unsystematic way of getting them would be embarrassing. Yet it is in the patient's best interest that they be kept secret from him, otherwise the patient would be in the position of having to pass judgement on a professional practice when he is, in fact, too involved to render an objective judgement.

that others are left floundering in the encounter as they grope for the new futures that the new identity implies.

This is all the more important in situations where roles are tightly linked together as in situations involving a division of labor. In one instance, a group of social scientists was presenting a progress report of research to a representative of the client subsidizing the research. The principal investigator's presentation was filled out by comments from the other researchers, his professional peers. Negatively critical comments were held to a bare minimum. Suddenly the principal investigator overstepped the bounds. He made a claim that they were well on the road to confirming a hypothesis which, if confirmed, would represent a major contribution. Actually, his colleagues (our informant was one of them) knew that they were very far indeed from confirming the hypothesis. They first sought to catch the leader's eye to look for a hidden message. Receiving none, they lowered their eyes to the table, bit their lips and fell silent. In the presence of the client's representative, they felt they could not 'call' their leader for that would be embarrassing, but they did seek him out immediately afterward for an explanation. The leader agreed that they were right, but said his claim was politic, that new data might well turn up, and that it was clearly too late to remedy the situation.

Careful examination of this case reveals a more basic reason for the researchers' hesitance to embarrass the leader before the client's representative. If their leader were revealed to be the kind of person who goes beyond the data (or to be a plain liar), serious question could have been raised about the kind of men who willingly work with such a person. Thus they found themselves coerced into unwilling collusion. It was not simply that their jobs depended on continued satisfaction of the client. Rather, they were unwilling to say to themselves and to the client's representative that they were the kind of researchers who would be party to a fraud. To embarrass the leader, then, would have meant embarrassing themselves by casting serious question upon their identities as researchers. Indeed, it was their desire to cling to their identities that led, not long afterward (and after several other similar experiences), to the breakup of the research team.

Just as, in time, an identity may be discredited, so too may poise be upset. Should this occur, each must be able to assume that the other will render assistance if he gets into such control trouble, and each must be secure in the knowledge that the assumption is tenable. Persons will be alert for incipient signs of such trouble – irrelevant attitudes – and attempt to avert the consequences. Goffman has provided many examples in his discussion of dramaturgical loyalty, discipline and circumspection in the presentation of the self, pointing out protective practices that are employed, such as clearing one's throat before interrupting a conversation, knocking on doors before entering an occupied room, or begging the other's pardon before an intrusion (1959, pp. 212–33). [. . .]

Conclusion

In this paper, we have inquired into the conditions necessary for role performance. Embarrassment has been employed as a sensitive indicator of those conditions, for that which embarrasses incapacitates role performance. Our data have led us to describe the conditions for role performance in terms of identity, poise and sustained confidence in one another. When these become disturbed and discredited, role performance cannot continue. Consequently, provisions for the avoidance or prevention of embarrassment, or quick recovery from embarrassment when it does occur are of key importance to any society or social transaction, and devices to insure the avoidance and minimization of embarrassment will be part of every persisting social relationship. Specifically, tests of identity, poise and self-knowledge will be institutionalized in every society. Such devices, like all mechanisms of social control, are capable of manipulation and may well be exploited to establish and maintain power in social transactions. Yet, deliberate or not, embarrassment is as general a sociological concept as is role.

References

ANONYMOUS (1962), *Streetwalker*, Gramercy Publishing Co.
GOFFMAN, E. (1956), 'Embarrassment and social organization', *Amer. J. Sociol.*, vol. 62, pp. 264–71.
GOFFMAN, E. (1959), *The Presentation of Self in Everyday Life*, Doubleday.
GOFFMAN, E. (1963a), *Behavior in Public Places*, Free Press.
GOFFMAN, E. (1963b), *Stigma*, Prentice-Hall.
HUGHES, E. C. (1954), 'Dilemmas and contradictions in status', *Amer. J. Sociol.*, vol. 50, pp. 353–9.
JAMES, W. (1892), *Psychology*, Holt, Rinehart & Winston.
RIESMAN, D. and ROSEBOROUGH, H. (1955), 'Careers and consumer behavior', in L. Clark (ed.), *Consumer Behaviour*, New York, University Press.
RIESMAN, D., POTTER, R. J., and WATSON, J. (1960), 'The vanishing host', *Hum. Organization*, vol. 19, pp. 17–21.
STONE, G. P. (1962), 'Appearance and the self', in A. Rose (ed.), *Human Behavior and Social Processes*, Houghton Mufflin.
STRAUSS, A. L. (1959), *Mirrors and Masks*, Free Press.
ZORBAUGH, H. W. (1926), in E. W. Burgess (ed.), *The Urban Community*, Chicago University Press.

Part Eight
Training in Social Skills

One of the main practical applications of research in social interaction is in training people in social skills, and a number of training methods have been developed. Gage and colleagues (Reading 26) show that when feedback was given to teachers of how their pupils saw them their behaviour improved considerably. If such feedback could be made available, perhaps from a sympathetic trainer, training on the job could probably be made very effective. Another method of social-skills training, which is widely used, is the T-group method. There is considerable controversy over how effective this method is, and Bunker (Reading 27) reports one of the best of the follow-up studies which have been done. It will be noted that there was considerable improvement among members of the untrained control group. Other studies have found that some T-group trainees are emotionally disturbed by the experience and become worse rather than better. Another method of social-skills training is by role-playing, which can be supplemented by video-tape playback. McDonald and Allen (Reading 28) describe an experiment to find out which kinds of feedback are most successful in training teachers in this way.

26 N. L. Gage, Philip J. Runkel and B. B. Chatterjee

Changing Teacher Behavior through Feedback from Pupils:
An Application of Equilibrium Theory

N. L. Gage, Philip J. Runkel and B. B. Chatterjee, 'Equilibrium theory and behavior change: an experiment in feedback from pupils to teachers', in W. W. Charters and N. L. Gage (eds.), *Readings in the Social Psychology of Education*, Allyn & Bacon, 1963, pp. 173–80.

The practice of collecting ratings of teachers from their pupils has had a moderate vogue for about thirty years. Advocates of this practice have claimed many values for such ratings, among them the improvement of teacher behavior. After reviewing the literature on the matter, however, Morsh and Wilder (1953) concluded that the research evidence was insufficient to support such a claim. Savage's subsequent experiment, performed in 1956–7 with student teachers at the junior-high-school level, did not brighten the picture (1962). She was unable to demonstrate that the student teachers had changed their behavior as a result of learning how their pupils rated them. Studies focusing upon the ability of the teacher to perceive her pupils accurately have also yielded negative results (Gage, 1958).

Despite the paucity of empirical evidence, it seems reasonable that giving teachers information about the relevant feelings and wishes of their pupils would influence their teaching performance. Under everyday conditions, the teacher gets feedback by glancing at her class and noticing signs of interest or boredom, comprehension or puzzlement, favorable attitudes or resentment. She asks direct questions, gives tests and talks informally with her pupils. She also gets feedback from other teachers, parents, people in the community and her principal. Through this feedback, the teacher gauges the learning requirements of her pupils and makes her teaching more appropriate to their needs and desires.

The present experiment, designed and executed in 1956, attempted to examine part of this argument. We asked, To what extent does an increase in the amount of feedback to teachers regarding their pupils' perceptions of them as teachers – an increase over what is normally available to them – affect the teachers' performance and the accuracy with which they are able to estimate their pupils' perceptions of them? In brief, we gave an experimental group of sixth-grade teachers information as to how their pupils described their teaching behavior and how the pupils view the ideal teacher;

we withheld this information from a different, randomly equivalent control group of teachers. The information had been obtained during an earlier testing period when pupils in both the experimental and control classrooms had responded to a twelve-item form for rating teacher behavior. One to two months after the experimental teachers received a summary of their pupils' responses, the pupils again described their teachers on the rating forms. A comparison of changes in pupil descriptions of their teachers between the two testing periods, then, provided a measure of the amount of change in teacher behavior during the elapsed time. We hypothesized that teachers furnished with feedback concerning their pupils' responses would change more than those who received no such information and, more particularly, that these teachers would then more closely resemble their pupils' conceptions of the ideal teacher.

Data also were obtained from teachers in the two testing periods regarding their own behavior and regarding their estimates of the way pupils perceived them. These data permitted tests of several subsidiary hypotheses. We report here on one of these – the hypothesis that information feedback increases the accuracy with which teachers estimate their pupils' expectations of them.

Equilibrium theory

Why do we predict that teachers will change their classroom behavior when they are furnished with information regarding their pupils' expectations of them? Common sense might predict that the 'teacher knows best' how to govern her professional conduct in the classroom and that she would ignore discrepant ideas which pupils harbor. The theoretical framework which has often been called 'equilibrium theory' and which Zajonc (1960) has called 'consistency theory' offers a systematic way to consider the alternative causes of action open to a teacher and to understand her choice among them. This theory is represented by the recent contributions of Heider (1958), Newcomb (1959), Osgood and Tannenbaum (1955), and Festinger (1957). It will be sufficient to say a few words about the theories of Heider and Newcomb.

Heider

Heider's ideas hinge upon the concepts of unit formation, sentiment and balanced state (1958). The tendency toward the balanced state can be seen in a triadic system composed of a perceiving person, p, an observed other person, o, and a third phenomenal object, x, these being bound together by the relations of unit formation (e.g. belonging, owning, producing, causing) and sentiment (e.g. liking, respecting, admiring). Heider states the formal conditions of balance as follows: 'A triad is balanced when all three of the relations are positive or when two of the relations are negative and one is positive' (1958, p. 202). Further, 'If two negative relations are given, balance can be obtained either when the third relation is positive or when it is negative, though there appears to be a preference for the positive alternative.' (1958, p. 206).

Suppose the teacher is given evidence that o dislikes x, for example, that her pupils are critical of her behavior and would like it to change in a certain direction. At the same time she approves of her own behavior (p likes x) and continues to be attracted to, or to respect, her pupils (p likes o). We can infer that there will be an influence on the teacher to alter the system; one thing she might do is to change 'p likes x' to 'p dislikes x' (assuming that 'p likes o' will remain true). That is, the teacher can resolve the imbalance by beginning to 'dislike' her own behavior and to change in the direction of the pupils' ideal teacher. This will be likely if she has knowledge of the pupils' ideal and if changing in this direction will not send into strong imbalance other co-existing p-o-x systems.

Newcomb

'Communicative acts' in their simplest form, according to Newcomb, consist of one person (A) transmitting information to another person (B) about something (X) (1959). Suppose the teacher (A) has a positive orientation toward her pupils (B). Suppose we inform the teacher as to the pupils' orientations toward the teacher's behaviors (X). Then we set up what Newcomb labeled 'strain toward symmetry' (a concept similar to Heider's 'imbalance') on the part of the teacher. Such strain tends to make the teacher develop the same orientation toward X which her pupils have. What responses might a teacher make when she finds herself under such a strain'? From Newcomb's analysis, we can derive the following alternatives:

1. Influencing pupils toward her own orientation to the behaviors.

2. Changing her own orientation toward the behaviors, i.e. adopting the same attitude toward the behaviors as she perceives the pupils to have.

3. Cognitively distorting the pupils' orientation, i.e. reinterpreting her perception of her pupils' orientation so that it becomes more like her own.

4. Modifying her attraction toward the pupils, i.e. liking them less.

5. Modifying her judgement of her own attractiveness to the pupils, i.e. feeling that the pupils like her less.

6. Modifying her own evaluation of herself, i.e. liking herself less.

7. Modifying her judgement of the pupils' evaluation of themselves, i.e. perceiving the pupils to like themselves less.

8. Tolerating the asymmetry without change.

How likely is each of these alternatives under the conditions of classroom life? We interpreted Heider's theory by means of alternative 2: The teacher, becoming dissatisfied with her present behaviors after learning of her pupils' views of them, changes her behaviors to conform more closely to the pupils' ideal. It is also possible to interpret this kind of response to feedback from the pupils in terms of alternative 1: If the teacher feels that a certain behavior is very much like her own, while she is informed that her pupils do not consider it so but would like it to be so (i.e. they say it would characterize their ideal teacher), the strain toward symmetry will lead her to communicative acts intended to make the pupils also consider the behavior very much like her own. In the classroom, these communicative acts will probably take the form of performing these behaviors more frequently or conspicuously. Alternatives 1 and 2, or some combination of them, seemed to us the most likely outcome of strain toward symmetry among our experimental teachers. For lack of space we shall not set forth our reasons for considering the other alternatives to be less likely.

Obviously, our hypothesis ignores many other influences upon the teacher and variations among teachers in susceptibility to the kind of influence from pupils which we hypothesize. Our hypothesis implies that influence from pupils will be strong enough, relative to other influences, to make the predicted effects observable. Our experimental design sought to randomize the other influences.

Method

Because a number of instruments were used and because some important precautions were taken during data collection, this section will need to be rather lengthy. We chose sixth-grade classes for our experiment. At that grade level the pupils are mature enough to understand printed test materials. Also, since most sixth-grade classes are not departmentalized, the teacher and pupils are together throughout the school day.

Procedure in selecting subjects and collecting data

Our first step was to ask every superintendent of schools in Illinois (outside of Chicago) whose jurisdiction included a sixth grade to send us the name of the first teacher in the alphabetical list of all his sixth-grade teachers; we told him that we would in turn invite this teacher to participate in the research. We tried to retain every possible teacher and her class for use in the final working sample but, since the entire data collection and the treatment were conducted by mail, the beginning list of teachers was inevitably subject to attrition. Some returns came in too late, a few were indecipherable, some losses occurred in the mails, and the like. Of 489 teachers originally receiving our invitation to participate in the research, 208 finally returned usable materials from themselves and their pupils at both pre-test and post-test.

Teachers in departmentalized schools or in schools where special circumstances made parts of our questionnaire inappropriate were dropped. We ended, after attrition of various kinds, with 176 sixth-grade teachers in Illinois and approximately 3900 pupils. The teachers were assigned atrandom to the experimental and control groups at the time the pretest answer sheets of their pupils were received. The distributions of class size among the control and experimental groups were about the same; the median class size was twenty-two in both groups, and the quartiles of class size were also almost identical. There were twenty-five males and sixty-five females among the control teachers, twenty-five males and sixty-one females among the experimentals. The final sample was probably biased in having a more than representative proportion of teachers who were interested in what their pupils think of their actions and who were willing to trust information gathered for them by a university research bureau.

Developing the items of teacher behavior

Our experiment called for four kinds of protocol, each obtained near the beginning (pre-test) and end (post-test) of the fall semester, 1956–7:

1. *Self:* description by the teacher of *herself*.

2. *Perceived:* the teacher's *perception* of how she would be described by 'a pupil who belongs to the majority'.

3. *Actual:* descriptions by the pupils of their *actual* teacher.

4. *Ideal:* descriptions by the pupils of their *ideal* teacher.

All four of these protocols consisted of responses to the following set of twelve 'stimuli', or brief verbal descriptions of teacher behavior:

A. Enjoys a funny remark made by a pupil.

B. Praises what a pupil says in class discussion.

C. Tells pupils about some interesting things to read.

D. Explains arithmetic so pupils can understand it.

E. Suggests to pupils new and helpful ways of studying.

F. Talks with a pupil after school about an idea the pupil has had.

G. Asks a small group of pupils to study something together.

H. Shows a pupil how to look up an answer when the pupil can't find it himself.

I. Asks the pupils what they'd like to study in tomorrow's lesson.

J. Acts disappointed when a pupil gets something wrong.

K. Explains something by using examples from games and sports.

L. Asks the class what they think of something a pupil has said.

These items were intended to be meaningful to sixth-grade pupils; hence they were made brief, with few qualifying phrases. Each item was intended to describe a recognizable and reasonably frequent teacher behavior so that pupils could more easily agree with one another as to whether the behavior occurred. The items were intended to deal with attributes which the teacher could change (more or less) within the time-span of the research and which were determined by teacher-pupil interaction rather than by physical circumstances. (For example, an item asking whether the teacher 'shows movies often' might be determined primarily by her having a movie projector and films rather than by motives and attitudes that could be influenced by our feedback.) Finally, to maximize the teachers' acceptance of the procedure, we sought to avoid highly threatening items. From another point of view, however, 'threat' should be great enough to exert pressure on the teacher to change. We compromised between these two opposed criteria as well as our judgement permitted. The final items were selected only after a number of trial administrations and analyses.

Instruments

The covering letter and the introductory material in the Teacher's Questionnaire portrayed our project as offering a service to the teacher – that of providing her with information about her how pupils perceived her classroom behavior. (Eventually we did send every teacher a summary of the responses given by her pupils.)

The questionnaire for teachers. The questionnaire booklet was in three colors with sprightly drawings, designed with special care since we depended entirely upon it and a one-page mimeographed follow-up letter to solicit the teacher's participation in the study. The first seven pages described the project and invited the teacher to participate. The care taken with this booklet seemed justified; we got back 360 (or 74 per cent) of the 489 sent out. In view of the time, work and dislocation of daily routine asked of the teachers, this rate of return seemed gratifyingly high.

Although the Teacher's Questionnaire contained four sections, only two are pertinent to this report. Each section presented the twelve items listed above. Excerpts from the instructions for the pertinent parts of the questionnaire are given below. Section b asked the teacher to describe herself and Section d asked her to estimate how her pupils would describe her.

Section b: 'First, read the sentence which tells what a teacher might do. Then pick one of the six answers. Like this:

'Enjoys a funny remark made by a pupil.

☐ Very much *like* me.
☐ Somewhat *like* me.
☐ A little bit *like* me.
☐ A little bit *unlike* me.
☐ Somewhat *unlike* me.
☐ Very much *unlike* me.'

Section d: 'Please answer the items on the next two pages according to your best estimate as to how this pupil who is typical of the majority would answer them if he were asked to: "Read the sentence which tells what your teacher might do. Then make an 'X' in front of one of the six answers."'

The pupil-opinion booklet. The Pupil-Opinion Booklet contained the same sections as the Teacher's Questionnaire, but, of course, the instructions differed:

Section b: 'First read the thing which tells what your teacher might do. Then mark 'X' after one of the six answers.'

Section d: 'This time, think of the best teacher you can imagine. (Do *not* think any more about the teacher you really have.) Then mark 'X' after the answer which tells how much this thing would be like the best teacher you can imagine.'

These instructions were supplemented by mimeographed material for the teacher to read aloud as her pupils prepared to answer the questionnaires. Careful provision was made to assure pupils of the anonymity of their answers. The booklets were provided with separate gummed answer sheets which folded in the middle. The face of the booklet bore this legend:

'Your answers will be sealed up tight when you are finished. Then they will be sent to the University of Illinois. No one in your town – not your teacher, nor your principal, nor anyone else – will ever know how you answered these questions.'

The instructions to the teacher on administering the pupils' questionnaires strongly urged her to keep the pupils' answer sheets confidential in every way. One indication of the success of these instructions was that we received no unsealed answer sheet.

The post-test materials were identical with the pretest materials, except that the introductory part of the Teacher's Questionnaire was omitted.

Communicating feedback: the 'report on your pupil's opinions'. Each teacher in the experimental group received a special booklet filled in with data obtained from her own pupils. This 'Report on Your Pupils' Opinions', attractively printed, was designed so that individual information could be entered for each teacher. In each booklet, twelve charts appeared, one for each of the twelve items. The chart for each item had two parts: (a) a histogram concerning the actual teacher, showing how many of her pupils chose a 'Very much like my teacher', 'Somewhat like my teacher', etc., and (b) a histogram concerning the ideal teacher, showing how many of her pupil, chose 'Very much like a "best" teacher', 'Somewhat like a "best" teacher' etc. Also, on each histogram, an arrow was fixed to show the position if the median answer. Other explanatory material was also included in the Report booklet.

The experimental design

Our experiment embodied what Campbell has termed *the pre-test–post-test control group design*, taking the form shown.

Our design offers no basis for generalizing to unpretested teachers. In strict logic, our conclusions can apply only to teachers who not only receive

	Approximately mid October	Approximately early November	Approximately mid December
Experimental group	pre-test	feedback ('Report on pupils' opinions')	post-test
Control group	pre-test	no feedback (letter explaining delay)	post-test

feedback but who were also pretested, i.e. prerated by their pupils and by themselves. Since we would have had no information to feed back to the the teachers without the prerating by pupils, this limitation is a realistic and necessary one.

We relied on ratings as our measurement devices in this experiment. Ratings like those we obtained are intrinsically significant, quite apart from their relation to other measures of teacher behavior. Yet the generalizability of the present experiment is limited in that no measures other than ratings were used. To overcome this limitation, we should eventually use a variety of ways of describing teacher behavior, 'all having in common the theoretically relevant attribute but varying widely in their irrelevant specificities' (Campbell, 1957).

Results on change of teacher behavior

This section will discuss the results obtained from three protocols:

pre-*actual* the pupil's description of his *actual* teacher on the *pre*-test.
post-*actual*: the pupil's description of his *actual* teacher on the *post*-test.
pre-*ideal*: the pupil's description of his *ideal* teacher on the *pre*-test.

Adjusted post-actual

The most important single concern of this study was, would teachers – as described by their pupils – change more if given information about how their pupils described them and their ideal teachers than if not given such information? Specifically, would the experimental and control groups of teachers differ in the post-test descriptions pupils gave of their actual teachers.

A straightforward attack on this question would determine whether the 'post-*actual*' means on each item were significantly different. This approach would, however, neglect the possibility that the teachers in the two groups may have differed in their initial status – at the time of the pretest ratings. Such differences, even if not statistically significant, would affect the comparisons of post-*actual* ratings.

Analysis of covariance was used to control such initial differences. The pre-test rating (pre-*actual*) on each item served as the control variable, the post-test rating (post-*actual*) as the dependent variable, and the feedback as the independent variable. For each of the eighty-six teachers in the experimental group and the ninety teachers in the control group, the median pretest rating given her by her pupils on each item was determined. Using those median ratings, we performed an analysis of covariance to determine the adjusted post-*actual* means of the median ratings. For each item, then, the *adjusted* post-*actual* rating of a given teacher is the median post-test rating given by her pupils after the following quantity had been subtracted: the difference between (1) the post-*actual* mean predicted from the group's pre-*actual* mean and (2) the grand post-*actual* mean based on all teachers.

Means for each item of the adjusted post-*actual* ratings are shown in columns 2 and 3 of Table 1. As can be seen in the table, the means for the experimental group were closer to 1 (1 being the code for 'Very much like my teacher') than were the means for the control group on ten out of the twelve items; for four of these items, the difference between experimental and control groups was significant beyond the 0·05 level.

Adjusted post-actual minus pre-ideal

The analysis so far has not considered the direction in which the teacher's pupils might wish her to change. Is the difference between adjusted post-*actual* means in the direction of the influence exerted by the feedback? To answer this question, we referred to the means of the pupils' median pre-ratings of their ideal teacher (pre-*ideal*). That is, we hypothesized that the feedback given the teachers in the experimental group concerning their pupils' pre-*ideal* ratings would exert influence on the teachers to change in that direction. The absolute difference between adjusted post-*actual* and pre-*ideal* would then be smaller for the experimental group. The results shown in columns 6 and 7 of Table 1 bore out this prediction for ten of the twelve items. Item A was tied, and the remaining item (J) went against the hypothesis.

Table 1 **Means of adjusted post-actual and pre-ideal ratings**

Item (1)	Adjusted post-actual mean		pre-ideal mean		Adjusted post-actual minus pre-ideal		Is difference between columns 6 and 7 in hypothesized direction? (8)
	Exp. (2)	Cont. (3)	Exp. (4)	Cont. (5)	Exp. (6)	Cont. (7)	
A	2·57	2·57	2·20	2·20	0·37	0·37	No
B	3·46	3·61*	3·21	3·02	0·25	0·59	Yes
C	2·33	2·42	2·09	1·96	0·24	0·46	Yes
D	1·15	1·18*	1·13	1·12	0·02	0·06	Yes
E	2·22	2·30	1·60	1·51	0·62	0·79	Yes
F	4·07	4·20	3·31	3·14	0·76	1·06	Yes
G	3·35	3·46	2·81	2·83	0·54	0·63	Yes
H	2·19	2·16	1·66	1·57	0·53	0·59	Yes
I	5·29	5·30	4·06	3·83	1·23	1·47	Yes
J	4·27	4·33	4·54	4·44	−0·27	−0·11	No
K	3·24	3·44*	2·64	2·66	0·60	0·78	Yes
L	2·84	2·96*	2·77	2·80	0·07	0·16	Yes

* Significantly different at the 0·05 level (one tail) from the value for the experimental group.

Columns 6 and 7 of Table 1 make clear that there was ample room for influence among these twelve items. On no item did the mean adjusted post-*actual* rating in either group reach the mean post-*ideal* rating. (This was also true of item J, since the 'desirable' direction for this item was opposite to that of the other items.) The item on which teachers fell farthest from their pupils' ideal was item 1 (Asks the pupils what they'd like to study in to-morrow's lesson); the item on which they came closest was item D (Explains arithmetic so pupils can understand it).

It is invalid to make simple tests of the statistical significance of the combined results here (e.g. by using the binomial theorem or chi square) because each item does not constitute an independent experiment or replication; i.e. the same subjects (teachers and pupils) were involved in all items. The consistency in the direction of the results, however, does suggest that the hypothesized effect of the feedback did occur. We shall have to rely on such a judgement of consistency in this report.

While these results are difficult to assess statistically, the pattern seems clear enough. It seems apparent that the feedback booklet had an effect on the behavior of the teachers. Even so, these results do not seem strong enough to be of great practical importance. That is, the differences between the control group and the experimental group seem small. It should be remembered, however, that this experiment was primarily a test of a hypothesis, not an attempt to demonstrate the most effective strategy for influencing teacher behavior. One small booklet sent by mail constituted the entire influence exerted on the teacher. The booklet contained only twelve simple charts and a few explanatory remarks; it contained no exhortation or suggestion that the teacher do one thing or another; no explicit pressure or prestige was brought to bear. Furthermore, in most of the feedback booklets it was perfectly clear that some pupils felt the ideal teacher would have characteristics opposite to those felt to be ideal by the majority of the pupils. Such a 'minority report' must have weakened markedly the influence of the feedback. This study demonstrated that teacher behavior could be changed by a brief package of information about pupils' opinions. The demonstration of such an effect, beyond all other influences acting upon the teachers, seems to us to justify the claim that the effects of pupil expectations on teachers deserve further investigation.

Summary and implications

Can a teacher's behavior be changed by telling her how her pupils describe her behavior and that of their ideal teacher? In our experiment, some teachers (the experimental group) were given information concerning their pupils' opinions; the remaining teachers (the control group) were not given this information. A month or two later, the pupils again indicated how well the behaviors characterized the teachers. Briefly stated, our major hypothesis was that the experimental group of teachers would change its behaviors (as described by pupils) more than the control group. This hypothesis was derived from an equilibrium theory of social influence.

All in all, our results have the following theoretical and practical implications: Equilibrium theory is given support by the changes in teachers' behaviors, as described by pupils, resulting from the feedback of pupils' opinions. The feedback not only produced change in behavior; it also produced improvement in the accuracy of teachers' perceptions of their pupils' opinions.

For practical purposes, our results suggest that feedback of pupils' ratings can be used to improve teacher behavior. Whether a procedure specifically designed to maximize influence on the teacher would produce changes great enough to have educational significance, whether changes would be found if teachers' behaviors were described and measured by expert observers rather than pupils, whether the changes toward pupils' ideals are also toward educators' ideals – all these are questions for further investigation.

Finally, a couple of notes to researchers are in order. First, our instruments seemed to be highly 'reactive'; that is, they focused the attention of teachers on their classroom behaviors and seemed to produce changes even in the control group (without feedback). Only powerful statistical methods enabled us to detect the effect in which we were interested. The reactivity of this kind of measurement should be kept in mind in planning; a 'posttest only' group would have aided us in interpreting our results.

Second, the design of this experiment should not be confused with that of some other studies in which attitude change has been attempted through written persuasion. Our *Report on Your Pupil's Opinions* was a message from the teacher's pupils. No arguments attributed to some authority inside or outside the school were presented; in fact, the booklets contained no explicit argument or persuasion whatsoever. In no way did we reveal any opinion about whether the teacher should change her behavior, much less in what direction she should change it. Our intent was to test not the influence of written persuasion on teacher behavior, but rather the influence of opinions of the teacher's own pupils. The outcome of our feedback was left to the working of the processes described by equilibrium theory.

References

CAMPBELL, D. T. (1957), 'Factors relevant to the validity of experiments in social settings', *Psychol. Bull.*, vol. 54, p. 316.

FESTINGER, L. (1957), *A Theory of Cognitive Dissonance*, Harper & Row.

GAGE, N. L. (1958), 'Explorations in teachers' perceptions of pupils', *J. Teacher Educ.*, vol. 9, pp. 97–101.

HEIDER, F. (1958), *The Psychology of Interpersonal Relations*, Wiley.

MORSH, J. E., and WILDER, E. W. (1953), *Identifying the Effective Instructor: A Review of the Quartative Studies 1900–1952*, Texas.

NEWCOMB, T. M. (1959), 'Individual Systems of orientation', in S. Koch (ed.), *Psychology: A Study of Science*, McGraw-Hill.

OSGOOD, C. E., and Tannenbaum, P. H. (1955), 'The principle of congruity in the prediction of attitude change', *Psychol. Rev.*, vol 62, pp 42–55.

SAVAGE, M. L. (1962), 'Pupil ratings used in student teaching', *Amer. Vocational J.*, vol. 37, pp. 19–29.

ZAJONC, R. (1960), 'The concepts of balance, congruity and disonance', *Pub. Opin. Q.*, vol. 24, pp. 280–96.

27 Douglas R. Bunker

The Effects of Laboratory Education upon Individual Behavior

D. R. Bunker, 'The effect of laboratory education upon individual behavior', in E. H. Schein and W. G. Bennis (eds.), *Personal Learning and Organizational Change Through Group Methods*, Wiley, 1965, pp. 255–66.

Training in awareness of self and social processes by laboratory methods has been going on for most of two decades. While current approaches are diverse and innovation is continuous, both the behavioral scientists who staff training laboratories and most of the managers, leaders and educators who participate in them have in common an aspiration to promote more effective action in groups and organizations. In laboratory training, more than in most educational enterprises, increased intellectual understanding of the subject matter and altered attitudes are not enough. The aim, whether an individual or an intact organizational group is the unit in training, is to enable participants to make adaptive changes in their perceptions and behavior in their back-home organizational setting. From the theoretical perspective underlying this type of training, adaptive changes are likely to be those which improve self-understanding and the capacity for open, meaningful working relationships with others – relationships in which both collaboration and conflict can be rendered productive.

Inquiry into training processes and outcomes has paralleled the development of laboratory educational methodology (Stock, 1964; Durham and Gibb, 1960). Of the many studies which have investigated training laboratory phenomena, few have explored long-range consequences in the work environment. One such investigation reported by Miles (1960) was the point of departure for this study. In comparing a group of public-school principals who had participated in a laboratory-training workshop with both matched and random control groups of principals who had not, Miles, using an open-ended, perceived-change measure, found that experimentals were seen to have changed significantly more over a ten-month period than controls in sensitivity and behavioral skill. 'Change,' he writes, 'was more apparent in organization and group-relevant behavior than in global attributes of the self' (Miles, 1960). These results provide evidence that changes initiated in in the laboratory setting can be applied over time in work relationships in the home organization. Similar results have been obtained from research on internal training programs reported by Argyris (1962) and the Personnel

Research Department of a Canadian utility (Boyd and Elliss, 1962).

This study represents an effort to determine whether Miles's findings relative to behavior changes among school principals can be extended to an occupationally diverse, larger group of participants in training laboratories. A second purpose of this inquiry is to provide an empirical explication of the dimensions of change in on-the-job performance that might be associated with laboratory education. The focus of the inquiry is upon changes in individual behavior, but the research methods are designed to tap those types of change which are most visible and organizationally consequential.

Six separate educational conferences were selected to be evaluated. Although they were all conducted by the National Training Laboratories at Bethel, Maine, in the summers of 1960 and 1961, the staff of each conference was different, and the training design for each was unique in some respects. The three conferences conducted in the summer of 1960 were three weeks long, while those in 1961 were shortened to two weeks. In each summer, two of the programs were general human-relations training laboratories, having a heterogeneous population including participants from industrial, governmental, religious, educational, medical and social-service organizations. The other program included each summer was a special session conducted for educational leaders, ranging from superintendents of school systems to assistant principals, and including a few senior classroom teachers. With staff, training design and participant characteristics all varying, we should still recognize the invariant components of the educational situation which might be critical to the change induction.

The participants, though diverse, were for the most part self-selected – most having some at least tentatively favorable predisposition toward this type of educational experience. The training staffs overlapped somewhat, with a few staff members being involved in as many as three of the six conferences while others worked in only one.

Research design and methods

Miles (1960) has correctly observed that laboratory training research shares problems with other kinds of treatment evaluation research in social science. These include the difficulty of obtaining comparable control groups, the problem of separating treatment effects from normal or base rate change and growth, and the perplexities involved in selecting a criterion which is at once measurable and operationally meaningful. Confronting these difficulties, we made efforts to deal with them in a way that would provide data with which we could assess the effects of laboratory training. Basic elements of the design were adaptations from Miles (1960): A matched-pair control group was obtained by asking each experimental subject to nominate an appropriate control subject from his backhome setting, and an open-ended perceived-change questionnaire completed by several describers for each subject was the primary data source. The most important methodological innovation in this study is an objective coding scheme which increases scoring reliability and permits an assessment of the types of changes making up each subject's total change score.

Design for data collection

Because the focus of the inquiry was change on-the-job, participants were first asked to cooperate in the study eight to ten months after they had returned to the job setting. Beginning the collection of data after this much time had passed enabled us to tap whatever durable effects had survived the waning of immediate post-training enthusiasm and the erosive effects of organizational constraints. The separation of training and inquiry also had the advantage of reduced contamination of data from awareness of the training activity on the part of others in the organization who would be asked to provide change descriptions. At the same time, of course, the lag permitted a number of other events to intervene. Some of these (e.g. relocations and promotions) were reported, thus reducing the size of the research population; others (e.g. changes in organizational structure or participation in contaminating training activities), unknown to us, probably operated with mixed effects upon our criterion for both experimental and control subjects.

The general strategy was to obtain self-descriptions from both experimental and control subjects and, for each, an additional set of five to seven descriptions of observed behavior changes from peers, superiors, and subordinates. Control subjects were nominated by the experimentals on the basis of the following criteria:

1. Identity or close similarity of organizational role to that of the participant.

2. No prior participation in the type of training program being evaluated.

3. Openness or readiness, in the judgment of the nominator, to participate in laboratory training if the opportunity were offered. (This stipulation was added to reduce the probability that basic differences in orientation toward self and others might exist between members of the control and experimental groups). Describers were selected by asking all subjects to submit the names of ten people with whom they had continuing working relationships which dated back at least fifteen months. From these names seven people were randomly selected to receive questionnaires.

Criterion development

The open-ended question for subjects took the following form: 'Over a period of time, people may change in the ways they work with other people.

Since May of 1960 (or 1961) do you believe you have changed your behavior in working with people in any specific ways as compared with the previous year? Yes—. No—. If "Yes", please describe.' A similar item was used to elicit descriptions of subjects from their associates.

The great volume of verbal material contained in responses to these questions required that we employ an objective method of classifying and counting the responses so as to permit statistical comparisons. While our first inclination was to impose a previously used, theoretically meaningful set of categories upon the data, the notion of developing new categories inductively and thus learning something about the kinds of dimensions intrinsic to the descriptions also seemed reasonable. We followed the latter course on the ground that the more important discriminations were those made by people in the organizational settings in which we are trying to assess change. This was consistent with the prior decision to make the form of the question open-ended in order to permit respondents to describe behavior changes using constructs that are both personally meaningful and organizationally relevant.

Inductively derived categories for content analysis[1]

A. Overt operational changes – descriptive

1. Communication
S. Sending. Shares information, expresses feelings, puts ideas across.
R. Receiving. More effort to understand, attentive listening, understands.

2. Relational facility. Cooperative, tactful, less irritating, easier to deal with, able to negotiate.

3. Risk-taking. Willing to take stand, less inhibited, experiments more.

4. Increased interdependence. Encourages participation, involves others, greater leeway to subordinates, less dominating, lets others think.

5. Functional flexibility. More flexible, takes group roles more easily, goes out of way, contributions more helpful, less rigid.

6. Self-control. More self-discipline, less quick with judgement, checks temper.

B. Inferred changes in insight and attitudes

1. Awareness of human behavior (intellectual comprehension). More conscious of why people act, more analytic of others' actions, clear perceptions of people.

1. Scoring depends upon an explicit statement of qualitative or quantitative difference. Changes may be positive or negative reflecting increases or decreases in quantity and greater or lesser utility. Precise category fit according to scoring conventions required for sets of categories A and B.

2. Sensitivity to group behavior. More conscious of group process, aware of subcurrents in groups.

3. Sensitivity to others' feelings. More capacity for understanding feelings, more sensitive to needs of others.

4. Acceptance of other people. Able to tolerate shortcomings, considerate of individual differences, patient.

5. Tolerance of new information. Willing to accept suggestions, considers new points of view, less dogmatic, less arbitrary.

6. Self-confidence.

7. Comfort. Relaxed, at ease (must be specific as to setting or activity).

8. Insight into self and role. Understands job demands, more aware of own behavior, better adjusted to job.

C. Global judgements – Gross characterological inferences, non-comparable references to special applications of learning, and references to consequences of change.

Following a long period of inductive derivation and testing, category specifications were determined and a team of coders were trained. The scoring task involved assigning each mention of a specific change to one of twenty-one content categories. For each protocol a maximum score of one was assigned for each category in which there was one or more mentions. The categories were sufficiently fine that this did not waste any data, and the ease with which the scorers could make the present–absent discrimination had a salutary effect upon the interscorer reliability. Following training, the percentage of agreements between scorers in assignment of mentions to categories was consistently above 90 per cent.

Protocols were stripped of group identification prior to scoring so as to ensure a blind process. Also, at the end of the eighteen-month data collection period a mixed sample of 1960 and 1961 responses were independently re-coded by two persons to check drift in the use of the categories. Score stabilities over this period of time again exceeded 90 per cent agreement in individual coding decisions.

Questionnaire response

Since the rate of return for mailed questionnaires tends to be very low and the resultant problem of subject self-selection is so destructive of otherwise well-conceived research designs, special efforts were made to avoid this difficulty. The simplicity of the questionnaire, accompanying explanatory letters, numerous reminders, and commitments to provide a summary of research findings likely, combined to give quite astounding response statistics. Only a third of the control subjects and less than one-quarter of the experimental subjects did not reply or refused to cooperate. After others were eliminated because of job changes and intervening or preceding training experiences, 346 or 56 per cent of both the original experimental and control groups were included in the study. The describer response ratios were even more satisfactory. Eighty-four per cent of nearly 2400 describers who received questionnaires returned usable responses. On the basis of these figures, subject-selection can be eliminated as an important source of error variance in this study.

Change scores

By combining cell values (zero or one) in the matrix of categories and describers for each subject, a variety of scores were obtained. The most comprehensive indices are a total-change score based upon the matrix sum, and a verified-change score developed by counting the number of observations of a particular subject in which two or more describers concur. Separate scores for category sets A, B and C, and for self-ratings as differentiated from others', descriptions were also used.

Results and discussion

Group comparisons using summary scores

The first analytic slice into the data is a comparison of total-change scores for those who had participated in laboratory training with those who had not. Examination of Table 1, which presents this analysis with the distri-

Table 1 **Distribution of experimental and control subjects, according to total-change scores**

	Experimental subjects	Control subjects	Total
Upper 9–23	99 (43·2%)	16 (14·3%)	115
Middle 5 to 8	81 (35·4%)	34 (30·3%	115
Lower −3 to 4	49 (21·4%)	62 (55·4%)	111
N	229	112	341

$\chi^2 = 45·88$
$(df = 2)$
$p (\chi^2 = 45·88) < 0·001$

bution divided into thirds, permits us to say that a significantly greater proportion of experimental subjects than controls were in the middle and top thirds of the distribution of change scores. The probability of a value of chi-square as large as that obtained is less than 0·001 if the groups are not different. Further, when the same type of comparison is made independently for 1960 and 1961 data, subject and describer scores, and category-sets A and B, the pattern of results in Table 1 is reproduced.

Only when the experimental-control comparison is applied to set C data do we find no differences. A straightforward although somewhat after-the-fact interpretation of this negative result provides a reason to believe that the positive results obtained with total-change scores are not mere methodological artifacts. Category set C is the global and miscellaneous pit into which relatively non-specific and other marginally scorable descriptions of change are cast. When respondents are asked to accommodate a researcher by providing a change description and they want to oblige, but do not have a concrete and specific behavioral referent, they tend to put down vague and global descriptions. This happens for both experimental and control describers with about equal frequency and is likely an important component of the base rate of change. These set C results are instructive in their contrast with other findings and in the emphasis they give to the discriminating power of scores based upon specific descriptions.

Further contrast between experimental and control groups can be seen in Table 2, in which the groups are compared with respect to the frequency

Table 2 **The number of subjects with one or more verified changes** (percentages in parentheses)

	Experimental group	Control group	Totals
One or more changes verified by Describer concurrence	152 (66·7)	37 (33·3)	189
No Verifications	76 (33·3)	74 (66·7)	150
Totals	228	111	339

$\chi^2 = 33·75, p(\chi^2 \equiv 33·75) < 0·001$
$df = 1$

of agreement among describers. The significance of the difference between the proportions of subjects with one or more confirmed change permits further credence in the interpretation that laboratory training tends to facilitate changes in behavior in the job setting. The agreements in detailed descriptions of behavior changes make it difficult to attribute these differences to mere describer bias induced by awareness of the subject's participation or non-participation in training. It is more parsimonious to accept these independent but concurring change reports as largely objective.

The ways in which our subjects changed over the assessment period are revealed in the category descriptions for these categories were constructed so as to minimize the distortion of the original descriptions. We also need to know, however, what kinds of changes were reported most frequently and which categories discriminated most clearly between laboratory participants and controls. Data to answer these questions are provided in Table 3.

Table 3 An analysis by scoring category of the differences between experimental and control groups in proportions or subjects reported as changed

| Scoring category | Label | Proportions perceived as changed | | |
		Experi-mentals	Controls	Differences
A-1S	Sending	0·3275	0·2328	0·0947
A-1R	Receiving communication	0·3406	0·1638	0·1768**
A-2	Relational facility	0·3581	0·2069	0·1512**
A-3	Risk taking	0·3188	0·2241	0·0947
A-4	Increased interdependence	0·3843	0·2741	0·1102*
A-5	Functional flexibility	0·2271	0·1293	0·0978
A-6	Self-control	0·2620	0·1552	0·1068*
B-1	Awareness of behavior	0·3362	0·1638	0·1725**
B-2	Sensitive to group process	0·2402	0·0862	0·1540**
B-3	Sensitive to others	0·3450	0·1034	0·2416**
B-4	Acceptance of others	0·4934	0·2931	0·2003**
B-5	Tolerance of new information	0·4192	0·2328	0·1864**
B-6	Confidence	0·2882	0·1897	0·0985
B-7	Comfort	0·3264	0·2328	0·1296*
B-8	Insight into self and role	0·3581	0·2414	0·1167*

* $p < 0.05$.
** $p < 0.01$.

Eleven of the fifteen categories discriminate between experimental and control subjects beyond the 0·05 level of significance. The large number of sensitive categories and the fact that the most popular category includes only half of the experimental subjects indicate the degree to which laboratory training outcomes tend to be individual and varied. A close look at some of the original data indicates that some subjects are perceived by their describers as having changed adaptively in the direction of an increase in assertive behavior and more willingness to take a stand, while other subjects are approvingly described as having decreased their aggressive behaviour and become more sensitive to others' feelings. These findings indicate that in the training programs studied, there is no standard learning outcome and no stereotyped ideal toward which conformity is induced. In this respect these results are very similar to those reported by Boyd and Elliss:

There were also wide differences in kind of response. The comparison of the cafeteria, which someone has applied to this form of development, comes to mind. Far from absorbing some standard lessons, each evidently chooses for himself. There were the quiet ones who came out of their shell to speak with greater confidence and definiteness. There were some who learned to consider more carefully before rendering a decision, while at the same time others received a spur to make up their minds. There were some with a chip on their shoulder who relaxed their defensive stance. There were those in the habit of expressing strong opinions or of holding decisions close to themselves who found that others had more to offer than they had supposed, and learned to listen, to consult, or to delegate (1962, p. 7).

Although there are more frequent changes for experimental subjects in all categories, there are differences among categories in the proportion of subjects for whom change was reported. The cluster of categories with both the highest proportions of participants seen as changed and the largest experimental-control differences has increased openness, receptivity, tolerance of differences as its common content (B-4, B-5, A-1R). A second cluster (A-4, A-2, A-6) has a theme of increased operational skill in interpersonal relations with overtones of increased capacity for collaboration. A third major cluster has to do with improved understanding and diagnostic awareness of self, others, and interactive processes in groups (B-1, B-2, B-3, B-8). There are empathic as well as purely intellectual threads binding this third cluster. These three dimensions constitute the principal types of adaptive, self-directed changes accelerated by participation in laboratory education conferences.

A fourth cluster consisting of three of the categories which do not significantly discriminate between experimentals and controls arises from these data (A-1S, A-3, B-6). The common content of this set seems to be increased and more effective initiation and assertiveness. While at least one-third of the participants made changes in this direction, when compared with the other categories and to the proportions of control subjects observed as changing in these ways, it appears that the training programs did not have their major impact in this area. The fact that within the wide individual differences in learning outcomes some subjects are rated as making their major move in this direction, may indicate that it is not the nature of the training activity that limits change in this direction. The composition of the trainee population may be the critical determinant. If the participants were selected heavily from among those whose reticence and reactive tendencies were inappropriately passive for the demands of their work environments, we might expect this fourth cluster to be more important as an ultimate outcome. Since the majority of laboratory participants are persons with leadership responsibilities and at least moderate influence in their home organizations, the three principal classes of change discussed above may reflect the participants diagnosis of particular organizational requirements. Although further research is needed to clarify these issues, the best answer on the basis of these findings is that the long-term outcomes of laboratory education tend to be increased capacity for adaptive orientation to the participants' particular situation rather than the stereotyped enactment of an ideology. The roots of such behavior changes lie in improved methods of collecting and processing information about the organizational environment and increased personal freedom to act on the basis of that information.

Training processes and long-term change

One recurrent finding relates to the question of the connection between behavior in the training situation and behavior changes following return to the home environment. A central proposition underlying laboratory education is that, in the laboratory, conditions are provided (contrast of social setting with the familiar, emotional support, access to knowledge of results of behavior) under which participants may more freely experiment with behavior and find alternative ways of dealing with their interpersonal environment. Responsible experimentation toward the development of more effective ways of attaining individual and group goals is the most direct laboratory learning process. But, there are individual differences in readiness to experiment and receptiveness to feedback about the consequences of one's action.

Some members of training groups take more risks, receive more feedback, and make more adaptive behavioral adjustments than others. If this conception of the learning process is approximately correct, these more involved and exposed participants should be those who are more often seen as having changed their behavior in their home organizations as well. We should expect then that observational measures of learning and change in the training group will be directly correlated with change scores obtained in the work environment six to twelve months later. Miles (1960) reported a product–moment correlation coefficient of 0.55 ($p < 0.01$) between his laboratory change ratings and organizational change scores about a year later.

A second test of this relationship was made by pooling data from a study by Harrison (1962) on training processes and immediate learning outcomes with the Bunker data on long-range changes for the same subjects. The Harrison measure was based upon ratings by peers in the learning group of the amount of behavior change in response to feedback evidenced over the two-week training period. This measure and the Bunker verified-change score described above were found to correlate 0.32 ($p < 0.01$, $N = 57$). The laboratory rating was also positively correlated with the total change score ($r = 0.23$, $p > 0.05$) and with a composite score for category set A ($r = 0.24$, $p < 0.05$). Inspection of these data in Table 4 indicates that the principal

Table 4 The relation between an immediate measure of laboratory learning and long-range change scores

A.		Verified changes			Proportion of each row sum in H column
		L	M	H[a]	
Laboratory	H	8	5	11	0·458
Learning	M	9	3	5	0·294
Score	L	9	6	1	0·063

B.		Total change score			
		L	M	H	
Laboratory	H	6	4	14	0·583
Learning	M	8	5	4	0·235
Score	L	6	9	1	0·063

[a] The distributions were divided as equally as their truncated nature would permit into Lower, Middle and Upper Thirds for visual presentation. Statistical relationships are reported in the text.

contributions to covariance are in the upper thirds of the long-range change score distributions. Seventy-four (73·7) per cent of those in the upper third of the distribution of total change scores were in the upper third of the distribution of laboratory learning scores (proximal change). Back-home application of learnings appears to be much less probable for those who did not become actively involved in the training processes.

This pattern of results in which those who are most active tend to display long-term results supports a model of behavior change which approximates that described above. A parallel finding from these data is confirmation of the indication that some, but certainly not all, laboratory participants acquire transferable skills and attitudes that facilitate their interpersonal performance at work.

A very recent finding by Harrison and Oshry (1965; personal communication) bears upon the issues just discussed. In a study of an organizational laboratory training program, they found that those who learned most in a T-group and applied their learnings most effectively tended to be those who were described by supervisors and peers before the training as being open to new ideas and to the expression of feelings. In the diagnosis of organizational problems they were seen as avoiding the assignment of blame to others and to the system. Those who were low in measures of learning and learning applications were described before the laboratory as inconsiderate of others and closed to new ideas. Their perceptions of organizational problems placed the causes outside themselves, in others and in the organization. If this pattern can be confirmed by other findings, it will appear that trainability has similar dimensions to training outcomes. Those who are open to new information can learn to become more so. The same characteristics and behaviors which block effective performance in working with others prior to laboratory participation seem to impair the ability to learn about self and social processes by laboratory methods.

The past five years have seen a good many new starts on research efforts to explicate the dimensions of laboratory training processes. Studies recently completed or under way examine individual personality factors, trainer characteristics and trainer behavior, group composition, group process variables, and features of training designs as determinants of laboratory education outcomes. In most cases, however, the outcome criteria have not included objective measures of long-range behavioral changes. Now that improved criterion measures are available, the next step is the systematic investigation of the relationship between each of these classes of determinants and application outcomes. There is strong evidence that groups, individuals and entire training programs have differential learning outcomes, but as yet there is no systematic evidence concerning the links between particular design components and observed applications.

References

ARGYRIS, C. (1962), *Interpersonal Competence and Organizational Effectiveness*, Dorsey Press.

BOYD, J. B., and ELLISS, J. (1962), *Findings of Research into Senior Management Seminars*, Toronto Personnel Research Dept., Hydro-Electric Power Commission of Ontario.

DURHAM, L. E., and GIBB, J. R. (1960), *An Annotated Bibliography of Research, National Training Laboratories, 1947–60*, Washington, D.C., National Training Laboratories.

HARRISON, R. (1962), 'The effects of training on interpersonal perception, Bethel, 1961', Yale University.

MILES, M. B. (1960), 'Human relations training: processes and outcomes', *J. Counseling Psychol*, vol. 7, pp. 301–6.

STOCK, D. (1964), 'A summary of research on training groups', in L. P. Bradford, J. R. Gibb and K. D. Benne (eds.) *T-Group Theory and Laboratory Method*. Wiley.

28 Frederick J. McDonald and Dwight W. Allen

The Effects of Self-Feedback and Reinforcement on the Acquisition of a Teaching Skill

Excerpt from F. J. McDonald and D. W. Allen, *Training Effects of Feedback and Modeling Procedures on Teaching Performance*, Stanford University Press, 1967, pp. 27–58.

The experiment described here applies well-known principles of reinforcement theory to a training problem. The training paradigm involves applying a reinforcer to an emitted response. The prediction is that the rate of responding will increase.

Two aspects of the training procedures do, however, depart from those typically used in reinforcement studies. First, the reinforcer is not given while the learner is actually emitting the response. In this study, the subjects were videotaped while emitting complex responses (teaching) some of which were to be reinforced. After the actual behavior sample was collected the subject viewed his performance in the presence of an experimenter. When the desired responses appeared on the videotape, the experimenter reinforced their occurrence. If results similar to those obtained in other studies occur in this situation, reinforcement concepts are widely applicable. Also training procedures or complex skills can be developed which use these principles and concepts in ways directly analogous to the procedures used in laboratory studies where the utility of these concepts has been amply demonstrated.

The second characteristic of the training procedure which departs from the usual laboratory methods is that the behaviors to be learned occur in the context of many other behaviors and are relatively more complex than operants conditioned in laboratory studies. They are more analogous to the kinds of behaviors that have been verbally conditioned in psychotherapy sessions. Here, as in these other complex verbal interaction, it is literally impossible to reinforce every instance of the operant being conditioned. The immediacy of the reinforcement, for similar reasons, is also somewhat variable. Again, if comparable results are obtained, the generalizability of reinforcement concepts is supported.

Since the subjects in this experiment are humans it was also possible to test the efficacy of a cue-discrimination procedure. This procedure consisted of pointing out to the subjects those cues to which the reinforced operant was attached. In this way the cue-response chain is clearly indicated which should be facilitating.

Since human subjects are being used, it is also possible that they can re-inforce themselves or, more generally, provide their own feedback. Video-tape recordings of a trainee's behavior sequence can be given to him so that he can view himself as a behaving organism. With instructions he can note the presence or absence of the desired response. However, it is dubious if such a procedure is likely to be highly facilitating since the subject may not attend well, may be easily distracted, may be highly subjective in his viewing. The effectiveness of this training procedure remains to be tested, however.

This experiment, then, tests the relative effectiveness of three training procedures, each representing an application of reinforcement principles. The three procedures represent points on a continuum from self-adminis-tered feedback or reinforcement to experimenter-administered reinforce-ment with cue-discrimination training.

The prediction is that the order of training effectiveness will be in the same direction, with the self-administered feedback the least effective and the experimenter-administered feedback with cue-discrimination training the most effective.

Method
General procedure

Intern teachers were videotaped on four separate occasions during the first twenty minutes of regular classroom lessons. In the intervals between each of these taping sessions they received differential feedback as part of their regular supervision. The treatment or supervision sessions were alike for all subjects in that they viewed videotape playbacks of their earlier teaching performance. The mode and amount of feedback given each intern was varied by manipulating the reinforcement and discrimination training provided by an experimenter.

Before the pre-test videotapes were recorded, all subjects were told when they would be taped and were asked to present a discussion-type lesson in which teacher–pupil interaction could be observed. This was not a new or unusual experience for them as they had been frequently exposed to the videotaping-playback-supervision process during the previous three months of the Stanford Intern Program.

Pupils in each of the classrooms were informed by the interns beforehand that the portable TV equipment would be present in the room, and that the cameras would be focused on the teacher, not the class.

Treatments

Mode of feedback, type of reinforcement and amount of discrimination training were varied for four experimental groups of interns.

Controls: Group (C): At the beginning of the first playback session these subjects were given written instructions which suggested that as they viewed subsequent playbacks of themselves, they try to determine their effectiveness in relation to: the aims of the lesson; use of examples; effectiveness of teacher-questions; amount of pupil participation; pacing of the lesson; and teacher–pupil rapport. Following this, they viewed the first and all subsequent playbacks alone. E started the machine and left the room. He returned as the tape finished, stopped the machine and told the intern when to expect the next taping and the date for the following playback session. As for all subjects, Group C (controls) viewed playbacks of the preceding lesson within three days of its taping. Lessons were videotaped within two days of each playback session.

Self-feedback: Group (S-F). These subjects followed the same basic schedule as the controls, except that they received a different set of written instructions. The instructions discussed the educational relevance of increasing pupil participation in certain types of lessons; defined pupil participatory responses (PPR) as a clearly observable nonverbal or verbal response that was considered desirable; and provided brief examples of such behavior. It was also suggested that the intern immediately reward a PPR when it occurred as this would tend to increase pupil participation. Examples of teacher responses – both verbal and nonverbal – were then provided. Finally, a simple rating chart was attached so that the intern could classify his responses to PPRs as 'teacher rewards'; 'teacher ignores'; 'teacher punishes'; or 'can't classify'. As with the control group, self-feedback subjects viewed each playback alone.

Reinforcement-only subjects: Group (R). These interns received the same written instructions as those in the self-feedback condition. However, E viewed each of the three videotaped playbacks with them, and verbally reinforced all observable instances of these Group (R) interns reinforcing PPRs. Whenever the intern was observed to reinforce a PPR, E responded by saying 'Good!'; 'That's it!'; etc. Beyond this, he did not comment upon the intern's teaching performance.

Reinforcement plus discrimination training: Group (R + D): These interns were first given written instructions which were identical to those administered to Group (S–F) and Group (R) subjects. In viewing subsequent playbacks with them, E provided differential reinforcement as in the Reinforcement-Only treatment. In addition, he provided discrimination training. This consisted of pointing out salient cues to which reinforcement should be attached, suggestions related to the immediacy, affect-loading and types of reinforcement the teacher could use, and finally, the effects of such behavior upon pupil participation. In general terms, then, it might be said that Group (R + D) subjects received 'maximum supervision' and Group (S–F) subjects received 'self-supervision'.

Experimental playback sessions for all groups were thirty minutes in length. When E viewed playback with Group (R) and (R + D) subjects, he reduced the sound momentarily when providing discrimination training, and spoke over the tape when providing reinforcement. Interns in all groups were informed that they could have the tape stopped or reversed and played over again at any point during the playback. Playbacks were stopped occasionally by E when he was working with the supervised groups. However, since the sessions were limited to thirty minutes, only one or two brief stoppages in sessions two and three were possible.

Subjects

All Stanford intern teachers preparing to teach English, social studies, and mathematics were included in the study. Approximately equal numbers of interns from each of the subject-matter areas were assigned to each group. In addition, groups of interns teaching in the same school were distributed throughout the four groups. In this way, systematic bias due to subject-matter major or pupil characteristics based on socioeconomic status was avoided. [There were seventy-one teachers in the experiment, seventeen or eighteen in each condition.]

The dependent variable

The dependent variable was defined as the relative frequency with which the teacher positively reinforces pupils' participatory responses during teacher–pupil interaction in the classroom. PPRs were defined in training sessions with the interns as any *desirable* or *relevant* pupil comment, answer or question. For purposes of measurement, however, desirability and relevancy were not considered.

The basic strategy in defining the dependent variable involved classifying teacher responses into one of four major response categories. These include positive reinforcement, negative reinforcement, interaction and information giving responses. Pupil responses were also classified and considered in relation to teacher responses. Each of the above response categories are defined in the following discussion. A summary of the classification system appears in Table 1 (experiment 1).

Teacher positive reinforcement. A teacher response was defined as positively reinforcing if it met one of two conditions: First, the response had to immediately follow a PPR. Second, it had to be classifiable under one of the following response categories.

Table 1 The dependent variable defined in terms of selected response categories

Teacher responses		Teacher–pupil interaction	
Positive reinforcement	*Negative reinforcement*	*Pupil initiated*	*Teacher initiated*
+Verbal Reinforcement (+V R)	−Verbal Reinforcement (−V R)	Volunteer Comments (V)	Direct Question to one individual (D S I)
+Non-Verbal Reinforcement (+N V R)	−Non-Verbal Reinforcement (−N V R)	Volunteer Questions (V?)	
+Qualified Reinforcement (+Q R)	−Qualified Reinforcement (−Q R)		Direct Question to Group, then Individual Specified (D S G–I)
Post Hoc Reinforcement (P H R)		No Response (P N R)	
Teacher No Response (T N R)			Teacher question directed to the group followed by volunteered pupil response (D S G–V)

1. *Teacher Positive Verbal Reinforcement* $(+VR)$: Immediately following a PPR, the teacher uses words and phrases such as 'Good', 'Fine!'

2. *Teacher Positive Non-Verbal Reinforcement* $(+NVR)$: The teacher in responding to a PPR, nods, smiles, leans or moves toward the pupil, or writes the pupil's response on the blackboard.

3. *Teacher Positively Qualified* $(+QR)$.

4. *Post Hoc Reinforcement* (PHR): The teacher emphasizes positive aspects of pupil responses by reorienting class attention to earlier contributions by a given pupil (PHR), or by differentially reinforcing the acceptable components of a partially adequate response $(+QR)$.

Teacher negative reinforcement. A teacher response was defined as negatively reinforcing if it immediately followed a PPR, and was classifiable as the obverse of one of four types of reinforcement outlined above $(-VR; -NVR; -QR)$.

Teacher–pupil responses independent of reinforcement classifications. Certain responses that occur frequently in interaction and yet are not classifiable as some form of reinforcement were included in the definition of the dependent variable. These included information-giving by the teacher, teacher-initiated interaction (i.e. questions directed to a given pupil or to the class in general), pupil initiated interaction (i.e. volunteered comments or questions), teacher-no-response and pupil-no-response.

In general, the dependent variable included evaluative and informational signals which the teacher may use in the classroom. There was a tendency to emphasize socially rewarding operants since it could be expected that such behavior would tend to increase pupil participation.

Both in the training and measurement phases of the study, the PPR was presented as an S^D which served to cue the teacher or rater that a desirable (or classifiable) teacher response was about to occur.

Measurement procedures. Four videotapes for each intern in each group were analysed by raters trained for this purpose. Throughout the rating phase of the experiment, they worked on the tapes in a random order so that they neither knew the treatment condition nor the number of the teaching trial of the tape being rated. Operators ran the television equipment and selected tapes using a list of random numbers.

In addition to recording the frequencies of each of the behaviors defined as components of the dependent variable, the raters recorded other relevant behaviors and lesson characteristics as well. Frequencies were recorded for the total number of pupils who responded, the number of responses they emitted, and the sex of each responder. The raters also recorded the length of each videotape to the nearest tenth of a minute, and determined how much time was spent in discussion, group work, or individual study.

The unit of measurement. In analysing pupil–teacher interaction, one may record discrete responses, or measure in terms of some unit such as the uninterrupted utterance. Raters were trained to define an interruption as a comment or question. 'Partial' responses that teachers commonly emit during pupil speech ('um-hum', 'yes', etc.) were not defined as interruptions. All forms of verbal and nonverbal reinforcement were scored in terms of discrete responses. For example, if the teacher said, 'Good!', 'Good!', 'That's fine!', the rater coded all three operants.

Training of raters. Eight raters were initially given intensive training on intern videotapes. Once they had achieved at least 90 per cent interrater agreement on all of the major response categories, and better than 95 per cent agreement on teacher reinforcement responses, the analysis of experimental tapes was begun. Reliability was maintained throughout the analysis by scheduling frequent joint rating sessions where raters checked the percentage of agreement and referred to definitions of relevant responses so that systematic rating biases would not develop. Neither ratings taken during training, nor those produced in the joint sessions were used in the statistical analysis of results.

The ratings upon which the reliability coefficients were acquired in the following way. As each block of thirty or forty tapes were completed (a total of 269 were actually rated), each of the six raters who did the bulk of the rating then rated a given tape. This was done without the rater's knowledge. Eight tapes, two from each trial, and two from each group were rated by all six raters in this way. As can be seen, interrater agreement was very high.

A certain amount of data was lost between initial videotaping and the final statistical analysis. Some tapes were technically poor, and could not be rated. Some tapes were inevitably less than the required twenty minutes, and were also omitted. However, if a given tape was over fifteen but less than twenty minutes, the obtained ratings were prorated to a twenty-minute base. Of the original set of 284 videotaped lessons, twenty-five were omitted at the outset, and fifty-one tapes were prorated before statistical analyses were performed. The T statistic was used to determine whether or not certain cells in the matrix were biased by the inclusion of a disproportionate number of adjusted tapes. T was nonsignificant.

Results

Three types of analysis were performed upon the data. Analyses of covariance were employed to test for the significance of differences between each of the groups (treatment differences). In addition, T tests were used to determine the significance of differences within a given group from one trial to the next (training differences). Finally, a multiple regression analysis was performed on all of the major response categories to determine significant relationships among these teacher–pupil behaviors.

Treatment differences. Positive teacher reinforcement constitutes the major response category of the dependent variable. Using trial one scores as covariants, the groups were found to be significantly different from each other. It was found that the differences were significant for both positive verbal ($p < 0.001$, 0.005 and 0.025 for trials 2, 3 and 4) and nonverbal reinforcement ($p < 0.025$ and 0.005 for trials 2 and 4). When the two types of positive reinforcement are taken together the R + D group outperformed all other groups. Figure 1 presents the change for positive verbal and nonverbal separately.

Negative verbal and nonverbal teacher reinforcement occurred infrequently throughout the groups. All three of the experimental groups consistently emitted fewer negatively reinforcing responses over trials while control-group responses increased. These differences appear to be fairly stable, but do not reach an acceptable level of significance. Figure 2 illustrates group trends in negative reinforcement. The data here are also based on adjusted treatment means (see Figure 2).

Training differences. Table 2 summarizes the significance levels obtained when within-group treatment means were compared using the t statistic. As can be seen, Group (R + D) interns significantly increased their rate of positive reinforcement by trial 2 ($p < 0.01$). They increased from a base rate of reinforcing approximately 60 per cent of all PPRs to a rate of 76 per cent by trial 2. In trial 4 the rate dropped to 67 per cent and this combined with considerable variation within the group, produced before and after treatment differences that were non-significant ($p < 0.10$). However, when trial 1 versus trial 4 differences were tested on the assumption that the population variances were unequal, significance well beyond the 0.05 level was obtained (required $0.05 = 2.13$; obtained $T = 4.19$). Group (R + D) subjects also increased their rate of positive nonverbal reinforcement from trial 1 to 2 and following two treatment sessions, ended ($p < 0.10$) to use less negative verbal reinforcement.

Increases in mean positive verbal reinforcement and a concomitant drop in negative reinforcement can be most clearly seen in Group (R) subjects. The higher significance levels result from considerably less within-group variation.

The control group showed no significant within-group shifts in

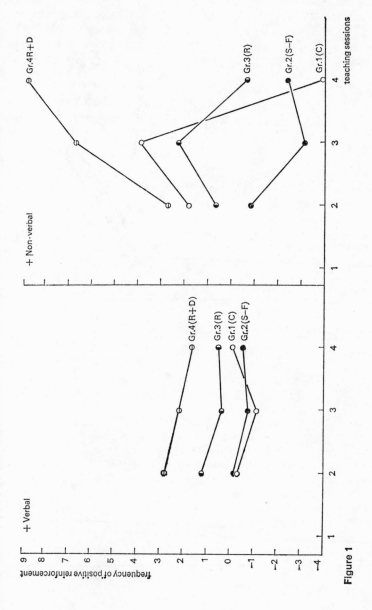

Figure 1

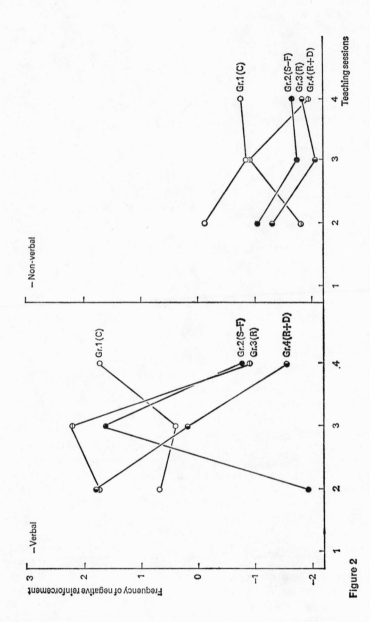

Figure 2

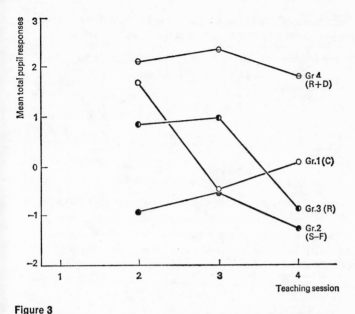

Figure 3

reinforcement from trial 1 to trial 4. Note that the control group subjects tended to increase their negative verbal reinforcement rate throughout treatment.

Pupil responses. What are the probable effects of the above types of teacher training on pupil behavior? To answer this question, total pupil responses and relevant component responses were analysed. A summary of the analyses of covariance (Table 3) performed on total pupil responses with trial 1 scores as covariates, shows that shifts in pupil responses closely followed concomitant shifts in teacher positive reinforcement (see Table 2). While the increase in the Group (R) pupil sample appears shortlived, Group (R + D) pupils maintain significantly higher response levels in trial 4 ($p < 0.005$) as well as for trials 2 ($p = 0.001$) and 3 ($p = 0.01$). These data are illustrated in Figure 3 (see Figure 3). Note that while the control group initially showed a higher mean frequency of responses it dropped slightly over four trials. Group (R) and (R + D) pupils increased from trial 1 to trial 4.

The increase in total pupil responses immediately leads one to ask whether they are due to increased teacher positive reinforcement, or perhaps more simply, to increased questioning by the teacher. While it is clear that differential feedback and reinforcement affected teacher behavior, it does not

Table 2 **Significance of differences for the four experimental groups from trial to trial, on major response categories of the dependent variable***

Response category	Group 1 (control)	Group 2 (S–F)	Group 3 (R)	Group 4 (R+D)
	Direction of difference from trial to trial and level of significance			
+VR	NS	NS	$T_1 < T_2$ (0·01) $T_4 < T_2$ (0·05)	$T_1 < T_2$ (0·01) $T_1 < T_4$ (0·10)
+NVR	NS	NS	NS	$T_1 < T_2$ (0·10)
−VR	NS	NS	NS	NS
−NVR	NS	$T_1 > T_3$ (0·10) $T_1 > T_4$ (0·10)	$T_4 < T_1$ (0·05) $T_3 < T_1$ (0·05)	$T_4 < T_1$ (0·10)

* Significance levels were tested by the T statistic for comparisons among treatment means (Winer, 1962, pp. 65–70).

Table 3 **Summary of the analyses of covariance for the experimental groups, with trial one scores as covariants and total student responses as the dependent variable**

	Group 1 (C)	Group 2 (S–F)	Group 3 (R)	Group 4 (R+D)	df	F
	Adjusted means and standard errors					
Trial 2	72·59 5·5354	47·39 5·2296	65·93 5·3014	83·29 5·1161	3/60	8·267***
Trial 3	58·97 7·6169	54·26 6·0530	60·06 6·3019	84·31 5·9179	3/62	5·082**
Trial 4	56·92 6·604	44·94 6·517	47·82 7·752	74·12 6·309	3/52	4·004*

* 0·05 level of significance
** 0·01 level of significance
*** 0·001 level of significance

necessarily follow that increased positive reinforcement as defined here had an effect on pupil behavior. A comparison of volunteered pupil responses as opposed to teacher-solicited pupil responses is relevant. If increased pupil responses were largely due to increased questioning by the teacher then one would detect an increase in directly solicited answers, and a decrease or no change in pupil-volunteered statements and questions. This does not appear to be the case.

Discussion of results

It is clear that feedback conditions proved to be the most effective training arrangement. Perhaps of greatest interest are what appear to be those variations in feedback which are most effective. Clearly, adding cue discrimination to the training method substantially improves the procedure. This procedure, however, is the most 'costly' in that it requires the active involvement of the experimenter to describe salient cues and to suggest ways of reinforcing participating behavior that the subject could use.

Variations in the effectiveness of this procedure might occur when a variety of experimenters are used. Informal observations suggest that not all trainees responded equally positively to this condition. Trainee characteristics probably interact with experimenter characteristics, and such interactions probably influence differentially the effects of feedback and cue-discrimination training.

Equally interesting is the relative ineffectiveness of the self-feedback condition, attractive because it is the least costly procedure. This method is probably ineffective because the desired response is not adequately cued. Even if trainees had a limited response repertoire of reinforcing responses, they still could have used them consistently, if somewhat monotonously. But, the rate increase is not likely to occur if the trainee does not 'know' when to emit the desired response. Both of the other feedback conditions cue as to appropriate response in some form.

This self-feedback condition might be improved by introducing some cueing procedures. Or, a combination of viewing models and self might be effective. The results obtained in this experiment indicate only that a limited kind of self-viewing, presumed to be a self-feedback condition and designed to be so, is not highly effective in producing behavior change.

The results of this experiment suggest that the operant conditioning model may be extended to situations in which the learner is not actually behaving but merely watching his performance after the actions have occurred. This extrapolation, if further substantiated, greatly increases the application of this particular paradigm. However, further research must also be directed to an analysis of the viewing conditions – characteristics of the persons viewing, time interval between enacting and viewing, the kind of behavior being reinforced, and similar conditions which might reasonably be expected to enhance or to limit the effects of the reinforcement procedure.

Also of theoretical interest is the possibility of modifying the operant conditioning paradigm by instructing subjects. This procedure shortens the time and cost of shaping the desired behavior through a series of successive approximations. The learning paradigm of this arrangement needs explication and analysis.

Reference

WINER, B. J. (1972), *Statistical Principles in Experimental Design*, McGraw-Hill.

Further Reading

General

M. Argyle, *Social Interaction*, Methuen; Atherton, 1969.

The biological and cultural roots of social interaction

I. Devore, *Primate Behaviour*, Holt, Rinehart & Winston, 1965.
E. Goffman, *Relations in Public*, Allen Lane The Penguin Press, 1972.
R. Hinde (ed.), *Non-verbal Communication*, Cambridge University Press, 1972.
T. Rowell, *The Social Behaviour of Monkeys*, Penguin, 1972.
T. A. Sebeok (ed.), *Animal Communication – Techniques of Study and Results of Research*, Indiana University Press, 1967.

The elements of social behaviour

R. Birdwhistell, *Kinesics and Context*, University of Pennsylvania Press, 1971.
R. V. Exline, 'Visual interaction: the glances of power and preference', *Nebraska Symposium on Motivation*, University of Nebraska Press, 1971.
P. Ekman, W. V. Friesen and P. Ellsworth, *Emotion in the Human Face*, Pergamon, 1972.
P. Ekman and W. V. Friesen, 'The repertoire of non-verbal behaviour: categories, origin, usage and coding', *Semiotica*, vol. 1, pp. 49–98, 1969.
E. T. Hall, *The Hidden Dimension*, Doubleday, 1966.
A. Mehrabian, *Nonverbal Communication*, Aldine-Atherton, 1972.
R. Sommer, *Personal Space*, Prentice-Hall, 1969.

Perception of the other during interaction

M. Cook, *Interpersonal Perception*, Penguin, 1971.
J. R. Davitz, *The Communication of Emotional Meaning*, McGraw-Hill, 1964.
R. Tagiuri and L. Petrullo (eds.), *Person Perception and Interpersonal Behavior*, Stanford University Press, 1958.

Two-person interaction

E. P. Hollander, *Principles and Method of Social Psychology*, 2nd edn, Oxford University Press, 1971.
S. M. Jourard, *Self-Disclosure: An Experimental Analysis of the Transparent Self*, Wiley, 1971.
D. L. Krebs, 'Altruism – an examination of the concept and a review of the literature', *Psychological Bulletins*, vol. 73, pp. 258–302, 1970.
S. Moscovici (ed.), *The Psychology of Language*, Markham, 1972.
P. Robinson, *The Social Psychology of Language*, Penguin, 1972.
A. Siegman and B. Pope, *Studies in Dyadic Communication*, Pergamon, 1972.

Interaction in groups and organizations

M. Argyle, *The Social Psychology of Work*, Allen Lane The Penguin Press, 1972.

B. M. Bass, *Organizational Psychology*, Allyn & Bacon, 1965.

A. P. Hare, E. F. Borgatta and R. F. Bales, *Small Groups*, Knopf, 1965.

R. Likert, *New Patterns of Management*, McGraw-Hill, 1961.

V. Vroom, *Work and Motivation*, Wiley, 1964.

Personality and social interaction

R. C. Carson, *Interaction Concepts of Personality*, Allen & Unwin, 1970.

K. J. Gergen and D. Marlowe, *Personality and Social Behavior*, Addison-Wesley, 1970.

W. Mischel, *Personality and Assessment*, Wiley.

W. C. Schutz, *FIRO: A Three-Dimensional Theory of Interpersonal Behaviour*, Holt, Rinehart & Winston, 1958.

P. Watzlawick, J. H. Beavin and D. D. Jackson, *Pragmatics of Human Communication*, Norton, 1976.

The self and social interaction

E. H. Erikson, 'The problem of ego identity', *American Journal of Psychoanalysis*, vol. 4, pp. 56–121, 1956.

E. Goffman, *The Presentation of Self in Everyday Life*, Edinburgh University Press, 1956; Penguin, 1972.

G. J. McCall and J. L. Simmons, *Identities and Interactions*, Free Press, 1966.

R. C. Wylie, *The Self Concept*, University of Nebraska Press, 1961.

Training in social skills

L. P. Bradford, J. R. Gibb and K. D. Benne, *T-Group Theory and Laboratory Method*, Wiley, 1964.

R. J. Corsini, M. F. Shaw and R. R. Blake, *Role Playing in Business and Industry*, Free Press, 1961.

E. H. Schein and W. G. Bennis (eds.), *Personal and Organizational Change through Group Methods*, Wiley, 1965.

A. R. Wight, *Cross-Cultural Training: A Draft Handbook*, Center for Research and Education, Colorado, 1969.

Acknowledgements

Permission to reproduce the Readings in this volume is acknowledged
to the following sources:

1 Macmillan & Co. Inc.
2 American Anthropological Association
3 The Clarendon Press
4 American Anthropological Association
5 North-Holland Publishing Company
6 Macmillan & Co. Inc.
7 American Psychological Association
8 McGraw-Hill Book Co.
9 *Psychiatry*
10 Tavistock Publications Ltd and Springer Verlag New York Inc.
11 Academic Press Inc.
12 American Sociological Association
13 American Psychological Association
14 Allen Lane The Penguin Press
15 Macmillan & Co. Inc.
16 Harper & Row Inc.
17 Routledge & Kegan Paul Ltd and Chandler Publishing Co.
18 *Personnel Psychology*
19 Pergamon Press Ltd
20 *British Journal of Clinical Psychology*
21 American Sociological Association
22 *Journal of Abnormal Psychology*
23 American Sociological Association
24 Duke University Press
25 University of Chicago Press
26 Allyn & Bacon Inc.
27 John Wiley & Sons Inc.
28 Stanford University Press

Author Index

Adorno, T. W., 345
Allen, D. W., 369
Altmann, S. A., 19, 31
Anderson, R. L., 113
Argyle, M., 14, 104, 105, 132, 161, 249
Argyris, C., 255, 383
Austin, G. A., 345

Bales, R. F., 67, 219, 250
Bamforth, K. W., 275
Bancroft, T. A., 113
Barker, R. G., 65, 319
Barnard, C. I., 273
Bass, B. H., 233
Bastian, J. R., 31
Bavelas, A., 251
Beall, G., 126
Beldoch, M., 119
Bernstein, B., 15, 48, 56–8, 60, 71
Brandis, W., 48, 57, 58
Bertalanffy, L. von, 272, 274, 283
Bion, W. R., 150
Birdwhistell, R. L., 11, 63, 88, 95, 98, 132
Blake, R. R., 295
Blau, P. M., 219, 253, 255, 257, 272, 283
Block, J., 343, 352
Bloomfield, L., 95
Boomer, D. S., 132, 164
Borgatta, E. F., 67
Bourguignon, E., 212
Boyd, J. B., 384, 391
Brannon, C., 174, 175, 297
Broadbent, D. E., 81
Brown, R., 114–15
Brown, R. W., 71, 72
Bruner, J. S., 344
Buchsbaum, B., 189
Budner, S., 297
Buettner-Janusch, J., 19, 22
Bunker, D. R., 369
Burtt, H. E., 260, 262

Campbell, D. T., 378
Candell, P., 189
Carment, D. W., 287, 289, 290, 295
Carpenter, C. R., 18
Cervenka, E. J., 96
Cervin, V. B., 287, 289, 290, 295
Chahbazi, P., 298
Chamberlain, C., 73
Chatterjee, B. B., 389
Christie, R., 297
Cicourel, A. V., 47
Clark, W. E. L., 17
Clemes, S., 326
Cohen, B. H., 123
Conklin, H. C., 66

Cook, J., 58
Cooley, C. H., 331
Coons, A. E., 262
Cornelison, F. S., 132
Cronbach, L. J., 320
Crook, J. H., 23
Crutchfield, R. S., 289

Danehy, J. J., 70
Daniels, D., 316
Darwin, C., 96, 132–3
Daugherty, B. N., 297
Davis, E. A., 164
Davitz, J., 121
Davitz, L., 121
Dean, J., 105, 163
DeCharms, R., 344
DeNike, L. D., 171
DeVore, I., 10, 15, 22–5, 27
Dill, W. R., 252
Dimock, M. E., 254
Dittman, A. T., 132, 316, 324, 325
Dornbusch, S. M., 331
Drucker, P. F., 275
Durham, L. E., 383

Edwards, A., 166
Efron, D., 95
Ehrlich, D., 304
Ehrlich, H. J., 304
Ekman, P., 119, 170, 324
Elliss, J., 384, 391
Emery, F. E., 219
Endler, N. S., 316, 320, 325
Erikson, E. H., 329, 340
Ervin-Tripp, S., 63
Ex, J., 77
Exline, R. V., 103, 173, 174, 175, 177, 180, 297
Eysenck, H. J., 289–90

Fairbanks, G., 121
Farbman, I., 316, 325
Feffer, M., 161, 188, 189
Feldman, S. S., 174
Ferguson, C. A., 70, 72, 75
Festinger, L., 233, 372
Field, P. B., 289
Fischer, J. L., 71, 73
Fishman, J., 47
Flavell, J., 188
Fleishman, E. A., 219, 260, 262, 269, 270
Ford, M., 71
Fordham, P., 213
Franks, C. M., 295
Freedman, N., 132
Frenkel-Brunswik, E., 345
Freud, S., 133

Subject Index